RL LN7091
18.99
41195

European States and the Euro

D0928289

European States and the Euro

Europeanization, Variation, and Convergence

Edited by
Kenneth Dyson

OXFORD
UNIVERSITY PRESS

OXFORD
UNIVERSITY PRESS

Great Clarendon Street, Oxford OX2 6DP

Oxford University Press is a department of the University of Oxford.
It furthers the University's objective of excellence in research, scholarship,
and education by publishing worldwide in

Oxford New York

Athens Auckland Bangkok Buenos Aires Cape Town Chennai
Dar es Salaam Delhi Hong Kong Istanbul Karachi Kolkata
Kuala Lumpur Madrid Melbourne Mexico City Mumbai Nairobi
São Paulo Shanghai Singapore Taipei Tokyo Toronto

with associated companies in Berlin

Oxford is a registered trade mark of Oxford University Press
in the UK and in certain other countries

Published in the United States
By Oxford University Press Inc., New York

British Library Cataloguing in Publication Data
Data available

Library of Congress Cataloging-in-Publication Data
European states and the Euro : Europeanization, variation, and convergence / edited by
Kenneth Dyson.
    p. cm.
   Includes bibliographical references and index.
   1. Monetary unions—European Union countries. 2. Monetary policy—European Union
countries. 3. European Union countries—Economic policy. 4. Europe—Economic
integration. 5. Economic and Monetary Union. I. Dyson, Kenneth H. F.

   HG3942 .E974 2002   337.1′42—dc21   2001047455
   ISBN 0-19-925026-X
   ISBN 0-925025-1 (Pbk.)

10 9 8 7 6 5 4 3 2 1

Typeset by Graphicraft Limited, Hong Kong
Printed in Great Britain on acid-free paper by
T.J. International Ltd., Padstow, Cornwall

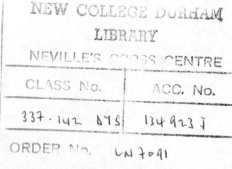

Acknowledgements

This study follows on from three previous books. *Elusive Union* (1994) examined the historical and structural conditions that made Economic and Monetary Union (EMU) possible. *The Road to Maastricht* (1999, with Kevin Featherstone) was based on the findings of a research project funded by the Economic and Social Research Council (ESRC). Based on extensive elite interviews and access to personal papers, it investigated in depth how EMU was negotiated. *The Politics of the Euro-Zone* (2000) was concerned with the nature and implications of an ECB-centric Euro-Zone, in particular its character as a 'stabilization' state. With this volume the emphasis changes to EMU as Europeanization. This change of emphasis was encouraged by the historic transition to stage three of EMU on 1 January 1999. From that date a new supranational institution, the European Central Bank (ECB), made monetary policy for the Euro-Zone as a whole. The eleven member-states in stage three began to reinforce their co-operation in the Euro-Group. It was both timely and important to consider how EMU was affecting EU states both inside and outside the Euro-Zone. In doing so, one had to remember that EMU had not begun on 1 January 1999. Its effects as a process could be traced back to the establishment of the European Monetary System (EMS) in 1979 and beyond to the Snake mechanism. These effects had been demonstrated at different times and different tempos, with France for instance facing a critical juncture in 1983. Hence the study of EMU as Europeanization needs an historical sense.

The book was made possible by the generosity of the British Academy in funding a conference in September 2000. This conference provided an invaluable opportunity for authors to present first drafts of their chapters for discussion. Particular thanks are due to Rosemary Lambeth at the British Academy for the courteous, patient, and efficient way in which she organized the conference and to the Public Understanding and Activities Committee of the British Academy for its financial support. The editor and two authors (David Howarth and Claudio Radaelli) are also grateful to the British Academy for awarding small grants to support fieldwork in France, Germany, and Italy.

In addition, the final revision of chapters benefited greatly from the comments of those who served as discussants at the British Academy conference. A special debt of gratitude is owed to: Professor Iain Begg (South Bank), Professor Alastair Cole (Cardiff), Professor Paul Furlong (Cardiff), Dr Erik Jones (Nottingham), Professor Richard Layard (LSE), Professor Christopher

Pierson (Nottingham), Professor Jim Rollo (Sussex), and Christopher Taylor (NIESR, London).

Thanks also to Amanda Watkins and the team at Oxford University Press for their support at every stage of the book. And last, but not least, the unfailing good humour and the dedication of the contributors deserve a special mention. Any shortcomings in the final product remain, of course, the responsibility of the editor.

Kenneth Dyson

University of Bradford
k.h.f.dyson@bradford.ac.uk

Contents

PART I European and Global Contexts

PART II Domestic Political and Policy Contexts

PART III   Sectors, States, and EMU

List of Figures

List of Tables

Notes on Contributors

Colin Crouch is a Professor of Sociology at the European University Institute, Florence. He is also an external scientific member of the Max-Planck-Institute for Social Research in Cologne. His recent books include *Industrial Relations and European State Traditions* (Oxford University Press, 1993); *Social Change in Western Europe* (Oxford University Press, 1999); *Are Skills the Answer?* (with David Finegold and Mari Sako, Oxford University Press, 1999); and (edited) *After the Euro: Shaping Institutions for Governance in the Wake of European Monetary Union* (Oxford University Press, 2000).

Kenneth Dyson is Professor of European Studies at the University of Bradford. He is a Fellow of the British Academy and an Academician of the Learned Society of the Social Sciences. In 1996 and 2001 he chaired the Higher Education Funding Council research assessment panel for European Studies. His recent books include *Elusive Union: The Process of Economic and Monetary Union* (Longman, 1994); *Culture First: Maintaining Standards in the New Media Age* (with Walter Homolka, Cassell, 1996); *The Road to Maastricht: Negotiating Economic and Monetary Union* (with Kevin Featherstone, Oxford University Press, 1999); and *The Politics of the Euro-Zone: Stability or Breakdown?* (Oxford University Press, 2000). He was adviser to the BBC 2 series on the making of EMU. His main research interests are in German policy and politics, European economic policies and politics, and the EU. He is co-editor of the journal *German Politics* and currently working with Klaus Goetz (LSE) on a project on Germany and Europe.

Andrew Gamble is a Fellow of the British Academy and Professor of Politics and Director of the Political Economy Research Centre at the University of Sheffield. His research interests lie in comparative political economy, public policy, and political theory. He is joint editor of *The Political Quarterly* and *New Political Economy*. Recent publications include *Hayek: The Iron Cage of Liberty* (Polity, 1996); *Politics and Fate* (Polity, 2000); *The Political Economy of the Company* (Hart, 2000, co-edited with John Parkinson and Gavin Kelly); and *Fundamentals in British Politics* (Macmillan, 1999, co-edited with Ian Holliday and Geraint Parry).

David Howarth is Lecturer in Politics at Queen Mary and Westfield College, London. He specializes in the study of French economic and European policies and policy-making. He is the author of *The French Road to European Monetary Union* (Palgrave, 2000).

Gavin Kelly is Senior Research Fellow at the Institute for Public Policy Research in London.

Ingo Linsenmann is a researcher at the University of Cologne. He is carrying out a research project on the institutionalization of the European Economic and Monetary Union, together with Wolfgang Wessels. He is co-author of the *Eurospectator 1999* report on Germany (European University Institute Working Papers LAW No. 2000/6).

David McKay is Professor of Politics at the University of Essex. His recent books include *Federalism and European Union* (Oxford University Press, 1999) and *Designing Europe: Institutional Adaptation and the Federal Experience* (Oxford University Press, 2000).

Martin Marcussen is Associate Professor of Politics at the University of Copenhagen. He specializes in economic and monetary union and the role of ideas in public policy. He is author of *Ideas and Elites: The Social Construction of Economic and Monetary Union* (Aalborg University Press, 2000).

Michael Moran is Professor of Government at the University of Manchester. He has written widely on the politics of market regulation. His most recent work is *Governing the Health Care State: A Comparative Study of the United States, United Kingdom and Germany* (Manchester University Press, 1999). He is presently writing a book on *The British Regulatory State* for publication by Oxford University Press.

Claudio Radaelli is Professor of Public Policy at the University of Bradford. His recent books include *The Politics of Corporate Taxation in the European Union: Knowledge and International Policy Agendas* (Routledge, 1997) and *Technocracy in the European Union* (Pearson, 1999). He specializes on European public policy, international tax policy, and Italian government and politics.

Martin Rhodes is Professor of European Public Policy at the European University Institute, Florence. His recent books on welfare include *The Future of European Welfare: A New Social Contract?* (Macmillan, 1998, edited with Yves Mény) and *Recasting European Welfare States*, a special issue of *West European Politics*, Vol. 23, No. 2, 2000 (edited with Maurizio Ferrera). His publications are mainly on issues of European welfare state and labour market policies.

Geoffrey R. D. Underhill is Professor of International Governance at the University of Amsterdam. His recent work has focused on patterns of international cooperation for the regulation and supervision of global financial markets and on the impact of regulatory change in financial markets on the global monetary system and the wider economic development process. He has edited *The New World Order in International Finance* (Macmillan, 1997); *Regionalism and Global Economic Integration: Europe, Asia and the Americas* (with William Coleman) (Routledge, 1998); *Political Economy and the Changing Global Order* (with Richard Stubbs) (Oxford University Press, 2000, 2nd edn); and *Non-State Actors and Authority in the Global System* (with Richard Higgott and Andreas Bieler) (Routledge, 2000).

Amy Verdun is Associate Professor of Political Science and Director of the European Studies Programme at the University of Victoria, British Columbia, Canada. She specializes in European monetary integration, integration theory, issues surrounding democracy and accountability in the EU as well as the role of knowledge and expertise in the policy-making process. She is the author of *European Responses to Globalization and Financial Market Integration: Perceptions of Economic and Monetary Union in Britain, France and Germany* (Macmillan/St Martin's Press, 2000). She also co-edited, with Thomas C. Lawton and James N. Rosenau, the volume *Strange Power: Shaping the Parameters of International Relations and International Political Economy* (Ashgate, 2000).

Wolfgang Wessels is Jean-Monnet Professor of Political Science at the University of Cologne and Visiting Professor at the Colleges of Europe in Bruges and Natolin. He is chairperson of the Trans European Policy Studies Association (TEPSA) in Brussels. His recent books include *Die Öffnung des Staates* (Leske und Budrich, 2000), *The European Union and Member States* (Manchester University Press, 1996, co-edited with D. Roemetsch) and *Fifteen into One?* (Manchester University Press, 2001, co-edited with A. Maurer and J. Mittag).

Introduction: EMU as Integration, Europeanization, and Convergence

Kenneth Dyson

Recent years have seen a growing output of publications dealing with Economic and Monetary Union (EMU) in Europe. Within this output certain themes stand out: how an EMU agreement was possible (for example, Cameron 1995; Dyson and Featherstone 1999; Marcussen 2000*a*; McNamara 1998; Moravcsik 1998; Verdun 2000*a*); the relationship between globalization and EMU (for example, Gill 1995; 1998; Rosamond 1999; Young 2000); what kind of institutional arrangements are emerging at the European level (for example, Begg *et al.* 1998; Dyson 2000*a*); the basic institutional deficits and lack of 'embeddedness' of EMU (Crouch 2000); broad effects on the European political economy, for instance on fiscal deficits and unemployment (for example, Frieden, Gros, and Jones 1998); and general implications for sovereignty (for example, Cohen 1998). In the media and public debates there have been regular vague allusions to the impact of EMU on European states. This impact has also been treated in some books (for example, Cobham and Zis 1999; Giordano and Persaud 1998; Jones, Frieden, and Torres 1998; Moss and Michie 1998). But what is lacking is a systematic evaluation of the ways in which EMU—as a policy paradigm and an institutional framework of rules, procedures, and styles—is affecting European states. These effects are profound and cover public policies, political structures, discourse, and identities. By seeking to offer a balanced, in-depth assessment of EMU's impact on EU member states this book tries to fill an important gap in the literature.

Unlike other books treating the topic of the impact of EMU on member states, this volume is explicitly situated in the new theoretical literature on the process of Europeanization (for example, Börzel 1999; Featherstone 2001; Goetz 2000; Green-Cowles, Caporaso, and Risse 2001; Hay and Rosamond 2000; Morlino 2000; Radaelli 2000). This literature draws attention to the interpenetration and complex interaction of European and domestic policies and politics, notably how lack of 'closeness of fit' between the two levels can serve as a condition for domestic change. It also analyzes the different dimensions of Europeanization: its scope, the direction of political and policy change that it imparts, and the mechanisms by which it produces its effects. Above all, it focuses on the roles of domestic institutions, political leadership, and specific forms of discourse in shaping the responses of European states. Finally, it deals with questions of convergence and variation among member states. These issues are directly relevant to understanding how EMU affects European states, in particular whether the direction of change is convergence around an Anglo-American neo-liberal model of market liberalization or the persistence of institutional and cultural variability with distinct national models of capitalism (Dyson 2000b; Hay 2000a; Schmidt 2001).

In talking about EMU and member states it is important to maintain some clear analytical distinctions, not least so that one is clear about the boundaries of Europeanization as a concept (Radaelli 2000). At the same time EMU as Europeanization is bound together in complex, interdependent feedback loops with two other phenomena: EMU as European integration and EMU as convergence/divergence. The story of EMU as Europeanization is intimately connected with these two other stories. EMU as European integration constitutes and structures the context of Europeanization. It prescribes a particular policy paradigm—'sound' money and finance—and a specific institutional model—an ECB-centric Euro-Zone and a model of implicit macroeconomic policy coordination (Dyson 2000a). In this way it provides a particular ideational context of narratives and understandings in which domestic elites are structurally embedded and on which they can draw as a strategic resource. The effects of EMU as European integration are discernible in two ways. It alters the configuration of strategic constraints and opportunities within which actors behave, privileging certain actors and certain courses of action. It also changes the way in which domestic actors define their interests and form their identities. In these ways EMU as European integration shapes the scope of, and provides a particular direction of change to, Europeanization. Convergence of policies and outcomes is one possible outcome of Europeanization. In turn, the mix of convergence/divergence in domestic processes, policies, and outcomes defines the parameters for EMU as European integration. The greater the convergence of policies and outcomes, the more likely are state elites to identify further macroeconomic coordination as in their interests. The result is increased Europeanization.

Hence, looked at in a macro-sense, EMU involves complex feedback loops in which its effects on member states are embedded (cf. Stone Sweet, Sandholtz, and Fligstein 2001). EMU as Europeanization remains analytically distinct but part of bigger and more complex processes of integration and convergence/divergence. Member states are a part of these processes but only imperfectly able to control them. Hence uncertainty, contingency, and indeterminacy are vital parts of the story of how EMU affects member states.

Approach

The book is organized around case studies combined with a thematic treatment, with contributions from authors who are established experts in their fields. It moves in a logical manner from globalization, through the EU level, to member states and, finally, specific sectors. No attempt has been made to impose a particular theoretical approach or methodology on contributors. This caution—which some might interpret as lack of theoretical ambition and scientific rigour—stems in part from the fact that Europeanization remains a relatively new theoretical interest and has produced more questions than answers. A mix of approaches also seems better adapted to the challenge of explaining the complex reality and range of issues with which the literature on Europeanization deals. This literature pictures Europeanization as a dynamic process unfolding over time, the complex interactivity of variables, and its diverse, contingent, and contradictory effects—for example, Olsen (1996); Dyson (2000b); Featherstone (2001).

On good scientific grounds one can resist the notion that EMU's effects on states follow the determinate cause-effect relations of Newtonian physics. More consistent with the simultaneous presence of pattern and randomness that Europeanization reveals is a model that stresses the fusion of cause and contingency and the role of contingency as a cause. Werner Heisenberg's principle of uncertainty in theoretical physics and complexity theory in mathematics caution against the expectation that we can assess the relative contribution of particular variables, indeed against taking the notion of causality too seriously in the first place. The power of EMU varies across space and time, expressed in terms of its capacity to break down resistance to change.

Hence this volume shies away from the narrowly focused, Aristotelian argument that a 'prime mover' is waiting to be discovered at the end of a causal chain. One such argument concentrates on distinguishing the variable that functions as the first cause so that one has a comprehensive causal explanation of how EMU impacts on member states. This prime mover has been variously identified as ideas of 'sound' money (McNamara 1998), domestic institutions (Milner 1995), political leadership (Dyson and Featherstone 1999), and domestic 'political opportunity' structures (Oatley 1997). Another argument of this type revolves around the question of whether EMU is the main determinant of market liberalization and welfare-state retrenchment in Europe or whether EMU is merely an epiphenomenon. This question revolves around whether globalization—in particular, freedom of movement of capital and the unfettered power of multinational corporations—is acting as the prime mover (Hay 2000a). Such arguments rest on the very contestable assumption that what we are observing at the level of states must logically trace back to a single primary entity and that a comprehensive causal explanation is possible.

It is important to try to establish how EMU impacts on states, not least by contextualizing it. But the search for a prime mover neglects the complex interactivity at work, both of structure and agency and of domestic, European, and international levels. In seeking to unravel this complexity one uncovers a multiplicity of causes, each itself having many causes, producing an infinity of original causes rather than just one prime mover. EMU's impact on member states is correspondingly associated with variation, contradictions, paradoxes, and problems (cf. Wright 1994: 102). The search for a prime mover also does too little justice to the basic ontological disagreements about the nature of social reality that underpin different views on causality and on what should be the focus of enquiry (Hay 2000b). These differences are not susceptible to empirical resolution and suggest that one cannot expect contributors chosen for their excellence in particular areas to share a single approach.

No less seriously, the search for a prime mover is made more difficult by the way in which the reality of domestic politics and policy is in substantial part constituted by the contrasting ideas of elites about EMU and about how it relates to such other factors as globalization and the 'new' economy. Discourse about EMU reveals the range of meanings given to it and its use in ordering and making intelligible social, economic, and political developments and in enabling change. Different constructions of EMU shape how state actors respond and the kinds of outcomes that emerge. They reflect the importance of the cognitive dimension of EMU. As these meanings are in part historical and embedded in specific institutional milieus, and in part the products of agency, they impart further complexity and variety to the effects of EMU on member states. Ideas about EMU play an independent causal and constitutive role in producing the effects attributed to Europeanization. Europeanization does not represent a causal factor or process working independently of the beliefs of domestic elites. Hence this book pays attention to the discursive mediation of domestic change in terms of Europeanization and the strategic use made of Europeanization as legitimization for reforms.

In particular, it highlights the distinctiveness of the domestic contexts within which EMU as Europeanization is debated.

Questions

Hesitancy about imposing a particular approach does not justify a lack of unity in an edited collection. Hence this book seeks to establish a basic coherence by a set of core questions raised by the impact of EMU on member states. These questions have also been designed to ward off the risk of theoretical prejudgment of EMU's significance. The book seeks to avoid too rigid a research design in favour of an approach that 'contextualizes' EMU (cf. Goetz 2000).

First, what are the implications of globalization and the institutional design of EMU for member states? What general tendencies do they impart to domestic political and policy changes? How EMU affects member states is bound up with the larger question of the international sources of domestic change, stressed in the 'second-image' perspective in international relations (Gourevitch 1978). Underhill takes up the issue of the relationship between globalization, EMU, and member states. He considers whether EMU is a mediating variable on behalf of an Anglo-American form of capitalism or whether it enables the retention of a distinctive European social model. Wessels and Linsenmann concentrate on EMU's impact on national institutions. McKay investigates the nature of the EU's fiscal regime in the context of monetary union and sets it in a comparative context.

Though the questions of the relationship between globalization and EMU and of the nature and implications of the EU's fiscal regime are centrally addressed in these early chapters, they inform all the chapters. The country-specific case studies highlight the different ways in which national elites construct both globalization and EMU on the one hand and the relationship between them and the degree of domestic accommodation to the fiscal regime on the other. They show that the relationship between globalization and EMU is highly contested in domestic politics and yields different answers across space and time. Underhill, Wessels and Linsenmann, and McKay offer a more 'top-down' and 'outside-in' view of how EMU is affecting European states, independently of their macro-characteristics. Wessels and Linsenmann emphasize the differential nature of the effects, comparing monetary, fiscal, and economic and employment policies. From these chapters one gains a sense of the international sources creating pressures for convergence among EU member states.

Second, how is EMU affecting discourse, identities, political structures, and public policies in member states? This question is addressed in the country-specific case studies. They provide a more 'bottom-up' and 'inside-out' view of EMU, focusing on domestic institutions, political leadership, discourse, and temporal sequence as explanatory variables. The picture that emerges is of the contingent character of convergence in policies, outcomes, and processes. Domestic institutional and cultural distinctiveness supports a variability in how EMU as Europeanization affects member states.

Finally, in what ways and with what consequences is EMU affecting key policy sectors? What conditions the degree of convergence discernible in different sectors? Moran focuses on financial market regulation; Crouch on labour-market and wage policies; and Rhodes on welfare-state reforms. Here again the impact of EMU is 'contextualized'. Many of the most fundamental challenges appear to have little to do with EMU. Sectoral differences are clear, with for instance financial markets deeply embedded in globalization while processes of labour-market, wage-negotiation, and welfare-state reform are more deeply conditioned by domestic institutional arrangements. The authors do not detect a single process of convergence around neo-liberalism. The stress is on how different domestic settings affect the scope, pace, and terms of sectoral reforms.

EMU as European Integration

EMU as European integration describes the process by which linkages among member states emerge and are stabilized over time by rules and procedures (Stone Sweet, Sandholtz, and Fligstein 2001). These linkages are both vertical —between the EU and member states—and horizontal or transnational— between officials in different member states. The study of EMU as Europeanization is about the domestic effects of EMU as European integration. These effects are prima facie powerful because EMU is the most important step in European integration since the Treaty of Rome in 1957 legitimized the customs union and a single European market as objectives. It has the attributes of a parameter shift in European integration, changing fundamentally the underlying basis of the EU and how it operates. The EU shifted from being principally a 'regulatory' state to being a 'stabilization' state (Dyson 2000a). It specializes in the essentially technocratic functions of regulation and economic stability.

With the Maastricht Treaty, negotiated in 1991, member states bound themselves to a policy paradigm of 'sound' money and finance (Dyson 1994;

McNamara 1998). This paradigm was institutionalized in rules and procedures. A European Central Bank (ECB) was mandated to secure price stability
—its independence guaranteed by treaty provision—and empowered to define
its own price stability objective. A 'no bail out' provision and the prohibition
on monetary financing of deficits safeguarded financial and monetary discipline. This discipline was further demonstrated by tightly defined convergence
criteria governing inflation, budget deficits, public debt, long-term interest
rates, and exchange-rate stability as conditions for entry into stage three.
These criteria were designed to ensure the achievement of a high degree of
sustainable convergence. An excessive deficit procedure was put in place
to monitor compliance (Dyson and Featherstone 1999). EMU embedded in
institutional terms a clear European model of 'sound' money and finance.
In so doing, EMU privileged a particular discourse and reform strategy. It
selectively empowered central bankers and finance ministry technocrats. The
European paradigm of 'sound' money and finance has implications both for
the programmatic activities of member state governments and for the way
in which domestic political and policy change is 'framed' and legitimized to
publics.

Before examining its effects on member states it is important to note that
EMU as European integration was not completed with the Maastricht Treaty.
Since then it has become institutionally 'stickier' in terms of rules and procedures relating both to financial discipline and to 'soft' or 'open' coordination
in the economic union pillar. The Stability and Growth Pact of 1997 tightened
fiscal discipline in stage three and introduced monitoring of convergence
programmes, in effect 'hard' coordination with sanctions in the background.
It was followed in 2000 by tax policy guidelines that defined sensible policies
for tax cutting over the economic cycle. The Euro Group was established for
stage three to deliberate on common economic policy problems.

A series of initiatives sought to redefine EMU as a project for growth and
employment, in a manner consistent with Social Democratic values, and
to strengthen macroeconomic policy coordination under Art. 103 (Dyson
2000a). A first step was the employment chapter of the Amsterdam Treaty
of 1997 and the so-called Luxembourg process, including new employment
policy guidelines and national employment action plans. This was followed
by the structural economic reform process initiated at the Cardiff European
Council in 1998. These two processes were brought together in the European
Employment Pact agreed at the Cologne European Council in 1999. Central to
the Cologne process was the new Macroeconomic Dialogue which draws in
the social partners, alongside the European Commission, national governments, and the ECB, to encourage compatible action in wage bargaining,

fiscal policies, and monetary policy. Multilateral surveillance of economic policies was strengthened at the Helsinki European Council in 1999 by broadening the agenda of the Broad Guidelines of Economic Policies to include structural reforms and more stringent monitoring of individual states. At the Lisbon European Council in 2000 the philosophy and methodology of 'soft' economic policy coordination was spelt out as a process of sharing experience and benchmarking best policy practice. Hence Europeanization was not just about the effects of the Maastricht Treaty. It was bound up in a continuing process of integration, especially focusing on 'soft' coordination of economic policy. To complicate the task of this volume, the variable whose impacts it studies has undergone change.

Despite this evolutionary character of EMU as integration, the striking aspect is the compatibility between this process of 'filling out' the institutional rules and procedures of the economic union pillar and the established paradigm of 'sound' money and finance. The ECB-centric nature of an Euro-Zone as 'stabilization' state remains intact (Dyson 2000a). It is tempting to see a 'path dependency' at work as the founding conditions of EMU limit how the institutional framework of the Euro-Zone develops. This framework embodies a particular form of structural power, understood as the ability to shape the context within which political strategies are formulated. Hence there is a striking continuity in the influence of the assumptions underpinning the 'sound' money paradigm. In adopting this paradigm as the guarantee of economic stability member-state governments had also implicitly committed themselves to the notion that money was neutral with respect to growth and employment and to the model of implicit macroeconomic policy coordination. In short, EMU came as part of a whole discursive structure which established its legitimacy as technocratic. EMU's technocratic character was strengthened by the new emphasis on benchmarking best practice as a methodology and by the Macroeconomic Dialogue. Member-state governments committed themselves to a pragmatic learning process about what works best, for instance in generating employment. But direction was given to that learning process by the paradigm of 'sound' money and finance and monetary policy leadership.

The questions being addressed in this book mean that it is not concerned to test different theories of EMU as integration. These theories do, nevertheless, shed light on an important issue that bears on Europeanization, namely the extent to which member-state governments are in control of the larger process. In one type of theory European integration is pictured as essentially controlled by these governments and their defence of national interests. Developing Milward's (1992) approach, EMU is another example of the

European rescue of member states. It strengthens the allegiance between states and their citizens by helping states to better perform their basic functions of security and welfare, notably by institutionalizing fiscal discipline and enabling a more effective functioning of automatic stabilizers. For Moravcsik (1998) EMU is a process of intergovernmental bargaining defined by convergent economic interests. Because economic policy interests are not convergent in a Euro-Zone economy characterized by structural differences, it is not possible to move beyond 'soft' coordination in this area. In both cases the image is one of tight control of the integration process by member states.

Conversely, neo-functionalist theory and theories of the logic of institutionalization stress that member-state governments are embedded in an integration process that they do not control and that is a product of what has developed in the past. These theories see politics as important at the micro- rather than macro-level. In neo-functionalist theory integration has a momentum of its own, imparted by spillover effects from one area to another and by technocratic rationales. Thus Verdun (2000a: 191) identifies spillover effects to EMU from the European Monetary System (EMS), the single European market programme, and liberalization of capital movement in particular. Similar effects might be identified within the Euro-Zone. Thus, an optimal performance of monetary policy in securing price stability at low cost to output and employment draws the issue of stabilizing unit labour costs on to the EMU agenda. The result is a new preoccupation with wage bargaining and welfare-state reforms in stage three.

Sweet Stone, Sandholtz, and Fligstein (2001) explain integration as generated by complex feedback loops or 'loops of institutionalization'. The result is a self-sustaining dynamic of integration. In EMU the key feedback loops might be visualized as between loss of autonomy in economic and monetary policy making, EMU rule-making and procedures, performance in macroeconomic convergence, and elite identity with EMU (Fig. 0.1). The synergy between globalization and the single European market in the 1980s laid the foundations for EMU. In globalized financial markets, characterized by the free movement of capital, EU governments are more constrained in monetary policy. They are also threatened by potential disruption of internal EU trade by exchange-rate instability and potential adverse policy interactions in an increasingly interdependent economic area, with negative consequences for employment and growth. New rules and procedures to stabilize and then irrevocably fix exchange rates and coordinate other policies offset the costs of this reduced autonomy in economic and monetary policies. These new rules and procedures for EMU in turn force governments to reappraise what they can best do in domestic economic policies, especially

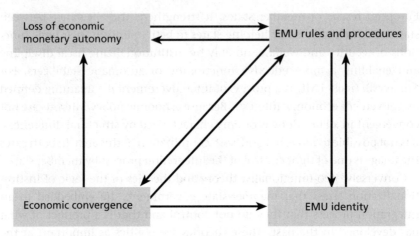

Fig. 0.1 EMU as a self-reinforcing mechanism of integration

by containing unit labour cost development and prioritizing structural economic reforms. A second feedback loop is between EMU rules and procedures and economic convergence. There appears to be a correlation between increased economic convergence and new EMU rules and procedures. New rules and procedures, like exchange rate coordination and then a single monetary policy, serve in turn to underpin and reinforce convergence. Equally, convergence increases confidence that these new rules and procedures can be made to work in the general interest. A third feedback loop involves a greater identity of national officials and central bankers with the institutional mechanics of EMU as it becomes clear that key decisions are being taken there. The more identity shifts to the European level, the readier officials are to endorse closer rules and procedures to strengthen coordination. This greater identity feeds back into greater compliance with EMU rules and procedures. Improved compliance feeds back in turn into a readier acceptance of macroeconomic coordination. Hence EMU appears as a self-sustaining process, characterized by a parameter shift in the period 1985–9. During this period the launch of the single market programme and increased economic convergence associated with the Exchange Rate Mechanism (ERM) set in process a complex set of interactions that led to a dynamic growth of EMU rules and procedures and of elite identity with EMU.

Neo-functionalism and the theory of the logic of institutionalization underestimate the difficulties facing EMU as a consequence of its political and institutional deficits, notably the absence of common economic policy instruments—like a fiscal transfer system—and of system-wide labour mobility (Crouch 2000). Political and institutional inertia associated with the diversity of national capitalisms and the lack of embeddedness of EMU is likely to make problems of economic convergence difficult, if not intractable. Protracted and deepening problems of convergence may force member-state governments to behave in new, less accommodative ways not predicted by the logic of institutionalization or neo-functionalism. Spillover and feedback mechanisms might be disrupted by a growing negativity towards EMU, with politics becoming important at the macro-level. The prospect is that EMU as integration process becomes highly politicized as regions and individuals attribute direct and negative effects to it. Theories of EMU as rescue of the state and as intergovernmental bargaining are also problematic. They underestimate more sociological and endogenous processes of interest definition and identity formation.

Instead of EMU rescuing states, the process of institutional refinement of economic policy coordination can be interpreted as European states seeking to rescue a potentially fragile and vulnerable EMU to which they have acquired a sense of belonging (cf. Milward 2000). In short, state elites come to redefine their interests as ensuring the Euro-Zone works and supporting the credibility of the ECB. Both types of theory identify certain tendencies within EMU as integration process. However, neither is able to capture adequately the uncertainty, contingency, and indeterminacy that surround it and the role of ideas and changing constructions of EMU in the complex causation of the integration process.

EMU as Europeanization

Though EMU as Europeanization is intimately bound up in this integration process, it is concerned with the effects of that process—the paradigm that it embodies and the institutional form that it takes—on member states. The potential scope of these effects embraces discourse, identities, political structures, and public policies (Morlino 2000; Radaelli 2000). Particular attention has been paid to the cognitive dimension of Europeanization, especially dissemination of a particular European policy paradigm and the distinctive ways in which domestic policy and political changes are framed and legitimized in different domestic contexts. However, the strategic use of EMU as a structure shifting opportunities and constraints to exercise power at the domestic level is also important.

The Scope and Direction of Effects

One key aspect of EMU as Europeanization is its effects. This issue is reducible to the scope of its effects and the direction of change that it imparts. The effects seem more obvious on public policies and discourse than on identities and on political structures, like party systems and representative structures. Within discourse the effects are more discernible at the elite level of programmatic activity than in the framing of specific policy changes for the purpose of legitimization to general publics. At the same time policy effects serve to transform how structures operate. This phenomenon is apparent within the executive branch where EMU has privileged central bankers and finance ministry officials. An ECB-centric Euro-Zone also has implications for elite identity, especially of central bankers making monetary policy for the zone as a whole and for finance ministry officials looking at aggregate effects of policy from the same perspective (Dyson 2000a). But these identity changes are confined to a very narrow technocratic elite and raise questions about the relationship between elite attitudes and public sentiments when publics have not been closely involved in approving the design of EMU.

The direction of change is defined by the 'sound' money and finance paradigm. By selectively empowering domestic actors and restructuring strategic opportunities, EMU serves to reinforce certain trends, for instance to technocratic empowerment. But the key issue is whether there is a 'goodness of fit' between this paradigm and domestic ideas and institutional arrangements. For instance, a depoliticized monetary policy has problems of compatibility with the French republican tradition. Its belief in the centrality of the nation as the fount of values suggests that government is responsible for the conduct of general economic, including monetary, policy. In consequence of differences of ideational and institutional compatibility, states exhibit varying responses to EMU. Radaelli (2000) identifies four responses. *Accommodation* means that EMU is compatible with domestic structures, policies, discourse, and identities. This response seemed most characteristic for Germany which succeeded in Europeanizing its monetary policy model. *Transformation* involves fundamental challenge to domestic structures, policies, discourse, and identities from a lack of 'goodness of fit' with EMU's framework of monetary and financial discipline. At times Italy has demonstrated this characteristic. *Inertia* involves a lack of change due to a combination of deeply entrenched domestic institutional veto players, a lack of political will, and the extent of incompatibility with the EU policy paradigm. Again Italy provides examples. *Retrenchment* involves the paradox of negative Europeanization. In this case lack of 'closeness of fit' with EMU strengthens the opposition to reforms and leads to counter-tendencies.

The threat of retrenchment acts as a constraint on the pressures to Europeanize. EU elites hesitate to push domestic elites into confrontations that they cannot win and would be counterproductive in effect. In this sense public sentiments remain a key independent variable. They constrain action by limiting the range of alternatives that elites are likely to perceive as legitimate (Campbell 1998). EMU challenges strongly entrenched and different identities to be found in national trade unions and social democratic parties. These identities help determine which issues of labour-market and welfare-state reforms are seen as worth contesting. In practice, astute elite management, notably in framing reforms and timing—typically deferring them—has contained this threat. Hence retrenchment has not been so evident as inertia or a transformation that attributes less significance to Europeanization than other factors. Framing has often been about avoiding attribution of the reasons for reforms to Europe. Hence a discursive gap emerges—for instance, in Germany—between programmatic endorsement of Europeanization of policy and the way in which elites communicate with the public about specific reforms. Far more typical than retrenchment are complex combinations of accommodation, transformation, and inertia, varying over space and time.

Cognitive and Material Mechanisms: Discursive Constructions of EMU

A second aspect of EMU as Europeanization is how it produces its effects. Several mechanisms are at work, cognitive and material, direct and indirect (Fig. 0.2). Materially, EMU alters the parameters of state action. In a direct sense the policy instruments for economic adjustment are changed. The loss of interest-rate and exchange-rate instruments forces labour-market and wage flexibility on to domestic agendas. In an indirect sense, EMU has material effects on the context of state action through transparency of prices

	Material	Cognitive
Direct	Loss of exchange-rate and interest-rate policy instruments	Institutionalization of sound money paradigm: vertical diffusion of ideas
Indirect	Intensified market Competition	Competition in economic policies: horizontal diffusion of ideas

Fig. 0.2 Effects of EMU

and costs, more intense market competition, and accelerated merger and acquisition activity. Its effects are mediated through a more competitive environment and structural adjustment.

Direct cognitive effects follow from the way in which EMU institutionalizes a European model of 'sound' money and finance, affecting the basic goals of state action. More broadly, EMU involves framing domestic policy reforms in a technocratic discourse. This discourse facilitates cognitive convergence around a paradigm of 'sound' money and finance. It also fits in with how historically the EU has legitimized its role (Radaelli 1999). Indirect cognitive effects are more apparent in economic policies. Here EMU protects states against direct intervention. An asymmetry between economic union and monetary union is expressed in the model of 'soft' coordination in economic policies. This emphasis on decentralization and sharing experience is legitimized by the higher principle of subsidiarity in the economic-union pillar of EMU. At the same time domestic effects are anticipated from the new methodology of 'benchmarking' best practice in policies for growth and employment. This effect suggests a horizontal rather than 'top-down' mechanism of transnational diffusion of policy ideas.

The cognitive effects of EMU are complex, as the domestic case studies show. However, certain basic patterns in discourse about EMU as Europeanization are discernible (cf. Hay and Rosamond 2000; Rosamond 1999). These patterns in construction of EMU reflect particular domestic conditions.

1. *EMU as the 'internalization' of the external economic imperatives represented by globalization as a force for disciplinary neo-liberalism* (Gill 1995; 1998). This discourse favours the adoption of domestic market-conforming policies of neo-liberalism, consistent with a view of EMU as reinforcing globalization's characteristics of free capital movement, open trading, and threats of exit from mobile transnational businesses unless domestic tax and regulatory costs are reduced. Those who advocate a model of 'market' or 'liberal' capitalism define these effects as benign and non-negotiable. Politically, this discourse is represented by EU central bankers, like Hans Tietmeyer at the Bundesbank and Otmar Issing at the ECB, the Kohl government in Germany between 1996 and 1998, and Tony Blair in Britain. It finds expression in attacks on supply-side rigidities and the radical, inevitable nature of the changes required if the Euro-Zone is to be sustainable. This type of discourse emerges when political elites perceive domestic reforms as urgent and unpopular and identify the positive associations of free capital movement. Conversely, they wish, like Kohl in relating structural reforms directly to globalization, to protect what they see as a potentially vulnerable EMU from a domestic political arena in which it might be contested if identified as the prime cause of painful

reforms. They may also be responding, like Blair, to a historical context in which there has been an arms-length and distrustful relationship to European integration and in which powerful economic interests are wedded to the model of 'market' capitalism.

2. *EMU as an inexorable process of dissolving national identities, undermining domestic political structures, and removing national sovereignty over economic policy.* Its effects are seen as principally cultural and political and defined as threatening. Politically, this discourse is represented by opponents of EMU across the EU, notably in Britain and Denmark and from political parties that appeal to a national populism. It finds expression in the idea of the surrender of national sovereignty and of EMU as a force for homogenization. This type of discourse arises when Europeanization has negative associations, when identity and sovereignty are viewed in absolutist terms rather than in terms of coexistence and sharing, when national governments are seen as powerless over European integration, and when domestic reforms are seen as unpalatable.

3. *EMU as a means of resistance to the external dependence on the US implicit in a globalization that is seen in essentially negative terms.* Globalization is pictured as the unaccountable power of financial markets and multinational corporations, a 'race to the bottom' in tax rates and in environmental and social standards, and the 'hollowing out' of the state and of democracy. EMU is defined as a counterweight to the erosion of traditional social solidarities by creating a new reality. Its effects are demonstrated in the preservation of a distinctive European social model and a new international activism on behalf of the regulation of the global economy. Politically, this discourse is represented by the pro-EU French Left under Leonard Jospin and by Oskar Lafontaine in the German Social Democratic Party. It finds expression in the idea of an EU-level 'economic government' and an interventionist approach to managing capitalism. This type of discourse arises in the domestic context of a positive view of European integration and a negative view of globalization and of a view that national governments are better able to influence the EU than to influence global institutions.

4. *EMU as a means of reconciling the European social model to the new realities of globalization.* This discourse reflects the values of 'managed' capitalism, with its emphasis on product quality, reliability, and flexibility and on the importance of effective retention and productive use of skilled employees (Iversen, Pontusson, and Soskice 2000). The result is a stress on managing globalization through neo-corporatist social dialogue embracing government, employers, and trade unions. Globalization is defined in positive terms, subject to a requirement of negotiated change so that the interests of potential

losers are safeguarded. Politically, Gerhard Schröder in Germany and Wim Kok in the Netherlands represent this discourse. It finds expression in the idea of a cooperative capitalism, for instance as embodied in the Macroeconomic Dialogue, the Wassenaar process in the Netherlands, and the Alliance for Jobs in Germany. This type of discourse is apparent in domestic contexts in which both European integration and globalization are seen in positive terms and in which there is little dissension over both. Governments define their role as enabling and orchestrating consensus about fundamental reforms consistent with the principles of a market economy. Restructuring is also seen in a longer timescale than in states attached to the model of 'market' capitalism.

Who is Affected?

A third aspect of Europeanization is who is affected and how. This question brings out the significance of actors and their strategic empowerment and disempowerment by EMU. EMU has been bound up, in a complex interactive process of cause and effect, with the creation of transnational networks of policy professionals. The presence of such networks, notably in central banking, made EMU possible and helps explain the asymmetry between monetary union and economic union. Shared knowledge among central bankers—in effect, an epistemic community based on shared professional knowledge—facilitated early agreement in the Delors Committee on the principle of an independent ECB as the focus for bargaining (Dyson and Featherstone 1999; Verdun 2000a). In turn, the process of negotiating EMU and then of managing the long transition to stage three reinforced the solidarity within these transnational networks (Dyson 2000b). The ECB, the Economic and Financial Committee and the Euro Group represent the epicentres of these networks. This intense interactivity, the associated socialization effects into the values of the Euro-Zone, and a new sense of shared identity combine to make the sense of Europeanization very pronounced in Euro-Zone finance ministries and central banks. In contrast, though brought into the EU orbit over employment policies and policies to create a European knowledge-based economy, other ministries have not spawned equivalently dense transnational professional networks. Also, EU finance ministries and central bankers have ensured their continuing professional control over the Broad Economic Policy Guidelines, the Employment Policy Guidelines, and the Macroeconomic Dialogue. The net effect of EMU has been to strengthen the domestic power of finance ministries over structural economic reforms.

At the same time, as we saw above, domestic elites have used EMU in different ways. EMU has been contested as elites have attributed contrasting meanings to it. This contest has been more muted among central bankers and finance ministry officials where the positive endorsement of both globalization and Europeanization has led to a dominance of two types of discourse: EMU as 'internalization' of globalization's imperatives and, to a lesser extent, EMU as social dialogue. The discourse of EMU as a defensive mechanism against globalization finds more resonance in social affairs and employment ministries, though even there it sits alongside the other two types of discourse. EMU as cultural and political threat is more strongly represented on the far left and far right of the party political spectrum and within public opinion, especially those with unskilled jobs and lower levels of educational attainment (Dyson 2000a).

EMU as Convergence or Diversity

A third question about EMU is concerned with its outcomes and whether these outcomes involve convergence or continuing diversity of institutionally and culturally distinctive forms of national capitalism in Europe. The central issue is whether EMU leads to convergence around common outcomes, specifically a neo-liberal form of welfare-state retrenchment, labour-market and wage flexibility, financial market deregulation, tax competition, fiscal discipline, and loosening of the ties of business with government and trade unions. This convergence may be attributed to EMU as an independent variable or to EMU as an epiphenomenon of a globalization that is predicated on an ascendant Anglo-American model of neo-liberal economic ideology.

EMU involves a common pressure for convergence from the loss of the exchange rate and the interest rate as policy instruments for domestic economic adjustment to asymmetric shocks. The effect is to favour policy strategies that place greater weight on labour markets and wages in adjustment processes. Conventional explanations rooted in neoclassical economics emphasize EMU as a pressure for convergence through heightened capital mobility, mimicking and reinforcing the effects of globalization as capital mobility (for example, Ohmae 1996). Heightened capital mobility in new large and integrated financial markets denominated in euros encourages the threat of exit by firms from high-cost locations and induces a process of competitive deregulation towards convergence around the model of 'market' capitalism and 'shareholder' value. In short, by encouraging a more perfect capital mobility, EMU imparts a particular bias or tendency to domestic policy changes that facilitates convergence of policies and outcomes around neo-liberalism. Convergence takes on an evolutionary, 'catch-up' form consequent on a process of benchmarking best practice in handling the implications of this capital mobility. In this respect the conclusions of the Lisbon European Council can be interpreted as underpinned by neoclassical economics and exemplifying its influence on discourse. Otherwise, convergence is forced by the exogenous shocks administered by EMU and globalization. They represent exogenous enforcement mechanisms on behalf of 'market' capitalism.

This focus on convergence around 'market' capitalism in neoclassical economics is replicated in neo-Gramscian theories of EMU and globalization (Gill 1998). Here EMU is pictured as part of a new international governance structure that is defined by a disciplinary neo-liberalism enforced by global financial market players and the social forces that support them. The result is convergence around an Anglo-American model of a flexible, deregulated, and privatized economy. This neo-liberal model of EMU is disseminated through the power and prestige of US multinationals and the reputation that comes from US economic performance (Gill 1998). Seen from this angle, French *dirigiste* ideas about imposing political will on global markets—EMU as 'regulated' capitalism—and Dutch and German models of negotiated change through social dialogue seem of symbolic rather than practical importance. They disguise the underlying structural realities of convergence around a neo-liberal discourse that identifies EMU, like globalization, as an objective and exogenous structure. At most, states wedded to traditions of 'managed' capitalism and state-centric capitalism delay—rather than divert—the process and are destined to fade away before the 'competitive imperative'.

In predicting convergence of policies and outcomes both neoclassical economics and the neo-Gramscian approach are insightful in identifying how a discourse of globalization and EMU as exogenous economic imperative has powerful political roots in developments in the international policy economy. But they also share serious weaknesses. They place too much weight on a discursive construction of an inevitable logic of market-conforming reforms. In fact, as we have seen, there are at least four different constructions of EMU, two of which have a market-reforming bias. In consequence, any process of convergence is bound to be contingent on the precise nature and effects of domestic contentions about EMU. Neo-Gramscian theory and neoclassical economics neglect the way in which domestic policy changes are embedded in a particular configuration of institutional arrangements and discursive practices. Hence their weakness is an under-specification of domestic policy processes and of the active role of domestic institutions in the formation and survival of norms, values, and practices. These processes reveal a great diversity. This diversity has implications for the prospects for convergence of policies and especially of outcomes, and not least for the effectiveness of reliance on benchmarking best practice elsewhere.

A large literature exists on the very different nature of capitalist organization, mainly from a political science and institutionalist perspective. Institutionalist accounts underline the varieties of capitalism and the individually specific nature of policy and political change (for example, Berger and Dore 1996; Crouch and Streeck 1997; Hall and Soskice 2001; Hollingsworth and Boyer 1997; Kitschelt *et al.* 1999). Thus Britain represents the model of 'market' capitalism in which a 'liberal' state ensures market-conforming behaviour. France articulates 'state' capitalism in which an 'interventionist' state organizes inter-firm collaboration and employer-trade union cooperation. Germany epitomizes the model of 'managed' capitalism in which an 'enabling' state facilitates cooperation in the management of change, especially between employers and trade unions (Schmidt 2001). This diversity is consequent on the 'path-dependence' of their political and economic institutions and the framing of their responses by historical memories and differing cultural norms. Particular, historically conditioned and culturally rooted forms of state-capitalism relations constrain the scope, direction, timing, and tempo of changes. In addition, globalization and EMU do not automatically privilege competition on cost and competitive deregulation. Though employers may seek reforms to 'managed' capitalism, for instance in Germany, they continue to value it as a means for containing unit labour costs, maintaining harmony in the workplace, retaining and upgrading skills, and ensuring product quality, reliability, and flexibility (Silvia 1999; Thelen 2000). In states like Denmark, Germany, and the Netherlands business strategy has underpinned the resilience of the model of 'managed' capitalism rather than followed the neoclassical logic of globalization and EMU.

Hence domestic policy changes tend to revitalize rather than displace distinctive national forms of 'managed' capitalism. The outcomes of EMU as Europeanization take the form of the reproduction of differences among EU economies over time (cf. Weiss 1998). In such accounts EMU as Europeanization takes place through the refracting prism of domestic institutional and cultural factors that militate against convergence in both process and outcome. The range of possible outcomes stretches from divergence to, at best, a contingent convergence that masks an underlying diversity (cf. Hay 2000a: 7) or a 'clustered' convergence that reflects the continuing impact of different models of capitalism.

The institutionally embedded nature of policy changes consequent on EMU has important implications for convergence. Thus, contrary to neoclassical economics, the demise of specific policy instruments like exchange rates and interest rates does not automatically enfeeble the state but can spur the development of new policy instruments adapted to particular institutional and cultural conditions (cf. Weiss 1998: 195). Common pressures do not mean policy convergence. The forms of policy response to such pressures have differed in labour markets and in welfare-state reforms. Even when policies converge, they are likely to have very different outcomes (Hay 2000a). For instance, how a single monetary policy works is conditioned by different monetary transmission mechanisms, reflecting the ways in which credit is organized. In consequence, the effects of an interest-rate change by the ECB may be felt quickly and sharply in some domestic contexts and more slowly and smoothly in other contexts. Similarly, convergence around fiscal discipline in the framework of the Stability and Growth Pact is consistent with diverse outcomes on taxation and public expenditure. Crouch, McKay, Moran, and Rhodes address these issues in their chapters.

Though institutionalist accounts add to understanding of the complex links between pressures, process, policies, and outcomes in EMU, they risk underestimating the specific ways in which EMU contributes to convergence. First, domestic institutions may exhibit greater flexibility than institutionalist accounts allow. This flexibility arises when institutions find themselves in a performance and legitimacy crisis (Morlino 2000: 8). In that context EMU as Europeanization can affect the process of reform and outcomes by 'selecting' winners and losers in domestic political argument and creating convergence through policy transfer. An example is internal processes of policy change on wage bargaining within trade unions. Thus in Germany trade-union supporters of a benchmark of productivity-based wage bargaining in order to stabilize unit labour costs defeated their opponents in 2000. Another instance is the catalytic effect of threat by the employers' federation to withdraw from management of the social security system in France.

Second, the scope for flexibility may be greater in the EU's southern periphery than in its core. EMU as an ideology of modernization has the potential to reduce the legitimacy and persuasiveness of institutions that are identified as traditional and to open the way for technocratic empowerment. In such a situation it may be more difficult to resist pressures for convergence, policy convergence, and process convergence. Hence the EU's southern periphery is likely to be subject to profound transformation from the 'disciplinary neo-liberalism' of EMU and the asymmetrical interdependence in which it finds itself within EMU (Gill 1995; Featherstone 2001).

Finally, EMU's impact is reinforced by the wider regional integration process of which it is a part, in particular by the scope of policy integration, the intensity of elite interaction, and the emergence—however limited—of a regional identity. For these reasons, as a regional mechanism of convergence EMU is likely to have a greater effect than globalization (Hay 2000a: 17). But just how far this proves to be the case depends on whether there is a dominant construction of EMU that emphasizes its role as a disciplinary mechanism on behalf of neo-liberalism. In this sense discourse as a means of legitimizing change has an independent causal effect on the direction, timing, and tempo of domestic change associated with EMU.

Conclusion

EMU is a complex force for change. It comprises cognitive and material aspects. It has direct and indirect effects. These effects began before 1 January 1999 and have demonstrated differences of timing, sequencing, and tempo. Moreover, EMU possesses a complex relationship to other forces of change, notably globalization and domestic sources of change.

EMU appears to be associated with certain general patterns. These patterns are discernible in the nature, scope, and direction of its effects. The cognitive effects involve the institutionalization of a 'sound money' paradigm, with a 'top-down' diffusion of ideas privileging price stability, financial discipline, and 'supply-side' reforms to financial markets, labour markets, wage negotiations, and welfare states. They also include a competition of economic policies and the benchmarking of best practice in promoting economic growth and reducing unemployment, through a 'horizontal' diffusion of ideas. Material effects are most apparent in intensified market competition and labour-market and wage flexibility. The result is systemic pressures for convergence of policies and outcomes. A pattern is also identifiable in the discursive constructions of EMU, which fall into four main types of policy narrative:

1. EMU as enforcing the economic imperatives of globalization;
2. EMU as eroding national identities and undermining domestic political structures;
3. EMU as a counterweight to US dominance of the global economy; and
4. EMU as a means of reconciling the European social model to the new realities of globalization.

These different ways in which EMU is defined and debated highlight the variability associated with its effects. There are differences in domestic institutional capacities to accommodate and to resist the changes linked to EMU. There are differences in the timing and tempo of its effects. Its effects on policies and outcomes are conditioned by their embeddedness in contrasting domestic political structures, types of national capitalism, and forms of discourse. They are also shaped by whether or not a state has already undertaken the types of reforms consistent with EMU. EMU has had very different relations to domestic economic liberalization and the entrenchment of 'sound' money ideas. Sometimes this process of paradigm shift in economic policy has preceded EMU—for example, Britain and Germany—sometimes accompanied EMU—for example, France—and sometimes followed EMU—for example, Italy.

Compared with globalization, EMU is a relatively discrete phenomenon. It refers to clearly identifiable and routinized decision processes. It involves a discrete set of actors, principally drawn from EU finance ministries and central banks. They are grouped around ECOFIN, the Euro Group, the Economic and Financial Committee and, of course, the European Central Bank. This degree of institutionalization and of specificity of actors makes EMU an easier concept to handle as an independent explanatory variable for domestic policy and political change than globalization.

We need, however, to be alert to some difficult challenges in handling EMU as a variable.

1. Since Maastricht in 1991 EMU has expanded in scope and its boundaries with other policy sectors have become more permeable. Hence we are dealing with a variable—EMU—that has changed. In particular, growth and employment have been added to the objectives with which the EU is concerned. New structures and mechanisms of coordination have been developed and existing ones strengthened for this purpose. On the other hand, a key theme appears to be a pronounced continuity in the 'vertical' diffusion of ideas from the EU level downwards. EMU remains the story of a dominant structure of discourse—the 'sound' money and finance paradigm—framing how EMU develops in institutional terms and the manner in which growth and employment objectives are conceived. In this sense EMU reveals the institutional power of path dependence and self-reinforcing mechanisms shaping and constraining its development.

2. The second challenge is how to disentangle effects attributable to EMU from those 'caused' by other variables. These variables include globalization, technological development, social and demographic changes, domestic policy regimes—for example, in labour markets and welfare state provision—and domestic politics—for example, party systems and electoral competition, the scope for executive leadership. The risk is of theoretical prejudging, of too easily finding what we are looking for, of too readily attributing to EMU what might be more persuasively attributed to other variables. Hence it behoves us

to be cautious and reflective in our scholarly judgements, recognizing that EMU needs to be set alongside other contextual changes and that EMU might be an intervening variable. The key is to clearly specify causal linkages between EMU and specific domestic policy and political changes.

3. The third challenge is causality. We have not tried to prescribe a particular view of causality that contributors must follow. They are at liberty to think about causality in multiple senses. In one view of causality, what is important is whether EMU is independently significant in constraining or enabling change. This approach has not been favoured by contributors. In a second view, to which contributors have proved much more sympathetic, EMU is significant as an intervening variable in mediating a variety of influences, whether social, economic, or political, global or domestic. In a third view, which is also strongly represented in this volume, the challenge is to trace temporal causal sequences. This view involves an historical approach to showing why actors respond in a particular way to EMU, how they react, and with what effect on outcomes. 'Thick' description of this kind is fine in looking at individual European states as long as it is set in an historical and/or comparative context. This historical view reminds us that EMU did not begin on 1 January 1999. We are concerned with an historical process that can be traced back over 20 years to the ERM and even beyond to the Snake. For many states the key critical juncture in taking on board the 'sound' money and finance paradigm was the ERM—for example, France in 1983, Italy in 1992–3. For others—for example, Britain and Germany—the adoption of this paradigm had nothing to do with Europeanization. There are very different domestic stories to be told about the time, timing, and tempo with which EMU has affected European states.

4. The fourth challenge is the 'level-of-analysis' problem and the risk of reifying either EMU or the state. We are examining the dynamic, intertwined relationship between these two and between them and the global level. To adequately conceptualize EMU we need to acknowledge three dimensions: the new European conditions of domestic political and economic dynamics that it represents; the domestic conditions that shape EMU-level dynamics; and the complex ways in which global developments interact with and constitute a key part of the character of what is happening at the domestic level and at the level of EMU. We must resist the temptation to prejudge the issue of causal significance by restricting our focus to one level of analysis. This means in particular avoiding a deterministic logic of structural inevitability in which EMU is seen as mapping a path to an end-state, for instance as a logic of neo-liberalism. EMU is perhaps better seen as imparting certain tendencies and invoking counter-tendencies. We might also expect contrasting processes

of causation in different policy sectors—for example, financial markets and welfare states. The constraints on convergence of policies and outcomes are linked to contrasting institutional frameworks, associated opportunities and constraints in relation to reform or blockage, and to different exposures to external constraints.

5. The fifth challenge is striking the appropriate balance between two types of account of EMU. One account takes an 'outside-in', 'top-down' approach. It focuses in a structuralist manner on the power of EMU as external constraint on European states. This tendency reflects the extent to which the literature on Europeanization is a reaction to state-centric 'realism'. A second account rescues the role of domestic politicians in the story. They are seen as crucial, as policy entrepreneurs in changing public agendas and as craftsmen of discourse in 'reframing' policies and seeking to shift public sentiments. This suggests the value of an 'inside-out', 'bottom-up' approach to EMU. In this approach the emphasis is on the ways in which the European dimension is 'imported' into, and used within, domestic politics and policies. How is it used in programmatic activity—for example, of political parties and governments? How is it used in the 'framing' of specific domestic policy reforms for domestic publics and business elites? Attention falls on the domestic institutional capacity for change; on the 'goodness of fit' between domestic ideology and ideas of EMU; and on the timing and tempo at which EMU is or is not absorbed into domestic policies. This volume seeks to capture *both* the power of external constraints *and* the significance of domestic stories. Individual contributors take up different positions on the relative significance of the two. Country-specific chapters gravitate to the 'inside-out' approach; sectoral and contextual papers, to a more 'outside-in' approach. This difference need not matter in the sense that ontological and epistemological differences amongst academics are perfectly normal and reasonable. They are not going to be resolved definitively by empirical research. But the onus is on us all to spell out how we see the causal mechanisms at work and to be aware of, and show respect for, alternative explanations. If interpretive disputes about EMU and European states cannot ultimately be resolved, we can at least make them more explicit.

6. The sixth challenge is to clarify the relationship between EMU as a material phenomenon, associated with changes in markets and in policy mechanisms, and EMU as a discursive construction or narrative. In one narrative EMU is thought to limit state action by requiring fiscal retrenchment, tax reductions, and downsizing of welfare states. EMU is used as a rhetorical device to discipline the expectations of others about what is politically, economically, and socially feasible. Here EMU seems to share an attribute with

globalization, namely, that by proving highly influential in policy circles it generates independent effects, causal and constitutive. In short, the discourse of EMU has its own significance in constructing a logic of inevitability, independent of its material effects. This is evident in the strategic use of EMU as legitimization for unpopular domestic policy decisions and as part of a deliberate attempt to create a 'crisis consciousness' as a means of impressing on the public the importance of reforms—for example, in Italy in the 1990s. The question is whether, and to what extent, EMU is also provoking a re-politicization of domestic political and policy debate and generating countertrends.

7. The seventh challenge is to discriminate the 'thin' and 'thick' effects of EMU on domestic elites (Dyson 2000b). 'Thin' effects point to behavioural changes induced by the changed incentives and constraints put in place by EMU. Elites are induced to accept compliance with monetary and financial discipline as rational responses to a new framework of rules. This behaviour is, however, calculative. It could alter if domestic electoral threat or intra-party opposition made the balance of advantage in compliance more problematic. Hence rationalist accounts of behaviour suggest a potentially weak compliance by states with the strictures of the Stability and Growth Pact. 'Thick' effects focus on how EMU changes the properties of states through socialization of elites, who internalize a shared set of policy ideas. State interests and identities come to be defined in terms of these shared ideas. Hence EMU has powerful endogenous effects, altering what are considered to be appropriate standards of behaviour. Its effects are felt at the level of elite culture. In practice, both effects are at work but are very difficult to distinguish, even for a particular individual. 'Thick' effects are limited to a very tiny elite. However, EMU has served to privilege this elite. It has also opened up the possibility of domestic cleavages between those 'thickly' affected, those only 'thinly' affected, those not affected at all, and those negatively affected.

8. The eighth challenge is to distinguish between what EMU is doing to domestic policies and politics and what it is doing to the state itself. Policy effects can be assessed by levels of change, ranging from objectives at the highest level, down through instruments used, to how instruments are used. The direct, second-order effects from loss of the interest rate and the exchange rate as policy instruments are clear, as are the indirect effects on other instruments like labour-market and wage policies. But how important EMU is for first-order paradigm change to objectives varies cross-nationally. Thus it was not important in the British and German cases but was very important for France and Italy. Political effects include the role conception of political parties. EMU can be seen as bound up with the long-term shift from

parties as mobilizers of a core electorate to efficient managers of the capitalist economy. Its effects might also be evident in electoral campaigning and behaviour, notably the rise of national populism. A third political effect is on organized groups: witness the rise of neo-corporatism in the 1990s. The bigger question of EMU's effects on the state focuses on decline or transformation. One interpretation is that EMU embeds states in a new form of regional governance in which powers are shared in ways that make the notion of sovereignty associated with the Westphalian state system problematic, even redundant. But EMU does not seem to be creating a new, 'post-sovereign' world. It is about the redefinition of sovereignty to suit new conditions in which EMU shifts monetary sovereignty to a supranational level and induces a sharing of power over financial and economic policies. The central political issue is whether domestic politicians and publics can accept the political norms of this 'semi-sovereign' politics in which power is dispersed in these ways. Faced with this challenge, the possibility emerges that EMU will create divisions among European states: some accommodating this development —for example, Germany and the Netherlands; others faced with difficult problems of domestic transformation—for example, Italy; and those retrenching or displaying inertia—for example, Britain.

9. The ninth challenge is to set the theme of this book in the wider debate about European integration. Two debates come to mind. First, Majone (1996) has written about the emergence of the 'regulatory' state at the EU level. The EU specializes in the function of market regulation in a manner consistent with its essentially technocratic legitimacy. It is a 'non-majoritarian' institution dedicated to economic efficiency. With EMU the EU's depoliticized character appears to be evolving as it takes on an added functional specialization in providing macroeconomic stability. This suggests a 'macroeconomic stabilization' state at the EU level (Dyson 2000a). The implication is that member states specialize in the more politically sensitive functions of distribution and redistribution, to which their democratic legitimization makes them better suited. A second debate is about network governance as the predominant feature of the EU as a political system *sui generis* (Kohler-Koch and Eising 1999). This mode of governance is disseminated into the member states. The actual negotiation of EMU had more of the attributes of 'statism' as a mode of governance. Core executive actors controlled the agenda and negotiations in the pursuit of national interests. But, once EMU was institutionalized, it revealed different attributes. Monetary union is characterized by supranational governance. The ECB is endowed with the authority to pursue the common interest of the Euro-Zone. In contrast, economic union has the main attributes of network governance: that is, it is based on

multilateral negotiations as a means of coordinating the interests of various stakeholders. In both these respects—as supranational governance and as network governance—EMU's effects push domestic elites to go 'beyond the nation-state'. EMU enlarges the scope for political action and opens a window of opportunity for domestic change (Kohler-Koch 2000). It widens the political space beyond member states, undermines the principle of territorial rule in favour of functionally specific action, and alters understandings of how best to organize legitimate rule.

PART I

European and Global Contexts

I

Global Integration, EMU, and Monetary Governance in the European Union: The Political Economy of the 'Stability Culture'

Geoffrey R. D. Underhill

From 1 January 2002, the European single currency will become a reality to millions of Euro-Zone consumers. Since 1 January 1999, it has been a reality for the global monetary system, European central banks, and Euro-Zone governments. For some time, invoices, pricing, and bank statements for businesses and consumers alike have been jointly denominated in euros. The vicissitudes of the international system of floating exchange-rate management has offered its share of policy dilemmas to the European Central Bank (ECB) and the Council of Economic and Finance ministers (ECOFIN) and to other national monetary authorities responsible for exchange-rate management and cooperation. A robust market in euro-denominated corporate and government bonds and stock market listings has emerged (Bank for International Settlements 2000: 128), trade invoicing and company accounting in euros has developed throughout the EU—including non-euro countries like Britain—and a wave of corporate restructuring across economic sectors has characterised the period leading up to, and immediately following, the introduction of the single currency.

This chapter aims to set the context for this volume, examining the relationship between the EU as a monetary space and the global monetary and financial system, and the implications of this relationship for Euro-Zone member states and corporate governance. In this sense the chapter is responding to the first question posed by Dyson in the Introduction: what are the implications of global integration processes and of the institutional design of EMU? To a lesser extent it also responds to the second question: how is EMU affecting public policies, identities, and the political economy of member states?

This chapter therefore sets itself a complex task, and the analysis implies a wide range of actors and processes cutting across levels of analysis: the global, regional, national, and the increasingly transnationalized private sector. In terms of monetary and financial management in this situation of multi-level governance (Marks *et al.* 1996), the Euro-Zone and wider EU has developed the notion of the 'stability culture'.[1] The provision of basic monetary stability through the ECB's monetary policy, combined with the other forms of macroeconomic prudence required by the Stability and Growth Pact of 1997 (European Council 1997) and other agreements, will provide a strategic framework within which the different institutional levels of the governance process and the private sector can formulate strategies and coordination in a market-oriented setting. This provision would not require centralized management of the sort once undertaken by national governments or the central coordinating role envisaged for the IMF in the original Bretton Woods plan of 1944.

Analytical Focus and Argument

The political economy of the emerging 'stability culture' is a broad and complex subject (Germain 1999). It would, therefore, be helpful to narrow the focus. In the first place, the chapter will keep to the traditional distinction between monetary governance and financial governance employed by Michael Moran in Chapter 10 in this volume, thus respecting the division of labour between us. This chapter will largely discuss issues of monetary governance, though my arguments are not particularly at variance with Moran's discussion of financial market governance, especially as regards (1) his treatment of the reflexive interrelatedness of levels of analysis—global, regional, national —and (2) his argument that the creation of the Euro-Zone 'elevates the management of financial markets to the centrepiece of economic policy and insulates the development of policy from the institutions of liberal democracy, representing the triumph of one long-term tendency in financial market government in Europe and the defeat of another'. However, because

---

[1] The reader will note some ambiguity about whether the 'stability culture' should refer uniquely to the 'Euro-Zone 12' member states in the single currency, or to the entire EU-15. The issue is that even the—currently three—member states outside the Euro-Zone are subject to the budgetary and other disciplines of the monetary union. Furthermore, it is the firm intention of the British and the Swedish governments to enter the single currency if and as soon as domestic political conditions permit. This chapter does not propose to resolve this ambiguity, which stems from the Treaty itself (European Council 1992).

the management of the financial system is intertwined with matters of monetary and exchange-rate policy—systemic financial stability often depends on the monetary climate and vice versa—and because the characteristics of the financial system—the level of openness to capital mobility, the extent of internationalization in the corporate sector—affect policy options in the monetary domain, financial system issues will be referred to from time to time.

Second, analytical focus can be developed by advancing four central observations concerning the policy tensions inherent in the Euro-Zone as an intermediary and so far only nascent level of governance, situated between the global monetary and financial system and the member states. Each observation corresponds to a level of analysis, and for each observation an explanation is offered as to how the situation might play out over time. The chapter will then discuss each observation in detail in four separate sections, aiming to understand better the emerging political economy of the Euro-Zone as a peaceful experiment with integration unparalleled in the history of the modern state system. The aim is not simply to provide a 'top-down/outside-in' view of EMU but also to demonstrate that this view can only with difficulty be separated from 'inside-out' perspectives focusing on the domestic level or on corporate governance.

The first observation is that there is a central paradox concerning the place of the Euro-Zone as an economic unit in the structures of the global monetary and financial system: the EU is relatively self-sufficient in terms of international trade but is deeply integrated into the structures of global financial markets and investment flows. The second observation is that, while there is a clear mandate for managing monetary policies in the Euro-Zone, emphasizing perhaps unduly the goal of price stability among possible policy objectives, there is a lack of clarity in terms of exchange-rate policy and other crucial policy domains such as negotiations on the nature of global financial architecture. Both of these characteristics, it is argued, tend towards the neglect of the exchange rate as a tool of macroeconomic policy. Third, at the level of the member states there is, on the one hand, considerable pressure for convergence in terms of macroeconomic management and corporate governance practices but, on the other, there are the intense bottom-line pressures of political legitimacy in terms of social policies, national—and other—identities and the role of national democracy in an increasingly integrated economic unit. This is often perceived as the 'sovereignty issue', though the debate usually has little to do with national sovereignty in strict terms of international law; the debate is probably better characterized as one about identity and policy autonomy, which are not the same as sovereignty. Fourth, following the third point but at the level of corporate governance, the Euro-Zone can be seen as a radical extension of the single European market programme, extending the incentives for EU-wide restructuring and corporate structures and strategies that cut across borders. Yet this integration process is juxtaposed on what remain distinct political systems with their own internal dynamics. The economic development and adjustment process associated with the single currency will furthermore prove asymmetrical (Padoan 1994; Feldstein 1997; 2000). The Euro-Zone will consequently encounter its share of disagreements among its members as the economic development process yields differentiated distributional consequences across the national economies. The latter two points imply, as Dyson argues in the Introduction, that pressures for convergence are not the same as the process through which the eventual outcome is generated. Indeed, *pressures* for convergence do not necessarily result in convergence as an *outcome*, but might end in stagnation of the integration process, the emergence of new forms of diversity, or an outright unravelling of the integration arrangement itself. Political legitimacy remains as always the bottom line (Underhill 1999*b*).

Seen in the light of these four observations, the Euro-Zone looks very much like unfinished business. The underlying argument of this chapter is that 'unfinished business' is precisely how we should understand and characterise the emergence of the single currency and all its related policy dilemmas elaborated in the four observations and detailed in the body of this chapter. Some of these policy dilemmas are simply inherent in the complexity of governance in the global monetary and financial system under conditions of capital mobility. But it has long been argued in the literature that the entire EU project should be understood more in terms of what it is *becoming* than of what it *is* at any one time. If political agreement fails in this regard, the future of the single currency will be a difficult one. For now, it is to be hoped that at least *within* the Euro-Zone and EU-15 the 'stability culture' will be successfully embedded in corporate and government practice so as to prevent the restructuring process from disrupting the idea of the EU itself.

The unknown factor in the eventual success of the stability culture is, however, external to the Euro-Zone: the periodic eruption of monetary and financial crisis at the global level, such as engulfed in turn Mexico, Japan and the Asian newly industrializing countries (NICs), Russia and Brazil among others and, more recently, Turkey and Argentina. Can the Euro-Zone stand out as the island of monetary and financial stability for which its architects hoped? Given the transmission mechanism for contagion and spillover provided by the process of global financial integration, doubt must surely remain on this point. It should be noted that the institutions and coordinating mechanisms for such crisis management, prudential supervision, and over-sight of the financial system are woefully underdeveloped at the level of the Euro-Zone and remain essentially the stuff of national jurisdiction.

The Euro-Zone and the Global Financial and Monetary System: Dependence versus Autonomy

The Euro-Zone is highly integrated into the global monetary system and the structures of financial markets, but is relatively self-sufficient in terms of international trade. In terms of trade, both the Euro-Zone and the EU-15 member-state imports and exports have a strong intra-regional bias;[2] if Euro-pean Economic Area and aspiring member states are taken into account, the result is a reinforcement of the trend. The issue of whether the euro comes to rival the US dollar as a reserve and investment currency in the private sector and among national currency reserves means that the Euro-Zone has a considerable interest in the role of the euro in the global financial system in relation to euro-denominated asset markets and global investor confidence in the European economy. At the same time, the Euro-Zone has relatively little interest in the precise level of the exchange rate because exchange-rate fluctuations will have a relatively limited impact on trade in the Euro-Zone economy overall. Monetary policies are thus likely to be self-regarding on the whole, and the exchange rate will be managed in line with the time-honoured principle of 'benign neglect'. In this sense, the market will be the principal determinant of the role of the euro in international financial trans-actions, payments and settlement, and the politics of global exchange-rate management. Global capital flows, not trade patterns, will mediate between the Euro-Zone as a monetary space and the international monetary system (Cohen 1998: Chs 1–2). This serves to emphasise the increasingly market-based nature of the internal Euro-Zone economy.

The first point concerns the relationship between the euro and the global monetary and financial system.[3] The arrival of the euro is almost as big an event for the global monetary system as it is for the EU member states. Euro

---

[2] In 1998, 62.9% of total EU member-state exports and 62.5% of imports were intra-EU-15 (Eurostat 2000b: 50). Likewise, in 2000, extra-regional exports of the EU-15 constituted only 10.1% and extra regional imports only 10.4% of total GDP at market prices (European Commission 2000c: Tables 39 and 43). In contrast, *intra*-EU exports constituted as much as 50% of GDP for Belgium/Luxembourg and Ireland, 39% for the Netherlands, though was considerably lower for some of the larger members (European Commission 2000c: Table 38).

[3] This section draws on the arguments of an earlier article (Underhill 1999a).

exchange-rate relationships will be determined by trade and capital flows and influenced by official policies. What sort of relationships will these be? Will the euro be 'strong' or 'weak'? In historical terms, the question for Europeans has often been: will the introduction of a single currency enhance or reduce the capacity of Europeans to manage their own monetary environment and, by implication, their freedom to choose their model of economic development? Will the euro reduce dependency on the dollar and allow Europeans more latitude in determining the rules of the monetary and financial game?

The answer to these questions is essentially as follows: the underlying structure and characteristics of the financial market system will determine the type of political economy that the Euro-Zone becomes. In a system characterized by financial openness, it is in the underlying financial structures that state monetary and exchange-rate policies are embedded, not the other way around as is often perceived. Some time ago Europe played the financial globalization card decisively in drawing up the legislation which governs the single market. The introduction of the euro will *enhance* the market nature of the system and will facilitate greater global integration of European markets as a result. The die is cast, but, as shall be seen, the future is not without choices. Those choices will, however, be hard ones for Europeans seeking to recover policy autonomy quite deliberately ceded to the forces and agents at play in the market—which includes central banks! EMU will do little to free Europeans from their current worship of the global markets, well though it might have done.

How is the monetary system embedded in the financial structure, and why is the financial system so central to the operation of a capitalist market economy? The key to understanding this question lies in the distinction between official monetary and exchange-rate policies—monetary governance —and *regulatory* and *supervisory* policies—financial market governance. How market-oriented will the system be? What sorts of linkages will there be with financial institutions outside the state in question?[4] If changes in regulatory policy of the kind increasingly seen on a global scale introduce a greater degree of transnational financial transactions and therefore a growing level of short-term international capital flows, the power of the market players is greatly enhanced and the objectives of state macroeconomic policy must increasingly be subordinated to the constraints imposed by agents in the market (Cohen 1993; Underhill 1996). As the financial system has changed, so has the role that official monetary and exchange-rate policies can play. The result is restriction on the autonomy of elected governments to realise

---

[4] These policies form the basis of discussion in Chapter 10 in this volume.

the socio-economic objectives associated with maintaining their legitimacy in the eyes of their electorates.

The primary way in which the EU accelerated global financial integration was through the single European market programme. As Story and Walter (1998) put it, it was a 'battle of the systems'. The EU legislation developed a single financial area oriented towards capital markets, with the City of London at the heart of the financial system, thereby constraining the pursuit of individual national macroeconomic policy objectives. Since the implementation of the single market legislation, domestic reforms from Germany to Greece have been oriented to developing securities markets, the better to compete with London, and there may yet be a single European equity market in the future. The bond markets were transnationalized some time ago. Financial institutions that develop successfully their securities arms have a growing competitive advantage over those that do not.

If the financial structure of the single market emerging in the EU is increasingly integrated with global capital markets, the money issued and nominally controlled by the ECB is in fact the plaything of large, transnational, private-sector agents. The euro will be embedded in the globalized financial structure; it will rise or fall as a currency on the basis of its acceptance by these market makers, public and private alike. Most of the constraints that affected the macroeconomic policies of EU states will affect the ECB and ECOFIN as they attempt to forge monetary and exchange-rate policies. This is not to argue that the introduction of the euro will make no difference to the global political economy or that of the EU; it will. But the changes that it brings will be in the context of the very global financial structures in which it will be embedded unless there is a dramatic change in the nature of the financial system itself.

Furthermore, the terms of the Maastricht Treaty reinforce the policy orthodoxy that the prevailing financial structure suggests. The Treaty favoured price stability and the fight against inflation over growth, employment, and social policies. Monetary policy and day-to-day exchange-rate management will be in the hands of a highly independent central bank, not at the discretion of elected governments. The budgetary criteria associated with the Treaty likewise speak of sober fiscal management, thus imposing fiscal constraints on states as well—though the terms are not as tight as is generally believed.

The balance sheet is not negative, however: the introduction of the euro gives the Euro-Zone states greater influence in international *monetary* relations. This increase in power at the bargaining table with the US and Japan can have a direct impact on the perceptions and reactions of market players. ECB monetary policies are seen as among the most important signals in the global economy, affecting capital flows and patterns of trade alike. These policy decisions will not be made in isolation from the perceptions of market players and, in fact, are designed to play on their expectations. The bargaining power of Europeans will be greater if the euro takes on the characteristics of an international reserve currency: if the ECB becomes, like the US Federal Reserve, a banker to the world. This is more likely if the euro is perceived as a stable asset as well as a currency that is readily available to make international payments. The greater investor confidence in the euro, which is interdependent with the ECB and EU member-state policies, the more important will be the role of the euro in the global economy and the greater will be the structural power of European monetary authorities. The policies of other governments and central banks will also be important. If Asian and Latin American central banks choose to hold reserves in euros, perhaps offsetting their vulnerability to the vagaries of the dollar, the euro's international role and the structural power of the ECB will be enhanced. This does not *release* the EU from the imperatives of financial orthodoxy, but it does enhance manoeuvrability.

Second, the reserves of the ECB will be much larger than those of any one member state in the past. The ECB will have a very substantial buffer against market movements in and out of the currency. If there is cooperation with the US and Japan, it should be possible to moderate market reactions. This larger buffer will be no substitute for 'prudent' macroeconomic policies in line with market expectations about economic fundamentals, but the buffer should help. In short, size is a help, but only if deployed sparingly and strategically.

There is another aspect to the question of size. The euro should accelerate the pace of integration of EU financial services markets. These markets may increasingly rival US markets in terms of size, liquidity, and coherence. This means that EU regulatory practice will be increasingly influential for market players, and EU interests more important in international regulatory cooperation. However, this emerging EU financial space is contiguous with global financial markets. The EU has already taken a substantial step towards Anglo-Saxon regulatory practices through the single market legislation. Furthermore, the influence of US market rules and corporate practice will not go away. US financial institutions are part of Europe and have been for a long time through the City of London.

Third, if the euro becomes a strong and stable currency, stability will have its own rewards. A currency that maintains its relative exchange value over the *long* run and that can be widely used for transactions in the global economy, such as international trade and investment, will be sought after by market agents. The *cost* of a strong euro will, however, be a constant process of economic adjustment to a strong currency and *that burden will not be equally borne within the EU*. The less competitive economies and firms will find it more difficult than those that have already adjusted well to global competition. If as a result there is internal EU conflict over monetary policies, the perception of stability may be undermined and the financial markets could flee the currency with destabilizing consequences. The ECB may be formally independent but, should consensus over the policies behind the euro break down, the ECB will have greater difficulty fulfilling its mandate.

Yet, if the above analysis is correct, the introduction of the euro means at a stroke the *externalization of instability*. Intra-EU exchange-rate fluctuations will no longer frustrate monetary policies and economic conditions in the way they typically did in the 1990s and before. If there is instability, it will be external, with the yen and the dollar. Such external instability can, of course, have a dramatic impact on the monetary policies of the ECB, but the insulation from the exchange-rate pressures which are generated by financial markets and payments imbalances is real.

In other words, even if the Euro-Zone gains greater weight against the global capital markets in terms of exchange-rate policy, it is unlikely that the ECB and ECOFIN will choose to employ this weight in the service of a deliberate exchange-rate policy. This is particularly the case because the EU as a whole is among the most self-sufficient economic zones in the global economy. Hence the Euro-Zone's exchange-rate policy is more than likely to resemble that of 'benign neglect.' Exchange-rate management in 2000 seems to bear this out. The euro's debut on the foreign-exchange markets was marked by a prompt and considerable devaluation relative to the dollar, a development not altogether expected given the underlying fundamentals. The ECB was in the end willing to intervene only when the decline of the exchange rate appeared to threaten inflation targets (ECB 2000*a*, *b*, *c*).

Institutional Lacunae in Monetary and Financial Management

The points raised in this section are related to those above and in fact strengthen the argument that the exchange rate is unlikely to emerge as a deliberate tool of policy. The Maastricht Treaty assigned clear institutional responsibility for monetary policy to the ECB, with an unusually strong accent on price stability as the key criterion of policy. However, the Euro-Zone as a monetary space is institutionally weak when it comes to either international exchange-rate cooperation or negotiations on international financial architecture. A coordinated approach to these policy issues appears difficult as a result of these institutional weaknesses. This lends further weight to the argument that the market will be the essential arbiter of the relationship with the outside world, with due allowance for the impact of Euro-Zone monetary and fiscal policies.

The Maastricht Treaty is quite clear on the issue of monetary policy. As has been pointed out (Dyson and Featherstone 1999; Artis 1992), the ECB has a particularly high degree of independence for both setting a price-stability target and the implementation of monetary policy (European Council 1992: Art. 107, title VI 'Monetary Policy'). Neither the member-state governments nor ECOFIN may interfere or attempt to influence the ECB in exercising its mandate. Furthermore, price stability is—unusually—the sole policy objective that the ECB is to pursue in exercising this independent mandate (Art. 105). This contrasts, for example, with the mandate of the Federal Reserve Board in the United States and is even stronger on price stability than the mandate of the highly independent German Bundesbank. Both their mandates were designed to take into account broader economic criteria in determining the direction and implementation of monetary policy.[5] Also, the legislation governing the roles of both central banks required ongoing accountability of bank decision-making to elected representatives, and this is much less clear in the Maastricht Treaty. So the mandate of the ECB in terms of monetary policy is starkly and simply defined.

This is not, however, the end of the story. Under conditions of capital mobility, the relationship between the management of monetary policy and the management of the exchange rate is a difficult one (Cohen 1993; 1996). Suffice it to say here that changes in monetary policy are likely to have an influence on the exchange rate, and vice versa: the two policy domains must be viewed as interdependent. But institutional responsibility for the determination of exchange-rate policy objectives is far less clear in the Treaty. Article 105 para. 2 states that foreign-exchange operations are the responsibility of the ECB. This makes sense in that, if intervention is to take place, the ECB is the obvious institution to carry this out and the obvious vehicle through which tensions between exchange-rate targets and monetary policy goals can be coordinated.

---

[5] The statutes governing the US Federal Reserve System do not specify the objective of price stability (Henning 1994: 106–7); in the case of the Bundesbank, price stability is specified as a primary objective, but the Bank must also 'support the general economic policy of the federal government' and must weigh responsibility for both the internal and the external value of the currency (see Kennedy 1991: 13, 21–8). In this sense, the ECB mandate takes the Bundesbank model one step further by specifying price stability as the primary objective *tout court*.

Yet Art. 109 para. 2 states that the Council may formulate the 'general orientations for exchange-rate policy'. Furthermore, Art. 109 para.1 grants the Council the right to set up or to abandon formal agreements with other states on an exchange-rate system. If a policy on exchange-rate management were to emerge, there are at least two institutional constraints. First, ECOFIN, with no doubt some important de facto role for the informal Euro-Group, would need to develop a unified position on policy objectives for the active management of the exchange rate. Given the contrasting interests of Council member states and potential tensions between Euro-Zone and ECOFIN, there would clearly be difficulties. Second, the determination and eventual implementation of an exchange-rate policy must involve consultation with the ECB—which anyway is responsible for foreign-exchange operations—and be 'without prejudice to the primary objective of price stability' (Art. 109 para. 2). If there is to be active management of the exchange rate, it seems that the coordinating mechanisms between the Euro-Zone states, ECOFIN, and the ECB need greatly to be strengthened. This may involve further development of the Treaty framework or a less formal operational framework.

But what happens when pursuit of exchange-rate targets conflicts with the *primary* objective of price stability in the EU? With whom will Japanese, American, and other monetary authorities negotiate, assuming internal EU agreement—the Council, the ECB, or both? And how would differences between the two be resolved? It seems that the ECB holds the ring. If the ECB takes the de facto leading role, this would complicate the already considerable problems of democratic accountability for Euro-Zone member states in this vital policy domain (Verdun 1998a). Of course, none of this matters much if there are international exchange-rate and balance of payments equilibria. But the global payments system is far from being in balance, with the US current account deficit reaching record highs recently, and an outbreak of exchange-rate volatility is certainly imaginable in the short to medium term.

The likely net impact of this set of institutional weaknesses is the neglect of the exchange rate as a conscious instrument of Euro-Zone policy. Institutional complexity in developing either practical coordination mechanisms or further altering the Treaty stacks the deck heavily in this direction. The Euro-Zone's exchange rate is thus likely to be determined by market responses to the ECB's monetary policy as it interacts with the evolving current and capital account situation in the global monetary system. 'Benign neglect' looks to be the rule of thumb.

The underlying assumption behind the successful operation of this system is that the pursuit of monetary—that is, price—stability by the ECB and by the US and Japanese authorities will result in the relatively stable evolution of the exchange-rate parities through market mechanisms. A tripartite float may have the relatively benign impact that it had throughout the 1990s, and intervention can safely be disposed of as a tool of exchange-rate policy, though the historical record of floating is not encouraging. If intervention is to be employed, then it will most likely be when exchange-rate parities threaten price stability, as when the ECB intervened on the foreign-exchange markets in autumn 2000 to support the euro when rising import prices, particularly oil, pushed inflation towards, and eventually over, the ECB's stated 2 per cent ceiling (ECB 2000c).[6]

So benign neglect of the euro exchange rate becomes integral to the political economy of the 'stability culture'. This stability culture of the Euro-Zone is furthermore the central element of governance throughout the EU, in fiscal, monetary, and financial terms. At its core is a macroeconomic policy designed around a market-led financial and monetary system in Europe, leaning on the assumption that monetary stability in the Euro-Zone equals financial and monetary stability just about everywhere else so long as the US and Japan play the stability game. The single currency and the stability culture are *the* solution to the exchange-rate crises of 1992–3 and presumably all others to come.

Yet a paper by Moutot and Vitale (2001)[7] casts some doubt on this optimistic scenario. They observe that a wide range of states now agree upon price stability as a primary ingredient of long-run growth in a situation of integrated goods, services, and capital markets, and that this goal has been and is being successfully pursued. This very success means that 'relative long-term growth prospects, debt and financial stability issues and the quality of communication between market participants and monetary authorities have become increasingly important in the explanation of international economic interaction and, in particular, in the determination of exchange rates' (Moutot and Vitale 2001: 338). Setting aside the issue of financial stability, one need not worry unduly if the important economic zones experience relatively uniform patterns of growth and cyclical fluctuation. But this is far from being the case. The US, Japan, and Europe are not at all on a path for convergence of either productivity and real growth rates or even of business cycles. International payments balances and growth rates are in considerable disequilibria. This is illustrated by (1) stagnation plus current account surplus juxtaposed with the emergence of an enormous fiscal deficit in Japan,

---

[6] A rise in interest rates might have accomplished the same goal but at a potential price in terms of growth for in particular the German economy, which at the time showed signs of weakness.

[7] Moutot and Vitale are themselves ECB officials, though in this paper they make it clear that they are not expressing the views of the Bank.

currently some 130 per cent of GDP (*Financial Times* 2001*c*); (2) rapid economic and productivity growth plus record current account and private-sector deficit levels in the US (Bank for International Settlements 2000: 13–16, 31–2; European Commission 2000*c*: Table 44; *Financial Times* 2001*d*), by 2001 mixed with a risk of recession (OECD 2001); and (3) more moderate growth and rough current account balance in the Euro-Zone/EU (Bank for International Settlements 2000: 32; European Commission 2000*c*: Table 44).[8] This situation implies not only that central banks need to be more clever in designing and implementing their monetary policies but also that a degree of coordination, not to mention cooperation, is necessary among the important monetary authorities in the global system on issues of growth levels, payments equilibria, and debt. The political difficulties of cooperation on these matters are well known, as the relatively successful case of the Plaza and Louvre episodes illustrates (see Funabashi 1988; Webb 1995). The relative lack of successful cooperation since then enhances the point, but the case for engaging in such exercises is strengthened: 'The efficiency of the fora for ad hoc cooperation, i.e. their design, their mandates, and their procedures, is also an essential determinant of an adequate international financial structure' (Moutot and Vitale 2001: 348), and this includes supervision issues.

In view of the analysis in this section, how well prepared in institutional terms is the Euro-Zone/EU for participation in such coordination? Politically, who will call the shots? How will a common position be reached across member states and the institutional fabric of the stability culture? As payments imbalances and capital market integration increase at one and the same time, how will the necessary degree of coordination with other monetary authorities be achieved? Filling the institutional lacunae is not merely an abstract issue but so far it is the market, with its frequent tendency towards volatility, that will have to decide.

Member States, Global Financial and Monetary Pressures, and the Euro

The market-led nature of the stability culture, characterized by integration with the global monetary and financial system, is reinforced by the pressures

---

[8] The EU's current account moved from surplus to deficit 1999–2000, constituting approximately 0.5% of GDP in 2000 (Eurostat 2001*b*); there were differences depending on whether one looks at current account, trade balance, or Euro-Zone versus the EU-15 (Eurostat 2000*b*; 2001*a, b*), but the average picture is as described in the main text.

that the system generates for member states. The argument here is relatively straightforward, has been rehearsed elsewhere (Underhill 1999b; Underhill and Zhang forthcoming 2002), and carries across into section four below. It has already been claimed in the first section that the Euro-Zone will be embedded in the global system of capital-market integration. This gains the advantages of market-led adjustment but forfeits defensive use of the new currency zone against the external volatility of global capitalism. Under conditions of capital mobility and a high degree of market integration based on economic openness, states also face a number of pressures for the convergence of their economic policy choices and their financial and economic systems with those of the dominant financial centres (Cohen 1993; 1996; Webb 1995). It becomes increasingly difficult for individual states to sustain and develop the sorts of independent policies that helped distinguish them as different models of capitalist development in the immediate post-war period.

The first site of convergence may be identified in the domain of financial regulation. Already the single market legislation established a relatively homogeneous financial space in Europe (Underhill 1997). What Story and Walter (1998) described as the 'battle of the systems' was decided in favour of the British capital market model of financial system. The distinctive national financial systems, which were integral to the distinctive forms of economic adjustment and welfare-state provision often characterized as competing forms of capitalism, are eroding rapidly as a result of combined EU-wide and global pressures. Regulatory harmonization has played its role, then, and the intensification of market competition associated with the removal of national currencies will accelerate the pressures.

But arguably the most powerful pressures for policy and system convergence come from the macroeconomic domain. This pressure involves the impact that changes in the global financial system have on the capacity of states *to formulate independent and distinct macroeconomic adjustment policies* and have to do with changes in the role of the state itself under conditions of financial integration (Baker 1999; Cerny 1997; Underhill 2000). The discussion in the second section has already indicated that capital mobility greatly complicates the design and implementation of monetary policy and exchange-rate policy. Investors increasingly pass judgement on the macroeconomic and regulatory environment in particular economies, creating significant incentives for convergence towards market-based adjustment policies and macroeconomic policies of the 'stability culture' variety. Furthermore, the single currency implies that states must further compromise their domestic autonomy in the name of effective cooperation, and the fact that the Euro-Zone is so closely integrated with 'global' financial space intensifies the need for relatively intrusive forms of cooperation.[9] There are the corresponding pressures on government fiscal and social policies working through the convergence criteria and the Stability and Growth Pact.[10] The single market and introduction of the single currency are thus an advanced version of state policies aimed at creating a more market-friendly economic and policy environment in order to attract global investment and render local firms more competitive. This places the different forms of European capitalism and their corresponding social and labour market adjustment policies in direct competition with each other and increasingly exposes governments to the preferences of international business.[11]

As argued in the first section, policy autonomy might be regained through the single currency by pooling responsibilities and exercising them collectively in a highly developed form of cooperation, including cooperation on the social dimension. But at least three requirements must be fulfilled if citizens are to perceive that room for policy discretion has been enhanced.

1. The institutions responsible for policy-making have the clear intention of using their strengthened hand for improving their discretionary room for manoeuvre, and a debate is engaged about how the several means of attaining policy objectives are to fit together. The underlying norms of the stability culture and the single-minded focus on price stability indicate that this is not the case.
2. The required institutional mechanisms for the coordination of the different aspects and instruments of policy are in place. This includes mechanisms for interacting with the global monetary system and the negotiating

---

[9] For example, the EU Commission recently censured Ireland's 2001 budgetary and tax plans, despite the sterling performance of the Irish economy over a number of years; *Financial Times* (2001*a*, *b*); *Irish Independent* (2001).

[10] It should be noted that the budgetary provisions of the convergence criteria in the Treaty apply to the transition to EMU and afterwards, and furthermore the Treaty refers to 'Member States', not to members of the Euro-Zone (European Council 1992: Art. 104c), meaning that the budgetary provisions apply as much to those out as to those in the single currency, *including* those permitted an opt-out clause for the single currency (European Commission 1992: 10). The same reference to 'member states' applies to the terms of the Growth and Stability Pact (1997).

[11] This does not rule out social policies but on the evidence has made their reform necessary; there are claims that capital mobility need not endanger social policy unduly (Garret 1998) and that a negotiated social dimension to capitalism may be a source of competitive success in a range of industries (Iversen, Pontusson, and Soskice 2000). See also Rhodes in Chapter 12: while he agrees that the pressures on social policies are there, he argues that they need not necessarily result in convergence and a reduction in social protection. I agree with the general thrust of his argument in that pressure for convergence is unlikely to result in a uniform outcome, but reform and adjustment of policies is certainly high on the agenda of a wide range of states in Europe and elsewhere.

forums for the governance of the financial system centred on Basle. The analysis in this chapter implies that this is not the case.

3. There are adequate mechanisms for the democratic accountability of those responsible for making monetary and exchange-rate policies, which is certainly not the case with the ECB and only partially so in relation to ECOFIN. Without such mechanisms, the ways of providing the institutions with sufficient sensitivity to concerns of political legitimacy are extremely limited for something so crucial as the monetary and exchange-rate policy domains in a highly diversified Euro-Zone economy. As long as 'they' get it right, the issue may be academic. But if and when 'they' get it wrong, even if it is not their fault, this problem will become clear.

However, these three requirements also imply a level of internal consensus within the Euro-Zone sufficient to develop both a sense of strategic self-interest and the institutions and policy process. This is sometimes difficult in federal societies with a relatively established history of central monetary governance combined with participation in global monetary and financial negotiations—Canada, Austria, and especially Germany post-unification. It will certainly be difficult in the EU where different economic development models still compete with each other. Thus, it is difficult to deliver the extra policy autonomy that the single currency theoretically makes possible. Mechanisms aimed at a 'European-level' model of social capitalism, which would externalize many of the costs of such a development, may be absent for the foreseeable future.[12]

Corporate Restructuring, Models of Corporate Governance, and Competing Forms of European Capitalism

The external pressures for convergence carry on through the corporate restructuring process and the way in which it affects models of corporate governance in European member states. One aim of policies that integrated the EU with global market structures was to encourage corporate restructuring in an ongoing fashion, with firms moving capital resources from one economic zone to another much more easily. Increasingly this happens in response to market conditions and to the relative competitiveness of producing services in one place as opposed to another. It also places different forms of corporate governance and entrepreneurial strategies in competition and thus under the

---

[12] Assuming that sufficient agreement for such a project could ever have been mustered in the first place.

scrutiny of financial market investors. Some may not cope, and restructuring or cross-border mergers and takeovers can result in the importation of models of corporate governance. Over time corporate cultures become less embedded in their original domestic setting. Market-based systems are all about greater autonomy for market actors, at least within the regulatory framework established by political authorities of various kinds. Firms over time feel less attached, perhaps even less committed, to specifically national models of economic development and the political bargains in terms of social and labour market policies that they embody.

Thus the national firms embedded in national models of economic development and welfare provision will increasingly compete in globally integrated as opposed to 'inter-national' market structures, adapting their corporate governance as they go. This is not just an economic phenomenon; it is a highly politicized process. Firms burdened with unfavourable home- or host-state forms of corporate practice and regulation may use their political resources to seek new compromises, or they may exercise their 'exit option'. Different national forms of corporate governance, central to the socio-political compromises which make national models of capitalism different in Europe, are thus subject to pressures for convergence. Broader changes in the European financial system, intensified by the single market/Euro-Zone integration processes, may therefore unsettle and perhaps destabilize these relationships. The result is changes in corporate governance, new relationships between finance and industry, altered relationships between labour and the employers, and thus a possible change in the distinguishing characteristics of the model of economic development itself.

The simultaneous financial integration processes at European and global levels represent precisely this sort of financial system change. Shareholders increasingly scrutinize the performance of corporate groups in the new climate, and capital can more easily escape the national socio-political bargain if this is perceived as too costly, particularly where labour-market adjustment and welfare provision are concerned. The financial system and corporate governance nexus, which lay at the heart of social democratic or developmental state institutions in post-war Europe, may over time *wither from within* as corporate managers adjust their behaviour and strategies to focus on shareholder value in global securities markets, just as they must anyway adjust to intensified global competition. The corporate restructuring process will in time yield trans-European and indeed global groups embedded not in their individual political economies but in the political economy of the stability culture.

The forces of convergence are therefore in evidence, though one should not argue that this convergence process is inevitable. Differences in corporate governance and culture die hard, as a number of transnational mergers have revealed, and the evidence is bound to be mixed for some time. But EMU is such a pervasive and dramatic form of integration that it seems difficult to argue that it makes no difference at all. Intricate socio-political compromises, closely linked to the political legitimacy of democratic regimes in Europe, can be undermined from within by these changes in the state and the increasingly disembedded corporate sector. It does not render social-democratic and corporatist compromises impossible, but it does render them more difficult and less likely in political terms.

In this sense the advent of EMU may have a considerable impact on the legitimacy of member states. Electorates are of necessity less mobile than capital and less pliable than the strategies of firms and systems of corporate governance. Yet national governments will continue to be accountable to domestic constituencies which may not always benefit from the integration process and its inevitable restructuring processes and consequent reshaping of the political economy.

EMU's stability culture implies that the failure of states to attend to the economic bottom line will get them into trouble with global investors, and thus into trouble themselves because they will not deliver economic growth for their electorates. Strapping governments to the mast through EMU (Dyson, Featherstone, and Michaelopoulos 1998) will enhance legitimacy despite short-term pain and adjustment. The argument in this chapter, by contrast, implies that the bottom line should instead be understood in terms of political legitimacy: does the stability culture deliver results in line with the expectations—diverse across national political economies—of the citizens of the new Europe, still intimately engaged in national-level democratic processes and identities with contrasting dynamics?[13] A failure to attend to the bottom line in terms of political legitimacy may get the whole stability culture in trouble. A continuous process of structural adjustment, and certainly an outbreak of serious financial or other economic turbulence, would call into question the underlying principles governing the Euro-Zone. In the end, monetary governance in the EU, which would always have been problematic with or without the single currency and whether all member states belonged to the Euro-zone or not, must face squarely the need to link up the plethora of national-level political bargains in terms of social and labour-market policies with the broader market-oriented governance of the EU/Euro-Zone itself. Will this be accomplished by national-level processes or Euro-level processes? If history is anything to go on, probably a combination of both.

---

[13] On national identity and European-level democracy, see de Beus (2000a).

Conclusion

This chapter has made four interrelated observations about the nature of EMU, its relationship to global integration processes and the international monetary system, and its consequences for the member states. It has focused on the question of monetary governance, but, given the close relationship between the monetary and financial systems, has inevitably strayed into the territory of financial governance primarily occupied by Chapter 10. These observations about EMU as monetary governance draw attention to the policy tensions across levels of analysis, across multiple institutional layers from the national to the global, and across policy domains: monetary, financial, social, labour market. These tensions are brought together in the restructuring of both state policies and corporate sectors in response to the new, essentially market-based political economy of the stability culture.

The first observation led to the argument that, even though the Euro-Zone is heavily interdependent with the global monetary and financial system, there exist strong structural incentives for policy-makers at national and EU levels to commit the management of the euro's exchange rate to a policy of 'benign neglect'. The second observation led to the argument that the institutional lacunae in the management of the euro—the lack of clear institutional responsibility for the management of the exchange rate and for cooperation with other authorities in this regard—reinforced this tendency to a policy of benign neglect. Internal monetary stability is the primary concern of the 'stability culture', but little is said about how the EU as an entity might manage the extent to which adjustment costs might be externalized and therefore imposed on others in the global monetary system. Even less is apparently said about the extent to which external monetary and financial *in*stability might interfere with the internal stability culture. This external instability might well be exacerbated by a latent Euro-Zone policy of benign neglect of the exchange rate. The highly interactive relationships across levels of analysis and across policy domains risk undermining the very objectives which the stability culture sets out to achieve. A major failure in this regard would be an enormous problem of variable dimensions for individual member states and a serious blow to the internal cohesion of EMU itself.[14]

[14] A prime example concerns the continued fragmentation of the prudential supervisory process in the EU, juxtaposed on increasingly integrated markets at both the regional and global levels. The Treaty (Art. 105) states that the ECB shall 'contribute to the smooth conduct' of prudential supervisory policies by member states and permits the eventual transfer of supervisory responsibility to the ECB, but for the moment the member states retain responsibility under the home-country control provisions of the single market legislation. The fact that monetary governance

The third observation led to the conclusion that there are considerable pressures for the convergence of the macroeconomic policies of the member states away from traditional post-war forms of social-democratic governance, based on broad socio-political compromises and institutionalized concertation among erstwhile social partners, and towards more Anglo-American, market-led adjustment processes. The institutional and legal basis of EMU, with its emphasis on sound fiscal policies and price stability, makes this tendency more likely though not inevitable. None the less, member states are left with a series of policy dilemmas concerning social and labour-market adjustment policies in particular.

The fourth observation led to the conclusion that this pressure for convergence was strengthened by developments at the level of corporate restructuring and corresponding changes in models of corporate governance. Patterns of corporate governance are historically integral to national models of economic development and the political and social bargains that underpinned them. Should the pains of corporate restructuring prove severe, distributional tensions are likely to be exacerbated in the corporate sector and labour markets and across national economies. This might invoke problems of political legitimacy for the project if the consequences of EMU-plus-globalization—which is what it is—in democratic context is perceived as constituting a decisive failure of the stability culture.

The clear assumption of EMU is that the stability culture will translate into sustainable growth such as to alleviate socio-political tensions and to resolve, or at least attenuate, some of the tensions across policy domains and levels of analysis. The joker in the pack may well be some form of global monetary or financial turmoil from which the stability culture may provide scant protection. Over time, mechanisms of governance in the EU will need to grapple with these tensions, and the focus will be on the distributional consequences and the potential polarization of social and political tensions within and across member states. If the stability culture is not good enough for enough of the people enough of the time, it will be in jeopardy. Need one be

occurs at ECB level, with a series of institutional weaknesses and lacunae with regard to exchange rates in particular, and that financial governance takes place at the national level and this admits of further institutional fragmentation, means that no one is comprehensively minding the shop when it comes to the linkages between the two through EU-wide prudential oversight. This happens at a time when the Bank for International Settlements has quite rightly warned that central banks must be more vigilant in the prevention of asset bubbles in the design of their monetary policy (Crockett 2001). To make matters worse, national central banks have been losing their prudential supervisory role to new agencies as such as the Financial Services Authority in Britain. In this regard, President Wim Duisenberg of the ECB condemned a German government plan to strip the Bundesbank of its supervisory oversight functions (European Central Bank 2001a).

reminded that, in the case of these sorts of difficulties, there is no centralized system of governance available to the Euro-Zone in terms of either relations among member states or relations with the global monetary system and world economy.

This may appear a rather pessimistic analysis, implying missed opportunity and careless institutional design at Maastricht and afterwards. It implies that Europe's long experiment with monetary cooperation is of questionable merit and may be prone to failure. The central thrust of the project is towards the marketization of the adjustment process and of economic space across the EMU; and, if Polanyi (1944) had anything to say, the difficulties of market-driven projects, in the absence of effective governance mechanisms, are prone to unpredictable social reactions. But the ledger need not project as gloomy a picture as all that.

In the first place, social policies have not disappeared. As Rhodes argues in Chapter 12, there is so far little evidence of a 'race to the bottom' in social standards under EMU. Second, and more importantly, the Euro-Zone constitutes unfinished business, and furthermore was intended to be so. The European integration process has always constituted unfinished business in this fashion, with some rather imprecise goal of 'ever closer union' looming far enough in the future to be ignored. If Polanyi (1944) is correct, then there *will* be reactions to the new market-led adjustment processes and to the new forms of state which are emerging, and they need not be ugly or disintegrative. As has been remarked earlier, indicating that there are pressures or tensions does not indicate the way in which these will be resolved.

There *is* a need for a further round of political and institutional innovation to develop EMU in a politically sustainable direction in a transnational, quasi-federal context. The entire EU integration process has been premised on this sort of logic, the logic of policy spillover. Furthermore, EU integration was a way around the zero-sum politics of balance-of-power, inter-state competition and war, and so far it has worked.

As the lacunae, both institutional and in terms of practice, are filled in; as the policy dilemmas are handled first in ad hoc and perhaps later in a more systematic fashion, the normative lacunae of what appears at this time a purely market-driven accord will be filled in as well. In fact, the process of filling the normative void has tentatively begun. EU member states have developed a more social dimension in the Amsterdam Treaty (European Commission 1999c: 11), and at Nice (European Council 2000). Much remains to be done to develop this dimension, but member states know that they must come to terms with the problems. Enlargement renders the task more urgent. The sound money and finance paradigm, while certainly very strong in EMU, was the starting point of the stability culture—and was certainly more sensible and sustainable that what was going on in the 1970s and the 1980s—not the end point.

So much of what constitutes the political economy of the stability culture remains to be established. The problem of political legitimacy will not go away, and member states and the Commission know it. If the ECB does not, it will soon find out. Despite its considerable institutional insulation, the making of monetary policy will never be successfully depoliticized and decoupled from other policy domains. The monetary and financial system is too central to governance for that.

There are, of course, competing visions with which to fill the normative lacunae, and by implication the institutional and political as well. Individual members states would have had to grapple with all these issues and tensions, regardless of EMU. Each national economic development model implies a set of—sometimes only implicit—normative preferences in terms of the way the adjustment process is carried out. Yet arguably there is a widely shared consensus in the Euro-Zone about the need for policy concertation and social justice in some form or other, though this consensus does not extend across the entire EU 15 states quite so effectively, especially where Britain is concerned. Problematically, each state has its own path-dependent way of realizing this underlying consensus. All this means, though, is that a Euro-Zone consensus will take time and will be imperfect, but anyone with experience of federal societies could hardly be surprised. Dyson's account in the Introduction of the emergence of a 'Kantian' EU culture may be a vision of things to come, fits well with some of the implicit premises of the stability culture, and does not need to contradict the sound finance macroeconomic policy framework. The relative insulation of the Euro-Zone, as a monetary space, from the rest of the global economy is important here; it provides some running room to work these matters out. It is to be hoped that a major episode of global monetary and financial stability does not force anyone's hand, as this is likely to resolve matters in favour of individual, national solutions as the pressures of the democratic process and the dynamics of political legitimacy push in that direction.

2

EMU's Impact on National Institutions: Fusion towards a 'Gouvernance Économique' or Fragmentation?

Wolfgang Wessels and Ingo Linsenmann

The observation and analysis of the impact of Economic and Monetary Union on national institutions raises highly intriguing political and academic issues. Taking the new treaty provisions and subsequent acts as independent variables, this chapter compares the impacts of three sets of significantly different modes of governance—supranational policy making, 'hard' coordination, and 'soft' coordination—on domestic actors and institutions in the 15 member states with varying politico-institutional as well as socio-economic backgrounds.

Following institutionalist approaches, the core assumption is that institutional developments on the European level will trigger changes in domestic institutions and on domestic actors: the 'top-down' approach. They will affect both opportunities for and constraints on national actors and institutions as well as the belief systems of domestic actors and even collective understandings and meanings attached to domestic institutions.

Two alternative scenarios serve as points of reference for describing and explaining empirical developments on both the European and the domestic levels. Will we observe *common trends* towards a vertical and horizontal fusion leading to a '*gouvernance économique*', or are indicators pointing to a scenario with fragmentation trends across policy areas and levels of interaction? With this analysis of EMU as modes of governance and their evolution we hope to have a spill-over towards to general theoretical approaches related to the EU system.

Part of our material presented here has been developed in a research project supported by the Deutsche Forschungsgemeinschaft directed by Beate Kohler-Koch in the priority area of European governance (http://www.mzes.uni-mannheim.de/projekte/reg_europ/dfg.htm; http://www.uni-koeln.de/wiso-fak/powi/wessels/forup/wwu.htm).

Impact Analysis: Our Approach

Methodological Opportunities and Difficulties: A Ceteris Paribus *Test?*

To discuss the impact of EMU on national institutions and member states in general is as relevant as it is difficult. From the perspective of the EU as a multi-level game, the 'top-down' view from Brussels and from Frankfurt—the ECB—is as necessary as the alternative 'bottom-up' view from national capitals to the EU arena. The political relevance derives from the vital importance of monetary, fiscal, economic, and employment policies for the evolution of national welfare states (Scharpf and Schmidt 2000) and for the EU system in general. The academic interest stems from the opportunity to compare three different 'modes of governance' (cf. H. Wallace 2000: 28–35; Kohler-Koch 1999: 20–6) within a 'single institutional framework'—Art. 3 Treaty of European Union—and over the same period. Some forms of governance are even described as models for the EU system in general (cf. H. Wallace 2000). However, Schmidt (1999), Risse-Kappen (1995), Héritier and Knill (2000), Radaelli (2000), Börzel and Risse (2000), and Green Cowles, Carporaso, and Risse (2001) argue that there is no sufficient ground to present a reliable, tested set of causal links, or at least to rely on a valid set of indicators to be used for empirical work on the relationship between the evolution of the EU level and domestic change (cf. Dyson's Introduction).

Faced with various possibilities for analysing EMU's impact on national institutions, this chapter starts with a 'top-down' approach, if only for the sake of presenting explanations offered by a broad set of integration-related theories for further empirical research. Our test arrangement (see Fig. 2.1) starts from the assumption that 'para-constitutional' changes—in this case the three sets of treaty provisions on EMU and subsequent relevant acts—will challenge actors in national institutions to pursue a reflected multilevel strategy (see Figs 2.2–2.4) (cf. Wessels, Maurer, and Mittag 2001). It follows institutionalist approaches (Olsen 2000; Peters 1999).

The major puzzle is, if actors *use* the new and/or amended legal empowerments in the final stage of EMU, then, depending on how they use it, the causal links *after* 1999 have to be tested with reference to the question of continuity and discontinuity. We assume that we witness a 'new' game where actors have to play according to rules different from those of the last 20 years and even different from those since 1992. The major thesis is, therefore, that the provisions will lead to the creation, evolution, and even transformation of new and different modes of governance in a multi-level polity, and are therefore part of the overall evolution of the EU system.

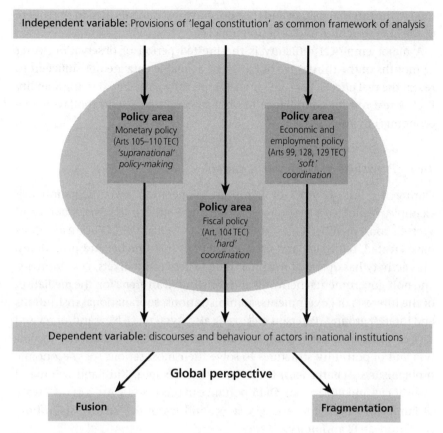

Fig. 2.1 Causal links for the analysis of the development of EMU policies

EMU researchers are presented with a highly interesting opportunity for testing theories at the macro level. They can use three distinct sets of EMU provisions and observe their simultaneous impacts on at least twelve countries in the Euro-Zone and on the three 'outs' as the Stability Pact on fiscal discipline and the economic and employment policies also affect the other member states. Thus we have some kind of *ceteris paribus* constellation, a rather rare occasion in social sciences. Furthermore, these new modes of governance differ distinctively from the 'traditional' models of EU governance, especially from the regulatory model (Majone 1996) and the 'Community method' of a policy cycle based on an institutional quadrangle of the European Commission, the Council, the European Parliament, and the European Court of Justice (cf. H. Wallace 2000: 28–30). Also, the instruments used differ from the traditional regulative, distributive, and partly redistributive Community instruments, especially with regard both to the legal mechanisms used in the internal market and the budgetary instruments used in the sphere of the EU's structural and cohesion policies.

A major empirical difficulty is the limited period of observation. After 24 months of the third stage of EMU, the available data are not sufficient to reveal the real effects. For some modes, especially with regard to the Stability Pact, a real test for compliance has not materialized due to the favourable economic environment.

Treaty Provisions as Independent Variables

During the last 50 years of European cooperation and integration (for example, Weiler 1995; Dyson 1994; Dyson and Featherstone 1999; Maurer and Wessels 2001) member states' governments as well as the EC/EU institutions have created, reformed, and used a variety of instruments and procedures. This activity has operated within a triangle between markets, governments, and non-governmental networks and constituted an arena for 'the mediation of the interests of governments, administrations, supranational institutions and interest groups' (Peterson 1995: 77–8; also Ayral 1975). New and/or revised sets of provisions offer European and national actors additional incentives and opportunity structures to solve their most serious socio-economic problems (see Scharpf 1997; Olsen 2000; Bulmer 1994; Knill and Lehmkuhl 1999; Börzel and Risse 2000). Of importance in this case are Art. 2 of the Treaty of European Union and Arts 2, 3, 4, 99, and 125 of the Treaty establishing the European Community.

We start from the 1993 treaty provisions as *independent variables*; they themselves are products of 'the road to Maastricht' (Dyson and Featherstone 1999). On the basis of collective learning processes over the last decades and guided by core executives (Dyson 1999c), the 'masters of the treaty' (German Constitutional Court 1995; Ipsen 1994) have created a complex set of rules allowing national and European actors to get involved in the EU policy cycle and to use instruments with an increasing impact on the domestic arena. These rules have been further developed in recent years at meetings of the European Council from Luxembourg in 1997 to Lisbon in 2000. Governments have formed institutional and procedural channels for running their 'business' more effectively.

EMU is not a single-rule exercise. It includes three sets of provisions resulting in three modes of governance: a 'supranational' policy making in monetary matters (Art. 105), a 'hard' coordination in fiscal policy (Art. 104 and the Stability and Growth Pact), and a 'soft' coordination on Macroeconomic and employment issues (Arts 99 and 128). Each of these provisions and their 'institutional designs' (Fligstein and McNichol 1998) allocate different instruments to the EU level and enable access and participation for different groups of governmental as well as non-governmental domestic actors. The respective incentives and constraints of the rules vary considerably. Even more, the installation of new and/or the development of existing committees has reinforced administrative interactions and cooperation among key domestic actors. The EC treaty gives far-reaching mandates to two high level committees: the Economic and Financial Committee (Art. 114.2) (cf. Hanny and Wessels 1998; 1999; Hägele and Wessels 2000) and the Employment Committee (Art. 130) (cf. Hörburger 1998; Tidow 1999; Maurer 2000), accompanied by the Economic Policy Committee (cf. Council of the European Union 1999).

In monetary policy, treaty provisions, the statutes of the European System of Central Banks and the ECB, as well as secondary legislation, including the rules of procedure of the ECB bodies, have laid down rules for a distinct institutional setting and policy-cycle style as patterns of behaviour which can be labelled as 'supranational' policy-making. The ECB is solely responsible for decision-making in monetary policy and in principle is constrained only by the treaty provision that this function is pursued in order to maintain price stability (Art. 105). Instruments, at least those concerning interest rates and other direct monetary instruments, will be applied after simple majority voting in the Governing Council, with no formal decision-making role assigned to the Council of the EU or any other European institution (cf. Levitt and Lord 2000; Eijffinger and de Haan 2000). The applicability of these decisions for the Euro-Zone is direct and immediate. In a typology of ideal modes of governance, we identify some kind of 'statehood' pursuing a European interest based on command and majority voting (for a typology, see Kohler–Koch and Eising 1999: 6–7) as central features of this supranational governance. Formalized participation rights in monetary policy for domestic actors on the European level are granted to national central banks only, which, however, are key actors (see Fig. 2.2).[1]

In fiscal policy, member states have established distinct rules for a 'hard' coordination in the procedures laid down in Art. 104, completed by the fifth protocol to the Maastricht Treaty and further elaborated by the provisions of the Stability and Growth Pact of June 1997, to put into practice the

---

[1] Note for this and the two subsequent figures that the arrows usually signify participation rights of actors and/or formalized cooperation provisions: submitting reports, right to submit recommendations, and so forth). The arrows do not necessarily indicate (co-)decision rights.

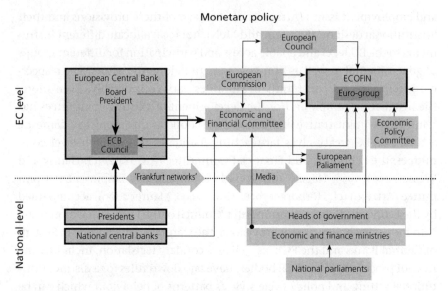

Fig. 2.2 The institutional setting of monetary policy

excessive deficit procedure (cf. Council of the EU 1997*a*, *b*). These rules include supervisory roles on national budgets for the European Commission and the Economic and Financial Committee, leading to Council recommendations against a 'sinner' state. 'Hard' coordination in fiscal policy refers to the procedure enabling the Council to decide, voting by qualified majority, on considerable financial sanctions against a member state in case of a continuous breach of the provisions (Art. 104.11). The procedures assign no decisive role to other European institutions, as the European Parliament is informed only afterwards and member states cannot appeal to the European Court of Justice.

For domestic actors, formalized participation rights at the European level are granted to political and administrative actors from finance and economic ministries as well as national central bankers. National finance ministries and parliaments are directly concerned, and many other actors indirectly, as fiscal policy is formally located at the national level with budgetary decisions affecting citizens and welfare-state groups directly (see Fig. 2.3).

In employment and macroeconomic policy, 'soft' coordination procedures have been introduced in Arts 128 and 99 with instruments such as monitoring policy processes and outcomes, providing general policy orientations, benchmarking, and the publication of 'best practices' (cf. Biangi 1998; Mosley and Mayer 1999; Odile 1999; Sciarra 1999). In contrast to the Art. 128 procedure,

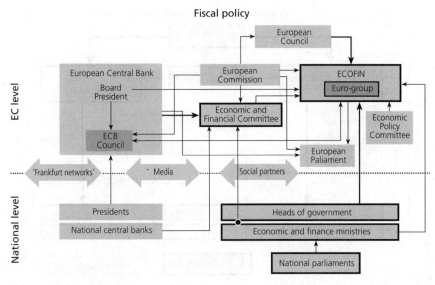

Fig. 2.3 The institutional setting of fiscal policy

Art. 99 on the Broad Economic Policy Guidelines foresees a recommendation of the Council to a member state deviating from the principles laid down in the treaty (cf. Conseil d'analyse économique 1998; Jacquet 1998: 35–46; Lamfalussy 2000). The Council can decide that these recommendations should be publicized, thus exposing the member state concerned to public debate on this issue (cf. the case of Ireland in February 2001).

These coordination procedures can be labelled 'soft' since the instruments have no direct legal impact for the member states and do not include any sanction mechanisms as does the 'hard' coordination of fiscal policy. EU institutions other than the European Commission are involved to a limited extent as the European Parliament is granted 'only' *ex ante* consultation and *ex post* information rights, and Art. 128 foresees the *ex ante* consultation of the Economic and Social Committee and of the Committee of the Regions.

In addition to the Art. 99 procedure, the member states agreed in 1998 to enhance the deliberation and interaction process on economic policy by establishing the so-called 'Cardiff Process' on structural reforms in the member states. To complement the various processes on employment and economic policy coordination, they established in 1999 the so-called 'Cologne process', constituting a Macroeconomic Dialogue at Community level between all relevant policy actors, including the social partners.

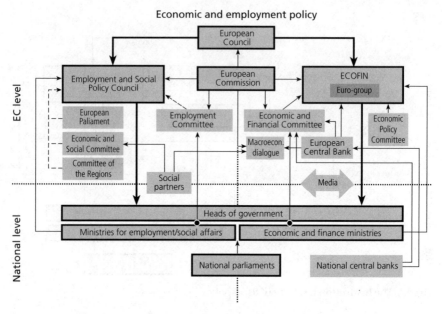

Fig. 2.4 The institutional setting of economic and employment policy

Formal participation rights of domestic actors on the European level are spread even wider than in fiscal policy, incorporating the labour and social affairs branches of governments. In addition to the Economic and Financial Committee and the Economic Policy Committee, the Employment Committee as well as the Macroeconomic Dialogue provide different access for national actors. On the domestic level, both employment policy and economic policy involve a greater number of governmental and non-governmental actors (see Fig. 2.4).

Dependent Variable: Institutions and Actors on the National Level

How these sets of legal constitutions affect the 'real constitution' on the national level is of major importance (cf. Olsen 2000). Thus, as dependent variables we examine the pattern of behaviour of domestic actors and institutions as well as possible institutional adaptations (cf. Mittag and Wessels 2001). For observing trends and evolutions we use a typology of four basic models of adaptation (see Fig. 2.5). We look at 'veto points' enabling 'weak' or 'strong' patterns of access and participation in national and EU phases of

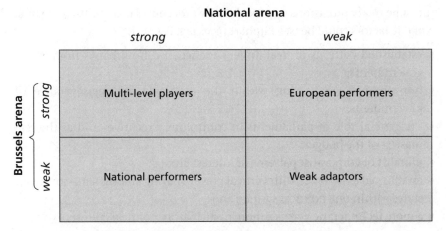

Fig. 2.5 Adaptation models of domestic institutions
Source: Mittag and Wessels (2001)

the policy cycle. Essentially, domestic actors who are directly involved at the European level are structurally advantaged by the wider range of opportunities at their disposal to respond to the new provisions. Compared with these multi-level players, national actors who are passive in 'Brussels' are more like objects of the amended provisions, facing increased adaptational pressure to compensate for the lack of European channels.

We expect some kind of mutually reinforcing logic: opportunities and constraints at one level will affect positions in the arenas of the other level. National central banks could be able to transform themselves from strong national performers to European performers within the ESCB or even become strong multi-level players. Though national parliaments might be able to maintain their positions as strong national players within the fiscal and economic policy fields, they will lose autonomy and turn into weak adaptors. National administrations might use additional opportunities to reinforce their position as strong multi-level players, while domestic social partners and civil society groups will not just remain national performers but also become active in the Brussels arena.

Domestic adaptation processes are likely to vary across member states. From other studies (cf. Mittag and Wessels 2001; see also country chapters in this volume), we expect at first only limited systemic convergence, that is, no uniform type of behavioural patterns. Two reasons can be identified. First, fundamentals of political systems will have major effects on the extent to which, and the ways in which, national institutions and actors as objects of the same treaty provisions can use the new procedures in a multi-level game. Notable factors could be (see Lijphart 1999: 248, Fig. 14.1)

- established patterns of 'real' independence of central banks from 'their' governments;
- horizontal power-sharing within the executive and perseverance of governments;
- the general role of parliaments in controlling executives and as the real masters of the budget;
- pluralist or corporatist patterns of interest groups;
- established experience with vertical power-sharing among semi–sovereign states within one political system; and
- a more technocratic versus a more participatory political culture.

These fundamental patterns of political systems are relevant in two ways. Following suggestions by scholars looking at Europeanization and domestic change, we expect that these domestic variables will 'frame' the perception, discourses, and interactions of domestic actors with regard to EMU provisions (Knill and Lehmkuhl 1999; Radaelli 2000; Börzel and Risse 2000; Green Cowles, Caporaso, and Risse 2001; Mittag and Wessels 2001). Thus, the way European provisions are compatible with domestic provisions will affect the preparation and implementation of European acts on the domestic level (cf. Dyson's Introduction). Furthermore, the compatibility, that is the 'goodness of fit', between new European institutions and rules on the one hand, and fundamental national structures as well as the real patterns on the other hand will affect the degree of adaptational pressures emanating from the European level (cf. Radaelli 2000).

Second, attitudes and behavioural patterns towards the integration construction *in general* (cf. Niedermayer and Westle 1995) might impinge on the use of EMU as it is an integral and vital part of the EU. However, whereas this factor has been of major importance for entry into EMU—and still is for the 'outs'—implementation studies indicate that it may not determine day-to-day work (Siedentopf and Ziller 1988; Mittag and Wessels 2001). On the other hand, the propensity of political parties to use EMU matters for populist electoral campaigning might be higher in those states where the general attitude towards the EU is rather sceptical.

A Dynamic Global Perspective: Fusion versus Fragmentation

For observing the real patterns of national actors we confront two scenarios as extreme cases.

Table 2.1 The evolution of three modes of governance: *ex-ante* expectations

Policy fields	Scenarios	
	Fusion	Fragmentation
(1) Monetary policy	Joint deliberations	Autonomous actions
(2) Fiscal policy	Compliance	Renationalization
(3) Economic and employment policy	Broad consensus	Evasion

Europeanization of National Actors Leading to Horizontal and Vertical Fusion

Basic assumptions: an economic governance 'in the making'

A first scenario expects that actors in all three sectors of EMU will:

(1) shift their attention to the EU level—our definition of Europeanization (cf. Rometsch and Wessels 1996; Wessels, Maurer, and Mittag 2001);

(2) merge their national resources with EC instruments—which we call 'vertical fusion' (cf. Wessels 1997; 2000); and

(3) create an institutional arrangement on the European level bringing together core actors from several institutions, networks, and bodies— here labelled 'horizontal fusion'. This 'collective governance' (cf. W. Wallace 2000: 541–2) is defined as a mutual participation pattern in a multi-faceted institutional and procedural network.

Vertical fusion and horizontal fusion are based on mutually reinforcing dynamics. Processes of horizontal and vertical fusion on the European level will continue in the coming years (cf. European Commission 2001a). Thus, what evolves in this perspective on the European level might be labelled an emerging *'gouvernance économique'* (cf. Teló 2000; Jacquet and Pisani-Ferry 2000: 26). This *gouvernance économique* is characterized as:

• a 'non-hierarchical' (Kohler-Koch 1999) 'core network';

• with the participation of governmental and non-governmental actors;

• from different regulated networks 'without a single centre' (Luhmann 1981: 22; Marks *et al.* 1996; Held 1991), that is, without executive government in the conventional sense;

• based on a 'shared commitment to the common enterprise . . . within a framework of shared experience and assumptions' (W. Wallace 2000: 532–3), that is, in our case the common—monetary and fiscal policy—paradigm (cf. Dyson and Featherstone 1999: 774–82);

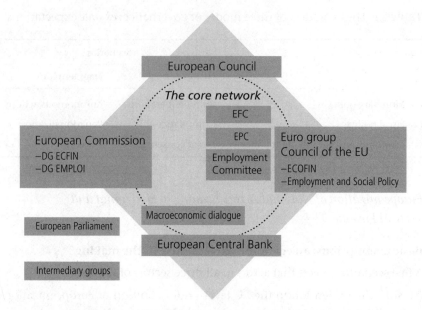

Fig. 2.6 The 'core network' of EMU on the European level

- informally pooling their respective instruments (Wessels 2000: 122–37), even in those cases where legal provisions foresee procedures and instruments formally allocated to specific institutions; and
- establishing a coordinated policy mix with regard to the formal and informal coordination of monetary, fiscal, macroeconomic, and employment policies.

These assumptions are different from those analyses expecting a small 'core executive' group within a 'hollow core' (Dyson 1994: 301–22; 1999c: 105–18) because the interaction patterns within this 'core network' will be sufficiently strong to develop a '*communauté de vue*' and to exist even without an institutional centre. It might be viewed as some kind of modern variation of the demands calling for the establishment of a *gouvernement économique* (Commissariat Général du Plan 1999; Jospin 2001). This concept is still being promoted by the French government and has created political controversies (cf. Sachverständigenrat 1997/1998: 235; von Hagen 1998: 44–5; Linsenmann and Müller 2000: 69–70, 104–7).

We expect national actors to increase their efforts to get access and 'voice options' (Hirschman 1970) in those decision-making processes that have repercussions on their own domestic policy cycles. They also try to influence policy-making processes, if possible, in those cases where treaty provisions do not formally provide for direct points of access (Stadler 1996: 160; Louis 2000; 2001a; Levitt and Lord 2000: 214–20). As a consequence, horizontal interaction and participation patterns will evolve on the domestic and European levels, where national as well as European actors will endeavour to pool their resources and instruments in order to reach more effectively and efficiently those policy aims which have been allocated to the European level.

The EMU provisions are interpreted in a broad sense, stressing the fact that both national and EU actors are involved in each phase of the policy cycle. Participating reciprocally in the institutions described above and interacting in various compositions within the three different EMU sets, they will increasingly perceive the growing interdependencies of the various policies. The differences between the modes of governance, as far as these are fixed in the legal constitution, will become less relevant in the real world of EMU. Not only are the links between monetary, economic, fiscal, and employment policies functional; as well, the Euro-Zone—if not the EU as a whole—will increasingly be perceived as a single economic and monetary entity. This will lead to increased efforts by actors in national and European institutions to try to combine various instruments of economic and social policies in order to produce a successful 'policy mix' which will also be in line with the treaty objectives (Arts 2, 4, and 105.1).

According to the assumptions of this scenario, national actors will not turn to the European level in order to defend their narrow 'vital' national interests in their quest for a suitable policy mix, but rather will contribute to a shared understanding and to common problem-solving mechanisms. The effectiveness and efficiency of European institutions will be a shared responsibility that is not perceived to be in opposition to their national interests. Domestic actors will be interested in a successful policy cycle at the European level since it will further strengthen their positions in the national context and reinforce their positions as strong multi-level players.

In this scenario, we will observe a redistribution of opportunities and constraints: those actors participating in the core network have a structural advantage over those outside this emerging structure. In essence, the main institutional effect of this emerging *gouvernance économique* at the national level is to reinforce trends visible in other studies: the strengthening of national administrations as strong multi-level players vis-à-vis parliaments, which are scarcely adapting their institutional procedures to deal with the new multi-level coordination policies (cf. Mittag and Wessels 2001). We expect national administrative and political actors from the ministries concerned, as well as those linked to the heads of state or government and from national central banks, to gain from these new forms of governance, whereas national parliaments will be more constrained by their exclusively national arena. Thus, the fusion process and the development of a coherent policy mix stretching into other policy fields limit the policy options available for those actors whose main instruments are still located at the national level. National policy-making procedures are thus losing out to a coordinated approach at the European level by administrative bodies such as the Economic and Financial Committee and/or the Economic Policy Committee, with informal backing from the Euro Group and pushed forward by strategic decisions taken by the heads of state or government at European Council meetings.

In such a scenario, the fundamentals of political systems (see above) will lose their relevance. The EU opportunity structures will have a growing impact on traditional patterns, and a convergence of national systems towards some kind of more uniform patterns of multi-level game can be expected.

Supranational governance of monetary policy: towards joint deliberations

These general assumptions about fusion processes can be further elaborated by examining each mode of governance in more detail. In monetary policy, member states have at the beginning of stage three of EMU finally and irrevocably allocated their national monetary instruments to the EU level and thus established a supranational set of rules. In the process of fusion, the ECB Governing Council, as the decision-making body with institutional hegemony and as a 'core executive' (Dyson 1999c: 117), turns into a multi-level 'technocracy' or 'expertocracy' (Scharpf 1998: 91; Wessels 2000: 104–5, 117–20). It is situated in an 'epistemic community' (Haas 1992; Verdun 1999a) between formalized actors from both the European and the national levels and produces broadly accepted outputs.

Horizontal fusion processes evolve based on the 'epistemic community' in monetary matters. This community includes not just a closed network of European and national central bankers in the centre of policy-making, but, as Fig. 2.2 shows, also the administrations of the economic and finance ministries, as well as—at the European level—the relevant directorates-general of the European Commission. The authorized decision-makers of the ECB engage in secretive coordinative deliberations of a 'problem-solving' style (Scharpf 1997: 130, 152) in formal and informal institutions and informal groups, especially in the Economic and Financial Committee and in the Euro Group. In consequence, they will turn into active shapers of a common understanding of what will be appropriate to do (cf. DiMaggio and Powell 1991). The doctrine of monetary stability and ECB independence, as developed over the last 20 years (McNamara 1998; Dyson 1999c; Dyson and Featherstone 1999: 774–82) and 'frozen' in the treaty, will be the common narrative and further elaborated on the grounds of its analytical validity and accepted legitimacy among the experts.

Monetary policy of the ECB would thus not be based solely on the monetary strategy of the ECB as such—that is, the two pillars of monetary policy (ECB 2000a)—but also on deliberations of the ECB within the broader institutional set-up. This will be further strengthened by equivalent activities on the national level, that is, cooperation among national central bankers and governmental as well as non-governmental actors at home.

Another feature of Europeanization will evolve as the output is debated intensively both in the European and in national arenas. With common points of reference—that is, the decisions of the ECB and the exchange rate of the euro—the objects, agenda points, and timing of these public discourses will become similar in the member states. Over time we expect to observe a broad Europeanization of the debate, with additional networks of banks and academics developing around the Euro Tower in Frankfurt, in the 'shadow of hierarchy' (Scharpf 1997: 197) of the ECB. European and domestic actors as well as the public will increasingly form a European public space on monetary matters. In this space the ECB will play an energizing role as an 'activator' (Kohler-Koch 1999: 26), keen to communicate to their reference and peer groups (see among others Dornbusch, Favero, and Giavazzi 1998: 12) aiming to 'sell' their message and organize some kind of intellectual elite support. In limited circles we will observe basic traits of a 'deliberative democracy' of a public good (Scharpf 1997: 161; Kohler-Koch 1998: 280–3).

Domestic structures and national framing of conceptions will be linked to each other and to the EU to allow trends to establish a permanent EMU-wide coordinating governance with a 'permissive consensus' (Inglehart 1971; Reif 1993: 23–40) for the ECB. In national discourses about economic performance, the monetary policy of the ECB will not become 'nationalized' and evaluated according to the perceived effect it has on the *national* economic performance. Since monetary instruments are no longer available for domestic policy-making but are handled at the European level for the Euro-Zone as a whole, national actors will turn towards the opportunity structures provided for at the European level. Here they will seek to influence the formal decision-makers, that is, the national members of the ECB Governing Board and those advising them. Also, within party-political discourse at the national level references will more and more be focused on European events.

The use of instruments formally allocated to the ECB is thus part of an overall broad consensus between different actors and maybe public discourses. The ECB then turns out to be an agent taking the formal monetary decisions based on such an agreed strategy to increase the 'output-legitimacy' (Scharpf 1997) of the system.

'Hard' coordination governing fiscal policy: compliance with the EMU rules

For the Stability Pact we expect that deliberation within ECOFIN and the Euro Group, as well as within the top administrative bodies such as the Economic and Financial Committee and the Economic Policy Committee, will be characterized by an argumentative style. This style will focus on the proper application of the indicators in the EC Treaty and in the Stability Pact, without a major political controversy about the accepted fundamentals of the norms to be followed by member states. As they are both participating in European institutions and involved in national policy-making processes, domestic governmental and administrative actors will submit to the 'hard' coordination rules. They will comply not only because of the threat of sanctions but mainly because the 'sound finances and money' paradigm has entered the economic beliefs of national policy-makers as a 'collective identity' (Dyson 1994; 2000b; Marcussen 1999; 2000a; cf. also Sabatier 1988). The key message resulting from the European institutions will be that the provisions are to be followed rigorously, that is, the rules on the timing and on the criteria will be interpreted literally and even when the Council imposes considerable fines member states will stick to the rules. Thus, the compliance rate will be high.

Furthermore, as public debate—at least within the specialized and elite-oriented media—has been Europeanized since the introduction of the euro, the European public and, above all, international financial markets put pressure on European and domestic actors to comply with the criteria. As the success of the euro is to a large extent measured by its exchange rate against the US dollar, as has been the case in 1999 and 2000, any watering-down of the provisions of the Stability Pact will lead to a negative perception. It would impair the necessary confidence of the financial markets.

With regard to horizontal fusion on the national level, the implications of this scenario for national institutions and actors are twofold. The Stability and Growth Pact has redistributed powers and resources between domestic actors in favour of governments and administrations. Administrations have more relevant experience and, as a result, a better understanding of the requirements resulting from the Pact for domestic policy-making. They can also use their knowledge about the behaviour of other member states and EU institutions to their strategic advantage. Hence we can consider national civil servants as the main domestic actors in this 'hard' coordination procedure on the European level (Fig. 2.3). Acting either on their 'Europeanized' beliefs or from rational self-interest considerations, administrations will seek to maximize their resources at the national level vis-à-vis other actors. This analysis might be valid in relation to the political leadership too, as administrations are part of the preparation processes inside the Council structure, with the Economic and Financial Committee acting as a 'separate Coreper' for ECOFIN and the Euro Group (cf. Levitt and Lord 2000: 215).

Second, social partners and other interest groups, as well as political parties and parliaments, will not challenge the amended opportunity structure and will not strive to use veto points such as the annual budget processes to act against the European consensus. Having incorporated the strong disciplinary mood into their own institutional belief system, parliaments will not object to even unpleasant decisions by the EU Council and thus become 'decision takers' in an area of their original parliamentary sovereignty (cf. Putnam 1988 for the term). As rational actors, political parties and social partners will not challenge governments' draft budgets which are 'close to balance or in surplus', as public perception will 'punish' them for acting against the spirit of the European consensus, whether directly through elections or indirectly through negative media coverage.

'Soft' coordination in economic and employment policy governance: building a broad economic consensus

In the governance of economic and employment policy, this scenario assumes that the opportunities for access and participation established by the set of treaty provisions, secondary legislation, or European Council conclusions will be used by European as well as national actors as channels to pursue own interests. They will get involved in the numerous 'soft' coordination and monitoring mechanisms according to the time-frames laid down in the treaty provisions. An indicator of a continuing trend of vertical fusion is the consecutive creation of additional 'soft' processes: 'Luxembourg', 'Cardiff', 'Cologne', and, to a certain extent, also 'Lisbon'. They show the efforts of European and domestic policy-makers to complement the treaty provisions with a set of additional instruments for establishing a policy mix within the EU.

The horizontal fusion of 'soft' coordination processes at the national level will take the form of actors continuing to increase the efficiency of these instruments. They will carefully adjust and fine tune the different processes inside the appropriate institutions by consensus and fit national policy cycles to the European timetable (cf. Council of the European Union 2000). In this case, adaptation processes at the national level will lead to higher convergence of national policy formulation and policy-making and further orientate national policies to European constraints, even if 'recommendations' for adjustments will not be formalized but will be part of an increased effort for coordination. This effort includes stronger horizontal links at the European level between various Council formations which will have to prepare their input into the Broad Economic Policy Guidelines and will therefore have to synchronize their administrative preparatory committee work with the policy cycle in economic policy (cf. Council of the European Union 2000).

As the various processes are concentrating on benchmarking and the publication of 'best practices', a European space for discussion, decision-making, and ranking will be established and will be open to manifold actors, be they governmental within the European procedures or non-governmental within national—and to some extent even European—procedures. This will reinforce fusion processes in both dimensions.

Given this wide range of 'voice' options (Hirschman 1970) provided by the manifold processes and coordination policies, domestic actors will find it less difficult to adapt to new opportunity structures as almost all governmental, administrative, and non-governmental domestic actors will benefit from the new participation and interaction patterns. Policy preferences can be articulated in an even wider set of institutions. As there is no intensive re-allocation of resources amongst domestic actors, direct and formal adaptational pressures are only moderate and do not challenge the core of national tradition in policy-making (cf. Haverland 2000). Those actors who are part of the core network will be able even further to change the political climate at the domestic level in order to increase support for those domestic reforms contributing to the success of the European policy mix. This outcome will in turn strengthen the effectiveness of the whole process (cf. Knill and Lehmkuhl 1999). Based on different collective understandings attached to the various institutions (cf. Risse, Green Cowles, and Caporaso 2001) domestic actors will use different paths to contribute to European deliberations and decision-making. They will thereby foster an intensive though productive competition between different Council formations, including some kind of overall consensus within the Jumbo Council between ECOFIN and the Employment and Social Policy Council. We will even witness corresponding informal domestic procedures to prepare European procedures, for example, informal macroeconomic coordination between ministries, national central banks, and social partners before European Macroeconomic Dialogues.

Horizontal and Vertical Fragmentation

Basic assumptions

An alternative scenario expects that in the policy areas concerned national actors will:

(1) focus on domestic policy arenas and on domestic discourses;

(2) only partially merge domestic policy instruments with EU instruments, leading to vertical fragmentation; and

(3) compete with each other so that policy areas will remain separate on both European and national levels where actors of different policy networks follow disconnected and diverging discourses, creating horizontal fragmentation.

In this scenario, the establishment of an identifiable *gouvernance économique* is not expected. On the contrary, the various institutions will use their respective instruments separately, according to the treaty provisions, without pooling them. Some of the central institutions such as the Economic and Financial Committee, the Economic Policy Committee, as well as the Euro Group and ECOFIN will formally or rhetorically call for a coherent approach to the policies concerned. However, the different policy networks will try to preserve their separate competencies and discourses. Even more, the dynamics of each policy area will lead towards increased institutional competition, for example between the Economic and Financial Committee and the Employment Committee. Contrasting doctrines will dominate the debate, being continuously reinvented by those actors who are part of the specific policy network. We expect a failure of specific attempts at the European level to coordinate the coordination policies (cf. Council of the European Union 1999) due to the stickiness of the existing institutional set-up and due to the disregard of, or inertia by, the actors involved (for the terms, Börzel and Risse 2000).

Fragmentation in the vertical sense means that institutions and procedures on the national level will remain exclusively oriented towards the agendas of the member states, such as electoral cycles. Hence we will not observe a convergence of political discourses between the member states (cf. Euro Spectator Series 2000). National institutions and actors will take account of incentives and constraints at the European level, but efforts at real adaptation will be an exception (cf. Chapter 8). These efforts will follow different domestic structures and path dependencies and be framed by national demands and discourses.

While acknowledging the usefulness of a policy mix that includes monetary, economic, and employment as well as fiscal policies, domestic and EU actors will still consider it a national issue to establish such an approach. Hence governmental actors will concentrate on those preferences articulated by domestic societal groups which they may present in an aggregated form within European institutions (cf. Moravcsik 1993). Member states will therefore engage in European coordination policies to the extent that it coincides with their own preferences and without accepting policy outcomes that might be unfavourable for them at the national level. As veto points for domestic actors are numerous, national administrations in the separate policy fields will have to aggregate these diverse domestic demands without being able to pursue a coherent approach at the European level. European institutions in charge of coordination will not be able to accommodate these various policy preferences and will choose more general and ambiguous positions (Tsoukalis 2000: 174).

Those domestic actors who are not directly participating in European institutions dealing with the relevant policy issues will try to limit constraints stemming from coordination policies. Most of these policies are without direct legal implications at the national level and therefore do not induce direct adaptational pressures on domestic policy-making processes or institutions. Accordingly, policy outcomes at the European level will be absorbed at the national level by domestic procedures. Accommodation is facilitated by the rather general recommendations or reports from Brussels. Policy cycles are followed to the extent that deadlines for the submission of reports or programmes are met; requested documents are sent to Brussels and meetings attended. But the effect of these coordination procedures is limited to the workload of divisions within ministries.

In national administrations, only those departments interacting at the European level deal with the policies, with no transfer taking place to other ministries. These ministries or divisions can be labelled 'isolated' or 'specialized' (Wessels 2000: 63–8). Interministerial coordination between the divisions in the ministries for finance, economics, and labour and social affairs, dealing with the different modes, reflects a 'negative' coordination without common positions and strategies (Scharpf 1997). The result is further complications for policy coordination and coherence on the European level (Kassim, Peters, and Wright 2000). Divergences in national fundamentals will not vanish but, under pressure, might even be accentuated.

Supranational governance of monetary policy: an independent ECB acting autonomously

If we look again at the modes of governance, the picture will be different from the fusion scenario. As a consequence of horizontal fragmentation, the ECB will use its instruments independently and without the interference of national and other European political actors. Inter-institutional interaction and shared participation rights at the European level will have only one-directional effects and will influence neither the decision-making institutions nor the individual actors of the ECB. Monetary policy of the ECB will be conducted within its Governing Council. Members of the Executive Board, senior ECB staff members, and senior officials from the national central banks will participate in inter-institutional set-ups. But these interactions will be used only as a tool to communicate the ECB's monetary strategy towards the political actors and to advocate the 'sound money' paradigm in case some political actors might choose to ignore it. Thus, the ECB will safeguard its role as supranational policy-maker. Based on the treaty provisions, the ECB will not favour a policy mix which would open up monetary policy to complementary and alternative concepts of macroeconomic policy. Instead it will take care to exclude monetary policy from such considerations.

Efforts of domestic political actors to tie the ECB and the national central banks—as the ECB's 'branches' in the member states—into a policy mix will be in vain. These efforts will either cease after some fruitless exercises—see the debate of former finance ministers Oskar Lafontaine and Dominique Strauss-Kahn in 1999 and early 2000—or continue to be a constant threat to the ECB's independence (cf. European Commission 2001a). Once the very favourable economic conditions at the start of the third stage end in an economic downturn, national politicians might increasingly press the ECB into policy outcomes that would take into account specific national economic problems and that put less importance on price stability.

National public debates on monetary policy will remain fragmented as they concentrate on national consequences of the ECB's strategy, especially for other national policy fields. This characteristic will be most apparent in those member states that suffer from 'asymmetric shocks' and in those states that are less important for overall monetary strategy due to their insignificant percentage of the Euro-Zone GDP. A real European debate will not develop apart from disconnected Brussels and Frankfurt networks which only have the ECB as a reference point and are isolated from public opinion in Europe. Thus the cleavage in perceptions of the euro between political and economic elites on the one hand and the general public on the other will continue.[2] Governors/Presidents of national central banks will continue to participate in national deliberations, be they formal or informal, public or within the policy-making structures. But the main aim will be to communicate the official policy of the ECB to the national arena. Domestic actors and institutions will perceive the national central banks more as a 'Trojan horse' of the ECB than as a useful channel for domestic policy-makers (for the term, Ciavarini Azzi 1985).

---

[2] For the latest figures, European Commission (2001b: 73).

'Hard' coordination in fiscal policy: non-compliance and re-nationalization strategies

In view of the horizontal and vertical fragmentation in fiscal policy, the debate will be about the interpretation of the 'hard' provisions, in procedural terms on the timing, on the substance of the legal provisions, and even more about their fundamental *raison d'être*.

At the national level, the constraints on national fiscal policies from the 'hard' coordination procedures will be considered far too demanding to be followed by actors in domestic institutions. The cost of compliance will lead to an intensification of national debates in and by national parliaments, which will stress their legitimate functions as budgetary 'decision makers', and by interest groups concerned by cuts in public spending. The controversies will be oriented towards national issues and will turn out to use 'Brussels' as a scapegoat for institutional misfits and the Commission as an unapproachable 'supranational bureaucracy' (Wessels 2000: 120–1). Neither epistemic communities nor interest groups will use European-wide networks for deliberations on fiscal policy, as they do not offer any added value in the power game which continues to take place in the national arenas. The propensity for evasion and non-compliance will be large, especially depending on national election cycles (Artis and Winkler 1998; Vaubel, Bernholz, and Streit 1998).

Some member states might even find 'loopholes' at the national level where stability pacts with sub-national governments have been introduced, for example in Italy and Austria (cf. Chapter 8; Baumann and Lang 2000; for Germany, Hellermann 2000). The constraints on the budgetary powers of the member states from the Stability Pact might therefore become a controversial issue not only between parties but also between different levels of government.

Though the opportunity structure of the Stability Pact is not geared towards 'exits' (Hirschman 1970), the political battle at the European level will grow, especially if and when an economic downturn hits more than one country. EU member governments will lead a political debate on how to change and especially how to explicitly or implicitly soften the fiscal criteria. National actors in ECOFIN and the Economic and Financial Committee will look for loopholes in the interpretation and avoid taking any tough decision with financial sanctions, whatever the provisions of the Stability Pact envisage. Recommendations of the European Commission and warnings of the ECB will be ignored, and majority voting will be shelved as a supranational 'sin' against the legitimate rights of sovereign states and their parliaments. Even if fines are imposed, member states will block their payment. The procedures will not achieve the objectives set by the formal provisions (see mainstream economics contributions like Spahn 1996; de Grauwe 2000b: 210; Artis and Winkler 1998; Sachverständigenrat 1996/97: 218).

If the rules are not followed according to the provisions in one case—one or more countries—the credibility of 'hard' coordination will collapse. The provisions will then not produce their own legitimacy by being regarded as a successful and respected rule but lose their normative weight by a self-destroying prophecy. The letters of the treaty will be dead, and we can expect at a certain moment a Council procedure to revise or adapt the legal framework on 'hard' fiscal policy coordination, eventually leading to some kind of 'soft' coordination.

'Soft' coordination in economic and employment policy: evasion strategies

The increasing number of varied formulas passed by the European Council and by ECOFIN will offer national actors wide opportunities to evade any kind of 'soft compliance'. National employment and economic policies will depend exclusively on national electoral cycles and on isolated themes in the national discourse and not on the coordination and monitoring cycles of the employment title and the Broad Economic Policy Guidelines. Instead of shaping an intensive European discourse, they will just register the outcome of fragmented national debates. In a vicious circle, low policy importance and low actor attention will reinforce each other. Given the variations in the economic situation of each member state, given also the divergences in the structures of intermediary groups in member states as well as divergent positions about the relevance and the substance of common guidelines, the European Council will only rubber stamp general and ambiguous programmes. These programmes will have been prepared in routine procedures by a differentiated network of governmental and non-governmental actors, deliberately represented by low-level officials.

Due to the low level of adaptational pressure, domestic actors will have no incentives to change their policy preference structures and to reorientate their attention to European processes. The channels provided in the new coordination procedures are too few to offer a credible alternative to domestic opportunities in national policy-making structures. In addition, most non-governmental actors will participate only in national procedures, sometimes not even knowing that these emanate from the European level. Those societal groups taking part in European procedures such as the Macroeconomic Dialogue will not be able or willing to pass down results to the domestic level and thus will increase the ineffectiveness of these procedures.

Future Outlook: On the Way Towards a Supranational *Gouvernance Économique?*

The central aim has been to explore the effects of the three new forms of governance in the field of EMU on national institutions and actors in a broader macro view. These new forms, especially the 'hard' and 'soft' co-ordination procedures, might '[become] a typical mode in future EU policy-making as an alternative to the formal re-assignment of policy powers from national to EU level' (H. Wallace 2000: 33). Given the limited time of observa-tion, and thus the scarcity of data, we cannot predict whether we will witness a common trend towards horizontal and vertical fusion in the policy areas of EMU or whether trends towards a fragmentation across policy fields and levels of interaction will prevail.

Extrapolating from the dynamics of the EU system over the last decades, the EU's evolution signifies institutional and procedural growth and differ-entiation with a growing participation of several actors from different levels. This basic evolutionary trend might be sometimes overshadowed by cyclical ups and downs in the political and public mood (cf. for Nice, Wessels 2001). Each 'up' in the legal constitution leads to a ratchet effect by which the level of activities in the valley of day-to-day politics moves to a higher plateau (cf. Maurer and Wessels 2001; also historical institutionalist approaches: Pierson 1998; Peters 1999). Looking closer, we find a three-step type of integra-tion cascade. Member-state governments start with some form of loose intergovernmental procedures and then move to some kind of rationalized intergovernmentalism with limited roles of supranational institutions and unanimity voting in the Council. They finalize this process by establishing more efficient rules with a strong role for supranational bodies and qualified majority voting in the Council (cf. Wessels 2001).

From this perspective, we are able to locate the three modes of governance on different levels of this integration scale and as a part of the overall evolu-tion and transformation of the EU system. At a critical juncture in a few years, this might result in another attempt by the member states to improve the capacity for effective problem solving on the European level by taking another step in the direction set by previous cases in the fields of fiscal, economic, and employment policy. The European Commission (2001a: 6–7) proposes new and thus 'harder' coordination procedures in the field of economic policy, and similar ideas were launched by the French Prime Minister, Lionel Jospin (2001).

In order to 'improve . . . the democratic legitimacy' of the EU (Declaration No. 23 of the Nice Treaty on 'the future of the Union') and to 'stabilize' national welfare systems and the emerging 'stabilization state' (Dyson 2000*b*), member states will eventually take further steps towards more supranational modes of governance in the field of fiscal, economic, and employment policy, adjusted to the specific characteristics of the policy field. In this respect, we expect that this new form of governance is transitional and not a dominant trend spreading into other policy fields of the EU.

This viewpoint is highly speculative as it is based on some general extrapolations that need more detailed analysis. However, it highlights the political relevance of the research as the real pattern, be it fusion of fragmentation, will have major effects on national institutions and on the EU system in general.

3

The Political Economy of Fiscal Policy under Monetary Union

David McKay

Few dispute that the adoption of Economic and Monetary Union (EMU) has great economic and political significance. Martin Feldstein (1997: 23) even went so far as to claim that it 'could be the most far-reaching political event of the 20th century'. Note that, along with many other academics, Feldstein identifies it as a *political* event (for economic perspectives, see De Grauwe 1994: 210; Fitoussi *et al.* 1993: 89; Tsoukalis 1993: 227; Boyer 2000; for political science analyses, see Moravcsik 1998; Dyson and Featherstone 1999). As might be expected given the short life of EMU, much of this literature concentrates on the origins of EMU rather than on its consequences. What EMU will bring in the medium or longer term must inevitably be speculative in nature.

Generally, it has been the economists who have ventured into this un-certain territory, largely because they are able to employ models that can make sensible statistical extrapolations from past experience. In almost every instance, the relationship between EMU and fiscal policy has been at the core of these analyses. There is, of course, a very simple reason: EMU will eventually achieve almost full monetary integration but virtually no fiscal integration. Economists have, therefore, been quick to identify the likely con-sequences of this asymmetry. Hence comparative applications of optimum currency area (OCA) theory have dwelt on such questions as conjunctural con-vergence in business cycles and the relationship between labour flexibility/ mobility and currency unions (in particular Bayoumi and Masson 1995; Eichen-green 1994; Bayoumi and Eichengreen 1992; Krugman 1993; von Hagen 1993*a*). Of necessity these studies have elevated the role of fiscal policy to a central position because of the crucial stabilization and equalization roles played by fiscal policy in established federations when faced with asymmetric economic shocks or when placating actually or potentially dissident states or social groups (Tondl 2000: 231–5 and sources cited). In other words, in federations fiscal federalism is used as a device to compensate for the spatial inequalities that result from the asymmetric consequences of economic change.

More recently, the focus of research has shifted to the role of the ECB and the working of the Stability and Growth Pact. Again, economists have dominated research and, again, the fiscal consequences of EMU are central to the analysis (Gros 1995; Allsopp and Vines 1996; Fatás 1998; Buti and Sapir 1998). This is clearly so given the Stability and Growth Pact's requirement that national governments adhere to limitations on national deficit and debt levels.

Finally, many economists argue that, for EMU—and indeed the single European market—to work at full efficiency, some degree of fiscal harmonization of national taxes, and in particular corporate taxes and VAT, will be required (CEPS 2000; Keen and Smith 1996).

Although rarely made explicit in the economics literature, these predicted changes in fiscal policy will have profound consequences both for the ways in which member states interact with national citizenries and for the ways in which member states operate within the EU. National sovereignty over monetary policy has been ceded to the ECB, while sovereignty over fiscal policy remains firmly in national hands. This asymmetry has the potential to produce major adjustments within European states and indeed may result in a major reshaping of the European nation state.

In this context, this chapter has three objectives: first, to outline the ways in which the fiscal dimension is likely to change the nature of domestic politics in European states; second, to place these changes in comparative context by reference to the experience of established federal states; and third, to speculate on the ways in which fiscal changes are likely to change the ways in which domestic political actors operate in the context of the institutional framework of the EU. Space limitations preclude a comprehensive coverage of these points. It is not intended to draw systematic distinctions between member states; the country chapters in this volume help provide this detail. Instead, the purpose is to draw on those theoretical perspectives generated by recent research in economics and political science that provide the basis for informed judgements on the *general* affects of EMU on national polities in general and national fiscal regimes in particular.

The Fiscal Dimension and Domestic Politics

As earlier indicated, research shows that the fiscal dimension of EMU can be broken down into three components: fiscal federalism, the effects of the Stability and Growth Pact, and the pressures for tax harmonization.

Fiscal Federalism

A large literature in applied economics has established that, unless the economies that make up monetary unions are characterized by a high degree of homogeneity and labour market flexibility and mobility, then some degree of central—or federal—government intervention will be necessary. This intervention serves either to stabilize economies whose business cycles are not synchronized or to equalize social security and other benefits on grounds of equity. All economists agree that *some* degree of intervention or fiscal federalism will be necessary, but they disagree on the extent. In the case of the US and other federations some 25–30 per cent of every dollar lost in a localized economic downturn is returned in the form of federal aid either to local jurisdictions or directly to individuals (Sachs and Sala-I-Martin 1992; Bayoumi and Masson 1995; Eichengreen 1994; Bayoumi and Eichengreen 1993; Krugman 1993; Tondl 2000: 234–5). Nobody expects the EU remotely to approach this figure, in part because labour mobility and flexibility is much lower than in the US and in part because the political conditions for such massive inter-state transfers are simply absent (McKay 1999a). Instead, figures ranging from less than 1 per cent to around 5 per cent of EU GDP have been cited: compare Gros and Steinherr (1994: 76) with the MacDougall Report, which opted for as high as 5 per cent (MacDougall *et al.* 1977). Even a 1 per cent figure would represent a very substantial increase on the approximately 0.5 per cent of EU GDP accounted for by structural aid—the rough equivalent of federal grants-in-aid in the US and elsewhere, although they are designed for longer-term economic revival rather than short-term stabilization.

As earlier implied, while a strong economic case can be made for a system of fiscal federalism in the EU (see Tondl 2000), the political obstacles in the way of such a system are formidable. Any substantial increase in EU-wide taxation designed specifically for redistribution would be strongly resisted by potential donor states (see McKay 1999a: 472–85 and sources cited). None the less, if—perhaps when—the EU or part of the EU were to suffer a major economic shock, the pressures for increased central or federal aid will be substantial given the inability of economies to adjust through devaluation or the exercise of monetary policy. In the case of a seriously depressed economy, the use of domestic fiscal instruments alone would require deficit financing which might fall foul of Stability Pact rules.

The crucial element here is that a system of fiscal federalism would require voters in those member states that were least affected by recession to accept the transfer of their tax euros to the worst-affected states. Such redistributions are tolerated in existing nation states only because of highly developed national identities that have been forged over very long periods, sometimes over centuries (see McKay 1999a: 472–85). Indeed, constitutional settlements often follow periods of upheaval inspired by redistributive questions. And federations often experience 'stateness' problems because redistribution is implemented without the full consent of the all the participating states and provinces (Linz and Stepan 1996: Ch. 1).[1] Voters in existing member states have certainly not granted any such consent to the EU, whether explicitly through party manifestos or implicitly through appointed representatives to Brussels. In other words, significant centrally funded redistribution across member-state boundaries, whether to individuals or to national governments, has yet to be legitimized through established representative mechanisms.

While support for the EU in general and EMU in particular varies across member states, we have no reason to suppose that in a system of enhanced fiscal redistribution donor states would support large-scale redistribution. On the contrary, it is more likely that, as with existing EU expenditures and in particular structural and cohesion funds, they would fight to keep net contributions within reasonable bounds (Hooge 1996).

The Stability and Growth Pact

As indicated, member-state fiscal policy is potentially seriously constrained by the Stability and Growth Pact. All countries within EMU are required to report their budgetary data to the European Commission on a twice-yearly basis and to keep their budget deficits below 3 per cent of GDP. Countries that fail to do so initially incur a penalty in the form of a non-interest bearing deposit. If the situation continues fines can be levied at levels between about 0.21 and 0.5 per cent of GDP. Given the uncertainties of economic forecasting, countries are actually aiming for deficits substantially below 3 per cent, thus restricting them further. Fines would, of course, actually add to the deficit, so countries are especially keen to avoid them. Exceptions are made for member states whose real GDP has declined by 2 per cent in any one year. In the—much more likely—event that the decline is between 0.7 per cent and 2 per cent, then, on the advice of the Economic and Finance Ministers Council (ECOFIN), the approval of the European Council is required to avoid penalties.[2] Moreover, countries would have to demonstrate that their

---

[1] Distributive questions often act as surrogates for deeper ethnic, religious, linguistic, or cultural divisions (see Linz and Stepan 1996: Chs 1–3).

[2] Some ambiguity exists on the whether the 3 per cent rule can be suspended should an economy contract by 0.75 per cent. The actual wording is: 'In evaluating whether the economic downturn is severe, Member states will, as a rule, take as a reference point an annual fall in real GDP of at least 0.75 per cent' (European Council 1997: 2).

recessions were in some way 'exceptional' before approval was granted. These Council decisions will be decided by qualified majority voting—at present a concurrent majority of 71 per cent, rising to 73.4 per cent after 1 January 2005 should all the enlargement targets be met. At all times Council members will engage in 'mutual surveillance' procedures to encourage the 'naming and shaming' of offenders (see Eichengreen and Wyplosz 1998; on the administrative mechanisms Eijffinger and de Haan 2000: 87–95).

Although, after two years of operation, the Stability and Growth Pact has not resulted in the unwanted consequences predicted by some economists (von Hagen and Eichengreen 1996; Arestis and Sawyer 1999), it has yet to be tested by an economic downturn. Indeed, in 1999 the average budget deficit in the Euro-Zone was a mere –1.1 per cent, although in the USA, the UK, Denmark, Sweden, and Canada substantial surpluses were in place (*Economist* 2000). None the less, the misgivings of many economists seems justified if, as seems likely, all the countries of the Euro-Zone do not approximate to an optimal currency area (de Grauwe 2000*a*). In this case the 'one-size-fits-all' monetary policy together with fiscal restrictions of the Stability Pact will deny to those countries affected by a downturn the traditional instruments that are available to stabilize economies.

Optimists may argue that we are in the midst of a paradigm shift in economic management involving universal acceptance of balanced budgets, lower levels of public expenditure, and open economies. Shocks may occur but, after minor adjustment, will be absorbed by the workings of the markets. For example, the threefold increase in oil prices in 1999/2000 was absorbed with relative ease compared with the oil hikes of the 1970s. History, however, would suggest otherwise. The late twentieth/early twenty-first century virtuous cycle was in 2000 only half a dozen or so years old and was uneven in its application; Japan with its budget deficit of 7 per cent was notably excluded. More likely is a return to traditional business cycles whose peaks and troughs will be determined by a host of unpredictable domestic and international economic and political factors. In other words, economic dislocation will occur and will oblige governments to continue to use national fiscal policies as instruments of stabilization.

But Euro-Zone governments will be limited in the extent to which they can employ this option. They will, in addition, be restricted in their use of fiscal policy as an instrument of equalization. Indeed, current debate on the need for the Euro-Zone economies to 'adjust' means pruning welfare states, reforming 'unfunded' social security programmes, and loosening labour markets. Economists have been quick to see the connection between such neo-liberal reforms and the Stability and Growth Pact. Hence McKinnon

(1997), Mussa (1997) and others have argued that welfare-state retrenchment can be justified, and indeed sold to reluctant voters, on the grounds that it is required by the excessive deficit procedures of the Pact.

Bayoumi, Eichengreen, and von Hagen (1997: 84) go even further and argue the case for the centralization of all budgetary procedures in EMU states:

Centralized procedures empower the prime minister, the finance minister or the treasury minister to overrule spending ministers, limit the scope for parliamentary amendments to the government's budget and limit modifications to the budget law at the implementation stage . . . A still more ambitious approach would be to create independent agencies at the national level to monitor the budget . . . Still more drastic reform would establish in each country a national Debt Board with the power to set a binding ceiling on the annual increase in public debt.

But the requirement that national budgetary procedures become central-ized, labour markets reformed, and welfare states retrenched involves matters that are traditionally dealt with by national governments, not the EU. So far there is little evidence that voters in the EMU area have made a direct connection between the Stability Pact and such reforms. Should they do so, however, the consequences for domestic politics would be profound. Labour-market practices and social benefits have accumulated over time as a direct result of the workings of representative government and in particular the championing of redistributive policies by social democratic parties. The direct linkage between neo-liberal policies and EMU represents a sort of double paradigm shift. A social market economy is replaced by a neo-liberal economy and, in contrast to the construction of welfare states, the impetus behind this change derives from exogenous rather than endogenous forces.[3] While political scientists have expressed this problem in terms of a potential legit-imization crisis (Weale 1996; Beetham and Lord 1998; Verdun and Christensen 2000), how this crisis might manifest itself in individual countries remains to be seen. What is plain is that national responses to these pressures will vary considerably from state to state. This much is clear from the country con-tributions in this volume. Much depends on political traditions and public expectations. In some systems, such as the Netherlands, traditions rooted in compromise and consociationalism may already have arrived at workable

---

[3] Although it could be argued that all countries are now obliged to conform to neo-liberal policies—for example, the UK and New Zealand have undergone major transformations from social democratic to free-market regimes—in these and other cases the shift was not imposed on the citizens via centrally administered institutional rules, where the lines of accountability are blurred.

solutions (see Chapter 9), while in other systems, such as the French, restructuring may prove more difficult (see Chapter 6). Notwithstanding these variations, however, EMU has changed the rules of the game by 'supranationalizing' the reform agenda and making specific labour-market and welfare-state reforms matters of necessity rather than choice.

This debate would, of course, be moot if, as some argue, EMU is not the major agent of change in labour-market and welfare-state reform (see Chapters 11 and 12). While other forces may be at work in the same direction, notably the imperatives of international trade competition, there can be no doubting that, in terms of political discourse and elite perceptions, EMU is widely accepted as an accelerative factor in the restructuring of state sectors and labour markets.

If it is *perceived* as having this effect, then it is but a short step for voters in the Euro-Zone states also to make the connection. Crucially, of course, the true test for the effects of the Stability Pact has yet to occur. Restructuring state benefits and labour markets is much easier, and is less urgently required, during periods of economic growth than during economic downturns. If voters perceive that adherence to the 3 per cent deficit rules can be achieved only at the cost of reduced welfare and other benefits, then they may work to persuade political parties and representatives to break the rules. Many economists are agreed that the rules may indeed be broken. For example, Eijffinger and de Haan (2000: 92–3) argue:

. . . it is questionable whether these fiscal rules [of the Stability Pact] will be adhered to if a large number of member states get into serious fiscal problems. As long as there are 'good guys' who are willing to exert peer pressure on the 'bad guys', the functioning of the Stability Pact is secured. However, this is less certain when (1) the number of 'bad guys' is large, (2) there is a common interest to lay aside the stipulations laid down in the Pact [fiscal deficit and public debt rules] . . . or (3) a country is not willing to comply with the sanctions of the Ecofin Council, knowing that there is no ultimate penalty like exclusion from the EU. The Council does not have the competence directly to intervene in national fiscal policy-making, for instance by cutting expenditures or increasing tax rates.

While compliance with the existing rules may be difficult to enforce, *some* form of fiscal discipline is necessary for EMU to work. Unchallenged fiscal recidivism on the part of some members would damage the euro on the foreign exchanges and, via imported inflation, might undermine the whole project. Indeed, in a number of existing federations it is precisely because central governments are unable to control runaway spending by state authorities that the national currency is weakened (World Bank 1997; Ter-Minassian

1997: Chs 1, 2). So whatever the inadequacies of the present arrangements, it seems improbable that ECOFIN, the ECB, and the Commission will forgo some form of regulatory regime. One obvious alternative would be to combine the stick of deficit rules with the carrot of fiscal federalism. But, as was discussed in the last section, this would, of course, itself raise legitimacy and equity problems that would not be easily resolved.

Fiscal Harmonization

The classic statements on fiscal decentralization argue that local fiscal autonomy can involve large gains in welfare and economic efficiency. Hence Tiebout (1961), Musgrave (1969), and Oates (1972) argue that fiscal autonomy encourages tax competition and drives down overall tax rates. However, in the context of globalized capital others have argued that highly differentiated levels of direct corporate taxation encourage capital flight to low-tax areas (see Ter-Minassian 1997: Ch. 2). Within both existing federations and the EU a case has been made for the harmonization of indirect taxes—sales and VAT receipts—to discourage capital flight, increase price transparency, and reduce accounting costs (see Smith 2000). Indeed, the Commission has long been committed both to the simplification of member states' VAT systems and to their harmonization, and the EU agreed to fix the standard rate of VAT at a minimum of 15 per cent in 1991. However, while there has been some progress towards standardization, considerable variations in VAT rates continue to apply and national governments resist ceding control over VAT regimes with some vigour (Eijffinger and de Haan 2000: Ch. 4). VAT harmonization is not just a matter of rate differentials. Problems also exist in the area of accounting methodology. VAT could be charged at the point of destination—where goods are finally sold—or at the point of origin. The present system represents a compromise between the ideal of harmonization and the insistence by member states that they retain control over their own taxes. Naturally, high-tax states fear the loss of revenue that harmonization down to the EU average implies, while low-tax states fear the economic and political costs of the higher taxes implied by harmonization.

The same dilemma applies to excise duties and to corporate taxation. Excise duties represent up to 16 per cent of taxation in some countries, notably the UK, and harmonization would result in a considerable loss of revenue for them. A system of minimum rates has been agreed, but considerable inter-state divergence persists (Hoeller, Louppe, and Vergriete 1996).

Most controversy surrounds the question of taxation on company profits and on savings. Some economists argue that all taxation on profits is counterproductive as the welfare resulting from such taxes is less than that achievable in a tax-free regime. The Commission line is that corporate taxes should be reduced but harmonized so as to provide a level playing field for investors and savers (CEPS 2000). At the moment corporate tax rates vary from 8.6 per cent of GDP in Luxembourg and 4.58 per cent in the Netherlands to 1.76 per cent of GDP in Germany and 2.17 per cent in Italy.[4] At the same time, considerable political support both from the Commission and from individual member states exists in support of a withholding tax or a tax on interest on savings in order to ensure that all cross-border interest flows are subject to tax. The original proposal was that part of the interest on savings would be paid directly to governments in order to ensure compliance. Indeed at the Helsinki Council in December 1999 the institution of a withholding tax became declared EU policy (CEPS 2000: iii). A number of states oppose the idea, however, including the UK, which is particularly concerned about the taxation of non-residents and the effects of the proposal on the euro-bond market. Under both the Portuguese and French Council presidencies pressures to reach a settlement increased, and a compromise was eventually hammered out in late 2000. Under the agreement member states would, for a seven-year transition period, share tax information in order to reduce evasion. In the meantime, those states that wished to impose the tax could do so. Luxembourg, Austria, Belgium, Greece, and Portugal proposed to continue with their existing withholding taxes. The issue remains firmly on the table, however, and is unlikely to be satisfactorily resolved even in the medium term. As with VAT, the harmonization of corporate taxation involves more than merely agreeing on common tax rates. Few doubt that in the complex area of tax law even nominally standardized tax rates would fall foul of national variations in definition and accounting and collection procedures (CEPS 2000; *Financial Times* 1998: 3).

In sum, while there is no clear EU policy of tax harmonization, elements of VAT harmonization exist and pressures for some standardization of corporate taxation are considerable. At the same time many argue that the benefits of EMU and the single European market cannot be fully realized until full tax transparency is achieved. This implies true tax harmonization including the creation of a single administration and collection authority. As with the Stability Pact, tax harmonization goes right to the heart of the relationship between the state and the citizen in modern societies. The loss of member-state tax autonomy would, as far as budgetary matters are concerned, move the EU towards a federal-like entity, with a central fiscal authority

---

[4] In 1997, cited in Eijffinger and de Haan (2000: Table 4.4).

similar to that operating in a number of established federations, including the United States and Switzerland.[5] We will return to this point in the next section.

Fiscal harmonization relates directly to centralized controls on taxing and borrowing and to fiscal federalism. Mandatory harmonization—and it is difficult to envision any other variety—would further limit the freedom of governments unilaterally to adjust taxes in the face of economic shocks, even within the confines of the Stability Pact. This in turn would strengthen moves towards fiscal federalism. Clearly this would help confirm the 'semi-sovereign' status of EU member states. Put another way, by removing some degree of national control over taxation, fiscal harmonization would change the architecture of domestic politics. As with the Stability Pact and fiscal federalism, these changes would vary considerably from country to country. But the general consequence would be the creation of a supranational tax regime. When voting in 'first-order' elections or those elections that select the level of government that is most important to voters (Franklin, Marsh, and McLaren 1994), individual citizens would be unable to influence crucial aspects of tax policy. They would, instead, have to transfer their allegiance to candidates and parties operating in the EU political domain, most notably the European Parliament.

These tensions will in all probability be intensified by decisions of the European Court of Justice (ECJ). For while the Court has no direct jurisdiction over member states' tax law, it has an obligation to ensure that national taxes are levied in accordance with Community law. Thus it is clear from recent ECJ decisions that some degree of standardization will result in such areas as VAT collection (Russell 2000).

EU Fiscal Arrangements in Comparative Context

From the preceding analysis it is clear that the EU is in danger of drifting towards a problematical fiscal regime. It remains limited by the provisions of the Stability and Growth Pact, and there is near unanimity among both economists and political scientists that the Pact places too many restrictions on the freedom of member states to use fiscal tools as instruments of

---

[5] The argument that because the EU has a 'bottom-up' fiscal structure with virtually all taxes levied at the sub-federal level, the need for harmonization is greater than elsewhere, is only partly true. In Switzerland State and local taxes amount to 22 per cent of GDP compared with just 13 per cent for federal taxes, yet large variations in income and other taxes by canton exist and harmonization is effectively constitutionally prohibited (OECD 1997a: Table 8).

stabilization during times of economic dislocation (see Willet 2000 and sources cited). The Pact is, in addition, being used as a justification for welfare-state retrenchment and labour-market reform, even though it was never explicitly intended to have these effects. Many economists also believe that the efficient operation of a single currency will require a degree of fiscal federalism and, ideally, the harmonization at least of VAT and corporate tax rates. These fiscal implications of EMU are certainly being openly discussed, even if they are not yet on the agenda for future intergovernmental conferences. Once EMU is fully operational after 2002, the technical and economic costs of withdrawal will be formidable. When, at this stage, the economies of the Euro-Zone experience an economic shock—or shocks—the temptation to opt for a system of fiscal federalism may be irresistible, especially if institutional decision rules have been changed in favour of QMV or—in the context of an empowered European Parliament—simple majority voting. In addition, global competitive pressures may intensify calls for fiscal harmonization and for further domestic retrenchment in public expenditure and labour-market regulation.

While we can only speculate about the likely consequences of such events for the domestic polities of member states, we may be able to learn something from the experience of other systems and in particular established federations. There are two dimensions to this exercise. First, to what extent does the EU fiscal regime resemble that of other federal systems? And second, what can be learnt from these systems?

The EU is, by some criteria, not so very far away from some other federations in terms of the level of fiscal autonomy granted to state—or member-state—governments. Indeed, as can be seen from Table 3.1, both the US and Switzerland grant fiscal autonomy to their state governments. It is also interesting to note that these two federations, together with Canada, place no controls on state borrowing, although in the cases of Switzerland and the US the States themselves place constitutional and other limitations on their borrowing power. In fact, by most measures there is a greater distance between the highly centralized Australian system and the decentralized Swiss system than there is between the EU and Switzerland.

The same is true if systems of fiscal governance are compared. As Table 3.2 shows, in its bare essentials, fiscal decision making in the EU is not so dramatically different from those operative in other federations, and in particular Switzerland. In both, Upper House, or Council of Ministers, approval is required for tax changes; in both, territorial dimensions to decision-making exists; and in both major changes in federal—central—taxation require constitutional change. A further parallel exists in that constitutional

Table 3.1 Levels of fiscal autonomy in five federations and the EU

	Australia	USA	Canada	Germany	Switzerland	EU
State tax conformity[a]	Yes	Very little	Yes[b]	Yes	None	None
State tax uniformity[a]	Yes	No	Very little	Yes	No	No (except min. VAT rate)
Single tax admin. and collection	Yes	No	Yes[b]	Yes	No	No
Independent tax role of centre	Large	Large	Medium	Large (but with tax sharing)	Small	Very small
Extent of fiscal federalism via formula-led redistribution	High	Low	High	High	Low	Very low
Central control of state borrowing[c]	Yes	No	No	Yes	No	Yes[d]

[a] State tax conformity refers to the extent of conformity in tax types between states; uniformity refers to the application of uniform tax rates.

[b] Quebec has a distinctive base for the level and administration of the individual income tax.

[c] Excluding state constitutional limitations and conventions rather than rules.

[d] Via the Stability and Growth Pact.

Source: Adapted from McKay (2001: Table 8.6).

Table 3.2 Representation of States[a] in central fiscal decision-making and constitutional change in five federations and the EU

Country	Role of lower house in tax matters	De facto veto power of upper house in tax matters	Territorial dimension to veto voting	Role of first ministers conferences	Changes in federal taxation constitutionally enshrined	Frequency of constitutional amendment attempts	State legislative approval for constitutional change	State popular approval for constitutional change
USA	high	yes	no	none	no	low	yes	no[g]
Canada	high	no	n/a	high	no	medium	yes	yes
Australia	high	yes[b]	no	medium	no	low	yes	yes
Germany	high	yes	sometimes	medium[d]	no	low	yes	no
Switzerland	medium	yes	sometimes	none	yes	high	yes	yes
EU	low	yes[c]	yes	high[e]	yes	high[f]	yes	sometimes[h]

[a] Member states in EU.
[b] Limited to certain issue areas.
[c] Council of Ministers.
[d] Federal/*Länder* Inter-ministerial Committees.
[e] Intergovernmental Conferences.
[f] Via successive treaties.
[g] But State conventions can be called to approve a constitutional change with two thirds and Congress approving.
[h] Via popular—referendum—ratification of EU treaties in some countries.

change as it affects tax matters occurs relatively frequently and is subject to something more than simple majority decision rules; constitutional approval by the Swiss cantons theoretically gives a veto to the nine smallest cantons representing 11.5 per cent of the Swiss population. This excepted, there are a number of important differences between the two systems. First, the role of the lower house in EU tax decisions remains limited, despite recent reforms; and in federal systems it is lower houses that typically represent *federal* rather than *state* interests. Second, and related, is the fact that in the EU territorially based, rather than ideologically or party- based, decision-making dominates. This is not true of the Swiss Ständerat where ideology is more important than territory (Linder 1998: Ch. 2). Third, in the EU major changes in taxation derive primarily from intergovernmental conferences—the broad equivalent of first ministers' conferences in other federal systems. In Switzerland tax changes can come from a number of sources including popular referendums. Fourth, even in Switzerland, the federal government controls a fair pro- portion of taxes and spending—around 13 per cent of GDP.[6] In the EU this figure is just over 1 per cent of EU-wide GDP. This fact, above all, increases the pressures in the EU for central control of 'state' spending.

Despite these differences, the fact remains that only in Switzerland and the EU are major changes in taxation both constitutionally established and sub- ject to decision rules more demanding than the simple majority rule operat- ive in the lower houses of most political systems. Although the Swiss system is often derided as inefficient and a 'tax jungle' (Bird 1986: 25), the fact is that it has been shaped by constitutional imperatives including the requirement that all changes in federal taxes be subject to constitutional amendment. And the constitution can be amended only through super-majoritarian decisions that are rooted in territorial politics (Linder 1998: Ch. 2). The population broadly accepts the resulting conservatism of Swiss fiscal arrangements because its constitutional basis is underpinned by a widely held core belief system. In essence this consists of a belief that the cantons are sovereign and that federal, or central, power should be contained. Any substantial accretion of power to the centre should be subject to a double majority approval of both houses of the legislature and a majority of voters in each of the cantons.

But the mechanisms for fiscal change in the EU are even more formidable than in Switzerland: unanimity rather than super-majoritarian rules prevail. Moreover, these mechanisms are largely uncodified, for, although the pro- visions of the Stability Pact have been laid out with relative clarity, how they will work in practice will almost certainly depend on the particular composition

[6] See n. 5.

of the Council of Ministers. Ministers are in turn the representatives of member-state governments, many of which are made up of coalitions of diverse political parties. All are, of course, subject to multifaceted pressures from a range of domestic and international actors. This complex dynamic applies not just to the operation of the Stability Pact, but also to all major changes in EU taxes and budgets.

Related is the fact that a great deal of uncertainty surrounds the future shape of the EU fiscal decision-making system. This is because the full fiscal implications of EMU have yet to manifest themselves. How precisely the main actors will respond is largely unknown. Some observers predict that a degree of stasis will result. Hence Levitt and Lord (2000: 221) contend that '. . . simply by virtue of the number of players involved, the institutional-ization of budgetary co-ordination between public authorities is likely to be far more complex under monetary union than under any previous political system'. If this is the case, then it is likely that system will be even more con-servative than the Swiss arrangements. Unanimity rules on tax matters in the Council of Ministers are likely to prevail for the foreseeable future. Unlike the Swiss system, in the evolving EU fiscal regime lines of accountability will be blurred, and the body to whom decision-makers are formally accountable —the European Parliament—will be uncommonly fragmented. Evidence from other political systems, and indeed from the European Commission, sug-gests that this combination can lead to corruption and or/factional chaos (Schofield 2000: 297–8 and sources cited)

This perspective fits well with the work of Dahl (1964) and others who have pointed out that, under representative federalism, the more complex and heterogeneous the polity, the more likely are the decision rules employed to move in the direction of unanimity (also Abromeit 1998: 118–19). Decision-making pathologies may result, including logrolling and the 'pork barrel'. As Weale (1996: 56) puts it: 'the reason is that with perfect information and low transaction costs, rational egoists will have an incentive to misrepresent their preferences to get the bribe of being induced to join the proto-winning coalition, and under imperfect information, log rolling will produce specific and visible benefits'. Empirical evidence from Germany suggests that in some federal systems just such an outcome has ensued (Scharpf 1988). If, at the same time, economic imperatives are pressuring decision-makers to adopt policies that result in fiscal centralization, the potential for policy error will be compounded.

The possible scenarios are legion, but one obvious one would involve a recession with asymmetric effects. ECOFIN and the European Council would be pressured by some states to institute fiscal federalism or ease the rules of the Stability Pact, but would be constrained from doing so by those less affected by the downturn. At the same time a much-strengthened European Parliament, operating according to simple majority vote, might decide that, say, a system of fiscal federalism involving sizeable spatial redistributions was necessary. Logrolling and the pork barrel would produce a perverse grant-in-aid distribution unacceptable to donor states. Decision-making stasis and conceivably a degree of market chaos might ensue.

Domestic Policy Regimes and EU Institutions

In sum, the EU fiscal regime will be infused with a degree of national influence that is unknown in other federations, including the extraordinary complexities of the much-maligned Swiss system. As the proceedings at successive intergovernmental conferences, and in particular the Nice Summit of December 2000, have shown, the most important policy-making forum in the EU has been dominated by national politicians advancing national interests. At Nice, for example, the list of issue areas transferred to QMV status was modest. And those areas that were scheduled to be transferred, including tax matters and the distribution of Structural Funds, were subject to vetoes by interested governments.

In terms of federalist theory, the EU remains a highly peripheralized federation, characterized by institutionally powerful states and a relatively weak central government (Riker 1964: Ch. 4; McKay 1999b: Ch. 9). Uniquely, however, this institutionally decentralized federation has, in EMU, acquired a highly centralized policy instrument whose economic logic requires an enhanced degree of fiscal centralization. But, as has been shown, the EU's institutional structure cannot easily accommodate such a development. Instead, the interests and needs of individual national systems with long-established democratic linkages between citizens and the state are likely to prevail.

In this context, the EU's fiscal regime is likely to develop in one of two directions. It may, as in Switzerland, continue to be characterized by a high degree of complexity that most economists would describe as 'inefficient' or 'sub-optimal'. This is the assumption behind a large economics literature that constantly seeks to rationalize or simplify EU fiscal systems (see, for example, CEPS 2000; Keen and Smith 1996). Given recent developments, this seems the more likely outcome. The national veto is likely to be retained in the taxation and budgetary areas, including the allocation of Structural Funds. In the absence of institutional reform, and in particular of Council of Minister decision rules, something resembling the status quo is likely to be retained. Enlargement will almost certainly aggravate this problem: the larger the number of members, the greater the number of carefully protected national fiscal regimes and the greater the obstacles to centralization and harmonization.

It could be argued that global pressures exist to achieve fiscal rectitude and competitive tax rates, and member-state governments will, as a result, agree to standardized rules and procedures whose effects will be broadly similar to those intended by the Stability Pact and tax harmonization. Certainly, the experience of member states outside the Euro-Zone, and in particular the UK, suggests that there is something to this argument. However, there is a crucial difference between national governments responding to global pressures and national governments having to comply with EU- mandated rules and regulations. With the former, national tax regimes can be adapted according to local conditions. With the latter, centralization and harmonization have to be achieved in ways that accommodate a variety of fiscal regimes. Given the sheer variety and complexity characteristic of these regimes, this will be a much more formidable task.

Hence the prospects for the second possible outcome—the creation of an EU fiscal constitution—are, at least in the medium term, slight. As earlier indicated, some member states may be more prepared than others to sacrifice national sovereignty. Germany, for example, has long experience of playing the 'semi-sovereignty game' both in terms of Land-federal government relations and in the context of the EU (see Chapter 7). States with unitary political structures and more nationalistic political traditions, such as France, are less likely to accept the loss of sovereignty implicit in a new fiscal constitution.

The problem is that, in the absence of a fiscal constitution, the economic imperatives of a centralized and unitary monetary policy will constantly collide with the economic imperatives of decentralized and fragmented fiscal policies. As has been established, these fiscal policies are buttressed by long-established domestic political arrangements that are rooted in unique and complex political traditions. In this sense the EU may be on the road to achieving a *gouvernement économique* in some areas (see Chapter 2), but it is far from meeting this objective in the fiscal area. The more likely prospect is for the asymmetry between monetary and fiscal policy to generate more of the sort of EU politics witnessed at recent intergovernmental conferences such as Nice 2000. In essence, the fiscal dimension is more likely to encourage a Hobbesian rather than a Kantian style of intergovernmental bargaining. National-interest or utilitarian calculation will be given higher priority than communitarian and shared values (see Introduction). This is not to deny that some common positions can be forged. But in the fiscal realm, at least, these common positions are likely to be lowest common denominators that present little in the way of a challenge to the integrity of national tax regimes.

PART II

Domestic Political and Policy Contexts

4

Britain and EMU

Andrew Gamble and Gavin Kelly

The impact of economic and monetary union on Britain has been different from most other states in the EU. The British political class remains divided on the merits of deeper European integration and therefore on the need to Europeanize its institutions and domestic policy process by adopting the values of European integration as guiding principles. Since EMU has become the main driver of deeper integration in the EU, and also a powerful instrument of Europeanization through the changes in economic policy objectives that it obliges all participating governments to endorse, British governments have consistently sought to keep their distance from it. The economic policy community in Britain, based around the Treasury, the City, and the Bank, was reluctant from the start to accept the degree of Europeanization that EMU entailed and was also sceptical as to whether a politically imposed currency would be successful. The Conservative government of John Major accordingly negotiated at Maastricht an opt-out from the single currency, and the Labour government of Tony Blair exercised that opt-out when the single currency was launched in 1999.

Despite British scepticism, the majority of EU states pressed ahead both with EMU and with the euro. This sharpened the debate within Britain. Before the 2001 election neither of the two major parties, Labour and Conservative, ruled out joining the euro for ever, but the Conservatives under William Hague had become implacably opposed to early entry—defined as within the next Parliament—while Labour kept postponing a decision on whether to recommend entry and hold a referendum. At the same time public opinion swung decisively against early entry. The substantial popular majority opposed to participation in the euro increased after the euro was launched. In 1999, at the time of the European Parliament elections, the polls indicated that 61 per cent of the electorate would vote 'no' in a referendum; one year later this proportion had risen to 69 per cent.

Although Britain remained outside the euro, it was still part of the EU, a signatory to the Treaties, and therefore could not avoid being affected by the broader process of EMU with its separate dimensions of monetary policy, fiscal policy, and employment policy (Chapter 2; Levitt and Lord 2000). Britain opted out of the first dimension by refusing to participate in the second phase of the ERM and then in the euro itself, but it was involved in the other two through the Stability and Growth Pact and through the agreements brokered at successive EU summits.

As in other EU states EMU has therefore had a significant effect on British domestic politics. But the effects are naturally rather different from those in the countries which joined the Euro-Zone in 1999. In Britain's case it is exclusion from the Euro-Zone and whether that is a viable long-term option which is of greatest interest. Is it possible for Britain to reject EMU and to resist further Europeanization indefinitely while remaining a member of the EU, or will eventually its opposition be overcome? Can Britain be in Europe but not run by Europe, as William Hague claimed?

Radaelli (2000) distinguishes four ways in which states have responded to the process of EMU. The first is *accommodation*, in which EMU is deemed compatible with domestic structures, policies, discourses, and identities. The second is *transformation*, in which EMU poses a challenge to them. The third is *inertia*, in which the political will is lacking to impose change that would make EMU possible, against the resistance of powerful interest groups. The fourth is *retrenchment*, in which the existence of EMU strengthens the opposition to Europeanization and leads to attempts to roll back some of its progress.

The responses of the British state and the British political class since the Maastricht Treaty, and especially since the humiliating ERM exit in 1992, show strong signs of inertia and retrenchment. The lack of political will to commit Britain to EMU and to challenge the opposition of powerful interests, such as the anti-European newspapers and the City of London, has been marked, and this has led at times, particularly under the Major governments of 1990–7, to a stance of retrenchment. But the British response has also from the first involved accommodation, at least as far as structures and policies are concerned. One of the peculiarities of Britain's relationship to EMU and to the process of Europeanization is that in several respects the policy requirements of EMU seem tailor-made for Britain. It would have been relatively easy to adjust Britain's domestic structures and policies to those required by the single currency because the commitment to sound money, an autonomous central bank, and freedom of capital movements were policies which Britain itself adopted independently in the 1990s. It was, however, much harder for the British state to accommodate the implications of EMU for political discourses and identity in the UK because they threatened to rule out the kind of global projects which the British state had pursued in the past. As far as the British political class was concerned, therefore, the direct policy implications of EMU were not the problem; it was the way EMU challenged the British discourse about Europe and entrenched conceptions both of Britain's place in the world and the nature of the policy process. This aspect of EMU would be transformative for the UK, which is why most politicians as well as the economic policy community have so far shied away from it.

This chapter explores the impact of EMU on British politics by examining, first, the structures and policies of the British state; second, the political parties and public opinion; third, the evolution of policy from the ERM to the euro; fourth, discourses and identities in public debate; and finally, the strategic options for the British state.

Structures and Policies

The reluctance of the British political class and economic policy community to embrace EMU appears puzzling in the light of the strong tradition in the UK of support for international monetary arrangements which provide macro stability and which are to some degree detached from direct political control by the British state. From the nineteenth-century gold standard to the post-war gold exchange standard based on the dollar, the preference of the British state has been for arrangements which could ensure sound money and financial stability by imposing external disciplines on government. Considerable British energy and ingenuity were devoted to devising international rules and institutions which were 'politician proof' and which could provide a stable framework within which economic activity could proceed with a minimum of interference from central authority. Such an international regime for money was part of a broader attempt to create a liberal international economic order which both reflected Britain's position at the nerve centre of international finance and commerce and promoted it (Strange 1971; Gamble and Kelly 2000).

There were always dissenting voices within Britain against the dominance of the liberal view of economic policy with its emphasis on free trade, sound money, and laissez-faire (Semmel 1960). In the twentieth century Empire Free Traders and national planners of different political persuasions fought hard against the dominance of liberal, free-trade doctrines. They had some successes, particularly after the suspension of the gold standard in 1931 and during the high tide of national protectionism in Britain and the world economy from the 1930s to the 1950s. But ultimately the older tradition was successfully reasserted, in the changed circumstances of the US-dominated post-war global economy.

The liberal free-trade era bequeathed to Britain a particular institutional structure for both its economy and its state. Its most prominent feature has been the importance of the financial sector, the City of London, both economically and politically. The City of London forms with the Treasury and the Bank of England an extremely powerful economic policy community that has normally been successful in shaping the policy of British governments on major economic issues. Priority has generally been given to the interests and perspectives of the City rather than those of manufacturing or the trade unions in determining the national interest. It was no surprise that one of the Labour government's five economic tests which had to be satisfied before Britain joined the euro was the impact of membership on the City. There was no similar test for manufacturing.

The conception of the British economy which has guided policy has been an open, trading economy rather than a closed, investing economy. The Treasury has continued to favour international arrangements that promote financial stability, but only when these also protect the interests of the City. It is thus no accident that within the government the Treasury has tended to be more sceptical of the benefits of the euro than other ministries, especially the Foreign Office and the Department of Trade and Industry (DTI). Some key Treasury officials were from the beginning of the 1990s part of a cross-departmental policy community in Whitehall which developed to handle EMU and to shape it as far as possible in line with British requirements (Dyson 2000c). But the Treasury as a department remained rather detached from the consensus on EMU and the need for Europeanization which developed in other ministries, notably the Foreign Office. After the debacle of the ERM exit in 1992 opinion in the Treasury had moved in favour of relying on domestic institutions to ensure financial stability rather than on an external discipline.

The attitude of the Treasury reflected its own departmental interest but also the interests of the City, which as far as EMU was concerned were once again at odds with the interests of key manufacturing and trading sectors of the British economy. On balance, the City's interests were more likely to be served by staying out of the euro or at least delaying entry until it was clear that the euro was established and a success (Talani 2000), whereas many leading manufacturing companies based their strategic planning on the assumption that Britain would join the euro by 2006 at the latest. EMU was conceived from the outset as a framework of rules designed to promote financial stability, exactly the kind of regime that would normally have recommended itself to the City. But the fact that the euro was an untested regional currency, with no certainty of being accepted as a global currency, made many in the City cautious. The distinctive feature of the City had always been that it was an international financial centre which had been allowed great freedom by British governments to operate as such. There was no certainty that the ECB would allow such freedom, which might mean the loss of much of the City's traditional business to financial centres outside the EU.

The nature of the City as an international financial centre has always led it to favour a policy of openness to the markets of the whole world, not just Europe. It is not an accident that the business cycle in the UK has normally been aligned with the US economy rather than the European economy. This provides a practical obstacle to early entry; but, more than that, it symbolizes a different view as to where British economic interests lie. At the same time many in the City recognize that staying out of the euro also imposes costs on Britain and on the financial sector and that at a certain point in the future Britain may have no choice but to enter the euro if it becomes a successful currency. But on balance the City remains sceptical that the euro will be a success (Talani 2000).

British business, including the City, had been vociferous in the past in pressing the case for EU entry, mainly because of the economic advantages which were perceived to flow from the creation of first a common and then a single market. British trade with EC countries grew much faster in the 1950s and 1960s than with any other part of the world. Large companies, particularly export-oriented companies, tended to be pro-European. EMU was supported by most of British business because it was seen as a logical next step to complete the single market. However, while strongly in favour of the financial rules and commitment to financial stability proposed at Maastricht, business and the City were equally strongly opposed to any attempts to harmonize taxation or to promote any kind of economic government at the European level, or to adopt any measures that might reduce the openness of the British economy. The possibility that the adoption of the euro might lead to such changes produced strong doubts in the City about the merits of EMU as a whole and opposition to further European integration from a significant minority of British companies.

From the ERM to the Euro

Prevailing attitudes of public opinion towards the EU and the division within the political class are important reasons why the progress of Britain towards membership of the euro has been slow. No government has felt strong enough to take a lead on the issue, and this reflects earlier experience of the ERM. In 1978 when the ERM was launched there was a considerable debate in Britain, by then a full member of the European Community, about whether to participate. The Treasury produced a Green Paper (Treasury 1978) setting out the advantages of membership of the ERM as an external mechanism to impose financial discipline on the British economy. But, while the Conservative opposition under Thatcher supported entry, the Callaghan government decided against (George 1994; Gamble and Kelly 2000). Opinion among most economists was that the conditions were not right for entry, while Denis Healey, the Chancellor, argued that the ERM was an arrangement that would primarily benefit Germany, the strongest economy within it (Healey 1990).

Throughout the 1980s the question of joining the ERM was to dog the Thatcher governments. Nigel Lawson pressed strongly for entry supported by Geoffrey Howe, his predecessor, and by the Governor of the Bank of England, Robin Leigh-Pemberton. But Margaret Thatcher, encouraged by key allies and advisers like Norman Tebbit, Nicholas Ridley, and Alan Walters, became adamantly opposed (Thompson 1996). Thatcher eventually agreed to entry in 1990 only after Lawson's resignation and at the prompting of her new Chancellor, Major, supported by most of the Cabinet (Thompson 1996; Stephens 1996). The debate over the ERM revolved around the questions of the parity at which Britain should join and the benefits of tying sterling into an external arrangement. The financial stability of the D-Mark contrasted sharply with the instability of British macroeconomic management over the previous 20 years. The main attraction of the ERM for its advocates in Britain was its potential to provide an external exchange-rate discipline which could deliver much more stable macroeconomic outcomes (Lawson 1992; Hogg and Hill 1995; Thompson 1996).

Major's success in persuading Thatcher to enter the ERM in 1990—a decision she subsequently regretted—and his emergence as prime minister at the end of that year signalled a more pro-European policy. But, although he promised to put Britain at the heart of Europe and appointed a Cabinet with many prominent pro-Europeans within it, Major still insisted in the Maastricht negotiations in 1991 on an opt-out for Britain in respect of EMU and refused to sign the Treaty until the Social Chapter was excluded. The strength of Eurosceptic opinion in the party and in the Conservative press, as well as the doubts of the City of the London, were such as to make this the only outcome that could have commanded assent within the party. But for Major it was also a position of principle. He was opposed to a single currency for both political and economic reasons, although he accepted that if the other members of the EU went ahead and established a single currency that proved successful then it would become very difficult for Britain to remain outside (Major 1999).

Membership of the ERM was therefore not regarded by Major as a stepping stone to the single currency. But a period of successful membership through the 1990s would have greatly increased the chances of a Conservative government recommending entry at some point. After Black Wednesday, however, on 16 September 1992, when sterling's membership of the ERM had to be suspended in humiliating circumstances (Stephens 1996), the Conservatives' reputation for economic competence and their standing in the polls plummeted, and the position of the pro-European wing of the party was fatally undermined. Major faced major parliamentary rebellions from his MPs over the ratification of the Maastricht Treaty (Baker, Gamble, and Ludlam 1994; Major 1999) and constant pressure on his leadership. In attempting to keep his party together he was forced to move in an ever more Eurosceptic direction, often against his own instincts. Following his resignation after defeat in the 1997 election the party leadership was captured by the anti-European wing, and all the pro-Europeans were purged from the Shadow Cabinet.

The Labour party had been strongly in favour of Britain joining the ERM and the debacle of September 1992 would have been presided over by Labour with calamitous results for the party had it won the election in April. Under Neil Kinnock and then John Smith the party had moved in a more pro-European direction, abandoning its 1983 manifesto commitment to withdraw Britain from the EU. After Tony Blair's election as leader and the launch of new Labour, the party became strongly pro-European. The strength of anti-European and Eurosceptic opinion in the press and the electorate, however, meant that Labour still trod cautiously, and when John Major in 1995 conceded a referendum to approve any decision to enter the euro—against the wishes of his Chancellor, Kenneth Clarke—Labour followed suit. It was a major victory for the anti-Europeans because a referendum created a much higher hurdle for entry than a parliamentary vote would have done and greatly increased the prospects of delay.

An important difference between the debates over the ERM and those over the euro was the context of macroeconomic policy. During the ERM period the British economy was much more unstable than that of the ERM bloc, with higher rates of inflation and unemployment and much larger fluctuations in economic activity. After the departure from the ERM in 1992, however, the British economy experienced steady growth, low inflation, and falling unemployment, which contrasted with the performance of the European economy. This new macroeconomic stability was inherited by Labour, which sought to embed it further by giving operational independence to the Bank of England and putting in place tight fiscal rules. The success of the macro policy, however, did change the balance of the argument about the euro, particularly within the Treasury. The argument that Britain needed to join such an external arrangement in order to ensure financial stability was less compelling than it had been for the ERM, and it further contributed to the postponement of a decision, with the Governor of the Bank of England, Eddie George, acting as a sceptic over the advantages of joining the euro. The Labour government decided, amid some confusion and internal wrangling, as early as October 1997 that Britain was not ready to join in the first wave in 1999. Gordon Brown went further, ruling out membership of the euro for the lifetime of the Parliament and insisting that membership was subject to five economic tests which only the Treasury could assess (Treasury 1997):

- Are business cycles and economic structures compatible so that Britain and others could live comfortably with euro interest rates on a permanent basis?
- If problems emerge, is there sufficient flexibility to deal with them?
- Would joining EMU create better conditions for firms making long-term decisions to invest in Britain?
- What impact would entry into EMU have on the competitive position of Britain's financial services industry, particularly the City's wholesale markets?
- Will joining EMU promote higher growth, stability, and a lasting increase in jobs?

By this means Brown established a Treasury veto over policy on the single currency. Government ministers reiterated that there was no issue of constitutional principle why Britain should not join but insisted that entry would not be possible until the five economic tests were met. Only the Treasury could decide when that was. This created considerable tensions within the Labour government and its greatest internal Cabinet rift (Rawnsley 2000), which in part reflected the personalities and rivalries of individual ministers but also departmental interests and the rival interests of different economic sectors. Brown's victory over his colleagues and over Tony Blair represented the ascendancy of the Treasury's view of EMU within the government.

The economic obstacles to entry could have been overcome. The real obstacles were political: finding the moment to launch a successful campaign to win a referendum. At times ministers seemed ready to start that campaign;

a National Changeover plan was announced at the beginning of 1999. But in other respects caution prevailed; the government declined to give a lead and did little to prepare for entry to the euro. There was no attempt to put sterling back in the ERM and the civil service and the business community were not given clear signals as to whether the government intended to recommend entry or not (Dyson 2000c). The growing unpopularity of the EU in Britain during 1999 and 2000 and the declining value of the euro both contributed to putting off the decision, to the irritation of the pro-euro camp.

The Political Parties and Public Opinion

One reason for the hesitation was that the political class in Britain has been much more divided over the euro than the political class in other member states. Popular opposition to joining the single currency has also been strong in Denmark and Sweden, and the Danes voted narrowly in a referendum in September 2000 to stay outside. But the Danish currency is already pegged to the euro, and the Danish economy is more integrated within the Euro-Zone than the British economy is. The political class in Denmark, spanning the main parties, business, and the media, was united in recommending entry (Chapter 5) and in taking active steps to prepare for entry.

The political class in Britain, by contrast, has become deeply split, with one of the two major parties, the Conservatives, moving ever more firmly in a Eurosceptic and even anti-EU direction. The Conservative party was initially the party of Europe, conceiving Europe as an enterprise which was very much in the security and economic interests of the British state, as well as a new external challenge to replace the Empire. It was a Conservative government under Edward Heath that narrowly secured parliamentary approval of the terms of entry in 1971. It was the Labour Party whose leaders were prone to talk of 'a thousand years of history' and who were immensely distrustful of the Common Market because of the restrictions it imposed on national planning. Although a majority of the Labour leadership did eventually support British membership of the European Community, a majority of trade unions and Labour Party members remained opposed because of their commitment to national economic planning.

The turnaround in British politics on the question of European integration means that there is now a majority of the centre-left in favour of Britain joining the euro while the majority of the centre-right are opposed. In a 1998 survey of MPs 66 per cent of Conservative MPs agreed that joining the single currency would signal the end of the UK as a sovereign nation. 83 per cent of

Labour MPs disagreed with this statement (Baker, Gamble, and Seawright 1998). Britain's troubled relationship with the EU since its entry in 1973 has continued and even deteriorated in the debate over the euro. Despite the referendum in the UK in 1975 on the principle of Britain's membership of the EU, membership is still controversial. Many within the anti-euro campaign now openly question whether Britain should remain within the EU, while for the UK Independence Party the only way to halt Europeanization is to leave the Union. It is a sentiment with which growing numbers of Conservatives agree.

Pro-Europeans believe that Britain's refusal to join the euro at its inception reflects a pattern of behaviour that has been repeated several times. British governments begin by expressing reluctance to be involved in a new initiative and stand on the sidelines, the rest of Europe goes ahead, and eventually Britain joins up, although without enthusiasm, having seen that the alternative of staying outside is worse. On this view European integration is proceeding stage by stage, and although the British may grumble more than some other nations in Europe they have so far signed up to every stage. On this view it may take ten years, but eventually the British will be persuaded that it is in their interests to join the euro.

The single currency and EMU may, however, be different. Even if the government decided that entry was on balance right, it is hampered by the need to win a referendum. A referendum that rejected the euro would have far-reaching consequences for Britain and for its future relationship to the rest of the EU. It would alter the balance of domestic political forces and greatly strengthen those elements that wish to pursue an isolationist policy towards the process of European integration and resist Europeanization. It might set in train a reverse ratchet and be followed by other steps to disengage Britain from the EU. An attempt to join the euro might, therefore, mark the end of the attempt within Britain and within Europe to make Britain a full member of the Union.

This detachment of Britain is often interpreted in terms of sovereignty. Few British politicians have ever had much enthusiasm for European integration because they have been reluctant to cede powers to a supranational entity. Some, like the first Labour government of Tony Blair and pro-European Conservative governments of the past, support greater European cooperation as a means to maximize Britain's welfare and security. Anti-Europeans see the process of European integration as continually escaping the control of national governments. The spillover effects of integration mean that proposals for new concessions of sovereignty constantly arise.

For the anti-Europeans and the sceptics the EU is a dangerous semi-sovereignty game and they are reluctant to play according to its rules. For

many pro-European observers this is the heart of the problem. British attachment at least in rhetoric to outmoded forms of sovereignty and the resort
of so many British politicians to construct Europe and Brussels as a hostile,
alien other against which they must maintain constant vigilance means that
British arguments about Europe never seem to progress. Despite the very real
integration which has taken place in the last 30 years, British public opinion
seems no nearer to accepting the legitimacy of the semi-sovereignty game
which the EU inaugurated.

Although this picture captures the popular discourse—and distrust—about
Europe quite well, the deep scepticism and hostility towards Europe within
parts of Britain's political class cannot be understood simply as a defence of
national sovereignty against encroachment from Brussels. The sources of the
detachment of so much of the British political class from the EU lie not primarily in a nationalist rejection of a supranationalist entity, 'little England'
against a 'centralized superstate', but in the still potent global ambitions of
the British state. These ambitions are reflected in many complex ways, not
least in the relationship of the British economy to the European economy.
Sovereignty in British political discourse is often code not for a narrow 'little
Englandism' but for an alternative international project. It is the presence of
this alternative that makes the winning of the case for British membership of
the euro far from certain. There are different possible outcomes for Britain and
no inevitability about a European future. EMU will have a major effect on British
politics but the direction of this effect—whether it will promote further Europeanization or rather promote a disengagement from Europe—remains open.

The 1975 referendum is the only referendum so far held by the British state
on the question of Europe. If a referendum on the euro is held, it will be the
second. Before the 1975 referendum the opinion polls showed a two-to-one
majority against membership. Similar figures were common for the euro
after 1997, leading some pro-Europeans to argue that public opinion could be
turned around on the issue once again. But the two situations are not alike.
In 1975 the leaders of all the three major parties—Harold Wilson, Thatcher,
and Jeremy Thorpe—campaigned for a 'yes' vote and the media were almost
unanimous in recommending a 'yes' vote, as was the business community.
The campaign for the 'no' vote was led by Conservatives exiled from the party
leadership, like Enoch Powell, and representatives of the Labour left in the
Cabinet: Michael Foot, Tony Benn, Peter Shore, and Barbara Castle. It was
relatively easy for the opposition to EC membership to be branded as the
extremes of British politics against the solid reasonable centre. The 'yes'
campaign turned the referendum into the question of whom the electorate
trusted most (Butler and Kitzinger 1975).

A referendum on the euro held in the second term of the Labour government will be very different because the main opposition party, the Conservatives, will campaign for a 'no' vote, while the Labour Party, the Liberal Democrats, and the nationalist parties will campaign for a 'yes' vote. The press will be divided, with several leading newspapers—*The Times*, the *Daily Telegraph*, the *Daily Mail*, and the *Sun*—all certain to campaign strongly against. The business community will also be divided, orchestrated by rival organizations such as Britain in Europe and Business for Sterling. The two main employers organizations, the Confederation of British Industry and the Institute of Directors, will line up on opposite sides of the argument. The trade unions will be more united in favour of the euro, but some unions, particularly the Transport and General Workers Union, will be at best lukewarm. If the referendum is won, it will be seen as a victory for the centre-left in British politics and as a definitive repudiation of the Thatcherite line on Europe. But if it is lost, it will spur the momentum, at least in the short term, towards further disengagement.

Discourses and Identities

To understand why the euro, and Europe in general, remains such a divisive issue in British politics when in most other member states it is long regarded as having been settled, it is necessary to explore the terms in which the debate has been conducted. Three main positions are evident in the debate, represented in both the two main parties: Keep the Pound, Join the Euro, and Wait and See.

Keep the Pound

For the anti-euro camp the retention of economic sovereignty is the key issue. The pound sterling is treated as both a symbol of that sovereignty and one of the most important instruments of it (Holmes 1996). Without control over its currency a nation ceases to be a sovereign nation, in this view. This is an issue of principle that cannot easily be fudged, although it is noticeable that many of those against the euro, including the Conservative leadership, do fudge it by refusing to make it an issue of principle. The Conservative policy before the 2001 election was to rule out membership of the euro for the lifetime of the next Parliament. When pressed by journalists on whether this meant that after that the party might recommend entry to the euro, the leadership replied that it could not foresee the circumstances under which it would make such a recommendation. But they still left open the possibility.

This equivocation was tactical. Once the argument is constructed in terms of sovereignty the case against the euro becomes overwhelming. But the detailed reasons as to why the euro should be rejected differ markedly between left and right, depending on the use to which it is argued that sovereignty should be put. On the left, the argument against the euro echoes the earlier struggle against the principle of membership of the EC on the grounds that the rules of the Community made discretionary economic management more difficult. Similarly, participation in the euro is regarded as ceding crucial economic levers, in particular decisions over interest rates, to a body that Britain does not control. The main loss is therefore the ability of a British government to determine its own independent social and economic policy (Holmes 1996; Whyman, Burkitt, and Baimbridge 2000).

What underlies this approach is a particular conception of the national economy and democratic sovereign control of it. The national economy is conceived as a discrete economic space that needs first to be carved out against the forces of the global market and then protected from being invaded by them. Left to themselves, global market forces will drive down costs and living standards and will erode all institutions and structures designed to promote solidarity and welfare. Controls over the exchange rate, interest rates, and taxation are regarded as essential tools of stabilization policy and among the most tangible signs of the ability of a government to plan the national economy, setting its own targets and choosing the most appropriate means of achieving them. From this perspective the main problem with the euro is that it surrenders this control to an unelected and unaccountable ECB. This is the feature which most appeals to the advocates of macro stability, because it takes the euro out of national politics and makes it immune to the normal pressures and conflicts of democratic government. But, for left Eurosceptics, economic policy is sound only if it is subject to firm democratic control. The ECB represents an example of the new disciplinary neo-liberalism which seeks to remove crucial economic functions from elected national governments, entrusting them to a network of unaccountable supranational agencies and institutions (Gill 1998).

On the right there is a similar concern to preserve the capacity of national governments to manage the economy in a discretionary way, but the objects to which the discretion should be applied are very different. The chief objection on the right to joining the euro is not that it will inhibit national planning but that it will lead to the imposition of an economic policy regime that will destroy the policy regime built up under Conservative governments since 1979 and largely continued by Labour. This regime is characterized by low taxes, flexible labour markets, privatization, and deregulation. If Britain were to join the euro, the possibility of the British people choosing that kind of policy regime and maintaining Britain's comparative advantage against other European states would be lost (Holmes 1996). It is, therefore, the implications of EMU for harmonization of taxes, of labour-market regulation, and of corporate governance that are regarded as most deleterious, rather than the EMU institutions themselves, whose insulation from popular politics many on the right would normally be expected to applaud.

Underlying these positions, on the right as on the left, is a particular conception of the national economy and democratic sovereignty. Many on the right use the slogan 'one currency, one government' believing that, if states agree to the euro, the EU cannot be preserved as a semi-sovereign game. It must necessarily evolve into a full autonomous sovereignty in which the centre comes to exercise all the most important functions of the participating states. Resistance to surrendering the pound is so strong because of this belief that Britain cannot continue as an independent nation if it loses control of its currency. Even if the EU were indeed a stronghold of disciplinary neo-liberalism, this would still not compensate for the loss of national identity and control of a people over its own state.

As indicated earlier, however, and explored later in this chapter, this position is not simply a 'little England', national protectionist position on either left or right, although such views can be found. More prevalent is the idea that there is an alternative internationalism or global project which Britain could be part of, one much superior to the EU and EMU. On the left, this takes the form of various kinds of international solidarity but based always on firm local democratic control of national economies. On the right, it takes the form of seeing Britain as a global investor and trader whose interests are only partially engaged in Europe and the European economy. To take full advantage of Britain's position in the global market, one built up over three centuries, Britain needs to be free of entanglement in an economic policy regime which does not suit it (Howell 2000). The corporatist and interventionist policies of other member states of the EU are regarded as a straitjacket from which Britain needs to escape. The EU has a role as a trading association but little beyond. On this view, reclaiming British sovereignty requires a fundamental renegotiation of the treaties to take back many sovereign powers already surrendered and resistance to the loss of any more.

Join the Euro

The second broad position in the debate supports, with varying degrees of enthusiasm, Britain's entry into the euro as soon as possible. There are both minimalist and maximalist versions of this position. The minimalist position, associated in particular with many pro-European Conservatives such as Kenneth Clarke, the former Chancellor, as well as many in the Labour Party, argues that joining the single currency is part of the logic of the single market. Without a single currency the single market is incomplete and the full benefits of creating a unified economic space, in particular the reduction of transaction costs, cannot be realized. If the single market is in the British national interest, then the single currency must also be. To exclude Britain from membership will have damaging consequences for British businesses trading in the Euro-Zone and will reduce the attractiveness of Britain as a site for inward investment. Since 50 per cent of British trade is with the Euro-Zone, the advantages of Britain being a full member of that zone are self-evident for the advocates of entry (Corry 1996).

The minimalists also dispute that entry to the euro has any significant constitutional implications, denying outright the main contention of the Eurosceptics. They separate the political from the economic, arguing that membership of a currency union need not infringe the sovereignty of the nation-states participating any more—or less—than membership of a customs union. The euro on this view is merely the latest extension of the pooling of sovereignty between the members of the EU for common purposes. It does not signal the creation of a United States of Europe or any kind of federation. The nation-states remain the essential core of the Union.

The maximalist position goes much further than this, enabling the Eurosceptics to argue that minimalists are either naïve, failing to understand the nature of the project of which the euro is a part, or simply disingenuous, pretending that the euro has no implications for sovereignty while knowing all the time that it will have. The maximalists accept that there are implications for sovereignty but they argue that these are entirely positive because membership of the euro keeps Britain at the centre of the EU, able to shape its agenda. For the maximalists entry to the euro would still be desirable even if there were no economic benefits. It is much better in the long run for Britain to participate fully in the EU and to see its future as irrevocably bound up with it than to be isolated and marginalized on the fringes (H. Young 1998).

This argument echoes the early debates in the 1960s on the desirability of British membership of the EC. Against those who stressed the economic benefits, others always saw the main benefits as political, the strengthening of the Western alliance, the preservation of peace in Europe, and the creation of a new kind of association between the European nations. Among the maximalists today there are differences about the final form the EU should take. Relatively few of them are committed federalists who envisage the creation of a United States of Europe. Instead, the more common vision of the

EU is for a new kind of polity in which there is no single centre but over-lapping jurisdictions and a wide distribution of functions and competences among different levels.

Wait and See

The third broad position in the euro debate is quite a crowded space, inhab-ited by Eurorealists deploying a range of pragmatic arguments as well as arguments of principle. At their head is Gordon Brown with his insistence on the five economic tests which were used to delay an immediate referendum after the 1997 election. The pragmatic position was also at the heart of the interdepartmental consensus within Whitehall (Dyson 2000c).

Pragmatists had an open mind on the merits of the euro but needed to be convinced on a number of economic and political tests (Currie 1997). On the economic tests they sought tangible evidence of efficiency gains as well as clear signs that the economic cycles of the British economy and the European economy were converging. What also had to converge were the economic conditions and institutions in the different member states. Without such convergence pragmatists doubted that the EU would constitute a genuine optimum currency area, as economists defined it, for which a single currency would be appropriate and beneficial. If the single currency were primarily a political project, then joining it might subject parts of the British economy to inappropriate interest rates and therefore very painful adjustments of internal prices. This was a problem that had long existed within the British economy, with interest rates being set in response to the needs of London and the South-East to the detriment of the North, Scotland, and Wales. But the euro, it was feared, might make the problem still worse (Michie 1997).

This fear was closely linked to the political tests that the pragmatists wished to apply to Britain's membership of the euro. What worried them most was the lack of accountability of the ECB, an expression of the wider democratic deficit in the EU, and the absence of a clear constitutional framework specify-ing the rights and powers of the states as against the central European insti-tutions (Siedentop 2000). One consequence was that many EU institutions were not directly accountable, and the way in which the ECB had been set up under the Maastricht Treaty meant that it was largely immune to political pressure (Marquand 1997). There was considerable anxiety that the policy that it would pursue would have a strong deflationary bias and that it would not encourage a faster rate of growth in the European economy.

Some pragmatists therefore urged that, before Britain participated in EMU, institutional and structural reforms were necessary to ensure that the deflationary policy of the ECB was not the only economic policy pursued at the European level. Either the remit of the ECB needed to be widened and its accountability enhanced or there needed to be a broadening of the functions of the EU, an economic government of the kind proposed by the French, to allow the EU to develop a much more active regional policy and supply-side policy, intervening in the economies of member states to compensate for any harmful side-effects of establishing the single currency. For the pro-euro camp in Britain such arguments seemed to confirm the claims of the anti-euro camp that participation in the euro would inevitably lead to further pressure to give more powers to the EU.

Many of the pragmatists were genuinely undecided about the merits of the euro for Britain, but others like the New Europe group, founded in March 1999, were firmer in their opposition. The group was headed by David Owen, former Foreign Secretary and leader of the Social Democratic Party, and included two former Chancellors, Nigel Lawson and Denis Healey. Against the positions of principle of the anti and pro camps that the euro was a fundamental erosion of sovereignty or an opportunity finally to commit Britain's future to the EU, most pragmatists attempted to weigh the evidence for and against British participation. Since the evidence is inevitably contradictory, reflecting the complexity of the relationships of Britain to the European economy and to the wider global economy, highly plausible arguments can be developed on both the costs and benefits of entry (Baimbridge, Burkitt, and Whyman 2000). Hence it seems unlikely that the argument within the political class can be settled at that level. What will decide it is resolution of the deeper strategic question which confronts the British state and its political class.

The Strategic Dilemma

This strategic choice is between three alternatives for Britain's future in the global economy: hyperglobalism, intergovernmentalism, and open regionalism. Each of them proposes a different strategy for positioning the British nation-state in the face of the contemporary trends towards a more interdependent global economy.

Hyperglobalists

The hyperglobalists are distinctive for the emphasis that they place on the importance of Britain being fully integrated into the global market. The changes introduced by globalization are so profound that they have created for the first time a global economy which national governments are powerless to control (Held *et al.* 1999). They reject any kind of national protectionism or closed national economies. But at the same time they see the maintenance of strong nation-states as essential for facilitating the adaptation of each national jurisdiction to the needs of the global market. National independence is vital to success in the new global economy (Portillo 1998). Their argument, set out most clearly by the former Conservative Minister David Howell (2000), is that the EC made sense in the 1960s as a step towards a more liberal global economic order, and therefore the Conservatives as the champions of economic liberalism were right to support it. But from the late 1970s onwards the EC has changed into an obstacle to greater economic liberalism because of the desire of the European political class to create a European state and to treat the European economy as a closed economy within whose confines policies of high taxation, high public spending, regulation of industry, and employment protection can continue to flourish.

Having liberated itself from these policies in the 1980s and 1990s and reversed its relative economic decline against other European economies, Britain should not allow these same policies to be re-imposed by signing up to membership of the euro. In the contemporary global market advantage accrues to sovereign jurisdictions which actively promote the adaptation of their citizens to the changing requirements of global competition and remove internal obstacles to it. Those jurisdictions that have strong states able to formulate clear policies and with the capacity to implement them and stay relatively independent of interest groups are likely to do best in this competitive race. Britain qualifies as such a state while the EU does not. Not only does the EU have the wrong policy in relation to the global economy by seeking to preserve many institutions which need to be swept away, but it is also at best only an embryonic state, lacking legitimacy and the capacity to implement policies swiftly and decisively.

The hyperglobalists discount the importance of the EU as a trading partner for Britain, arguing that other parts of the world, particularly North America and East Asia, are as important as, or in certain respects such as flows of investment actually more important than, the EU. Britain's position as a global investor and trader depends on having maximum freedom and flexibility to adjust to new conditions in global markets. Economic sovereignty, including the power to set interest rates and influence the value of the currency as well as determining fiscal policy and supply-side policy, is crucial to this capacity. Some have taken the logic of this argument to its extreme, arguing that Britain should aim to become the Hong Kong of Europe, an economic space that is a haven for enterprise with much greater freedom and flexibility than the much larger continental economy which adjoins it. Preserving British independence from this larger continental economy, even though it means abandoning any influence over its internal decision-making, is seen as a price well worth accepting. Britain would negotiate a trading arrangement with the EU but nothing more.

Another aspect of this strategy has been the suggestion that, to avoid the clutches of the EU and of EMU, Britain should negotiate to join NAFTA. Many hyperglobalists believe that, since the US has now recovered its position as the indisputable leader of global capitalism, it makes far more sense to tie Britain to the North American economy than to the European. The British model of capitalism has long been seen as having more in common with the North American model than with either the European or the East Asian (Coates 2000). With the addition of the common language and cultural and defence links, the Atlanticist option comes to loom much larger than the European. Britain, it is argued, can prosper best in the future if it resists subordination to a culture and set of institutions that are inappropriate to its national style of capitalism. A closer connection with the North American world and a looser connection with the EU are presented as the correct strategic choice.

Intergovernmentalism

The intergovernmentalists also place great weight on the nation-state but tend to dismiss the hyperglobalist strategy as unrealistic. They see it as based on a false analysis that the world economy has evolved into a global economy rather than remaining an international economy which is managed through bilateral and multilateral negotiations between nation-states and in which the nation-state therefore remains the key administrative and political unit (Hirst and Thompson 1996). From this perspective the concrete advantages of the EU are too many to be easily set aside and the consequences of disengagement likely to be extremely harmful. The intergovernmentalists see no alternative to continuing to extend European cooperation. But they regard this process as always subordinate to the fundamental interests of nation-states and argue that only those rules and institutions which plainly benefit the national interest of each participating nation-state have been agreed (Milward 1996). In relation to EMU this means that participation has to be decided by each nation-state, and the resulting regime remains an intergovernmental one. Even though powers are delegated to the ECB, these could be revoked or amended if a majority of the nation-states wished it.

From this perspective Britain's participation in EMU depends on a hard-headed calculation of national self-interest. It really is a question of whether the economic benefits outweigh the economic costs. Since the EU is primarily an intergovernmental association, there is no obligation on nation-states to sign up for every policy. The pooling of sovereignty is instrumental; ultimate power remains with the nation-states, which means that there is no danger that participating in EMU carries implications for the creation of a European super-state. Similarly, not participating in EMU carries no dangers of permanent isolation or marginalization. It simply means that the complexity of the institutional structure of the EU is increased.

For the intergovernmentalists sovereignty is not the issue; there is no question of a permanent loss of sovereignty by Britain or by any other member state of the EU which participates in EMU. But this does also make it harder to take the decision to participate when the benefits and costs appear quite evenly matched and when there are vociferous arguments on both sides from different sectors as to the merits of joining the single currency. Business is not speaking with one voice on the euro. Both industry and, to a lesser extent, the City are divided. Those sectors which trade most with Europe, such as car manufacturers, tend to be keenest on Britain joining, while those which are focused on North America or other global markets tend to be opposed. There also appears to be a clear split between large and small companies. Some of the industrialists and financiers who support either Britain in Europe or Business for Sterling do so for ideological reasons, but many are swayed more by a simple calculation of where their best interests lie. On balance, most surveys continue to show a majority of businesses wanting entry, but the minority is strong enough and vociferous enough to mean that business is far from speaking with the united voice that it did on earlier crucial decisions on Europe. The trade unions are also divided, but again there appears to be a clear majority in favour of entry. The engineering union (AEEU) and the Manufacturing, Science, and Finance Union (MSF) are the strongest advocates on the grounds that preservation of manufacturing jobs and inward investment require participation. But other unions, like the transport workers (TGWU), are much more cautious, fearing the effects of a deflationary policy on regional employment. All the major unions accept, however, that Britain should ultimately join.

The effects of the euro on regional unemployment are crucial to the intergovernmentalist assessment of whether on balance the euro is a good idea for Britain. The absence of obvious institutional means to ensure labour mobility within the EU to compensate for variations in prices which might emerge in particular regions is cited as the main reason for caution and reinforces those who advocate the policy of wait and see. Only when there has been some experience of how the ECB copes with widely different levels of economic performance, it is argued, can a judgement be made as to whether Britain will benefit. On the other side, the harmful effects on many sectors of the British economy from the strengthening of the pound in 1999 and 2000 against the euro was used as an argument as to why waiting for more evidence was unnecessary.

Open Regionalism

The third strategic option sees the EU and EMU as something more than an intergovernmentalist initiative. It is rather a unique experiment which, although originating as an initiative of nation-states, has moved beyond intergovernmentalism by creating a new kind of state, one with many levels of governance and many overlapping jurisdictions. Where the open regionalists differ from the intergovernmentalists is that the new entity that has come into being is important in its own right and deserving of allegiance. It offers ways of leaving behind the old world of nation-states, creating a European space, new institutions, and new politics which cannot be reduced simply to the interests of sovereign nation-states.

Open regionalism accepts that globalization in the last 30 years has created a world economy which is in certain respects qualitatively new, but it rejects the hyperglobalist analysis (Perraton *et al.* 1997) and in particular the closed regionalism which the hyperglobalists associate with the EU. The regime and institutions that it seeks to create are steps towards a wider integration, not an attempt to close off a particular region as a self-sufficient bloc. In this way open regionalism signifies the creation of new forms of governance which are necessary for moves towards global governance. The development of new forms of regionalism in several parts of the world does not necessarily run counter to globalization but often helps promote it (Gamble and Payne 1996). EMU is a critical stage in the evolution of an open regionalism beyond the nation-state, establishing new forms of interdependence which do carry implications for other relationships. Regional blocs such as the EU are not primarily protectionist blocs; they remain open to world trade and subject to its rules. They facilitate the creation of a new political space which allows the discussion of common concerns and the elaboration of new forms of governance and collaboration. The strategic choice here is the recognition of the advantages that can flow from establishing such forms of cooperation, the acceptance of interdependence as the basis for governance.

EMU is a key building block for open regionalism, which is why those who favour simpler one-dimensional forms of jurisdiction argue that it is a step too far. The dynamics of a single currency area and a single market will alter significantly the context in which economic policy over a wide range is formulated and considered. For open regionalists that is what is attractive about it, the opportunity to find new and more effective ways of governing the economy, recognizing that many traditional goals of national economic management are now best pursued at the European level. From this standpoint EMU is a strategy for guaranteeing macroeconomic stability and permitting the gradual reform and adjustment of institutions and practices within the EU to ensure that Europe has labour markets and cost structures that enable European businesses to be competitive within global markets.

Conclusion

Britain has a different relationship to the euro from most other member states of the EU, and its political class remains more resistant to the logic of Europeanization. It is far from certain whether a popular majority can be assembled to vote for Britain's participation. This chapter has argued that the deep divisions in Britain over the issue are rooted in the legacies from Britain's imperial past. The strategic choice that Britain has to make is a painful one for much of its political class, and the balance of advantage is hard to determine. As with the arguments over free trade in the middle of the nineteenth century, EMU represents Britain with a strategic choice but also a strategic dilemma. It is not yet clear how it will be resolved.

Much will depend on immediate political factors such as the fortunes of the political parties and of the different personalities within them. But, whoever triumphs in the party game, hard questions will remain. John Major has bequeathed his dilemma to his successors, reflecting as it does the consensus of many civil servants as well as the City and many of the pragmatists in the British political class. They have been instinctively opposed to the project of a single currency as too risky and too premature in the current economic and political condition of the EU. Advocates of this position are, nevertheless, prepared to recommend entry once the new currency has proved its staying power and it has become clear that staying out is no longer an option. The problem is deciding when that point has come. A precondition for movement is that either the Treasury and the Chancellor lift their veto or the Prime Minister succeeds in wresting control of the issue from them.

The Labour government will decide in the first two years of its second term whether once more to rule out entry for another Parliament or whether to hold a referendum which it might not win. Joining the euro is a higher priority for the Prime Minister than for the Chancellor and the Treasury. Their differences will have to be resolved and the Chancellor's veto lifted if a referendum is to go ahead. If the referendum is postponed entry may not be possible before 2010. But by that time the euro will either have proved its critics right and placed such an unbearable political strain on the EU that it has had to be abandoned or it will have established itself as a major international currency and the advantages of being inside the Euro-Zone will have become irresistible, even for a Conservative government.

5

EMU: A Danish Delight and Dilemma

Martin Marcussen

Although Denmark is not a member of the third stage of EMU, the Danish polity has undergone profound developments in the 'EMU process'. The concept of the EMU process is a dynamic one in the sense that EMU in this chapter is considered to be the institutionalization of ideas, institutions, and policies over a period of three decades. The point of departure is that the roots of EMU are to be found in formal and informal monetary regimes, patterns of cooperation, and macroeconomic causal ideas which date back at least to the beginning of the 1970s. Furthermore, since the Maastricht Treaty was ratified in 1993, EMU has continued to be a moving target. 'Add-ons' and modifications, such as the Growth and Stability Pact, the Euro-Group, and the Luxembourg, Cardiff, Cologne, and Lisbon 'processes', are constantly changing our ways of understanding the factors behind and the impact of EMU. Hence, to study the consequences of EMU for the Danish polity means to study the development of the Danish polity throughout the period in which EMU has slowly materialized. It also means that the explanatory factor—EMU—has changed throughout the period of our investigation. This dynamic historical perspective leads us to expect EMU to have an impact on the Danish polity *throughout* the EMU process and not just from its inception on 1 January 1999.

Another consequence of such a dynamic and historical perspective is that it is difficult to identify the causal impact of EMU on the ways in which the Danish polity has been reshaped. From this perspective EMU is more than just a set of formal rules that regulate state behaviour. It also exemplifies a 'way of thinking' typical for the 1980s and early 1990s and defines a new set of actors—transnational and national—who are at the centre of the European macroeconomic organizational field. Therefore, apart from studying the formal regulatory requirements of adaptation, a full understanding of these processes of change requires us to consider informal pressures for change deriving from normative and cognitive elements of the European monetary regime.

Second, it is difficult to identify the impact of EMU on state adaptation because it must be seen in the context of a variety of other explanatory factors—transnationalization, globalization, domestic politics, and so forth—that have affected the ways in which the Danish polity is continuously being reshaped. Third, the relationship between the Danish polity and EMU is not one-dimensional. It is one thing is to study the impact of EMU on the Danish polity, quite another to study the ways in which EMU is being framed and reconstructed in the Danish polity. As mentioned above, EMU embodies formal institutions, policies, actors, and relations as well as cognitive and normative representations of these aspects. Within distinctive national institutional and cultural contexts these formal and informal elements of EMU take on very nation-specific forms in a very complicated political process in which social reality is continuously being reconstructed (Dyson 2000b).

Levels and Stages of Change

In the case of Denmark, changes related to the EMU process started in the 1970s and early 1980s. The process can, for the sake of simplicity, be divided into four stages, each presenting new challenges to the Danish polity. The first stage, from the mid-1970s to the early 1980s, was characterized by political and economic crisis. The second stage ran through the 1980s and is defined by the complete liberalization of financial and capital markets and the profound Europeanization of Danish corporatism and of the Social Democratic Party. The third stage was characterized by the development of common EMU institutions and procedures for decision-making, surveillance, and coordination. Finally, the fourth stage is the period after the Danish people's rejection of EMU in a referendum on 28 September 2000.

In each of these four periods there is variance and stability to be explained at four analytically distinct levels of investigation. The first level is *ideational* and concerns what social groups in the Danish polity commonly tend to take for granted. Here an important distinction is between the narrow consensual knowledge at the elite level and broader public sentiments. The second level is *institutional* and deals with constellations of political actors and the norms and procedural rules regulating their interaction. This second level should be seen in close connection to the third level of change, which concerns *public policy*, reform strategies, and other output decisions. The fourth level is *discursive* and rhetorical, including the styles and forms of various information

Table 5.1 Denmark in the EMU process, 1977–2000

Levels of change	Stages of change in the EMU-process			
	1977–1982	1983–1992	1993–2000	2001–
Ideational	The Sound Policy consensus and public scepticism	Europeanization of the social democratic party		
Institutional		Europeanization of corporatism		
Public Policy		Liberalized Capital		Europeanization of the welfare state?
Discursive			Framing the EMU issue	

campaigns and the ways in which EMU was framed in successive European referendums.

In each stage, and at each level, a combination of explanatory factors can help us understand how and why the Danish polity is being transformed in the EMU process. It is not possible—or relevant—to investigate each of these combinations, as a result of which six constellations of levels and stages have been chosen to form the overall argument (Table 5.1).

EMU: Ideas on the Move

Elites and the 'Sound Policy' Paradigm

When the Danish Social Democratic Minister for Economic Affairs, Ivar Nørgaard, wanted a devaluation of the Danish currency within the ERM in 1979, it sufficed to telephone the head of the EC Monetary Committee to confirm the size and timing of the adjustment. No particular meeting or explanation was required. Nor did anybody ask Nørgaard to present a plan for domestic reform prior to the adjustment. Three years later, in 1982, when Nørgaard went to Brussels with a similar demand, the other members of the EC Monetary Committee flatly refused his request. However, by promising profound changes to the national economy, Nørgaard obtained a small devaluation, about half the size of the one initially desired. Nørgaard felt that his central bank governor, Erik Hoffmeyer, as well as the other members of the EC Monetary Committee had let him down. He experienced the hard way that the rules for appropriate behaviour within the ERM had undergone profound changes in the intervening years.

In 1979 the Danish economy was in crisis, and currency adjustments constituted an acceptable economic instrument, even for members of the ERM. The Danish economy was still in crisis by 1982 but by then unilateral currency adjustments had stopped being part of the plethora of policy instruments that national economic ministries could apply as it suited them. By 1982, any member country of the ERM that aspired to bilateral adjustments had to convince the so-called strong currencies—the D-Mark and the guilder— that they had sincere intentions of promoting profound domestic reforms prior to the adjustment. This applied to big states—for example, France—as well as to small states like Denmark.

But Nørgaard did not succeed in getting inflation and interest rates down. Unemployment climbed and the budget deficit and the trade balance deteriorated. The Danish Social Democratic Prime Minister, Anker Jørgensen, resigned in September 1982, leaving governmental power to a coalition of Conservatives and Liberals headed by Poul Schlüter. Prior to the change of government Erik Hoffmeyer had summoned a group of opposition leaders to a meeting in the central bank. He made it clear that he considered the Danish economy to be in a very bad condition. Already, in January 1980, he had publicly described how Denmark was on the verge of economic disaster (Hoffmeyer 1980). This intervention had added to Hoffmeyer's popularity in the media and the population, and it caused considerable embarrassment to the Social Democratic government. During the short meeting in 1982, Hoffmeyer told the opposition leaders that a 'sound policy' was characterized by its definitive exclusion of the devaluation instrument and by the priority it gave to reducing the rate of inflation and the budget deficit. If the new centre-right government would publicly announce these priorities on assuming office, he promised to do all in his power to get sky-high interest rates down to a more acceptable level (Andersen 1994: 197).

The new centre-right government fulfilled its part of the deal. On 9 September 1982, the day before taking office, it announced that it had no intention of using the devaluation instrument under any circumstances. Furthermore, attention would be paid to sound finances and low inflation. A few months after the change in government, Hoffmeyer was able to fulfil his part of the deal. Long-term interest rates had halved from over 20 per cent.

During the 1980s devaluation disappeared from the political agenda (Iversen and Thygesen 1998: 72). The 'sound policy' strategy became consensually shared and achieved a taken-for-granted quality among the elites within the Danish macroeconomic organizational field. Business, trade unions, central bankers, civil servants, and ministers converged around a set of beliefs about how the economy works, about the priority of macroeconomic objectives, and about the instruments that could legitimately be used to achieve these objectives. When the centre-right government was replaced in January 1993 by a coalition of Social Liberals and Social Democrats, headed by Poul Nyrup Rasmussen, the macroeconomic ideational consensus remained unchallenged. Both Social Democratic and Social Liberal ministers were at pains to constantly underline that they were 'responsible' in the sense that they fully respected the established consensual knowledge in monetary and economic affairs.

In retrospect, the change of ideational consensus from Keynesian-inspired demand management towards a more monetarist conception of macroeconomic dynamics had its origin in the international macroeconomic crisis caused by the two oil crises in the 1970s. In the critical period between Nørgaard's two attempts at devaluation in 1979 and 1982, an international ideational change was under way. Within the European Monetary System (EMS) the 'strong' currency members adopted a new form of coercive leadership which placed serious pressure on top decision-makers in Denmark to consider alternative macroeconomic strategies. In the same period, the governor of the Danish central bank, Hoffmeyer, initiated a public campaign in favour of 'sound policy' in order to 'get out of the abyss'. Processes of coercive socialization within the EMS and ideational leadership within the Danish macroeconomic organizational field helped launch 'sound policy' ideas as a replacement for the ideas and strategies that had been tried in vain throughout the 1970s. The shift was already under way when the centre-right government took office in 1982. But a full-fledged adherence to the ideas of 'sound' finances and money was not implemented before 1982–3 (Marcussen 1998b; 2000a).

If an elite consensus centring on 'sound policy' illustrates a Danish *delight*, its combination with a broad public scepticism about European integration in general and EMU in particular clearly constitutes a *dilemma*. These broader value orientations can be traced back to the very first referendum on EEC membership in 1972, and they continue to divide elite attitudes from popular attitudes and to split political parties on both the left and the right.

The Danish People and Europe: An 'Impossibility Structure'?

Ever since Denmark's entrance into the EEC in 1973—and even before— Europe has been a controversial theme (Olesen and Laursen 1994; Rüdiger

1994; 1999). Until the start of stage three, the EMU-sceptical part of the population was in a comfortable majority. However, since 1 January 1999, when Denmark started to practise its position as a 'pre-in' or a 'country with a derogation', popular sentiment suddenly moved in favour of the euro. Partly because of this marked shift in popular attitudes and partly because of increasing pressure from the opposition parties, Prime Minister Poul Rasmussen decided in March 2000 to hold a referendum on Denmark's relationship to the EMU, which took place on 28 September (Marcussen and Zølner 2001). However, shortly after the public announcement of the euro referendum popular attitudes again shifted, and from June 2000 until the referendum all polls showed 15–20 per cent undecided and a 50–50 split between EMU-supporters and EMU-sceptics. The final result was a relatively clear 'No' vote: 46.9 per cent in favour, 53.1 per cent against, in a turnout of 87.5 per cent.

Danish business, especially the banking sector and the industrial sector, remained in favour of full participation. The same went for the civil service in the central administration. However, a change in attitude took place in the central trade-union organization, Landsorganisationen (LO), whose leaders publicly expressed their full support for EMU. Whether such an EMU-positive attitude corresponded to attitudes among the rank and file members of the trade unions was unclear. Some polls concluded that trade union-members were basically in favour of full EMU membership, other polls concluded the opposite. Within Parliament five small political parties announced their opposition to EMU and publicly campaigned for a 'no' vote: two right-wing parties, two left-wing parties, and the Christian Peoples Party. All the other parties, holding 140 seats out of 179, officially declared their support for EMU membership.

At a first glance, this depicts a political landscape massively in favour of Denmark's full participation in the EMU. However, one national newspaper, *Ekstra Bladet*, typically adopted a Eurosceptic attitude, and various national associations—JuniBevægelsen, Folkebevægelsen mod EU and Nationernes Europa—as well as internal party factions within the Social Democratic Party, the Conservative Peoples Party, and the Social Liberal Party launched Eurosceptic campaigns. The result was that the political establishment felt that 'anything can happen'. Constantly threatened by a negative result from one of the many referendums or European parliamentary elections, the Danish Prime Minister always runs the risk that domestic politics will be disturbed by so-called EU-scandals or that EU matters will be distorted by so-called domestic scandals. In other words, the link between domestic politics and European politics presents anything but an opportunity structure for Danish politicians. A political campaign in Denmark wins nothing from being linked to anything 'European': on the contrary. If opponents from both sides of the political spectrum aspire to trouble the Prime Minister, a typical strategy is to make a link between the domestic issues at hand and 'Europe', thereby attempting to delegitimize his actions.

Seen from the viewpoint of Danish public opinion, a strong and popular minister is someone who promotes Danish political issues in the EU and, in the process, fights what the Danish people regard as the overwhelming resistance from the EU machinery and the large EU member states. Similarly, a weak minister is someone who 'takes orders' from the EU or someone who resorts to EU-scapegoating when promoting domestic reforms. Exactly because these dynamics are well-known to the top politicians and their campaign organizers, Henrik Dam Kristensen, allegedly a strong and popular minister, was officially nominated as head of the euro campaign for the referendum.

The conclusion is paradoxical. A consensus about 'sound' and 'stability-oriented' macroeconomic policies was firmly established at the elite level together with broad elite support for the EMU project. But the population was split into almost two equally-sized camps in favour of and against the EMU project. Popular attitudes towards the EU in general and EMU in particular constituted an 'impossibility structure' for the government's attempts to sell the EMU project in a referendum. As we shall see below, European ideas cannot be sold as being purely 'European'. They have to be carefully framed so as to delimit the perceived misfit between European issues and domestic institutions and cultures. 'Europe' simply does not sell very well in Danish public debate.

The Europeanization of the Social Democratic Party

Throughout the 1980s, the Social Democratic Party was in opposition and against any further European integration in general. EMU did not play a significant role for the Danish social democracy until 1989. The case for discussing it was raised in September 1985 when, among others, Professor Niels Thygesen published a report for the Danish Economic Council of Wise Men (DØR 1985) arguing that increased capital liberalization was likely to lead to new political initiatives for EMU. Although the report had been commissioned by the Social Democratic parliamentary group, and although it was intensively discussed in the Danish Parliament, the official spokesperson on European matters, Ivar Nørgaard, did not pursue the EMU issue.[1] Instead,

---

[1] Ivar Nørgaard, 12 November 1985, Folketingets forhandlinger (Ft.) columns 2010–52.

a fierce critique of central bank independence and capital liberalization was offered. A second opportunity to take a stance on EMU was offered in December 1985 and January and February 1986 when the Single European Act was discussed in Parliament.[2] Although the Social Democratic group in Parliament rejected the Single Act, its spokesperson did not adopt a position on the short paragraph in its preamble about the gradual realization of EMU.

In its manifesto for the European parliamentary elections in 1989 the Social Democratic Party finally brought the EMU issue to the fore. This manifesto rejected the idea of pooling member states' sovereignty in order to counter-balance German dominance in the EMS: 'The Social Democratic Party says No. There is no basis for taking European monetary co-operation that far' (cited in Haahr 1993: 241).

The publication of the Delors Report on EMU provided the Social Democrats with another opportunity to clarify their position. During a parliamentary debate on 23 May 1989, their spokesperson, Ivar Nørgaard, lamented the fact that the central bank governors' conservative monetary positions had dominated the Delors Committee's work. However, a clear opening was made on the EMU issue. Now, rather than completely rejecting EMU as in their official manifesto, the Social Democrats made support for EMU conditional on integration of the employment objective.[3] Provided that this objective was given higher priority and that no country could be obliged to go further than the first stage of EMU, the Social Democrats supported the centre-right government's active participation in the Madrid European Council and its recognition of the Delors plan as a point of departure for further negotiations on EMU. This new opening of the Social Democrats towards further European monetary integration was extended in 1990 when the party leader, Svend Auken, emphasized that the party was clearly in favour of European integration and that EMU needed to be coupled more closely to the objective of employment.[4]

Ivar Nørgaard remained opposed to European monetary integration (Hardis 2000) but, in late 1989 and during 1990, the official stance of the Social Democratic Party seemed to change (Krogh 1999). Haahr (1993) even argues

[2] Ft. 10 December 1985, columns 4165–225; 21 January 1986, columns 5314–454; 28 January 1986, columns 5860–954; 30 January 1986, columns 6134–75; 4 February 1986, columns 6329–64; and 20 March 1986, columns 8687–714. See also 25 November 1988, columns 2605–66 and 25 January 1989, columns 5539–74.

[3] Ivar Nørgaard, 23 May 1989, Ft. column 10585. The social democratic position was repeated in the parliamentary debate which preceded the European Council meeting in December 1989 under the French presidency (Ivar Nørgaard, 30 November 1989, Ft. column 2578).

[4] Svend Auken, 18 April 1990, Ft. columns 8478, 8628. See also Ivar Nørgaard, 29 May 1991, Ft. column 7120.

that the party changed its attitude towards monetary integration between June 1989 and October 1989. In June 1989 treaty reforms occupied no prominent position in the European Parliament campaign. Not until October 1989, when the French Socialist President, François Mitterrand, proposed an intergovernmental conference on EMU, did the Danish Social Democratic Party gradually reformulate its position (Haahr 1993: 235). An indication of this change could be that the Social Democratic members of the European Parliament approved the Fernand Herman Report on EMU on 16 May 1990. Another indication could be that the chairperson of the Social Democratic parliamentary group, Ritt Bjerregaard, revealed her support for EMU in September 1990. She furthermore expressed concern that the German government was about to back down from the EMU plans (Haahr 1993: 246). By September 1990 the Social Democratic position had thus evolved from one of scepticism and opposition to one of active participation in the EMU negotiations.

Some researchers (Petersen 1994; Madsen 1996) emphasize the crucial changes in the European architecture—the fall of the Berlin Wall—as an explanatory factor for the U-turn in the Social Democratic attitude towards European integration. Others (Scharpf 1991; Pontusson 1992) point to structural developments in the relationship between capital and labour in Europe. According to this argument, social democracy has been more or less obliged to go for European rather than national solutions in order to remain the strongest political counterweight to the increasingly transnationalized financial and productive sectors. Seen from that perspective, the European option is considered by the Social Democrats as *faute de mieux* because national labour-capital compromises everywhere broke down during the 1980s. For instance, in Denmark, centralized wage bargaining collapsed in the late 1970s and early 1980s (Iversen 1996).

In consequence, since 1989–90 the Social Democratic Party has officially supported the ratification of the Maastricht Treaty on 2 June 1992 and of the so-called Edinburgh Agreement of 18 March 1993 which granted Denmark four opt-outs, including one on EMU membership. A final indication of how complete the U-turn has been is that an overwhelming majority of the delegates to the Social Democratic Party congress on EMU on 29 April 2000 voted in favour of full Danish participation in EMU: 501 for, 14 against. This position is in sharp contrast to the Social Democratic electorate.[5] But, with the congress vote, the long process by which the Social Democratic Party

---

[5] According to *Berlingske Tidende* (2000), 51 per cent of the Social Democratic electorate said 'Yes' to EMU, 46 per cent said 'No', while 9 per cent were undecided. At the referendum on EMU on 28 September 2000, 40 per cent of the Social Democratic electorate voted against Danish participation in the third stage of EMU.

was slowly Europeanized can probably be said to have been brought to a definitive end.

The Europeanization of Danish Corporatism

Corporatism is still going strong (Schmitter and Grote 1997), including in Denmark (Christiansen and Sidenius 1995; 1999; Christiansen and Rommetvedt 1999). The novelty is that Danish corporatism has been sectorized and Europeanized (Pedersen and Pedersen 1995; Esmark *et al.* 2001; Sidenius 1999). In so far as European monetary integration entails a pressure towards semi-sovereign forms of governance in which formal authority to make decisions and allocate resources is split between different levels and types of government, this tendency is consistent with the routines and political cultures already in place in Denmark. Although the question about formal sovereignty is highly politicized in the Danish context, semi-sovereignty is a completely taken-for-granted and accepted praxis in the Danish polity.

However, corporatism does not exist in the traditional sense (Schmitter 1974). Pedersen and Pedersen (1995) show that from the 1980s onwards a third generation of national corporatism has emerged. Corporatism in Scandinavia has, therefore, not necessarily been *weakened*, as argued by Blom-Hansen (2000: 171), but rather *transformed*. The second generation of Danish corporatism was characterized by the fact that important parts of the economy were governed by 'negotiated concertation' of wage bargaining in the labour market and 'cooperative policy-making' in the web of public boards. The policy arena was split vertically into various policy sectors in which institutional networks consisting of civil servants, members of political parties, trade-union members, and members of employer's associations developed formal rules of conduct. This corporatist legacy has played an important role in the adaptation of the Danish polity to European integration (Streeck and Schmitter 1991). A new third generation of Europeanized corporatism developed from the early 1980s. Two parallel processes evolved: a process of decentralization in peak organizations, wage negotiations, and labour-market regulation (Iversen 1996), and a pattern of negotiation and contacts between the Danish administration and the European institutions.

A so-called 'Euro-community' for the formation of transnational policies began to cross-cut existing vertical national policy communities. This Euro-community is horizontal and includes parts of the public administration and members of industrial and sectoral organizations who have developed close and regular links with a series of European agencies and institutions. It is above all professionalized, technical, and routinized in nature. The contacts between its members are rooted in Danish and European commissions, boards, working groups, and councils; they tend also to consist of informal, regular, and intensive personal contacts. Blom-Hansen (2000: 177) argues that 'Interactions between the state and organized interests are becoming less formal . . . [and] seem to have taken on a more lobbyist character'.

The Danish macroeconomic organizational field can be thought of as an EMU community. At its centre we find the Ministry of Economic Affairs, the Prime Minister's Office, and the Danish central bank. In a second circle Danish economic actors from other parts of the central administration and from private organizations are represented in special committees under the Ministry of Economic Affairs. In a third circle, the European Committee in the Danish Parliament plays the roles of controller and observer. When it comes to EMU issues, two parallel and interrelated decision-making procedures exist in two versions: formal and informal.

The *formal* 'traditional' EMU procedure can be grasped with the vocabulary of second-generation corporatism. It starts when the European Commission takes an initiative; it regularly includes a number of interest groups in formal negotiations; it involves parliamentarians on an equal footing; and the national borders delimit its scope. The *informal* version of the same procedure is quite different. On the EMU issue it is no longer the Ministry of Foreign Affairs which takes on the coordinating role but the Ministry of Economic Affairs. Rather than just relying on a set of formal contacts with regular interest groups, the Ministry of Economic Affairs has established a web of informal contacts with all relevant parties. Of course, such a network extends beyond the national borders and includes a wide range of actors within the European macroeconomic organizational field. Rather than exploiting these contacts whenever a new EMU-related initiative is taken in Europe, the contacts are continuously cultivated and involved in all stages of the formal decision-making procedure. The relationship between the actors in this informal network is shaped by the often very technical issues involved in the governance of the European macroeconomic regime. These issues typically preclude a systematic involvement of national politicians. What characterizes the third generation of corporatism and the EMU semi-sovereignty game is a fusion of national and supranational, semi-public, and private actors into a system of multilevel governance.

Parallel to the traditional EMU procedure, a 'special' EMU procedure involving only the core of the Danish Euro-community has been established on all EMU matters of some importance that do not need a formal mandate for negotiation. The origin of this procedure dates back to the crisis in July and August 1993 when the ERM band of fluctuation was expanded to plus or minus 15 per cent, and it has been maintained ever since. All matters concerning currency policy are the exclusive competence of the government and are, therefore, one of the main issues dealt with by this special EMU procedure.

Formally, when the Ministry of Economic Affairs deems an EMU matter to be of some importance, it convenes the so-called Committee of Currency Policy on which top civil servants from the economic ministries and the central bank are represented. The matter is then forwarded to the Prime Minister's Coordination Committee, consisting of the relevant economic ministers, who discuss the matter in a relatively informal way and form an opinion. The closed nature of the procedure and the limited number of actors participating in it can hardly be described in corporatist terms. Contrary to the traditional EMU procedure, in which the Ministry of Foreign Affairs plays an important coordinating role, the Prime Minister's Office and the Ministry of Economic Affairs are central to the special EMU procedure.

However, the special EMU procedure also exists in an *informal* version, which allows the inclusion of other actors into the decision-making process. These actors are private as well as public, national as well as supranational. The informal version of the special EMU procedure resembles the informal version of the traditional EMU procedure, whose horizontal, technical, pro-fessionalized, and transnational network also forms the basis of the special EMU procedure. The special procedure is very much centred on the personal network of the Prime Minister, the Minister of Economic Affairs, and the central-bank governor. These EMU-related networks are particularly cul-tivated in the European Council, ECOFIN, the Economic and Financial Committee, and other such forums. In other words, the special EMU proced-ure has its particular strength in its limited scope, its high level of authority, and its informality (see also Knudsen 2000). If this can be characterized as third-generation corporatism, it is corporatism at a very high executive level.

An interesting question concerns whether the existence of concentric circles in the Danish EMU community has an impact on the power relationships between those actors at the centre—particularly civil servants and ministers in the Ministry of Economic Affairs, the Prime Minister's Office, and the central bank—and the actors in the outer circles of the EMU community (Marcussen 2000b). Those within the national polity who have established closed and dense coalitions with equals within the European macroeco-nomic organizational field tend to possess power resources denied to those in the domestic polity with no international coalitions (Moravcsik 1994). Thus, the centre of the Danish EMU community has access to political and technical *information* which other actors in the Danish central administration cannot possibly get. The Ministry of Economic Affairs, the Prime Minister's Office, and the central bank closely follow and participate in the EMU decision-making processes from the very beginning, whereas politicians in the Danish Parliament are informed only in the very last stage of the process. Second, and partly as a result of this asymmetrical access to information, the core members of the Danish EMU community have an almost exclusive opportunity to set the agenda for the EMU debate. The core takes the *initiative* and drafts the convergence programmes and employment action plans. It monopolizes decisions about monetary and exchange-rate policy and is free to amend negotiation positions throughout the decision-making procedure. Third, the *institutions* that encapsulate the EMU procedures favour the core members. These core members participate continuously in the workings of the Economic and Financial Committee, the ECOFIN meetings, and the European Councils. These forums are closed, excluding actors in the outer circles of the Danish EMU community. Finally, the core members are not only the carriers of *ideas*; they also invent new macroeconomic ideas, promote them, and implement them. The core members have the privileged status of being the legitimate ideational entrepreneurs in periods of crisis and are responsible for 'selling' EMU ideas to the population in referendums and elections.

In conclusion, the third generation of corporatism since the 1980s, and particularly the creation of an EMU community, is highly compatible with European multilevel governance (Falkner 2000). Semi-sovereign structures of governance do not cause many organizational adaptation problems in Denmark; semi-sovereignty has become an integral part of political culture. However, these new structures of governance might have an impact on the social relationships between actors in the Danish EMU community. Some actors benefit disproportionately from the power resources emanating from their exclusive access to EMU information, their monopoly on EMU initiative, the closed EMU institutions, and their role as ideational entrepreneurs.

Liberalized Capital and Central Bank Power

In the late 1970s and early 1980s, pressures for capital liberalization came from two sources. First, within the EMS framework the two countries with the strongest currencies—Germany and the Netherlands—were increasingly unhappy that they were financing the currency adjustments of the weaker currencies. They argued that increased capital liberalization in Europe, which they had to a large extent already implemented, would force the weaker currencies to adopt stability-oriented policies with more emphasis on low inflation. However, in the late 1970s the Commission was no longer a driving force for capital liberalization. In the 1960s it had been in the forefront with new directives on capital liberalization, but in the 1970s such efforts were in vain. Hence, by the early 1980s, it was the German and Dutch representatives on the EC Monetary Committee who took the initiative to relaunch one of the original objectives of the EC (Art. 67): complete capital liberalization (Bakker 1996: 149).

The second pressure for general capital liberalization came from the change of government in Britain and Margaret Thatcher's overnight liberalization of all capital movements. A similar movement towards deregulation had been undertaken in the US and a change in mood was under way throughout Europe. Within the framework of the EEC, the entire dossier was left for the EC Monetary Committee, which convened numerous meetings in the course of 1983 and 1984 without really involving ECOFIN. Not until the informal ECOFIN meeting in Dromoland Castle, Ireland, in October 1984 was the general principle of full capital liberalization confirmed at a political level (Bakker 1996: 159). From 1985 the principle was fully integrated in Jacques Delors' White Book on the Internal Market, and it was introduced on the agenda of the intergovernmental conference convened in Milan on 28–9 June 1985, preparing the Single European Act.

In Denmark the new centre-right government from 1982 onwards willingly adopted the general deregulatory trend (Iversen and Thygesen 1998: 70). Denmark quickly became known as a complete convert to the gospel of capital liberalization and joined forces with Germany, the Netherlands, and Britain within the liberal coalition of the EC Monetary Committee.[6] The fourth directive on capital liberalization did not run into much resistance when it was debated in the Danish Parliament on 24 March 1988 and was implemented two years ahead of time.[7]

Capital liberalization—indeed monetary policy in general—has only rarely been debated in the Danish Parliament, although the Social Liberal Party and the opposition parties on the left tried on various occasions to raise the issue through parliamentary questions to the Prime Minister or Minister of Economic Affairs. However, on one occasion in December 1984 the Social Democrats and the Socialist People's Party formed a majority to demand that an expert report on Danish monetary politics be commissioned. The report

---

[6] On 1 May 1983 Denmark eased the restrictions on purchases of foreign securities and direct investment. On 1 January 1984 Denmark abolished restrictions on the purchase of foreign shares by residents. On 11 June 1985 Denmark implemented further liberalization measures. On 1 October 1988 Denmark abolished all remaining exchange control regulations two years before time (DØR, 1994: 131–4; Mikkelsen 1993: 266–72).

[7] 24 March 1988, Ft. columns 8943–89.

was published in September 1985 and started a unique debate in Parliament about capital liberalization and the role of the Danish central bank in the Danish economic polity.[8]

The expert report concluded rather frankly that monetary politics had been negotiated and adopted behind closed doors, without the involvement of Parliament. The main actors in this game had been the economic ministries and the central bank governor, and the scope of their power to liberalize capital movements had increased decisively since the centre-right government took office in 1982. The process of capital liberalization was, according to the report, irreversible and would inevitably lead towards demands for EMU, with common fiscal and social policies (DØR 1985).

In a foreword to the report the central bank governor, Erik Hoffmeyer, was given the opportunity to reply to these accusations about his role in monetary politics. He rejected the view that monetary union was anywhere near the horizon; he denied that the central bank was a closed and secret organization and that he had any responsibility for the exclusion of parliament in the area of monetary politics.

However, despite Hoffmeyer's disavowal, central banking was crucial in the Danish economic polity. The first reason is general for most central bankers in Europe: central bankers have become increasingly central to national and European decision-making processes (Dyson, Featherstone, and Michalopoulos 1995; Cameron 1995; Marcussen 1998a). After the breakdown of the Bretton Woods regime, central bankers developed and intensified their formal transnational relations: Bank for International Settlements, EC Monetary Committee, G10, Committee of EC Central Bank Governors, G7, and so forth. Within these circles central bank philosophy was that capital liberalization would enforce a 'sound policy' ideology on heads of government and their ministers of economics. Second, central banking has operated in a very permissive context in Denmark. Central bankers have been given wide scope for manoeuvre by the absence of a strong coalition between industrial capital and financial capital, by increasingly decentralized and fragmented labour organizations, and by consecutive centre-right governments explicitly supporting 'sound policy' measures (Epstein 1992). The third reason is specific to one person. In the 30 years from 1965 to 1995, Erik Hoffmeyer achieved an unprecedented position in the Danish economic polity from which moral as well as technical and political judgements could be diffused among economic elites. He wrote extensively in the press (Danmarks Nationalbank 1986) and achieved a reputation as reliable and

---

[8] 12 November 1985, Ft. columns 2010–52.

impartial. The newspaper *Børsens Nyhedsmagasin* has for many years published a list of persons whom decision-makers and other public persons in Denmark considered to be the most reliable. Hoffmeyer typically appeared second on the list, 'beaten' only by Her Majesty Queen Margaret. These three factors made the Danish central bank a very central actor in the process by which capital was liberalized. The fact that the process of capital liberalization was unpoliticized and rapid considerably eased Denmark's path towards participation in EMU.

With Denmark outside the third stage of EMU, central banking was still present in the public debate prior to the referendum on EMU. The central bank governor, Bodil Nyboe Andersen, indicated that she considered 'Danish membership of the EMU as being a natural continuation of the economic policy strategy which has been pursued over the last two decades' (B. Andersen 2000).[9] Otherwise, central banking took on a more background role following the ratification of the Maastricht Treaty in 1993. In the above-mentioned speech, Andersen provides us with an explanation for this self-chosen modesty. She argues that, through the Delors committee, central bankers had been able to place central bank independence and price stability on the top of the list of macroeconomic priorities in Europe. For that reason alone, there is no need to constantly speak about something that everybody seems to take for granted. Interestingly, Andersen argues that, because central bankers were involved in producing the Delors report, they now seem to express total loyalty towards EMU. EMU grants European central bankers an influence over European economics and a role in European politics that they would otherwise not have had.

In conclusion, Denmark is no exception when it comes to the general trend in Europe, which has seen central bankers achieve a pivotal, independent, and uncontested role in macroeconomic policy-making and seen capital markets liberalized. These structural developments have long been an integral part of the Danish economic polity and fully accepted by all actors within the macroeconomic organizational field (Iversen and Thygesen 1998: 79).

Framing EMU: The Sound Policy Paradigm vs the Danish Welfare State

In the 1980s and 1990s two themes formed the core of the official Danish macroeconomic discourse on both sides of the political spectrum: the

---

[9] See also *Børsen* (2000) and central bank economist Hanne Lyngesen (2000: 10).

sacredness of the sound policy paradigm and of the Danish welfare state. It is not legitimate for any political actor who aspires to membership of the macroeconomic 'in-group' to question the relevance or importance of these two key institutions. As we shall see below, in the 1990s the Social Democratic Party in office had problems in reconciling traditional welfare-state object-ives and stability-oriented policy strategy. The EMU process forced all Danish politicians to take a stand on these two issues and on the potential conflicts between them. Politicians had to frame these issues in public debate in such a way that they at least appeared as two sides of the same coin.

The problem of framing these two issues became visible shortly after the Social Democratic and Social Liberal coalition government took office in January 1993. With the 'A New Start' programme, new public investments were launched and the labour-market and tax systems underwent thorough reform. These measures were undertaken against a background of a budget deficit of 2.7 per cent of GDP, expected to increase to 4.1 per cent by the end of 1993 and to 4.4 per cent in 1994 (Økonomiministeriet 1993). Since then, the Minister of Economic Affairs, Marianne Jelved, and the Prime Minister, Poul Nyrup Rasmussen, have not missed an opportunity to emphasize their firm adherence to the dominant macroeconomic consensus within the Euro-Zone: a policy of sound money and finance. Politicians were busy assuring the financial markets, the opposition, and their colleagues in the European macroeconomic organizational field that the Danish 'kick-start' was tempor-ary, responsible, and fully in accordance with the main principles of sound policy. Thus on 27 January 1993, when Rasmussen delivered his first speech in Parliament as leader of the Social Democrat-led coalition government, he emphasized that the sound policy of the previous centre-right government continued to constitute the main pillar of the new coalition government.[10] Since then, this message has been repeated on many occasions.[11]

Rasmussen was also at great pains to underline that he endorsed further monetary integration in Europe and eventual full membership of EMU.[12] However, while praising EMU and the sound policy paradigm, he emphas-ized that EMU had changed its character since its inception in the early 1990s. He argued that EMU was firmly linked to a European commitment to job creation: 'In my opinion, Denmark is best served by adhering to the Euro

[10] Poul Nyrup Rasmussen, 27 January 1993, Ft. column 4746.

[11] For a recent example see Poul Nyrup Rasmussen, end of session statement in Parliament, 25 May 2000.

[12] Poul Nyrup Rasmussen, 5 October 1993, Ft. column 11; Prime Minster Poul Nyrup Rasmussen New Year's Speeches, 1 January 1999, http://www.stm.dk/taler/taler/tale20.htm, and 1 January 2000, http://www.stm.dk/taler/taler/tale52.htm

. . . This is all about employment and Danish jobs.[13] The Social Democratic way of reconciling its traditional focus on welfare and employment with the Europe-wide sound policy consensus that in the short run prioritizes low inflation over employment was to argue that EMU had fundamentally changed its character during the 1990s. The argument was that, compared with the 1980s, the EU was evolving a 'Social Democratic EMU' which *both* takes 'common sense' seriously—that is, assuring price stability—*and* is engaged with Social Democratic ideals—that is, job-creation. In this spirit, two Social Democratic spokespersons, Torben Lund and Jacob Buksti, stated that they clearly understood and accepted why Danes voted 'No' to EMU in 1992. Then, EMU was a markedly neo-liberal project that had low inflation rather than high employment as the prime objective. But the situation had changed because of the Luxembourg, Cardiff, and Cologne processes:

The present EMU is another kind of currency union than the one to which the Danes voted No in 1992 . . . In 1992 the EU was dominated by centre-right governments with neo-liberal approaches to economic policy-making. This clearly had an impact. In the 1980s and beginning of the 1990s unemployment was considered a secondary problem. Low inflation and large balance of payment surpluses were the most important objectives for Thatcher, Kohl, Juppé, Schlüter and Ellemann . . . On that basis it is not surprising that the Danes voted No to EMU . . . In short, another currency union has been realized after 1998 than the one we could have expected in 1992. (Buksti and Lund 1999)

In short, a recurrent line in official EMU discourse in Denmark has been that 'sound and stability-oriented policy' is uncontested and constitutes the foundation for the European integration process. However, it is also argued that EMU has changed its character since summer 1993 when employment was discussed at the Copenhagen European Council and was later institutionalized in the Luxembourg and other processes (see also Kristensen (1999)). In other words, EMU is basically framed as a Social Democratic project in which the traditional convergence criteria have been supplemented with a set of less formal and less legalistic criteria about active and Europe-wide employment policies (Marcussen 2000c).

The second key element in official EMU discourse is the Danish welfare state. As Knudsen (2000: 155) eloquently argues: 'An attempt by any of Denmark's important parties to roll back the welfare state would be electoral suicide. If a party wanted to cut spending, it would have to argue that these

---

[13] Prime Minister Poul Nyrup Rasmussen's opening statement in the Danish Parliament, 5 October 1999. See also *Søndagsavisen* (1999); *Nordjyske Stiftstidende* (1999).

short-run changes would *save* the welfare state in the long run.' The sacred-ness of welfare was, therefore, a critical point which had somehow to be decoupled from EMU if the euro was to have any chance of being 'sold' convincingly to the Danish electorate.

One prominent argument of the government and other EMU supporters about the consequences of EMU is that it has nothing at all to do with the Danish welfare state. To support this argument, EMU supporters typically refer to the Treaty's Art. 136 (ex-Art. 117), which states that the Community and the member states shall implement measures within the area of social and employment policy which take account of the diverse forms of national practices. They point also to Art. 137 (ex-Art. 118), which emphasizes that the provisions adopted within these areas shall not prevent any Member State from maintaining or introducing more stringent protective measures com-patible with the Treaty (Økonomi- og Finansministeriet 2000: 457).

Another argument that quite often appears in public debate about EMU is that it is not EMU that threatens the Danish welfare state but rather more general and unspecified processes of globalization. EMU should be seen as a shield that protects the existing European welfare-state regimes. Whereas globalization is presented as a harmonizing force that will lead to converging European welfare states at the lowest common denominator, EMU is pictured as the mechanism that guarantees national diversity and local specificity (Økonomi- og Finansministeriet 2000: 35).

On 11 April 2000, a debate about the Danish government's official report on 'Denmark and EMU' was held in parliament. Unsurprisingly, the question of EMU's consequences for the welfare state was a central theme. The Euro-sceptic spokespersons focused on the welfare issue from the beginning. They complained that the official EMU report had failed to closely examine the impact on the welfare state. The opposition knew that in the campaign the government could not publicly support a political project that could be interpreted as having detrimental effects on the welfare state.

In a very illustrative way, the political spokesperson for the Social Demo-cratic Party, Claus Larsen-Jensen, replied that EMU had nothing to do with welfare. He clearly knew that in Denmark it is impossible to legitimately argue that EMU somehow will trigger a reconsideration of some of the sacred elements of the Danish welfare state:

If the arguments against the euro are weak, then it is convenient to say: 'The wolf is coming', 'the welfare society will be undermined', 'the social model is disappearing', 'the tax-based system is disappearing', 'Denmark will stop being an independent country', 'the United States of Europe is on its way'. If this is what it is all about, I too would vote No. But this is not what we have on the agenda, and this is not what we are going to vote about, as a result of which it doesn't lead us anywhere to emphasize these aspects.[14]

The Minister of Economic Affairs, Marianne Jelved, used the same rejection strategy. It was also in her self-interest, if she was to appear trustworthy in the eyes of the public, to totally decouple the EMU debate from the issue of welfare: 'It is not about [the harmonization of welfare states], and this has nothing to do with the common currency.'[15]

On 2 May 2000, the government presented a bill for Denmark's participation in the common currency (L288). The bill explicitly stated that the EMU members remained solely responsible for their welfare policies and that EMU could be seen as a shield against globalization. By this defensive strategy of linking unpopular welfare-state reforms to unspecified and impersonal processes of globalization, politicians were able to evade responsibility. At the same time, EMU was constructed as an instrument that could be actively used to protect the sacred core of the Danish macroeconomic debate: the welfare state.

The bill was discussed in the Danish parliament on 17 May 2000.[16] The leader of the Conservative Party, Bendt Bendtsen, used the occasion to construct a public image of himself as a welfare-state protector. In doing so he gained added credibility in appealing to the Eurosceptic elements in the Conservative electorate. Bendtsen specified what was at the core of the Conservative referendum strategy, titled 'A Reflective Yes' (*Ja med omtanke*):

There can hardly be any doubt that in the years to come we will see initiatives from certain member states which wish more integration than we would like—for instance, when it comes to the issue of the Danish welfare state. But we have our limits, where we say No, and where we can say No. It's a national competence to map out the welfare state.[17]

Having noticed that the Conservative electorate was split into two almost equally sized groups, the party leader chose to emphasize that EMU, even if not directly linked to the welfare state, would not be allowed to affect the Danish welfare-state regime. A similar strategy had been pursued by the leader of the Danish Liberal Party, Anders Fogh Rasmussen, who in an attempt to appeal to the Liberal Eurosceptics argued that the welfare state was

[14] Claus Larsen-Jensen, 11 April 2000, Ft. column 6364.
[15] Marianne Jelved, 11 April 2000, Ft. column 6365.
[16] The parliamentary debate on 17 May 2000 was the first of three readings of the government's proposition for law about Denmark's participation in the third stage of EMU. The following two debates took place on 24 August 2000 and 6 September 2000.
[17] Bendt Bendtsen, 17 May 2000, Ft. column 8101.

sacred and that EU integration should not interfere in this area (Rasmussen 2000).[18]

In summary, it seems that the Danish elite's debate about the euro exhibits a Europeanization process which can be best characterized as 'bottom-up' (Dyson 2000b). The direct impact of EMU on Danish public ideologies, institutions, and policies—'top-down' or 'second image reversed' processes—is but one side of the coin of Europeanization. The other side is the ways in which EMU is framed in the national institutional and cultural contexts so that it appears comprehensible, feasible and, not least, legitimate to the actors involved, including the larger public. In the framing process, EMU can be constructed in various ways: as a political and/or economic project, as a neo-liberal or as a Social Democratic project, as fundamentally detached from welfare-related issues or as a means to protect the welfare state from globalization. The key point is that the chosen strategy of framing very much depends on the dominant ideas in the macroeconomic culture of the country in question. Thus, the framing process is all about constructing a convincing 'fit' (Börzel and Risse 2000; Cowles, Caporaso, and Risse 2000) between EMU —its institutions, procedures, and ideas—and consensually shared ideas at the national level. In the public debate before the EMU referendum in September 2000, the Liberal and Conservative party leaders projected themselves as 'protectors of the Danish welfare state' while Social Democratic leaders sought to guarantee a 'stability-oriented and responsible macroeconomic policy strategy'. These framing strategies were designed to achieve one sole objective: to appear faithful to the ideational core of the Danish macroeconomic culture—'sound policy' and 'welfare state'—and simultaneously as supporters of EMU membership.

Conclusions

This chapter has investigated the various ways in which the Danish polity has adjusted to EMU. This process of adaptation has taken place gradually and almost unnoticed by the broader population. Although the European issue has been widely discussed in Denmark since the early 1970s, such issues as capital liberalization, the Europeanization of corporatism and of the Social Democratic Party, and the emergence of an ideational elite consensus about the 'sound policy' paradigm have not been on the public agenda. The public

---

[18] On 28 September 2000, 28 per cent of the Liberal Party's electorate voted against Denmark's participation in the third stage of EMU.

debates have been about narrow economic benefits resulting from European integration, not about visions for the national and European polities.

This narrow economic focus is most clearly expressed in the debate about Denmark and EMU and is reinforced by reports of authoritative international economic organizations on the state of the Danish economy. The IMF, for instance, concluded that 'Denmark is well equipped to participate in the common currency' (Økonomiministeriet 2000*a*) and the OECD reminded the interested reader that 'there are clear economic advantages for Denmark in a common currency' (Økonomiministeriet 2000*b*). This chapter has gone beyond a purely economic assessment of Denmark and the euro to study the ideational and institutional aspects of the relationship.

Following the initial definition of four stages in the EMU process and four levels of change, a number of conclusions can be drawn. First, 'stability-oriented' or 'sound' macroeconomic ideas have long since been internalized and consensually accepted by elites within the Danish macroeconomic organizational field. This organizational field includes the various ministers, the central administration, the national central bank, and their counterparts on the European scene. In Denmark, it is simply not relevant to discuss the ideational foundation of EMU in these forums. These ideas are taken for granted. Nor is it legitimate to seriously question the basic macroeconomic objective of the ECB—low inflation—or the means by which this objective should be achieved—low national budget deficits and central bank independence. It is important to specify the mechanisms by which the EMU process has had an impact on this ideational shift among Danish elites. These mechanisms include ideational socialization through the EMS, ideational leadership by European central bankers, as well as ideational emulation of the German model of economic stability.

Second, at the end of the 1980s the main opposition party, the Social Democratic Party, also turned 'European'. From having questioned most aspects of the centre-right government's foreign policy and from expressing reservations with regard to most aspects of European integration, the party suddenly adopted an active stance on the European question. In the beginning, support for European monetary integration was conditional on the parallel introduction of European employment policies. But soon, and particularly once the Social Democrats took office in 1993, that support became close to unconditional. This U-turn by the Social Democratic Party was seen in terms of benchmarking practices taking place in the critical period after the collapse of the Soviet Union. Ideational emulation of the French Socialist Party and of the Socialist Group in the European Parliament was crucial in this respect.

Third, if the Danish economic and political elites were delighted with Europe in the late 1980s, particularly with regard to the main ideas and institutions on which EMU is founded, the Danish population has constituted a critical dilemma throughout the EMU process. A majority of the population was in favour of Denmark's full participation in EMU for only a limited period of time in 1999. At all other times a clear majority has been against. The EMU issue touches on feelings of social security and national identity and sovereignty, and most political parties have been split on these issues. The many referendums on Europe—in 1972, 1986, 1992, 1993, 1998, 2000, with probably four more to go—have made former senior civil servants propose that the referendum as an institution be abolished (Christensen and Ersbøll 2000). However, if the Danish population has clearly expressed itself against EMU, the Danes are manifestly in favour of Danish membership of the EU (European Commission 2001b: 37). The vote on 28 September 2000 was a vote against EMU, not against the EU.

Fourth, during the 1980s Danish corporatism has gone through a process of transformation into a third generation, characterized not just by its Europeanization but also by a decreasing level of formality and an increasing level of routinization and professionalization. The Europeanization of corporatism is manifested in the ways in which the Danish EMU decision-making procedures are organized. A 'semi-sovereignty game', with its dispersion of responsibilities and layers of transnational networking, is already visible in Denmark. The shift to the EU level of Danish corporatism was stimulated by the Single European Act, which made the European political space much more interesting for lobbying by Danish organized groups. The Single Act also encouraged Danish civil servants and politicians to do a much better job in forging EU coalitions rather than relying on their veto power and the typically narrow mandates from the European Committee in the Danish Parliament.

Fifth, during the 1980s capital and financial services were increasingly liberalized in Denmark and nearly all internal market directives were implemented in accordance with the first stage of EMU. In the process, the Danish central bank governor, together with his EU central bank colleagues, and top civil servants from the national finance ministries in the EC Monetary Committee played a dominant role. By liberalizing capital they redefined the rules of the European monetary game, thereby preparing the ground for further integrative steps. On the domestic scene, the Danish central bank governor helped consecutive Danish governments to define a set of sound policy objectives and strategies. In consequence, the instrumental and normative agenda within the Danish macroeconomic organizational field was changed. With the Danish central bank governor as a central actor in macroeconomic matters, the differences between the Danish financial system and the financial systems within the Euro-Zone became minimal. Thus, an additional potential barrier to an easy entry into full EMU membership was eliminated. The liberalization of capital movements can be seen, above all, as an attempt to comply with the rules of the internal market. However, Denmark liberalized its financial flows much faster than necessary, which indicates how willingly the country copied the international fashion in the area. In particular, the practices of such countries as Germany, the Netherlands, and Britain served as benchmarks for appropriate behaviour.

Sixth, there is the issue of how EMU was constructed in national public discourse. The top-down processes by which the Danish polity has undergone changes during the last three decades as a result of EMU represent only one side of the coin. The other side involves the important ways in which EMU ideas, institutions, and policies were framed in the national political processes (Dyson 2000b). The official EMU discourse contained a two-dimensional core: the attention paid to the sound policy paradigm and the continued relevance attributed to the welfare state. The imperative was to frame them in positive terms and to reconcile them so that possible contradictions were removed. In the public debates about the EU, EMU was sometimes entirely decoupled from the welfare issue and sometimes seen as the shield that could protect the Danish welfare state from unspecified processes of globalization. Other discursive strategies framed EMU in terms of political ideologies. On the one hand, the EMU was framed as a 'responsible' Social Democratic project that focused on welfare while respecting the Europe-wide 'sound policy' consensus. On the other hand, EMU was framed as a neo-liberal project that guaranteed sound public finances and money, thereby securing strong foundations for a further development of the Danish welfare state.

To sum up, during the last three decades the Danish state has, almost imperceptibly adapted to the EMU process and is therefore well-placed to play the full EMU semi-sovereignty game. EMU ideas are consensually shared, Danish corporatism has been Europeanized, central banking is at the centre of the Danish macroeconomic organizational field, capital markets have long since been liberalized, and the government is pursuing a 'stability-oriented' policy that would make any central banker sleep well at night. For these reasons, 'Denmark is extremely well equipped to harvest the advantages of EMU membership', said the Danish Minister of Finance, Mogens Lykketoft on 16 January 2000 (Lykketoft 2000). The following day, however, the official government EMU spokesperson, Henrik Dam Kristensen, added that 'In

Denmark it is difficult to narrow the public debate down to only dealing with the EMU—we have to discuss broader issues, because this is what our electorate wants' (Kristensen 2000). These two quotations illustrate well the dilemma in which Danish politicians find themselves with regard to European integration.

On the one hand, the Danish state has adapted almost completely to the EMU process. Under normal circumstances the Danish transition to the third stage of EMU would be painless and fast. These processes of state adaptation can be analysed in terms of five mechanisms of change: ideational leadership, ideational emulation, ideational socialization, direct EU-regulation, and market competition. On the other hand, there is a strong Danish tradition of involving the public in the general debate about the EU. The more than six months of EMU campaigning from March to September 2000 demonstrated once again that there is no way that Danish politicians can take Europe for granted. They will continue to be 'lonely riders' in Europe, delighted by EMU but recognizing the dilemma in which they find themselves.

6

The French State in the Euro-Zone: 'Modernization' and Legitimizing *Dirigisme*

David Howarth

French participation in the Euro-Zone is to be seen principally as a *self-imposed* 'semi-sovereignty game'. From the creation of the EMS in 1979, French polit- ical leaders have seen a European monetary constraint as a tool to reinforce domestic economic restructuring. In this sense, President François Mitterr- and's March 1983 decision to keep the franc in the ERM represented the final decision to end socialist reflation, embrace open competition in the EC, and conform—at least to a certain extent—to the German economic standard. The French pursuit of EMU demonstrated the desire to ensure the continua- tion of reform while simultaneously loosening the external constraint by sharing monetary power with the Germans. The tightness of this constraint was blamed for the excessive decline in French economic output and the growth of French unemployment, particularly in the period following German reunification.

This chapter examines the impact of EMU as part of the Europeanization of the French state, which has been explored in more general terms by Ladrech (1994), Guyomarch, Machin, and Ritchie (1998), and Cole and Drake (2000). The analysis of Europeanization is constructivist, focusing on the develop- ment of French state identity. The EMS and the EMU project have involved both weak and strong Europeanization. As 'weak' Europeanization, the EMS and EMU should be seen as intervening variables shaping the operation of the French state, policies, and outcomes. They were embraced by leading French policy-makers, starting with President Valéry Giscard d'Estaing, to reinforce domestic efforts to 'modernize' the state and economy and keep public spending under control despite widespread reluctance in the French population and political circles. This reluctance stemmed from worries about increased exposure to European and global competition, European competi- tion rules, and the comparatively heavy reliance on foreign capital to finance both public-sector debt and private-sector equity capital. EMU was in this sense 'bottom-up' Europeanization: improving the fitness of the French economy in order to keep the franc in the ERM and to participate in EMU (Alphandéry 2000; Boissonnat 1998). The EMS constraint and the EMU project influenced the timing and pace of some reforms to French policy regimes which have been adopted principally for other reasons: financial market liberalization, budget reform—including the reform of the social security budget and the structures controlling this budget—increasing labour-market flexibility, and privatization. This 'weak' Europeanization involved 'framing' individual structural policy reforms in terms consistent with persuading the Germans to accept mutual realignments in the ERM in the 1981–7 period, avoiding devaluation in the ERM from 1983, and respecting the convergence criteria of the EMU project and the Stability and Growth Pact.

In other respects, the EMU project functioned as a 'strong', 'top-down' Europeanization. Its role as an independent variable was seen in the imposition of central bank independence, sought by few French policy-makers, opposed by many, and directly contrary to the French republican tradition. This role was also apparent in the modification of the role of the French Treasury and the change in programmatic discourse, notably the medium-term stabilization plans in coordination with European partners to fulfil the terms of the Stability and Growth Pact. 'Strong' Europeanization was reflected in the considerable emphasis that the 'Plural Left' government of Lionel Jospin placed on counter-balancing both the power of the ECB in the Euro-Zone by strengthening a European 'economic government', and the 'sound' money bias of EMU by reinforcing European social and employment policies.

This chapter has two parts. First, it examines the discursive/ideological structure underpinning and shaping the impact of EMU on French state structures, policy regimes, and policies, and French strategic responses to the operation of the EMS and EMU. This discursive structure is shaped principally by a conservative liberalism—in the ascendant given the economic constraints reinforced by monetary integration—and a rearguard interventionism. Second, substantive state reforms and the strategic behaviour of French policy-makers in the Euro-Zone reflect the dialectic between these two ideologies. This dialectic and the substantive reforms have contributed to reshaping French state identity. EMU has acted as an intervening variable enforcing the reforms sought principally by conservative liberals dominant in the financial administrative elite. The result was a shift in state identity towards stabilization. However, this shift was couched in other long-standing themes of the French state. The constraints of monetary integration sat uneasily with a strong interventionist legacy. None the less, EMU increased

possibilities for improved EU-level coordination in economic and employment policies—'economic government'—in whose development the Jospin
government was in the vanguard.

The decision to embrace EMU should also be seen in terms of French
strategy to increase monetary policy-making power in relation to both the
Germans and the Americans. It was a reflection of the traditional assertiveness of the French state in the European and international arenas, backed
by widespread popular approval (Howarth 2001). In public discourse, EMU
was justified principally as containing the economic and diplomatic power
of reunified Germany, and the creation of the single European currency as
replacing the D-Mark and challenging the international role of the dollar.

The Economic Ideology of French State Strategies in the Euro-Zone

Reinforcing the Conservative Liberal Agenda

Conservative liberalism has been the dominant economic ideology in the
Treasury division of the Ministry of Finance, the Bank of France, and the
Financial Inspectorate, the *grand corps* which forms the leading part of
the French financial elite. However, the influence of this ideology has always
been limited by its fragmentation and weakness in French party politics
(Dyson, Featherstone, and Michaelopoulos 1994: 35; Hazareesingh 1994). The
creation of the EMS in 1979 corresponded to the hitherto rare predominance
of conservative liberalism in government under Giscard d'Estaing as President and Raymond Barre as Prime Minister. This ideology was inspired more
by the German model of low inflationary economic growth than Anglo-
American liberalism (Dyson 1994; McNamara 1998).

Conservative liberals uphold the self-adjusting nature of market mechanisms and reject state-led reflation. They seek exchange-rate stability, low
inflation, balanced budgets, and current account surpluses. Devaluation was
long opposed as a fundamental threat to a social order based on savings and
monetary stability. Conservative liberals embraced the EMS and EMU as
useful means to import German 'sound' money policies and budget and
wage discipline. They respect technical experience and expertise in economic
policy and the maintenance of a measure of autonomy from political interference in the formulation and implementation of economic policy—which
serves the interests of the Treasury and the Bank of France.

The EMS helped to reinforce the influence of the Treasury and the Bank
of France in relation to governments. EMU helped to further reinforce

conservative liberalism through the convergence criteria and the transfer of monetary policy to technocratic control in the Bank of France and the ECB. Members of the Treasury were very reluctant to embrace independent central banking as a necessary step to reinforce their economic preferences. However, the convergence criteria and the Stability and Growth Pact reinforced Treasury influence over the domestic reform agenda.

Core conservative liberal economic ideas formed the bedrock of 'competitive disinflation', the major French macroeconomic policy from the mid-1980s (Fitoussi 1992; 1995). The value of 'sound' money was linked to the idea that the weakening competitive position of French exports was due to structural problems that could not be resolved through competitive devaluations. Following Mitterrand's March 1983 decision to prioritize a stable franc in the ERM, intellectual and political support for this policy gradually solidified, labelled by critics *la pensée unique*. At the intellectual level, the extensive influence of the state in economic research, through the studies produced in the Treasury, the forecasting division of the Ministry of Finance, and the National Institute of Statistics and Economic Studies (INSEE), facilitated the rapid extension of these ideas into the academic economic community and their dominance. The ideological shift to 'competitive disinflation' was reinforced by the modernization and liberalization of the French financial markets in the mid-1980s, including the creation of the MATIF—the French futures market—as part of the drive to reform the 'overdraft' economy (Mamou 1987; Loriaux 1991). The objective of opening access to foreign capital to finance French debt was to control inflation and lower interest rates. This increased reliance on foreign capital made both attractive rates and a strong currency more necessary than previously.

In a French political class traditionally little concerned with inflation as an economic problem, 'competitive disinflation' helped to increase the acceptability of 'sound' money policies and the EMS constraint. The demands of French governments for a more balanced convergence suggest that their principal worry was not inflation per se but the inflation differential and trade imbalance with France's major trading partners. The label 'competitive disinflation' is thus revealing: disinflation was required principally to improve France's competitive position vis-à-vis Germany. The distinction is important because it demonstrates the shallowness of anti-inflationary sentiment in French political circles beyond the small conservative liberal hard core around Barre and Giscard and the Socialist modernizers, notably Jacques Delors and Pierre Bérégovoy. Moreover, this distinction introduces a different angle on the economic logic behind French support for the EMS constraint. The purpose of this constraint for many leading French politicians was not to reduce the level of French inflation as an objective in itself but to reduce the level of inflation in order to improve France's competitive position. Treasury officials and ministers of finance accepted, more or less, the need to lower inflation as an economic objective in itself. However, for a political class historically obsessed with the trade balance, notably in relation to Germany, the competitive element of the policy had much greater resonance. The greatly improved competitiveness of French companies in the 1990s and record trade surpluses from 1994 helped to legitimize a policy that was otherwise blamed for lost economic output and high unemployment.

The Continued Weakness of French Neo-Liberalism

Neo-liberalism has been weak in the Treasury, Bank of France, and French academic and political circles and of relatively limited influence in directly shaping French policy on EMU and economic reform. Likewise, France was largely immune to Anglo-American economic arguments criticizing EMU for not being an optimal currency zone (Rosa 1998). Neo-liberalism was most influential in the context of financial market liberalization started by Bérégovoy in 1984. This process was encouraged both by EMS membership— the search for non-inflationary sources of finance—and by continued EMS membership—increasing the need for monetary stability and raising French interest rates to attract foreign capital.

Neo-liberalism enjoyed a brief period of influence in the neo-Gaullist party (RPR) of Jacques Chirac in the mid-1980s, although this rhetoric was rejected after 1988 for electoral reasons. Overt neo-liberalism played only a limited role in the public debate on the EMS and EMU. Most frequently it has been invoked with a negative connotation by those on the left and the right opposing EMU as a neo-liberal device to reinforce the effects of globalization and undermine the French social model.

The Lingering Dirigiste Bias

Dirigisme as a manifestation of étatisme reflects a strong mistrust of market mechanisms, the economic utility of which is none the less accepted. It insists on the need for active state intervention in the economy, labelled volontarisme. Dirigisme has influenced a wide spectrum of French political and public opinion to different degrees, notably the Gaullist/neo-Gaullist parties on the right, the Socialist Party on the left, in addition to the elite technical corps of the French state, which had limited influence over monetary policy.

*Dirigiste*s tend to prefer the conservative liberal goals of a strong currency, monetary stability, and a trade surplus, although normally for different reasons. But these goals are secondary to state-led economic growth. *Dirigistes* also seek to place constraints on the operation of international financial markets and speculative capital. Jospin continued to call for the imposition of an international tax on speculative capital movements—the so-called Tobin tax—right up to the 1997 legislative elections.

In decline since the 1960s with the opening of the French economy to international markets, *dirigiste* strategies have been restricted in the context of the operation of the EMS and the EMU project and the corresponding 'modernizing' reforms. Paradoxically, this decline has worked to the disadvantage of the Treasury and the Financial Inspectorate. Their influence had profited immensely from post-war *dirigisme* and the extension of the public sphere. The decline of *dirigisme* reflected the rise of the Treasury's ideological bias of conservative liberalism, while greatly weakening the influence of the Treasury itself. None the less, the capacity of the French state, led by the Treasury, to persist in a policy of avoiding ERM parity realignments for twelve years from 1987 to the start of EMU, despite the considerable economic and political difficulties in doing so, reflects an important strength of the *dirigiste* tradition. In the 1980s and 1990s both the neo-Gaullists and the Socialists rejected many elements of *dirigisme*. At the same time electoral constraints— the public sanctioning of perceived excessive liberalism—forced both parties to continue to emphasize state-led action. Active state responses to the challenges of 'modernization', particularly in social and employment policies, and the political difficulties of managing the privatization of the public services demonstrate the institutionally embedded ideas that make French responses to the constraints of the Euro-Zone unique. Radical critiques of capitalist society remained very much embedded in the left wing of the Socialist Party and its coalition partners in Jospin's Plural Left government. Moreover, much of the electorate on both left and right continues to expect interventionist state responses. Even conservative liberals like Edouard Balladur, Edmond Alphandéry, and Alain Juppé made a spirited defence of French public services against European competition rules.

To justify reforms, leading Socialists have appealed to the Mendeiste left-wing tradition of economic modernization designed to challenge 'traditional centres of capitalist privilege'. From the early 1980s, social Catholics like Delors sought a 'Third Way' that would retain elements of *dirigisme* while accepting the predominance of market forces. What was common was the idea of 'reforming' capitalism in alliance with the technostructure of the French state. The idea of regulating and controlling markets in the context of what Jospin labelled a 'modern socialism' was an important element of Socialist Party discourse in dealing with the constraints of globalization (Jospin 1999; Marian 1999; Cambadélis 1999). Leading Socialists learnt from their defeat in the 1993 legislative elections that a continued *dirigiste* discourse and policy response was crucial to their electoral success by preventing the loss of support to other left-wing parties. In order to reinforce his government's left-wing credentials, Jospin also distanced himself from the 'social democracy' espoused in the Blair-Schröder Paper—attacked as 'social liberalism' by many in the French Left—and insisted on the plurality of European social democracy.

Officially, EMU was not to force the left into strategies that pushed 'modernization' in the direction of unacceptable liberalization. Jospin (1999) claimed that the *volontariste* state remains a crucial part of 'modern socialism' despite European and international constraints (also Marian 1999). The left accepts the central role of the market but insists that it must be regulated and 'governed' at both national and international levels. While interventionist strategies of the 'old' left are no longer valid, *volontarisme* remains crucial in three forms: what Jospin calls a 'strategic state' which encourages activity in areas of future growth, an 'investor state' which plays an active role in assuring the improvement of infrastructure, education, and research, and a 'facilitating state' which works to improve the quality of the operating environment of companies.

Jospin also placed emphasis on the construction of 'social democracy' at the European level as a means to counterbalance the monetary power of the ECB and to limit the worst effects of globalization. He stressed improved economic policy coordination in the Euro-Group, especially coordinated reflation, the development of European employment policy, the reinforcement of European social policy, and common European positions on international market regulation. If appropriately counterbalanced by EU-level economic policy coordination, EMU was a means to regain control of, and manage, the forces of globalization. This strategy reflects the strong negative connotation of globalization on the French left, demonstrated by the popularity of such books as *L'Horreur Économique* (1996) by Viviane Forrester. Equally, it illustrates the relatively positive perception of European integration in the Socialist Party established by President Mitterrand. In the 1990s EMU has been manipulated in the same way as the Single Market Programme from the mid-1980s: as a mechanism to make the economy more competitive while preserving the relatively generous social security system and working conditions (*les acquis sociaux*). The discourse of EMU as a means of reconciling the European social model to the new realities of globalization—notably in Germany—has been less present in France given the widespread hostility that 'globalization' inspires.

However, Jospin's Socialist-led government from 1997 placed clear boundaries around this *dirigiste* reflex. The brief return of neo-Keynesianism under Oskar Lafontaine in Germany was not matched intellectually in France. The Socialist Finance Minister, Dominique Strauss-Kahn, joined several Lafontaine initiatives calling for more European-led activism on growth and employment. Also, the two ministers issued a joint statement praising the drop in French and German intervention rates on 3 December 1998, from 3.3 per cent to 3 per cent in France. Their attempt to launch joint initiatives was apparent in their article in *Le Monde* on 15 January 1999. However, Strauss-Kahn refused to join Lafontaine's attack on ECB monetary policy-making.

At the international level and in business and financial sector forums in France, Strauss-Kahn was particularly active in promoting his government's modernizing credentials. He was frequently praised for his ability to present very different messages at different forums. During the twelfth anniversary meeting of the London-based Centre for Economic Policy Research (CEPR) in November 1998, he equated 'modern socialism' with 'modernization' and, in particular, 'sound' money and finance. He argued that there was nothing socialist about high deficits and debt (Strauss-Kahn 1998). Though his domestic public and party political speeches were decidedly more *volontariste* in rhetoric, the Jospin government accepted the need for continued 'modernization' in the face of increased competition in the Euro-Zone and globalization. It privatized more state assets than all previous conservative governments combined and refused to intervene in highly politicized factory closures—the Renault plant in Vilvorde, Belgium, in 1997—and massive lay-offs—Michelin in 1999—despite considerable pressure from coalition partners and trade unions. In consequence, the government was exposed to accusations that it had accepted the dominant conservative liberalism in economic policy-making and allowed an excessive Anglo-American style liberalization. In contrast, it had used a 'virtual' activism in EU and domestic social and employment policies in order to legitimize modernization (Desportes and Mauduit 1999).

Monetary Power Interests

From the creation of the European Coal and Steel Community, European integration—and the loss, restriction, and sharing of state powers—has been supported to the extent that it serves French economic interests, promotes French leadership in the European Community, and reinforces European power in relation to the United States. These preoccupations reflect long-standing French *Realpolitik*, discourse, and identity on European matters (Dyson 1999*d*); Dyson and Featherstone 1999; Howarth 2001). The establishment of the EMS was seen as a way to limit the dominant power of the Bundesbank and share the costs of monetary stability. The move to EMU was a response to failed French efforts to persuade the Germans to create a more symmetric EMS. EMU was thus embraced as a way to share monetary power with the Bundesbank and adopt interest-rate policies which corresponded more closely to French economic preferences. In the period following German reunification, the containment of growing German economic and political power in the EU framework became a—if not *the*—major public justification for EMU. The high interest rates and speculative attacks on the French franc of the 1990s were presented as additional reasons to move to EMU. The expanded use of the European Currency Unit (ECU) and the euro was viewed as a means to challenge the supremacy of both the D-Mark and the US dollar. For this reason, French negotiators sought a more powerful ECB from the start of stage two of EMU, empowered to promote the ECU. In 1998 French monetary power preoccupations were manifested in the dispute over the appointment of the first ECB president.

EMU and French State Reform

In addition to 'weak' and 'strong' Europeanization, the effects of EMU can be examined in terms of three of the four state responses listed by Radaelli (2000): accommodation, transformation, and inertia. There has been no retrenchment in France to date, due principally to the strong, albeit often not apparent, political commitment to EMU and to the relatively strong economic growth since 1997. Strong growth has made respect for the Stability and Growth Pact more politically manageable. The possibility of retrenchment was strongest between 1992 and 1996, when record high interest rates, sluggish economic growth, and rising unemployment, combined with republican and nationalist opposition to the loss of monetary power, made French support for EMU problematic. Opposition to EMU in France was more widespread than in the majority of the EU member states. Substantial sections of nearly all parties were opposed, with opposition increasing towards the extremes and especially within the more educationally and socio-economically disadvantaged groups (Howarth 2001). Much of this opposition owed less to the goal of EMU itself than to the perceived negative economic implications of EMS asymmetry and the EMU convergence criteria at the time. None the less, throughout this period, polls showed that a majority of French voters supported the core elements of EMU, and, unlike in some countries, the mainstream French press was on the whole supportive of EMU (Balleix-Banerjee 1999). The normally acquiescent business community began to turn against the ERM constraint from 1992, although the CNPF—the leading peak association of large-scale companies—remained officially silent on the matter and continued to support EMU (Aeschimann and Riché 1996).

No political party collapsed over the issue of monetary integration, despite the strong opposition of Eurosceptics in the Gaullist Rally for the Republic (RPR), including the large majority of the party's National Assembly deputies and leading members Philippe Séguin and Charles Pasqua. In 1999 Pasqua led a split from the RPR following the success of his Eurosceptic list, with Philippe de Villiers, in the European Parliamentary elections (Howarth 2000). Ostensibly, this split was due to his removal from the party after his refusal to accept the ratification of the Amsterdam Treaty. But long-standing opposition to EMU was a contributing factor. It remains to be seen if Pasqua's new Eurosceptic Gaullist party, the Rally for the French People (RPF), will remain a permanent element of the French party system and what impact it will have on the right.

The various French attempts to qualify the imposition of 'sound' money policies and technocratic control, outlined below, reflect French government efforts to prevent retrenchment. With the drop in interest rates from 1996, demands for withdrawal from the ERM and for the pursuit of a more expansionist economic policy gradually declined. Public opinion also warmed substantially to EMU. The threat of retrenchment created by the election victory of the Plural Left in 1997 proved to be only temporary—see below.

The element of accommodation to EMU was apparent in the 'sound' money policies that French governments had already successfully maintained and, during the Maastricht negotiations about EMU, in the perception that France would have little trouble respecting the convergence criteria. After German reunification, and with the sluggish economic growth of the early to mid-1990s, EMU became more closely associated with lowering interest rates, a French preoccupation from the early 1980s. As mentioned above, EMU was also compatible with traditional French *Realpolitik*, discourse, and identity on EU matters.

The start of stage three corresponded with a period of relatively strong economic growth in France, which helped reinforce the legitimacy of EMU as demonstrated in the very favourable opinion polls. France was reaping the rewards of a long period of domestic adjustment that started in the late 1970s and was reinforced by the success in avoiding devaluation of the franc from

1987 onwards. The strong trade surplus created by the policy of 'competitive dis-inflation' continued into the Euro-Zone, despite the strong rise in domestic consumption. A substantial fall in German and French short-term interest rates between 1995 and early 1997, in the period immediately before stage three, and during the first half of 1999 gave a much needed push to domestic consumption and investment. The substantial decline of the euro in relation to the dollar and the yen also suited French preferences. Throughout the 1990s, French governments argued that European currencies were overvalued in relation to the dollar. In a November 1996 article in the French weekly *L'Express*, former President Giscard d'Estaing, one of France's leading pro-ponents of EMU, called for a unilateral devaluation of the franc in the ERM. He justified it by the overvaluation of European currencies in relation to the dollar and the German refusal to lower interest rates to allow a devaluation of the D-Mark. The Plural Left established a lower exchange rate with the dollar and the yen as one of its four conditions for continuing with EMU. French calls for European politicians to avoid expressing views in favour of a weak euro, notably Gerhard Schröder, should *not* be seen as a reflection of the Jospin government's preoccupation with the slide of the European currency (*Le Monde* 2000). The gradual rise in European interest rates from November 1999 also suited French economic interests. Growth was strong in 1999 and 2000, while the economy had spare capacity well into 2000. A tighter but still accommodating monetary stance favoured French requirements. Germany, which was at an earlier stage in the cycle, preferred the lower rates. Reflecting the monetary power motives that drove French policy on EMU, the rate rise was seen as a manifestation of Germany's reduced influence in EMU—widely commented on in the French press—compared with its previous predominance in the ERM.

Adjusting to Independent Monetary Authority

The early benign economic impact of the Euro-Zone helped to legitimize the highly controversial transformation—'strong' Europeanization—that EMU imposed on France, notably central bank independence. Administrative and political opposition to independence was rooted in four factors (Howarth 1999a): the republican tradition, notably the indivisibility of French political authority; the perception of the appropriate link between monetary and economic policies; the belief that low inflationary policies do not require independent central banks; and the institutional power interests of the French Treasury. This opposition fed wider public concern about rule by 'technocrats' and democratic accountability.

Compared with other central banks, the Bank of France was normally considered to be one of the more 'dependent', with monetary power concentrated in the Finance Ministry (Goodman 1992). In the post-war period, the Bank had made repeated demands for increased autonomy. However, political and Treasury opposition to greater autonomy had been too great. The conservative liberal admiration of the 'German model' did not extend to support for central bank independence. On the left, autonomy was associated with a pre-war privileging of private interests, deflation, and inadequate investment. None the less, prior to the Maastricht Treaty the ERM, the stable franc policy, and financial market liberalization had already promoted a shift of relative power from the Treasury to the Bank of France, notably because of the increased importance of interest-rate policy on which the Bank had the greater expertise (Mamou 1987; Dyson, Featherstone, and Michaelopoulos 1994; Dyson 1997). The German insistence on the privileged position of the EU central bank governors in the negotiations on EMU also reinforced the position of the Bank in relation to the Treasury.

The rapid move to independence of the Bank in 1994—the start of stage two of EMU—was justified as building confidence in the franc in the context of record levels of speculation, not the desirability of independence per se. The intensity of the 1993 debate on the bill granting independence, opposed essentially by the same politicians who opposed EMU, and the necessary constitutional change—which required a special majority of three-fifths of both legislative chambers meeting at Versailles—demonstrated the unlikelihood that independence could have been achieved without EMU. The legislation on independence was initially blocked by the French Constitutional Council on the grounds that, under the constitution of the Fifth Republic, a government could not delegate responsibility for the conduct of monetary policy to an independent body.

Article 1 of the bill also attempted to meet republican objections to the ban on 'soliciting or accepting' outside instructions on the conduct of monetary policy by asserting that monetary policy must operate 'in the framework of the government's general economic policy'. The move to independence also provided the opportunity to transfer full power over banking supervision to the Bank of France, opposed by the Treasury and traditionally by much of the political class. However, this move was seen as a crucial in rebuilding confidence in banking supervision after the Crédit Lyonnais scandal. This scandal demonstrated the difficulty of maintaining effective Treasury control given the cosy networks of the Financial Inspectorate.

Independence and EMU transformed the role of the Bank of France in domestic policy-making. Governor Jacques de Larosière, former head of the

IMF, played a crucial role in the discussions on EMU leading to Maastricht both as a credible interlocutor of the Bundesbank and by his efforts, using a very active and public campaign, to convince Mitterrand and others of the need to accept German demands on independence. Bank of France governors had previously been known for their criticism of government policy, especially during the Fourth Republic. However, most demonstrated caution when commenting on government policy-making. Following independence, the Bank had to accommodate itself to a more active and public role in promoting 'stability' culture in France. Jean-Claude Trichet, the first governor of the independent Bank of France, made several thinly veiled attacks on presidential and government economic and monetary policy statements and economic policy decisions which appeared to menace the pursuit of 'sound' money policies, the move to EMU, and respect for the Stability and Growth Pact (Aeschimann and Riché 1996; Milesi 1998).

The process of appointment of the Bank's Monetary Policy Committee members created the possibility of strongly divergent perspectives on monetary policy-making and a less orthodox Bank leadership than that of the Bundesbank and, paradoxically, the pre-independence Bank. The appointment of six of the nine external members for staggered nine-year terms is shared between the presidents of the National Assembly, the Senate, and the Economic and Social Council. The other three, the governor and deputy governors, are appointed for periods of six years. By early 1997, a majority of the Committee—five of the six externally appointed members—were known for their anti-EMS credentials and opposition to the excessively high interest rates necessary to keep the franc in the ERM. The leading neo-Gaullist Eurosceptic, Phillipe Séguin, as president of the National Assembly nominated Jean-René Bernard and Pierre Guillen, appointed 3 January 1997. The latter, a former president of the metal-workers' federation, had actively opposed the Maastricht Treaty. This anti-EMS majority battled unsuccessfully for a rapid drop in French rates. In November 1996, two of the externally appointed members publicly expressed their disapproval of the EMU convergence criteria and argued in favour of an additional criterion emphasizing employment levels (*Le Monde* 1996a, b). Thus, the governing board of the independent Bank of France itself contributed to qualifying the emphasis placed on 'sound' money policies which had been established as its sole official objective in the 1993 statute. Paradoxically, in doing so, it may have reinforced the independent Bank's legitimacy on the left.

Bank of France independence also involved a shift in government discourse on monetary policy. In the context of strong domestic political pressures to stimulate economic growth, there was a strong temptation to use the Bank, and notably Trichet, as a scapegoat for the high interest rates in the EMS. Such scapegoating was highly problematic given the Bank's fragile legitimacy and public support, unlike its German counterpart. Leading Euro-sceptics and opposition politicians frequently attacked Trichet, whose name unfortunately approximates the French word 'to cheat' (*tricher*). More problematic were the attacks by President Jacques Chirac and the government of Alain Juppé. In the context of continued doubt about French willingness to maintain high interest rates and commitment to EMU, such attacks prompted speculation against the franc. Thinly veiled personal attacks against Trichet threatened to undermine his professional credibility and public acceptance of independence. Thus on 14 July 1995, in a televized interview, Chirac implicitly, but very clearly, took Trichet to task on two matters: high interest rates and the laxity of banking supervision in the late 1980s and early 1990s when Trichet was head of the Treasury. The Jospin government resisted criticizing the ECB or diverging in any way from public support for a strong euro. In part, this stance reflected policy learning. The long experience of foreign-exchange speculation made French governments, particularly Socialist-led ones, highly sensitive to the need for caution when discussing monetary policies. The risk of incurring the sanction of Euro-Zone partner governments also imposed greater caution. More importantly, the difficult economic and political conditions of the 1992–7 period had been lifted and were unlikely to be recreated in the near future.

The French Treasury had to accommodate itself to a very different kind of policy-making role. The loss of control over monetary policy and banking supervision were only two elements of the gradual decline of Treasury power. Other elements included financial market liberalization, privatization, and European competition rules. However, the Treasury regained influence in domestic policy-making, consequent on reinforced European coordination of economic policies in the Euro-Group and the Cologne process and on the medium-term stabilization plans which have largely corresponded to conservative liberal reform priorities. The Treasury remains very much the centre of economic intelligence in France. Although the Bank of France has increased its capacities in this field, it still depends on Treasury information in several areas, notably economic statistics and forecasting information. Treasury power was reasserted as the privileged partner in the Franco-German Economic Council, created in November 1987, and, alongside the Bank of France, in the Economic and Financial Committee—the rebaptized Monetary Committee—whose first head was Jean Lemierre, a former Treasury director and Financial Inspector. The appointment of former Treasury director and Financial Inspector Christian Noyer as ECB Vice-President, and thus member of both the executive board and the governing council, created a vital link between the French Treasury, the French financial elite, and the ECB. Noyer's appointment, although acceptable according to the ECB statute given his experience in the area of monetary policy, was unusual. He was the only member of the ECB governing council with no direct professional or academic experience in central banking.

Policy Regime Reform

Both transformation and inertia have been apparent in the different policy regimes where governments have sought to introduce reforms. The framework of monetary and financial discipline created by the EMS and EMU has been an explicitly manipulated driving force behind financial market liberalization as well as budgetary, fiscal, welfare-state, administrative, and labour-market reforms. This connection was made most prominently in the 1994 Minc Report, the most comprehensive package of reform recommendations to date. EMU as 'weak' Europeanization has been used by governments as a more politically acceptable way of 'internalizing' external economic imperatives represented by globalization. EMU as a justification for reform was presented as the central message of Chirac's public U-turn on economic policy on 26 October 1995, the Juppé Plan of the following November, and the shift in the Jospin government's budget policy in summer 1997.

EMU as a justification for reform has, however, run up against competing values. Ideologically inspired political opposition to reforms combined with trade-union opposition to modifications to social security regimes and to privatized public services which disadvantage public-sector employees. The result was some degree of inertia. Slower than expected change was due less to domestic institutional veto players than to the lack of political will to push reforms. The political difficulties of reform were manifested in the widespread strikes and public demonstrations of December 1995 and the frequent strikes and demonstrations in affected sectors. Public administration staff cuts—the non-replacement of retiring staff—have been recommended in diverse reports but consistently avoided by governments. In April 2000, Jospin sacrificed his Minister of Finance, Christian Sautter, and cancelled cuts in the number of tax officers which had sparked nationwide strikes. The aim of the cuts had been to set a precedent for other ministries. The French public-sector deficit remains one of the largest in the Euro-Zone, and there is peer-group pressure on France to make more sustainable cuts to public spending. With presidential and legislative elections in 2002, the Jospin government was unwilling to engage in further cuts that would enable it to meet the Stability Pact's aim of a budget surplus during a period of relatively strong economic growth. French public-sector debt hovers very close to the 60 per cent criterion, which makes more substantial cuts necessary after the 2002 elections.

Careful political management, increased emphasis on negotiation and good relations with trade-union leaders, and gradualism have become core elements of government reform strategies (Marsh 1999). The public reaction to the Juppé Plan of November 1995 demonstrated the dangers of pushing through ambitious reforms without adequate consultation and supportive coalitions (Howarth 1999b). The presence of Communist, Green, and left-wing Socialist parties in the Plural Left government made the management of reform particularly hazardous but has equally helped to contain opposition (Cambadélis 1999). Jospin placed considerable emphasis on open debate, although coalition partners increasingly complained that this debate was principally a technique to push through reforms that they found unaccept-able. In this context, resort to a government audit in 1997 was necessary to justify continued government spending cuts to meet the 3 per cent criterion. The Plural Left coalition had promised to stop these cuts.

Jospin also created the Council for Economic Analysis (CAE), attached to his office. This group consists of 38 academic economists, appointed by the Prime Minister, who meet once a month to discuss matters chosen by him or other ministers in advance. It was presided over by either Jospin himself or Pierre-Alain Muet, a leading French academic economist and member of his support staff (*cabinet*). The stated purpose of the CAE is to provide an opportunity for open debate on the major economic and social questions of the day prior to government decision-making. Its members produce reports requested by ministers, and these reports reflect, rather than suppress, the diversity of views. The CAE is intended to present a public challenge to the perceived excessively technocratic Treasury control over economic policy (interviews with CAE members; Victor 1999: 427). It plays the role of legit-imizer of controversial economic policy decisions and a means to contain the opposition of left-wing academic economists. More generally, the creation of the CAE demonstrates an attempt to respond to those who question the legitimacy of the highly technocratic EMU and the economic constraints that it imposes by demonstrating the continued capacity of the government to take an activist line on economic and social policies.

Financial Market Liberalization

Besides monetary policy, the financial market liberalization of 1984–8 was the first major French policy regime reform linked explicitly to the operation of the EMS. It was inspired more by Anglo-American neo-liberalism, which shaped the thinking of American-educated members in the Socialist Finance

Minister Pierre Bérégovoy's *cabinet*, than by 'sound' money ideas imported through the operation of the EMS. Still, the decision to maintain the franc in the ERM made financial liberalization both more acceptable and likely because French policy had to focus on market-imposed interest rates more closely. The continued participation of the franc in the ERM made the pursuit of low inflationary policies more necessary, whereas the provision of state-allocated credit in the *circuits de trésor* was inherently inflationary. The challenge of controlling inflation provided a useful logic that helped overcome the institutionally-rooted reluctance to accept liberalization in the Treasury, which had blocked previous reform attempts (Loriaux 1991).

Financial market liberalization in turn reinforced the ERM constraint and increased the logic of moving to EMU. The limited development of French institutional investors resulted in the dramatic growth of French dependence on foreign-held, largely American, debt, which amounted to roughly 40 per cent of total debt by the early 1990s, far higher than any of the larger EU member states. In consequence, French governments had to be particularly cautious about the perceived strength of the franc and attractiveness of French interest rates (Reland 1998). Liberalization also created new controlling interests—American pension funds—which increased the importance of shareholder value and discouraged interventionist strategies that were inconsistent with this value.

The need to maintain high real interest rates in the context of the asymmetric operation of the ERM encouraged the French to pursue its reform and led to the Basle-Nyborg accords on improved interest-rate policy coordination. The German refusal to accept further obligations that would make the EMS a more symmetric system encouraged French interest in more substantial reform. Increased reliance on foreign capital and the desire to build Paris as a financial centre also made capital controls imposed at the national level increasingly problematic. In consequence, France had less to lose from capital liberalization, which the German government had established as a precondition for discussions on EMU. None the less, French governments remained wary of the impact of liberalization on exchange-rate stability, given the persistent speculation against the franc well into 1987. Ironically, President Mitterrand had to impose capital market liberalization on Bérégovoy, the father of financial market reform, in the interests of making progress on EMU (Howarth 2001).

Budget Cutting

The 'sound' money policies pursued in the EMS constraint increased pressure on governments to keep public spending under control. Following financial market liberalization, budgetary restraint was deemed necessary to lower French interest rates. The justification of budget cutting involved a reinvention of discourse appealing to the preoccupation with unemployment. Dramatically reversing the reflationist discourse and criticism of the deficit convergence criterion of his presidential campaign, in October 1995 President Chirac explicitly argued that rapid cuts were necessary to ensure the move to EMU in 1999.

Budgeting cuts provide a major example of 'weak' Europeanization. EMU, German insistence on respecting the 3 per cent deficit criterion, and the Stability and Growth Pact placed budget reform high on the agenda. However, even without the external constraint, budget cutting would have been a priority because of record high tax levels and a decreased margin of manoeuvre in budgetary policy. A growing percentage of the total budget consisted of allocated expenditure. In 1993 the budget deficit reached an unprecedented 6 per cent of GDP. In his October 1995 interview, Chirac insisted that low budget deficits were a precondition of job creation, a core argument in conservative liberal discourse.

Governments were forced to examine possible cuts in government and social security spending, a tighter control over local government budgets, and also, more controversially, structural reforms. The ability of the Jospin government to meet the fiscal criteria to ensure that it was an uncontroversial candidate in 1998 depended largely on privatizations and transfers of French Télécom profits. More problematically, in 1996 the Juppé government had assumed state control over existing France Télécom pensions. In consequence, France Télécom transferred 37.5 billion francs to the state budget, which diminished the deficit by 0.45 per cent. Though vital to prove continued French commitment to EMU, it imposed a heavy financial burden on future governments.

Barring substantially higher economic growth rates, further structural reforms are required in order to respect the Stability Pact in the medium term. Budget cuts largely affected the Ministry of Defence. With one of the largest public administrations in Europe in terms of percentage of total jobs, cuts to staff numbers have been widely recommended. The Picq report of 1994 established the goal of replacing only one in three civil servants retiring from the administration in order to reduce the total number of staff to the 1980 level: a 15 per cent cut. However, in the context of record high levels of unemployment, and the strong and militant trade-union presence in the public sector, led by *Force Ouvrière*, cuts were postponed by the Balladur and Juppé governments. The need to start making politically difficult cutbacks, combined with an anticipated economic downturn, was one major consideration that led President Chirac to dissolve the National Assembly and hold the legislative elections in 1997, a year early. Just prior to these elections the UDF Minister of Finance Jean Arthuis promised to reduce personnel (*Le Monde* 1997). However, the Plural Left government of Jospin continued to delay total staff cuts. It used staff replacement as a political device to demonstrate its commitment to job creation in the public sector, allied with temporary youth employment schemes.

Improved budget management also came on to the agenda as another example of weak Europeanization. Bolstered by the Stability and Growth Pact's commitment to budget surpluses during periods of economic growth, Arthuis (1998) called for changes to the budget ordinance of 1959 in order to prohibit a deficit on current expenditure. Government deficit financing would be strictly limited to capital expenditure. This move would have been in keeping with the emphasis that Arthuis as finance minister had placed on the distinction between current expenditure and capital expenditure in preparing the 1997 budget. While this reform proposal had some support in conservative liberal circles, it is unlikely that it would have been proposed in the absence of the Stability and Growth Pact. There have also been growing calls, led by two former finance ministers, Arthuis (1998) and Alphandéry (2000), to increase parliamentary control over the budget. They sought increased powers and resources for the finance committees of the Assembly and the Senate, in particular to resist more effectively the adoption of supplementary credits by decree. But the well-entrenched opposition to the extension of parliamentary control over the executive prevented any significant early moves in this direction, demonstrating the clear limits of weak Europeanization.

The Juppé government was not, however, opposed to the extension of parliamentary control over the level of overall social security expenditure. This increased control involved a major challenge to the powers of the social partners—employers' representatives and trade unions—which previously had the final say over budgets in the mutual fund administrative councils. Opposition to this element of the Juppé Plan was one of the factors that sparked off the December 1995 demonstrations. None the less, the government proceeded with the necessary modification of the Constitution on 19 February 1996 and the legal process—a decree of 24 April 1996—to enable the reform. Decrees were also adopted to reform hospital administration and to control more effectively medical practitioners' standard consulting fees. Additionally, the Juppé government sought, unsuccessfully, to modify the pension regimes for public-sector employees in order to increase the number of contribution years to that of the private sector: from 36.5 to 39 years. Initial moves in this direction in November 1995, affecting train and metro conductors, were rescinded to end nationwide strikes.

Before the 1997 elections the Plural Left promised an end to budget cuts. But the Jospin government rapidly abandoned promises to run an activist budgetary policy and continued with cuts in government expenditure, notably in defence. None the less, the Jospin government maintained the rhetoric of margin of manoeuvre—vital for maintaining legitimacy on the left— promising an increase of 1 per cent in government expenditure, whereas the Juppé government had sought an expenditure freeze. In December 1998, the Jospin government announced its annual medium-term stabilization plan for a sustainable drop in the public deficit. The increase in government expenditure was to be only 1 per cent over 2000–2, or 0.3 per cent per year—a reinterpretation of the previous promise—lowering the public deficit from 2.3 per cent in 1999 to 0.8–1.2 per cent in 2002, depending on growth rates. From the start of 1999, the Jospin government announced that for the 2000 budget there would be no spending increase, demonstrating its decision to defer any increase to the lead-up to the 2002 presidential and legislative elections. The Socialist-led government recognized the unpopularity of cutbacks in its own constituency, much of which works in the public sector. Finance minister Christian Sautter failed in his efforts to decrease the excessively large number of tax administrators due to the unwillingness of the Socialist-led govern- ment to push through cuts in the face of stubborn trade-union opposition. He was replaced by the more politically astute former Prime Minister Laurent Fabius, who put all government cutbacks on hold. Relatively strong eco- nomic growth during the first three and a half years of office enabled the Jospin government to delay more substantial, sustainable cuts until after the 2002 elections.

The debate in early 2000 on the unexpectedly large budget revenue—the 'cagnotte'—due to stronger than predicted economic growth was revealing. The use of the cagnotte became a symbol of the Jospin government's priorities. Rather than using it to further reduce the deficit, Jospin was constrained by the Socialist left and the Plural Left coalition partners to increase government spending. Likewise, the government sought to prioritize income tax cuts— announced on 31 August 2000—for the first time in 15 years; French taxes are among the highest in the Western world. Tax reductions benefited all income groups, in particular the least well off, as well as companies, with the aim of stimulating further growth in order to lower the deficit.

Labour-Market Reform

The restriction of interest-rate and exchange-rate policies in the EMS and their loss with EMU, along with the increased wage competition in the Euro-Zone, placed increased pressure on French governments to modify labour-market policies and increase wage flexibility: another example of weak Europeanization. Reform took place in the context of high structural unemployment due to the high minimum wage and high social security charges imposed on French companies. It was constrained by the political diffi- culties of lowering the minimum wage—traditionally, new French presidents and governments raise the minimum wage above the rate of inflation— and by the lack of centralized wage bargaining which makes negotiated solu- tions more difficult. The attempt by the Balladur government in 1994 to introduce a lower minimum wage for young people met with stubborn student resistance and was dropped.

The combination of these factors led to two major policy responses to the problem of labour-market inflexibility. French governments relaxed rules on hiring by allowing greater scope for the creation of work of a limited duration—*contrats de durée déterminée*—and for part-time work. The Jospin government also created the possibility for greater flexibility in the context of the 35-hour week. It allowed companies, in collective bargaining about the implementation of the 35-hour week, the possibility of freezing wages and spreading the 35-hour week over the period of a year.

French Strategy to Modify 'Sound' Money Policies and Legitimize the EMU Constraint

At the European level, French governments of both left and right con- sistently manifested a desire to modify two core elements of the EMU project—the prevalence of 'sound' money policies and technocratic control over monetary policy—with more interventionist EU strategies. Despite the increased influence of conservative liberalism and the determined pursuit of low-inflation policies, this desire was reflected in long-standing French efforts to persuade the Germans to accept a more balanced economic conver- gence and to increase the obligations of strong currency states—Germany— in the EMS to decrease its deflationary impact. To reiterate, French interest in monetary cooperation and integration was based on accepting the need for an external constraint; but, equally, French governments opposed an excessively rigorous constraint. Since the early 1980s, French governments also actively pursued job-creating reflationary EU strategies. Notable was Chirac's success at the June 1995 Cannes European Council in persuading his European partners to accept a massive EU-wide infrastructural development programme—never put into effect. The continued attempts to modify and counterbalance 'sound' money policies were demonstrated by proposals to modify the EMU convergence criteria, to create an EU 'economic government'—including improved economic policy coordination and a strengthened employment policy—and to develop EU social policy. French governments consistently sought to modify the economic policy-making constraints imposed by EMU while accepting the EMU goal itself. They actively attempted to make the EMU semi-sovereignty game 'stickier' in order to satisfy French policy preferences whose fulfilment was excessively restricted at the domestic level. These government efforts should also be seen as an important legitimizing exercise on behalf of the EMU constraint and 'modernizing' reforms, appealing to the strong interventionist tradition in France: part of what Dyson (1999d) labelled the 'craftsmanship of discourse'.

National politicians, both in government and in opposition, had difficulty accepting the idea, central to 'sound' money policies, of the neutrality of monetary policy in terms of employment. Following German reunification, the unique situation of low French inflation combined with record high real interest rates to maintain the franc in the ERM did not help this process of acceptance. From 1991 to 1997, French governments were very critical of the Bundesbank and the Bank of France for their excessive caution in lowering interest rates. These criticisms tended to undermine the credibility of French monetary policy.

The modification of the convergence criteria, notably the 3 per cent deficit rule, was a consistent demand of French governments against the background of the economic difficulties of the mid-1990s, the dramatic rise in public-sector deficits, and the political difficulties associated with necessary cuts. The government had accepted the convergence criteria in 1990–1, France being one of the few states that could respect them at the time. French negotiators proposed the 3 per cent deficit criterion rule whereas the German Ministry of Finance had originally proposed a more relaxed calculation of deficits.

The Juppé and Jospin governments accepted the proposal for a Stability Pact, principally as a means to meet the demands of the Kohl government and to counter strong opposition to EMU in Germany. However, they sought to render it as innocuous as possible (Milesi 1998; Schor 1999). The Juppé government wanted to avoid the automaticity of fines sought by the Germans, giving priority to politically determined fines, in ECOFIN. After prolonged discussions, the French accepted automaticity. They then sought derogation in the event of economic recession. However, again the Germans largely prevailed: derogation was guaranteed in the unlikely event of recession beyond 2 per cent of GDP and politically determined in the event of a shrinking GDP between 0.75 per cent and 2 per cent of GDP. The Germans also succeeded in imposing the goal of budget surplus during periods of economic growth. The addition of the word 'Growth' to the Stability Pact was a French demand to ease the acceptance of the pact at home.

The Plural Left had promised the rejection of the Stability and Growth Pact as part of their wider push for a *'euro-social'*. To avoid a crisis that would put EMU at risk, the Jospin government reached a compromise with the Germans at the Amsterdam European Council in June 1997. This compromise involved the symbolic modification of the resolution on the pact by a general and vague resolution on growth and employment, topped by a common pre-amble which ostensibly granted equal weight to both. The Amsterdam resolution on 'growth and employment' included the 'urging'—no obligation was established—of the European Investment Bank (EIB) to increase its interventions in high-technology and small and medium-sized enterprise projects, as well as education, health, environment, and large infrastructure projects on the grounds that these tended to create jobs. In reality, this commitment did not amount to any real change. The EIB already took employment into account in its investment decisions, and there was no increased funding—which the Germans were quick to point out. However, a previously agreed EIB loan for small and medium-sized companies was announced at the Amsterdam summit and presented by the Jospin government as proof that the new employment policy had teeth. The Jospin government's efforts to ensure the participation of the Italians—another Plural Left demand—also reflected the desire to maintain a less rigorous Euro-Zone and limit German influence. French support for not penalizing Italy for its excessive deficit in 1999 reflected more relaxed attitudes to the application of the Stability and Growth Pact.

French preference for relaxing 'sound' money and technocratic control was reflected in constant demands for the establishment of a European 'economic government': a political counterweight to the ECB to improve economic policy coordination and establish an appropriate policy mix at the European level. Improved European economic policy coordination had been a French policy ambition from the oil crisis of 1973, normally with the aim of encouraging the Germans to reflate their economy—or lead an EC-wide reflation—or improved interest-rate policy coordination in the EMS, pursued in the Basle-Nyborg reforms of September 1987, to increase German responsibility for helping weaker currencies resist speculation. Pierre Bérégovoy first raised the need for a European economic government in 1988 to challenge the obvious predilections of the central bank governors meeting in the Delors Committee. In their draft treaty of January 1991 (Ministère de l'Économie, des Finances et du Budget 1991) French Treasury officials insisted:

Everywhere in the world, central banks in charge of monetary policy are in dialogue with the governments in charge of the rest of economic policy. Ignore the parallelism between economic and monetary matters . . . and this could lead to failure.

The draft treaty also proposed that the European Council, on the basis of ECOFIN reports, define the broad orientations for EMU and the economic policy of the Community. Within these orientations, ECOFIN would coordinate the policies of member states and make recommendations to individual governments while the ECB would manage European monetary policy. Bérégovoy insisted that the French draft treaty did not seek to challenge the independence of the ECB and the pursuit of the goal of price stability—which the Germans would have refused to accept (*Le Monde* 1991). French discomfort with having to accept unqualified central bank independence was reflected in the efforts by Socialist government politicians to avoid the issue during the 1992 Maastricht referendum campaign. On one significant occasion during the major televized debate on the Treaty in early September, President Mitterrand misleadingly claimed that elected officials would establish the economic policy framework for the formation of monetary policy: an interpretation of the Treaty inconsistent with its actual provisions (*Libération* 1992).

Likewise, French governments exaggerated the importance of subsequent developments at the EU level to the process of constructing an economic government. Thus the agreement at the December 1996 Dublin European Council to create a Euro-Council was presented by the Juppé government, and subsequently the Jospin government, as an important step towards economic government. Subsequently, it was downgraded to 'Euro-Group' given German opposition to the term 'Council' which wrongly suggested that the new body had legal powers. The new Economic and Financial Committee— the rebaptized Monetary Committee—was also presented as an element to reinforce the control of the Euro-Group over the economic framework in which monetary policy was made, and thus a step closer towards the creation of economic government (*Libération* 1999). Each reinforcement of economic policy coordination at the European level, including the Cologne Macroeconomic Dialogue, was seized on by the Jospin government as a victory of the French perspective. While some form of economic government is being created (see Chapter 2), the overriding goal of coordination has been to ensure the maintenance of price stability rather than the older French objective of stimulating economic growth.

As chair of ECOFIN during the French EU presidency of the second half of 2000, Fabius blamed the weakness of the euro on the lack of strong political leadership in the Euro-Zone, the absence of an EU equivalent to the American Secretary of the Treasury. In order to reinforce its arguments, the Jospin government created a group in the Planning Commission, chaired by the economist Robert Boyer, to provide a detailed plan of alternative scenarios for the reinforcement of strategic EU-level economic policy coordination and the construction of economic government (Boyer 1999). Boyer (1998) is a well-known critic of what he labels the 'political and institutional deficits of the euro'.

Economic government as expressed through the creation of a substantial EU employment policy was of particular importance for the Plural Left government as a reinforcement and legitimization of activist domestic employment policies and a modification of the Stability Pact. The Juppé government had accepted the German refusal to extend the EU policy remit to cover employment in the Amsterdam Treaty. Respecting campaign promises, Jospin reached a compromise with the Germans that involved the creation of the employment chapter, the resolution on growth and employment, and the formulation of a European employment strategy. As already noted, the resolution involved only vague objectives. The employment chapter involved no additional spending or obligatory measures but focused on information sharing, pilot projects, and benchmarking, as agreed at the Luxembourg and Cardiff jobs summits. French Socialist ministers consistently stressed, if not exaggerated, the significance of EU policy developments in this area (Howarth 1998).

The efforts of French governments to establish and then reinforce a European social policy from the mid-1980s can be seen as a French strategy to limit the competitive disadvantage, in the context of the single European market, created by expensive French social programmes and generous workers' rights, and by correspondingly high taxes and social charges on companies (Guyomarch, Machin, and Ritchie 1998). EMU reinforced this disadvantage by creating a new transparency in prices and costs. For Socialist governments, in particular, the EU social chapter has also been a legitimizing device to balance excessive emphasis on economic and monetary integration. French strategy was to establish a higher minimum European standard that acted as a buffer, protecting the French social security system from the competitive impact of globalization. In contrast, German and British governments sought to minimize European-level developments in this field. Overall, a lowest-common-denominator approach prevailed, challenging only states with the more basic standards—notably Britain. But even these limited developments were frequently presented to the domestic audience as victories for French governments. Tax harmonization has been another priority of French governments, anxious to challenge more competitive tax regimes that place French companies at a disadvantage and attract French capital.

Jospin's rallying cry, the core motif of his 'modern socialism', was 'modernizing' interventionism. As applied to domestic employment and social policies it meant 'yes to the market economy but no to the market society' ('*oui à l'économie du marché mais non à la société du marché*'). If the reinforcement of EU-level employment and social policies was a priority for his Plural Left government, domestic policy developments in these areas were of even greater importance. The legitimizing 'social democratic' element of Jospin government policy-making came principally in the guise of active intervention to create jobs and, in particular, jobs for young people. The Plural Left government promised to create 350,000 jobs in both the public and the private sectors. The targets were met thanks to the establishment of special low-paid and temporary contracts for young people in the public sector (*emplois-jeunes*) and improved economic growth in the private sector. The 35-hour week was an interventionist policy that did not contribute to the government budget deficit. It was presented very much in terms of social justice. However, faced with the need to increase labour-market flexibility and to lower unemployment, the government reneged on its promise that wages would not be affected. It allowed companies to freeze wages in the context of collective agreements with trade unions. Thus, as a legitimizing device the 35-hour week proved problematic.

The Plural Left government also placed considerable emphasis on social policy, although here rhetoric was not matched by large increases in spending. By 2001 the creation of 'universal health coverage' (Couverture Maladie Universelle, CMU) was the most significant social policy development. It financed the complementary health care of some 6 million poorest people. While this policy improved the left-wing credentials of the government, the organization of the payment for this programme demonstrates another underlying reform agenda that could transform the French social security system. The CMU's funding—a total of 9 billion francs—comes from the state, which contributes 1.7 billion francs, as well as from mutual funds and insurance companies. The government wanted to minimize the budgetary impact. Equally, the mutual funds sought to minimize contribution increases. Thus, private insurers took the opportunity to strengthen their position in the social security system, which could be a major market for them. This development should be seen in the context of cautious steps by Jospin to allow private insurers to cover extra complementary (*sur-complémetaires*) pension regimes, adopted in October 1998. Very controversial on the left, these initiatives seemed to represent a first step in the development of

Anglo-American-style pension funds, rendered more politically acceptable by 'socialist' frills: no fiscal advantages for higher-income earners and fund management by the 'social partners'.

The Jospin government's tax reform also displayed this Janus-like characteristic in the face of the growing pressures from the single European market and EMU to adopt a more competitive regime. On the one hand, the newly elected government adopted a series of tax measures designed to demonstrate its reformist left-wing credentials: a rise in the tax imposed on the most wealthy, a major increase of the CSG (*contribution sociale generalisée*) created to help cover the social security deficit, a slight increase in savings taxes, the progressive reduction of health-care contributions (*cotisations-maladie*), a temporary two-year increase in company tax, and the targeted drop of certain VAT rates to benefit low-income earners. The Jospin government argued that France had progressed far enough in the European race to lower taxes—even though French corporate tax rates remained among the highest in the EU. Notably, however, no new capital taxes were introduced, and few of the measures had a significant redistributive impact. At the same time, the government proceeded cautiously, despite considerable opposition on the left, with the lowering of the relatively high tax on company stock options. The Fabius income-tax cuts of 31 August 2000 benefited all income groups—although the CSG was cancelled for the lowest-income earners—as well as companies.

Conclusion

EMU as strong Europeanization involved reforms to the French state that most likely would not have been adopted given deep-seated domestic opposition—notably central bank independence and the management of domestic policy reforms through the medium-term stabilization plans. The operation of the EMS and EMU as weak, 'bottom-up' Europeanization helped French governments push through controversial domestic reforms. Monetary integration has been a self-imposed 'semi-sovereignty game', involving the 'framing' of several policy reforms in terms of improving the fitness of the French state and economy to cope with the combined challenges of EMU and the single European market. This approach was more politically acceptable than 'framing' reforms in terms of coping with globalization, given its widespread negative connotation in France as liberalism beyond the control of governments. In contrast, the EMS and EMU were presented as an extension of French state action and a reflection of French monetary power interests.

Europeanization has involved a redefinition of French state identity to embrace stabilization as emphasized by conservative liberals. However, this redefinition has been couched in terms of active state responses to the challenges of the single European market and globalization, in the areas of social and employment policies at the EU and domestic levels. It has also been bound up with the impressive ability of French governments to spread adjustment costs over more than a decade within the ERM constraint and to keep a politically tenuous and economically problematic EMU project on track. There may be different emphases placed on the role of the state by French governments of the right and the left, with the latter stressing more active state responses. Moreover, the constraints of European and global competition, reinforced by EMU, increasingly limit the scope of this interventionism. However, the degree of continuity is provided by the institutionally embedded *dirigiste* legacy and the domestic political difficulties involved in pushing through some reforms. In consequence, French responses to the constraints of the Euro-Zone remain unique despite the pressures to converge.

7

Germany and the Euro: Redefining EMU, Handling Paradox, and Managing Uncertainty and Contingency

Kenneth Dyson

This chapter begins by examining the complex discursive structure under-pinning and shaping German responses to EMU. It highlights how EMU came to be contested and the emergence of a new, complex, and tense domestic accommodation of EMU during the government of Gerhard Schröder. It then investigates the strategic behaviour of German policy-makers. This strategic behaviour is informed by the deeper inherited dis-cursive structure which is institutionally embedded. At the same time German strategic behaviour is a response to the new paradoxes consequent on the challenges, uncertainties, and contingencies with which EMU faces policy-makers. The changes in discursive structure outlined at the beginning are in turn shaped by these contextual changes. What emerges is a picture of complex, interactive changes in which discursive structure and the chal-lenges, uncertainty, and contingency associated with EMU emerge as power-ful, dialectically related factors in conditioning German responses.

EMU raises interesting questions about how it relates to the wider forces changing German policies and politics and about the role of discourse in mediating those changes. These forces have in substantial part been com-mon to other European states, notably globalization, the 'new' economy, and demographic developments. One force—German unification—has been specific to Germany and has been associated with a redefinition of Germany as a 'burdened' state less able to shoulder new external commitments. The domestic debate about *Standort Deutschland* predated German unification

This chapter was made possible by the British Academy's generosity in financing field research in Germany with one of its small grants. I would like to thank Alastair Cole, Stefan Collignon, Jürgen Stark, and Eirik Svindland for their comments on the first draft.

in 1990 (Dyson 1999a). However, by 1993 sharp, harsh 'de-industrialization' in the five new federal States, high unemployment consequent on low productivity and rising costs there, and huge fiscal transfers had given a new focus and impetus, and a specific German dimension, to problems of domestic policy reform. German unification—and the redefinition of Germany that went with it—acted as a new catalyst for domestic reforms.

What is interesting about the German case is the way in which a dominant domestic ideology of Ordo-liberalism conditioned and constrained the way in which key policy-makers responded to these forces for change. Specifically, before 1999 this ideology led policy-makers to construct Germany's problems as consequent on globalization, technological change, and unification and the rigidity of German goods, services, capital, and labour markets in the face of these challenges. They were viewed as creating an inexorable long-term logic of structural supply-side reforms and market liberalization (Bundesministerium für Wirtschaft 1998: 13–16). This logic challenged an outdated 'Rhineland' or 'managed' capitalism and its norms of consensus and co-operation in managing change. These norms, supported by an 'enabling' rather than 'liberalizing' state, were seen by Ordo-liberals as hostile to the flexibility and individual initiative required of the German economy.

This Ordo-liberal viewpoint both reflected and gained support from within the corporate sector. By 1995–6 the German corporate sector was legitimizing a wave of rationalization and direct investment abroad as making Germany 'fit for globalization' and ensuring that Germany was on 'the winning side'. Corporate pressures, channelled through the Federation of German Industry (BDI) and led by Daimler-Benz, Allianz, and Deutsche Bank, emboldened policy-makers in the Chancellor's Office and the Finance Ministry to adopt a new, tough approach to pushing through Ordo-liberal ideas of supply-side reform. The result was centrifugal forces that seemed to challenge the basis of the 'managed' capitalism model and to promise a more aggressive and conflictual climate of domestic policy making (Silvia 1999). Pressures for radical decentralization of wage flexibility to firm and plant level were reflected in threats of defection from the Federation of German Employers (BDA) which negotiated area-wide, encompassing collective contracts (*Flächentarifverträge*) with the trade unions. Tensions mounted between the BDI, which was most aggressive on globalization, and the other main peak economic associations, which had a stronger interest in the 'managed' capitalism model. The weakness and defensiveness of the German Trade Union Federation (DGB) was further exposed by the early collapse of the trade-union-sponsored Alliance for Jobs in March 1996 (Turner 1998). Globalization was associated with a newly assertive Ordo-liberalism. The industrial context was deep discontent with traditional collective bargaining arrangements among employers and support for subcontractual wages and working conditions from works councils in the East. The political context was the Kohl government' attempt to redefine itself as the champion of structural economic reforms and a 'reform blockade' (*Reformstau*) conducted by the opposition Social Democratic Party (SPD) under Oskar Lafontaine.

But, strikingly, Ordo-liberals were more cautious about attributing significance to EMU as a force for change. Their discourse focused on EMU as a force for structural reforms in other EU states and on the risk that EMU might add to Germany's problems rather than be a key part of the solution. This discourse was consistent with a preference for a 'controlled delay' over strict adherence to the Maastricht timetable. EMU's significance was really publicly recognized by Ordo-liberals only from 1998, once stage three was a fait accompli. It then began to be seen in more positive terms as a catalyst for necessary domestic structural reforms to labour markets, wages policy, and the budget. By institutionalizing fiscal and market discipline, and forcing German policy-makers to attend to the new realities, EMU promised to speed up the process of market liberalization.

As this chapter stresses, Ordo-liberalism remained dominant but was newly challenged on EMU. The New Keynesians around Lafontaine and—more significantly—the 'Rhineland' capitalists were quicker to recognize that EMU could be a force for change, for opening up what they viewed as a closed, conservative debate in Germany. One construction of EMU—the Ordo-liberal —gave way to contention and accommodation among three main constructions. Each attributed a different meaning to the euro. This contention was opened up with the election of a SPD/Green coalition government under Gerhard Schröder in September 1998. In this respect there were two parallel developments: the transition to stage three on 1 January 1999 and a new party political constellation in power. The change of power was itself a factor in shaping how EMU was constructed in Berlin.

But an examination of the discursive structure underpinning and shaping German responses to EMU tells us only part of the story. Another part is the strategic behaviour of German policy-makers in dealing with the paradoxes and uncertainties with which EMU faces them. Five paradoxes are striking:

(1) between export of the German model of economic stability and a new methodology of benchmarking best practice;
(2) between the Europeanization manifested in programmatic statements and the reticence about Europeanization in 'framing' and legitimizing particular reforms to the German public;

(3) between the fixed timetable for EMU and strict convergence;
(4) between the Bundesbank as the bank ruling the transition to stage three and the Bundesbank seeking a new role and structure to strengthen its position once EMU was in place; and
(5) between EMU and the 'managed' capitalism model.

Hence the transition to EMU threw up a whole complex of interrelated problems with which German politicians and officials had to grapple. Underlying all these problems were the new uncertainties created by EMU and the extent to which outcomes were contingent on many factors, outside the direct control of the German government. Economic growth was a key determinant of whether the fiscal criteria could be met and the timetable adhered to. Rising output and employment also facilitated structural economic reforms by the Schröder government. Another variable outside German control was the behaviour of other EU governments—especially France—in achieving fiscal performances that could be sold to the Bundesbank and the German public as consistent with a 'stability community'. A third variable was German public opinion and how German politicians chose to use it, whether for instance the SPD might be tempted to oppose the timetable for stage three and how the Bavarian Christian Social Union (CSU) responded to electoral threats from the extreme right. Public opinion also mattered in relation to the Ordo-liberal view that a strong euro required measures to strengthen political solidarity in the EU. German support for stronger Community institutions, like the European Parliament, was, however, vulnerable to erosion of the 'permissive' public consensus that had traditionally supported elite consensus on European unification. Hence a key theme is the management of uncertainty and contingency.

Economic Ideology and the Construction of EMU

Ordo-liberalism

Ordo-liberalism was the underlying economic ideology which gave direction to, informed, constrained, and legitimized German negotiating positions on EMU (Dyson and Featherstone 1999). It was a specifically German product, rooted in the lessons drawn from traumatic experience of two hyperinflations, the failure of the Weimar Republic and the Third Reich (Nicholls 1994). Its heroes were Ludwig Erhard, Walter Eucken, and Wilhelm Röpke; its victories, a post-war economic miracle and a strong and stable D-Mark; its leading combatant on EMU, Hans Tietmeyer and the Bundesbank; and its most unequivocal party political expression in the Free Democratic Party (FDP). The Bundesbank was Ordo-liberalism's institutional epicentre, and the strategic requirement to 'bind in' the Bundesbank in monetary and financial policy negotiations was a guarantee that Ordo-liberal ideas would dominate German policy on EMU (Dyson and Featherstone 1999). Support for Ordo-liberal ideas could be relied on from the Federal Economics Ministry, the Federal Finance Ministry, and the Council of Economic Advisers (*Sachverständigenrat*). It dominated among academic economists and within most of the six main economics research institutes. The history of EMU is one of its continuing impact and resilience in the face of challenge. Its continuing centrality within post-war German economic policy discourse means that the neo-liberal ideas of international bodies like the IMF and the OECD found a ready reception, with Ordo-liberals calling for market liberalization of goods, services, capital, and labour markets. Hence globalization as neo-liberalism did not so much change the terms of German discourse as strengthen and reinvigorate Ordo-liberalism.

Ordo-liberalism was influential in three ways in shaping how German policy-makers constructed EMU. First, it argued that EMU must be a 'stability community' based on economic convergence if it was to be sustainable. This meant Europeanizing the German model of economic stability: through absolute priority to the principle of open, competitive markets; an independent ECB pledged exclusively to price stability; rules on 'no bail outs' and proscribing monetary financing of budget deficits; and clear, strict, and automatically enforceable rules on fiscal discipline. The stress was on strict interpretation of the convergence criteria in the Maastricht Treaty. It was also on rules in the Stability and Growth Pact to ensure both a balanced or surplus fiscal position, to comply at all times with the 3 per cent ceiling for the public deficit, and a quasi-automatic triggering mechanism for sanctions.

Second, Ordo-liberalism argued against 'explicit', formal policy coordination at the EU level. Specific policy problems were to be clearly assigned to different actors who were responsible for solving them. Growth and employment were not seen as the responsibility of the ECB. Equally, governments and social partners were not to interfere in how the ECB discharged its responsibility for price stability. Ordo-liberals were on the whole unhappy with debates about EU-level economic policy 'coordination', preferring 'dialogue' and 'cooperation'. Their particular suspicion was directed at French talk of an 'economic government', at references to a more active exchange rate policy for the euro, and at references to the Euro 'Council' rather than Euro 'Group', implying that it had a formal status as a decision-making body. They were seen as devices for undermining the independence of the ECB.

Hence Ordo-liberals emphasized the principle of subsidiarity in economic policy, the individual responsibility of member states for growth and employment, and the competition of national policies (Bundesministerium für Wirtschaft 1998; Siebert 1998). At the same time the subsidiarity principle was clearly differentiated from the economic rationale for a monetary policy that is directed solely to price stability. There was a consensus that monetary policy aimed at price stability had to be supported by a responsible economic policy.

Third, Ordo-liberalism stressed that a strong euro depended on the ability of the EU to project itself as 'an autonomous political entity' (Deutsche Bundesbank 1990; 2001: 26–7). Hence EMU required an acceleration of European political union by strengthening Community institutions and a more effective coordination in such sectors as foreign and security policy, environmental protection, and interior and justice policy. Only by encouragement of a pan-European identity would it be possible to give the euro the political support that it required. But the Euro Group could not play this role without endangering the principle of the ECB's independence and hence undermining the credibility of the euro both externally and internally. Its role was limited to fiscal consolidation and to encouragement of cooperation in domestic structural reforms by means of peer pressure, especially decentralization of wage agreements and more flexible labour and goods markets. The Bundesbank ruled out any common financial policy instruments and both centralized and cross-national coordination in wage policies and structural reforms. It also stressed that the Euro Group must refrain from creating the public impression that it wanted to play a role in exchange-rate policy. By doing so the Euro Group put in question the ECB's independence in pursuing price stability. The Bundesbank's position was that European political union was more important than ever but that the Euro Group had to abstain from monetary policy.

Ordo-liberalism's association with the 'coronation' theory, according to which monetary union would be the final moment of a process of economic and political union, meant that its exponents had a reserved position on EMU. Strict convergence came before a fixed timetable; political union must accompany EMU to ensure sufficient solidarity; and a controlled delay was preferable to a poorly prepared EMU. In essence, the 'coronation' theory served as a critique of the readiness of the EU rather than of Germany itself, which was presented as the template for EMU. Hence Ordo-liberals were reticent about using EMU as a critique of German policies and politics. Their critique of Germany was linked to globalization, technological change, and German unification (Bundesministerium für Wirtschaft 1997). The

Ordo-liberal critique focused from the mid-1980s on the single European market programme as a welcome catalyst for overdue domestic reforms. But EMU was seen as a potential source of deeper problems for Germany in a global context rather than as a part of the solution. Hence the tax, social-security, labour-market, privatization, and utilities liberalization reform proposals of the Christian Democratic/Liberal (CDU/CSU/FDP) coalition from 1996 were framed more in terms of globalization than of EMU (Banchoff 1999).

This low profile of EMU as a factor in domestic structural reforms came to an end after 1998 for two main reasons. First, once EMU was a fait accompli, Ordo-liberals began to redefine it as a catalyst for overdue domestic supply-side reforms by subjecting the German economy to intensified competition, especially in the banking and financial sectors and in labour-market adjustment. In essence, EMU was redefined as an agency for speeding the impact of globalization, notably through a greater focus on 'shareholder' value (Siebert 1998). EMU was now valued as an instrument for an Ordo-liberal revolution in Germany eliminating 'managed' capitalism. From this perspective the Schröder government was not ultimately about correcting Ordo-liberalism in the name of social democratic values. Its role was the symbolic political management of necessary market liberalization, a role that seemed to be demonstrated when it abolished capital gains tax on the sale of shareholdings held by banks and financial institutions. This measure suggested a major advance for the 'shareholder' capitalism model. Hence Ordo-liberals had come to terms with EMU, attributing a greater causal significance to it, even if as an intervening variable.

Second, the SPD-led government was able to occupy a space between domestic Ordo-liberal ideology and the positions advocated by other EU governments of the centre-left within the Euro-Zone. Centre-left governments, notably that of Lionel Jospin in France, had a more interventionist bias on growth and employment issues. They were also more ideologically attached to the 'managed' capitalism model in which the state played an 'enabling' role in facilitating cooperation between employers and trade unions in macroeconomic management and structural reform. This greater ideological space between German Ordo-liberal thinking and change at the EU level opened up an opportunity for the Schröder government to play a more active role in developing an agenda of 'coordination' and 'dialogue', new keywords in Berlin. But this process was accompanied by new controversy. This controversy was at first within the new government—between New Keynesian ideas about 'coordination' and 'managed' capitalist ideas—and between the government and the Ordo-liberal establishment. It was followed by an accommodation that secured once again the primacy of

Ordo-liberalism but that pragmatically explored the potential to develop coordination within that framework. In that way a greater symmetry was achieved between the way in which European economic policy coordination was developing and traditional German practices of asymmetric coordination in which powerful employer and trade union organizations bargain within a framework of tough monetary policy discipline (Streeck 1995).

New Keynesianism

The key contest within the new government revolved politically around Schröder and Lafontaine. As new Finance Minister in 1998 Lafontaine saw an opportunity to open up German economic debate to new ideas, to use EMU as an instrument to rescue Germany from unemployment, and to safeguard the European social model from the thesis of globalization as an imperative. This opportunity was provided by the loss of authority of the Bundesbank over monetary policy and hence a weakening in the projection of Ordo-liberal policy ideas. Lafontaine sought to Europeanize the Finance Ministry and make it the powerhouse for new economic ideas, on the British Treasury and French Trésor models. Above all, he aimed to break the grip of what he saw as a conservative, inward-looking, and bureaucratized economic policy process dominated by the Council of Economic Advisers and the leading economic research institutes (Lafontaine 1999).

Central to this strategy was the transfer of key parts of the Economics Ministry to the Finance Ministry: notably, the traditional Ordo-liberal conscience and crown jewel of the Economics Ministry, its economic policy division (*Grundsatzabteilung*), and its responsibility for European policy co-ordination (Division E). By this means the Economics Ministry was prevented from acting as an intellectual and political counterweight on economic and European policies. The rationale was that German credibility and strength depended on a unified EMU policy to which the old checks and balances approach was inimical. A new European division was created to press the case for a coordinated EU policy mix involving financial policy, monetary policy, and wage policy. It reflected Lafontaine's view that to be effective SPD policies had to be European. In addition, New Keynesians were drafted into key positions, notably Heiner Flassbeck and Claus Noé as State Secretaries, Wolfgang Filc as head of the money and credit division, and Stefan Collignon into the European division.

Lafontaine had prepared these changes as party chair from 1995. He played a driving role in getting the SPD to see in EMU a catalyst for domestic economic reforms based on social democratic values. Lafontaine worked closely with the French Socialist Party to construct EMU as a project for growth and employment based on close macro-policy coordination, as the creation of a counterweight to US dominance of globalization, and as a European employment pact. These ideas, which were agreed at the special SPD conference in Hanover in December 1997, reflected the thinking of Jacques Delors and Lafontaine's commitment to using transnational collaboration with the French Socialists to redefine SPD programmatic ideas in a European context. He aimed to achieve domestic economic and social change through Europe.

The most controversial aspect was Lafontaine's sponsorship of a New Keynesian approach. Its intellectual basis was provided by the work of Francesco Modigliani, Robert Solow and James Tobin. Advised by Heiner Flassbeck, who was in close contact with work at Harvard and MIT, he focused on the German and Euro-Zone problem as, contrasted with the US, persistent negative output gaps over the previous 20 years (Collignon 1999). Excessively high interest rates had had a detrimental effect on investment, growth, and employment. The ERM had been the mechanism for the diffusion of the sharply deflationary policies of the Bundesbank to cope with the inflationary impact of German unification (Soskice 2000). The solution was not so much supply-side reforms on the 'market' capitalism model of the US and the UK as coordinated reflation. By more attention to the factor of demand it would be possible to strengthen the employment performance of states with institutional arrangements based on the model of 'managed' capitalism. Flassbeck, Lafontaine's State Secretary, placed emphasis on a flexible, growth-accommodating interest rate policy by the central bank, seeing the US Federal Reserve as the model (Flassbeck and Spiecker 2000). This policy necessitated strong policy coordination at the G-7 and EU levels, breaking the US grip on key international institutions like the IMF that propagated neoclassical economic orthodoxy and challenging the Bundesbank and the ECB to pursue growth and employment as part of their objectives (Lafontaine and Müller 1998).

Lafontaine's tenure of office was short—he resigned after six months—divisive, and highly controversial. Though his resignation was seen as a defeat, his impact outlasted him in the SPD and, to a lesser extent, in the Finance Ministry. Under Schröder German policy drew back from endorsing a New Keynesian construction of EMU. But the themes of social justice, macro-coordination, and demand management endured, albeit with a change of emphasis and style under Hans Eichel. For instance, in the German paper of 10 March 2000 for the Lisbon European Council the SPD's impact was discernible in two of the four strategic goals: 'renewal and securing of the European social model' and 'macroeconomic policy and economic policy

coordination for sustained growth'. The first goal involved maintaining minimum social standards and top priority to investment in human and social
capital; the second, avoidance of unfair tax competition and the pursuit of a
macroeconomic policy mix oriented to growth and stability. These Lafontaine-
type goals were, however, elaborated in a way that ensured their consistency
with the two main models—'managed' capitalism and Ordo-liberalism—and
reflected the political victory of Schröder in the contest with Lafontaine.

Within the Finance Ministry too the primacy of Ordo-liberal values
was reasserted. Policy routines returned to normal with a greater ministerial
respect under Hans Eichel after April 1999 for the detailed policy work within
divisions and sections. Nevertheless, the Finance Ministry continued to
argue the importance of an effective policy mix that embraced the demand
side as well as the supply side. It rejected the view of the Council of Economic
Advisers that unemployment had its sole roots in supply-side conditions
(Bundesministerium der Finanzen 2000: 83). This thinking was reflected in
Eichel's budget consolidation and tax reforms of 2000, which provided a net
stimulus to demand. Finally, and informally, the DGB kept alive the ideas of
macroeconomic coordination and active demand management. However,
it opted for a strategy of caution and stealth. Thus the DGB instituted new
regular private meetings with the incoming president of the Bundesbank,
Ernst Welteke. It also used informal meetings, involving the Bundesbank,
in preparation for the Macroeconomic Dialogue and organized within the
Finance Ministry. The DGB advocated Lafontaine's thinking but shore of his
confrontational style and Flassbeck's intellectualism. It preferred discrete,
behind-the-scenes influence in a pragmatic way.

'Managed' Capitalism

More influential in filling the policy space opened up by EMU was the
construction of EMU around the values of 'managed' capitalism. Here there
was a meeting of minds between Schröder, his economic policy adviser Klaus
Gretschmann, Eichel, Economics Minister Werner Müller, and Labour and
Social Affairs Minister Walter Riester. Much of this thinking had revolved
around the SPD in North-Rhine Westphalia, notably Bodo Hombach (1998),
minister in the Chancellor's Office till summer 1999. The keywords were cooperation, dialogue, and social consensus in managing supply-side reforms,
ensuring that labour-market flexibility took place within a framework of
social protection. As with Ordo-liberals the key source of change was seen
as globalization. But EMU was more than just a catalyst, forcing the pace of
structural reforms. It was an opportunity to regain control over economic

policy, to act as a counterweight to the US, to reassert the values of the German consensus model, and to achieve closer coordination of economic policy (Gretschmann 1998: 53, 60–1).

In contrast to New Keynesians, the emphasis was on the value of co-operation in managing the all-important details of change within the micro-economy of firms and sectors where competitiveness is created, innovation generated, and jobs created. Globalization, the single European market, and EMU were seen as increasing dependency of employers on skilled labour to ensure product quality, reliability, and flexibility in fast-changing, more competitive markets. The prime requirement was an 'enabling' state that would facilitate continuing skill-upgrading and social peace at plant level. German employers were in substantial part attracted to this model of capital-ism, not least because, by keeping away difficult distributive issues about wages, it supported a focus on production issues at plant level. Hence the Schröder government was able to sustain employer support for the Alliance for Jobs as the key domestic symbol of this style of capitalism. There could be serious tensions. An example was the Schröder government's proposal to extend the principle of co-determination through a requirement to establish works councils in smaller and medium-sized firms, not least to bring the 'new' economy within the framework of 'managed' capitalism. But overall German employers were unwilling to sacrifice a system that worked in terms of raising productivity, containing unit labour costs, standardizing a high level of skill training, and minimizing industrial conflict for the alternative of a deregulated capitalism (Silvia 1999: 115; Thelen 2000). The challenge for the Schröder government was to demonstrate the adaptive capacity of 'managed' capitalism.

Crucially—and unlike New Keynesianism—'managed' capitalism was consistent with long-established, institutionalized practices of cooperation in the German economy. These practices include coordination in wage bar-gaining, the role of works councils at the plant level, and a collaborative approach to vocational education and training, to the organization of innova-tion, and to the organization of social insurance. For Ordo-liberals such prac-tices represent multiple veto points on structural change and institutionalize inertia. From the angle of 'managed' capitalism they create 'stakeholders' who have an interest in the adaptability and effectiveness of the German system.

From the perspective of 'managed' capitalism, EMU had involved the export not of the German model, only its Ordo-liberal component. Hence EMU needed reform to strengthen social dialogue and cooperation and achieve a closer fit between the domestic 'Rhineland' model of cooperative capital-ism and the institutional design of the Euro-Zone. The key was to integrate wage bargaining into the EMU policy mix and to make possible a growth-supporting ECB monetary policy by ensuring that unit labour costs remain consistent with the price stability objective. But, in contrast to the New Keynesians, proponents of 'managed' capitalism did not see the need to challenge the exclusive dedication of the ECB to price stability.

This thinking lay behind the German initiative during its EU Presidency of 1999 to establish the Macroeconomic Dialogue—the Cologne process—as a means of promoting a better understanding of how policies interacted. Though it was not modelled on the new Alliance for Jobs (*Bündnis für Arbeit*) of the Schröder government, it reflected the same type of thinking. The Macroeconomic Dialogue brought together member-state governments, the Commission, the ECB, and the social partners, at both political and technical levels, to engage in dialogue about the most appropriate policy mix at the European level and, in particular, to draw wage policy into discussions. Another manifestation was in German ideas, adopted at the Helsinki European Council in December 1999, on strengthening economic policy coordination. The aims were to take better account of the interdependencies and spillover effects at work in EMU; to broaden the agenda beyond fiscal discipline; and to toughen up pressure on member states of the EU to deliver reforms. These measures involved extending the Economic Policy Guidelines to include structural reforms—for example, wages and labour markets—recommendations to individual member states of the EU, and monitoring of their implementation.

Towards a New Centre of Gravity in the Consensus on EMU

From 1998 onwards there were signs of a shift in the centre of gravity of the German consensus about the emerging Euro-Zone. This consensus involved some Ordo-liberals, notably Horst Köhler (1998: 7) who had negotiated the Maastricht Treaty, accepting that the Euro Group was more than just guardian of the Stability and Growth Pact. It was also an economic policy 'pole' in EMU, pursuing a tight coordination of economic policies, especially of structural reforms, and engaged in intensive dialogue with the ECB. Another aspect of this consensus, discussed below, was a stronger recognition that domestic economic policies were embedded in EMU. There was, in addition, a new consensus by 2000 on policy 'benchmarking' of best practice in economic policy as a method of 'soft' coordination. Benchmarking was useful because of its compatibility with Ordo-liberal premises of subsidiarity and competition of policies. It also promised a technocratic ground of expert determination of what works best as the basis for domestic reforms. Hence Ordo-liberals and 'Rhineland' capitalists could rally around it. German negotiators actively promoted benchmarking. Finally, Gretschmann and others promoted the notion of a new phase in European integration after monetary union. This phase involved creating the 'European innovation and know-ledge society' and drawing the Education, Science, Research, and Technology Ministry as well as the Labour and Social Affairs Ministry actively into EU processes of benchmarking best practices. Once again a technocratic basis for a consensual approach to EMU and to domestic policy reform was identified. The Lisbon European Council of March 2000 was seen as marking a better 'goodness of fit' between EMU and the German model. In these respects the Schröder government can be said to have moved the centre of gravity of the German consensus. Not least, benchmarking made it respectable to use argu-ments derived from experience in other states which were committed to the model of 'cooperative' capitalism to strengthen domestic political arguments for structural reform and overcome domestic 'veto points' on change.

But this shift needs qualification. First, tensions and potential for conflict accompanied the consensus. In strict Ordo-liberal terms, the Council of Economic Advisers continued to speak of a readiness for conflict as necessary for a long-term economic policy of supply-side reforms. It expressed scepti-cism about the value of both the Alliance for Jobs and the Macroeconomic Dialogue, arguing that they threatened to produce a confusion of respons-ibilities (Sachverständigenrat 1999). There was also disagreement between the federal government, which saw itself as taking a balanced approach to the demand and supply sides of economic policy, and Ordo-liberals who stressed supply-side reforms. Another instance, discussed below, was a difference of view within the Finance Ministry on the scope of Europeanization. Second, Ordo-liberalism retained a strong gravitational pull despite the weakening of the Bundesbank and of the Economics Ministry. It continued to define the limits on macroeconomic policy coordination—discussed below—to enforce respect for strict fiscal discipline, and to keep supply-side reforms high on the agenda: witness the budget consolidation and the tax reforms of 2000. In the preparations for the Cologne European Council Gretschmann ensured that the Finance Ministry's idea of an optimal macroeconomic policy mix was excised from the proposed Macroeconomic Dialogue in favour of stress on its information and communication functions.

The Paradox of Europeanization: From Exporting Model Germany to 'Benchmarking' Best Practice

EMU was associated with a seismic shift in German self-perceptions. The Maastricht Treaty had symbolized German monetary power, the successful 'Europeanization' of the German model of an independent, powerful central bank. It had been a substantial, if incomplete, vindication of German negotiating strength. The resulting 'goodness of fit' between German and EU policy paradigms of 'sound' money and finance meant that German policy-makers saw little problem in accommodating EMU. The problem rested with others who were required to undergo drastic domestic transformation. Paradoxically, the transition to stage three revealed the mounting problems of the German political economy, undermined its moral claims to a leadership role, and weakened its negotiating position in 1998–9 compared with 1991. German policy-makers began to embrace a more humble outward-looking attitude of learning from others' better practice in structural economic reforms.

This fundamental 'goodness of fit' applied not just to the ECB—the Bundesbank writ large—but also to the earlier ERM, anchored to the D-Mark, and the Stability and Growth Pact, subjecting budgetary policies to clear long-term rules. In each of these cases German domestic preferences had been successfully projected into EU-level agreements. Thus Köhler (1992), State Secretary in the Finance Ministry, spoke of 'exporting this fine piece of German identity to Europe'. In the Bundestag debate of 23 April 1998 Theo Waigel, the Finance Minister, argued that the German government was not giving up the D-Mark but continuing its history of success at the European level. For the CDU/CSU parliamentary party in a statement of September 1997 EMU was not a question of 'sacrificing' the D-Mark on the 'altar' of Europe but of 'investing it in the European cause'.

This successful 'Europeanization' of the German monetary-policy model was driven by the persuasive ideological conviction of Ordo-liberals. They preached the virtues of price stability and of a predictable, long-term framework of monetary and financial policy as the essential precondition for sustainable growth and employment. Consistent with this credo, the Bundesbank defined its role as the guardian (*Wächterrolle*) in preparing EMU and as the reliable, expert, and committed advocate of sustainable monetary stability in the Euro-Zone. With the arch Ordo-liberal Tietmeyer as its president during 1993–9, the Bundesbank forcefully pursued a pedagogic role on behalf of price stability. EMU was in this respect about a 'Germanized' Europe.

But Europeanization of the German monetary policy model had deeper roots than just a strongly articulated, impressively argued, and coherent Ordo-liberal theory. The quality and effectiveness of German arguments on EMU rested on strong economic fundamentals, on a powerful historical memory, and on the peculiar symbolic importance that Germans attached to the D-Mark. The strong economic fundamentals were represented by the superior performance of the D-Mark as a 'hard' currency, both internally and externally, compared with other EU currencies. In addition to benefiting from association with success, the Bundesbank was able to identify itself with German histor-ical memory of what damage inflation could wreak on economy, society, and democracy. The lesson was that the management of money must be depoliti-cized and conducted in a long-term and consistent framework. Historical memory fused with the post-war performance of the D-Mark to give a degree of political self-confidence to the Bundesbank lacking in other German insti-tutions, except perhaps the Federal Constitutional Court. Above all, it enjoyed a very high level of public support for its mandate (Kaltenthaler 1998).

Hence, politically, the Bundesbank had a powerful institutional veto posi-tion on EMU. 'Binding in' the Bundesbank was an essential precondition for keeping German public opinion behind EMU. This strategy was pursued in putting EMU back on the agenda in 1988—its president Karl-Otto Pöhl was appointed to the Delors Committee—and throughout the negotiation of the Maastricht Treaty and the transition to EMU (Dyson and Featherstone 1999). The political damage that could follow when the strategy of 'binding in' failed was revealed in 1997. Waigel's reputation as Finance Minister was seri-ously damaged by his abortive attempt to engineer a premature revaluation of the Bundesbank's gold reserves as a means of defraying the public debt (Duckenfield 1999). Bundesbank endorsement was the single most important domestic condition for persuading the German public to give up to Europe their most impressive postwar achievement, the D-Mark.

But, paradoxically, this successful Europeanization of German monetary policy—EMU as the projection of German 'civilian' power—was accompanied by an eroding credibility of 'Model Germany' from 1991 onwards. This eroding credibility reflected underlying structural changes (European Commission 1999b; Bundesministerium der Finanzen 2000). From 1993 the annual rate of economic growth fell below that of the EU-11 and EU-15 average. Germany's annual rate of growth of capital formation amounted to only 2.3 per cent in the 1990s compared with 5.7 per cent in the United States. Its unemployment rate doubled between 1991 and 1999. Ominously, it scored the second biggest fall in total employment in the EU between 1991 and 1998. Germany suffered from new budgetary problems—especially due to reliance on debt financing of huge fiscal transfers—unprecedentedly high Bundesbank interest rates to fight inflation, and, by 1995–6, failure to meet the Maastricht deficit criterion. The reason for this declining performance might be contested, notably between New Keynesians who pointed to demand deficiency and Ordo-liberals who stressed lack of structural economic reforms. But the effects were clear to all: a loss of negotiating power.

In short, Germany moved from being the model for fiscal discipline to a problem case. By March 1997 Tietmeyer was confessing that Germany was no longer the model economy for Europe—the Netherlands had a stronger claim—and asking whether EMU might be delayed by German weakness. A statement of the CDU/CSU parliamentary party in September 1997 broke new ground in pointing to the greater success of the Netherlands and other countries in pursuing economic and social reforms, the huge progress in Italy and Spain, and France's better record than Germany on inflation since 1992. As Germany began to contemplate the 'long overdue reforms' necessitated by EMU, a new humility was evident.

Most striking was the lack of initiative before March 1996 from the Chancellor's Office in addressing economic reform. A key factor was the politics of the electoral cycle. With a low Bundestag majority in the 1994 federal elections, Kohl was persuaded that it was better to defer reforms till after the key *Länder* elections in March 1996 so as not to weaken his position in the second chamber, the Bundesrat. But the effect was to create another problem of political timing. These reforms would occupy the last two years of the Bundestag, a time constraint that provided a strategic opportunity for the SPD to block reforms in the Bundesrat.

Kohl's new image as the Chancellor of economic reform was pressed on him by increasingly impatient employer and industry associations. They sought a political ambition to match the scale of rationalization measures being pursued in the corporate sector. Corporate concerns about the euro were expressed in the Petersberg Declaration—'Secure into the Future with the Euro'—of 1996. Here the German employer and industry associations pressed for more flexibility, especially in the labour market and in wage negotiations. But when in March 1996 the government adopted tough new positions on tax and welfare-state reforms, notably a cut in sickness pay, it drew back from legitimizing them by reference to EMU (Banchoff 1999). As in the 1970s and 1980s, reforms were presented as indispensable preconditions for improving international economic competitiveness and restoring credibility to Germany's economic policies. The urgency was justified by domestic political concerns about rising unemployment and by worries about Germany's international standing.

Germany's weight at the European level, especially in the transition to stage three of EMU, played more of an internal role within the political elite than in the framing of reforms. Internally, it was recognized that, unless Germany could demonstrate a will to reform, its preaching of the stability message to others would invite charges of hypocrisy. It would also be more difficult to rebut the claims of Italy and others to join stage three in the first wave. But reforms were framed for public opinion by reference to the imperatives of globalization.

Two features characterized the attempted economic reforms of the Kohl government of 1994–8. They appeared as too little, too late, undertaken by a tired and fractious coalition of CDU, CSU, and FDP. The reforms were trapped politically between an FDP demanding deep tax cuts and an SPD opposition hostile to major spending cuts and having a majority in the Bundesrat, the second chamber. More seriously, by trying to push through reforms in the latter part of the legislative period, they invited a 'reform blockade'. By 1997 'Reformstau' became a keyword to describe the condition of Germany. Against this background, and fearful of not meeting the Maastricht criteria, Waigel was tempted to launch his ill-fated proposal to revalue the gold reserves.

Schröder (1998) mounted his political challenge against Kohl in terms of his superior competence to handle the imperatives of globalization rather than in terms of EMU. But after 1998 the Schröder government proved unable, for internal political reasons, to take full advantage of its temporary posses- sion of concurrent majorities in both Bundestag and Bundesrat. Paradoxically, it was only after it lost its majority in the Bundesrat that it was at last able to negotiate a radical tax reform, in July 2000, following a radical budget consolidation programme. Its success in doing so rested on a greater internal unity and on Schröder's political strategy of seeking out consensus with the employer organizations and trade unions as a means of putting the CDU/CSU opposition and his own left under pressure to accept reforms. Even so the pace of reform was slow, with key welfare-state and labour-market reforms still to be tackled.

From 1996 onwards a new modesty crept into German discourse about EMU. This strain of modesty provided a greater ease of fit between Germany and a large rather than a small, core EMU. Indeed, there was a striking associ- ation between Germany's mounting economic and political problems in 1996–8 and the demise of what had become an informal consensus by 1995 that only a small core of states would proceed to stage three. The new modesty was also apparent in the spread of the idea of 'benchmarking' best practice elsewhere, deriving in part from the corporate sector, in part from Brussels, and in part from modernizers in the SPD.

The Paradox of Europeanization: The Gap between Programmatic Discourse and the Framing of Domestic Policy Reforms

Despite a political reluctance to politicize EMU by associating it with increasingly contentious structural reforms, Europeanization of economic policy through EMU was invested with new meanings. Policy-makers began to see EMU as a catalyst for domestic transformation rather than as a new reality which Germany could easily accommodate. This change of perception was most apparent in programmatic statements. How Europeanization was understood in Berlin was first made clear in the Annual Economic Report of 2000. It turned its attention to 'learning from "good experiences" in other states', focusing on Denmark and the Netherlands in labour-market and wage-policy reforms and also the United States (Bundesministerium der Finanzen 2000: 11–12). These states were seen as offering lessons about the kinds of macroeconomic conditions and micro-structural reforms required to modernize Germany. The report also recognized that the euro required a 'deepening and strengthening of coordination' of national economic policies, that German autonomy of action was further constrained, and that its economic policies had to be more strongly embedded (*eingebettet*) in the European macro-framework (Bundesministerium der Finanzen 2000: 19). The new European division in the Finance Ministry—Lafontaine's legacy—advocated the view that all domestic economic policies had a European dimension and argued the case for closer European coordination.

But also striking were the perceived limits on Europeanization. There was a greater readiness to justify structural reforms by international 'best practice' or 'benchmarking'—horizontal policy transfer—than by reference to the requirements of the euro—vertical policy transfer. 'Benchmarking' had two advantages as a concept. First, it situated the debate about domestic reforms in the arena of 'globalization' rather than the euro. This construction of reform reduced the association of the euro with negative effects for Germans and hence was politically expedient in protecting the European integration process, in which Germany had a vital national interest, from potential lack of consensus over structural reforms. Second, 'benchmarking' gave a technocratic rationale to reform. It framed painful reforms in a context of matching 'best practice'. This form of technocratic discourse also eased problems of gaining acceptance for measures of market liberalization within the SPD and the trade unions.

A further limitation stemmed from the arguments advocated by the economic policy division (*Grundsatzabteilung*) of the Finance Ministry, transferred from the Economics Ministry in 1998. The Annual Economic Report of 2000 reflected acceptance of its three arguments against the view that German economic policy had been completely Europeanized, and hence established a measure of continuity. It endorsed the basic principle of subsidiarity, according to which responsibility for growth and employment rested primarily at the national level. It stressed the subsidiary role of European coordination to coordination and discipline by the market. It also underlined the importance of policy competition for raising economic performance.

Though these arguments qualified the new emphasis on Europeanization in the Annual Economic Report, Eichel gave strong internal backing to the European division. This backing focused on two key considerations that favoured the thesis of Europeanization of German economic policy: that policy competition must be fair, notably in tax policy so that tax revenues were stabilized; and that benchmarking 'best practice' was a key to expediting structural reforms inside Germany. However, by 2001 a new political argument for qualifying Europeanization had been accepted within the Finance Ministry. Eichel was frustrated by the difficulty of developing a coordinated approach to economic reform with the French Finance Minister, Laurent Fabius, because of the veto role of Jospin, and by unwelcome French pressure to formalize economic policy coordination. Hence he found it strategically useful to stress the value of British participation in the euro as a means of preemptively blocking any new French initiatives on strengthening economic policy coordination. He argued that such initiatives would make it more difficult to persuade a sceptical British electorate to endorse the euro in a referendum.

Despite the new programmatic emphasis on Europeanization, the crucial budget consolidation programme, tax reform programme, and pension reform proposals of the Schröder government were conspicuously not framed in terms of the requirements of EMU. Strict discipline on public expenditure and continuing reduction of the budget deficit were legitimized in German terms. They were justified as essential for regaining domestic room for manoeuvre in financial policy, thereby enabling the government to better deliver on its political priorities. They were also framed in terms of the principle of intergenerational fairness. The tax reform was about better domestic conditions for investment, growth, and jobs, with the EU addressing problems of unfair tax competition. Pension reform was about adapting to negative demographic developments and about intergenerational fairness. In short, domestic political principles and arguments were far more important than EMU. EMU played a background and indirect role.

This background, indirect role was noticeable in the arena of federal-State financial planning. In 1997 Waigel presented proposals for a law on a national stability pact to ensure that State governments and local authorities accepted responsibility for meeting German obligations under the EU's Stability and Growth Pact. In doing so he stressed the threat to German credibility from a failure to match EU discipline with a parallel domestic discipline. He also threatened an appeal to the Federal Constitutional Court if Germany should find herself faced with sanctions and without a legal regulation binding the states. But negotiations broke down in the face of disagreement between the federal government and States and between rich and poor States about an appropriate formula for distributing deficits. Following rejection by the Financial Planning Council, it was agreed to take the Stability and Growth Pact into account informally.

Hence a gap remained between a new programmatic discourse of Europeanization within governmental circles and official documents and the actual framing of budget, welfare-state, and labour-market reforms in public debate. The motives were twofold: a domestic motive of being seen as a government to be pursuing reforms for good German reasons and not because 'forced' to do so; and a fear of diverting domestic criticism to the EU. EMU was too new, fragile, and important a project to be politically exposed. In so far as one was reforming to 'make the euro work' there was an inhibition about making a public admission.

Europeanization of economic policy took two forms by 2001. First, the Finance Ministry sought to change the remit of the Council of Economic Advisers by asking it to frame its analysis and proposals within the context of EU-level data, the Broad Economic Policy Guidelines, the German stability programme, and commitments entered into in the area of 'soft' economic policy coordination. This was an important means of Europeanizing the German economics profession which traditionally had been critically 'distant' on EMU. It was also important in reframing the domestic economic policy debate so that it addressed euro-level issues. Second, the Finance Ministry brought the relevant Bundestag and Bundesrat committees into debate about the Broad Economic Policy Guidelines in their draft form. In this way they were more involved in the process of economic policy coordination at the European level. By these means the Finance Ministry sought to anchor euro economic governance more firmly within professional economics and within the parliamentary arena and the arena of federal-State politics.

The Paradox of a Firm Deadline and Strict Criteria

The third paradox reflected a deep divide within post-war public opinion between 'civilian power' values and 'stability' values. On the one hand, there was a great deal of cultural and intellectual support for the idea that German interest was in multilateralism, 'good neighbourliness', and respect for international institutions and their rules. German interest in a peaceful and prosperous Europe meant meeting the Maastricht timetable with a large rather than a small 'core' EMU around Germany and unqualified respect for the treaty commitment to a clear timetable. On the other hand, German public opinion reflected great pride in the post-war heritage of monetary stability, symbolized by the D-Mark. Respect for this principle meant precedence to a small 'core' and an 'orderly postponement', if necessary.

The paradox of a firm timetable and strict convergence derived from the Maastricht Treaty itself but was given a specific German definition. Germany was committed both to moving to stage three on 1 January 1999 and to ensuring tough convergence criteria were met in order to qualify. By the time that the treaty was signed in February 1992 the issue of which came first—timetable or criteria—was already established as the central domestic political issue about EMU. From December 1991 onwards Kohl and Waigel were on the defensive, operating in a context of multiple uncertainties with an ambiguous political formula designed to offer reassurance to different audiences. Their strategic aim was to avoid a conflict between the timetable and convergence in a domestic context in which a strict interpretation of the criteria became critical. The basic strategic objective was to keep EMU in a framework of consensus defined in terms acceptable to Ordo-liberals.

The federal government was quick to recognize two failures in the Maastricht negotiations. First, not enough had been done to prepare German public opinion, handing the political advantage to those who feared losing a cherished national symbol, the D-Mark. Hence the political and economic case for EMU had still to be made. After Maastricht the agreed formula was to stress four German interests. A stronger EU through EMU would better help the East onto its feet. EMU would reduce the economic risks from a return to currency speculation. It would provide a more predictable environment for German exports and investment. Finally, EMU would increase the political acceptability of German economic strength to her neighbours. By 1996 Waigel was giving increased salience to the economic threat of an overvalued D-Mark to exports, investment, and jobs. The risk was a flight of capital into the D-Mark if EMU should fail or be delayed.

More broadly, there was a shared perception across the political elite that the established political parties risked being out of touch with popular sentiment. This translated into a recognition that political leaders must show themselves to be cautious and responsible in creating a sustainable EMU. It also meant devoting a great deal of attention to ensuring that the leaders of German industry and banking offered active support for EMU. Thus in 1993 the senior German EMU negotiator Horst Köhler took over as president of the association of German savings banks, a key presence in retail banking.

The failure most stressed by the Finance Ministry and the Bundesbank was that Germany had not secured clear enough achievements on European political union. This mattered because, as the Bundesbank argued, EMU could not work in the absence of a political union. The government dealt with this problem by keeping political union at the forefront in the 1990s. The weakness of the euro in its first two years provided the Bundesbank with the opportunity to reiterate the importance of this issue (Deutsche Bundesbank 2001). At the same time the government sought to contain criticism by reminding the Bundesbank that political union negotiations were a matter for the federal government and by stressing that the Bundesbank had a legal responsibility to support the policy of the government. In addition—and here it was in agreement with the Bundesbank—it pointed out that the Ordo-liberal stress on the principle of subsidiarity in economic policy—for example, in relation to employment policy—and on safeguarding the independence of the ECB qualified the degree of economic policy coordination that was desirable to support monetary union. Even so, the federal government had to be able to demonstrate progress on political union with the Amsterdam Treaty in order to insure against negative votes on stage three in the Bundestag and Bundesrat.

The principle of irreversibility left little room for interpretation. There was a fixed, final date for completing EMU. Kohl's agreement to this commitment at Maastricht was domestically controversial. In particular, Ordo-liberals feared the creation of an unsound EMU, with serious negative effects both on the German economy and on the larger European integration process. They doubted the availability of a 'stability culture' outside Germany as an essential underpinning for a sustainable EMU. These doubts and fears were expressed in the manifesto of 60 leading German economists in June 1992 condemning the undue haste and the laxity of the criteria. They were repeated in the letter of 155 German economists in February 1998 calling for an 'orderly postponement' as the deficit and debt criteria had not been adequately met by enough states. They were also shared within the Economics and Finance ministries and the Bundesbank.

'Irreversibility' was founded on a political definition of Germany's vital interests in European integration and on the argument that, following German unification, there was a greater responsibility on Germany to demonstrate its loyalty to this process. Giving up so important a symbol as the D-Mark was the ultimate test of Germany's trustworthiness as a good European. This political argument—stressing German 'responsibility' for Europe—was driven by Chancellor Kohl, shared within the Chancellor's Office and the Foreign Ministry and within the leadership of the CDU/CSU parliamentary party. Kohl reiterated that the timetable would be respected. He was also sensitive to the political argument that the original Six, including Belgium and Italy, must march together into stage three. Germany had an interest in EU solidarity. There was also an economic argument for a fixed timetable. A clear date put pressure on all states to pursue convergence, with the threat of exclusion operating as a preventive sanction against fiscal irresponsibility. In April 1997 Kohl justified his decision to stand again as Chancellor candidate in 1998 by the vital importance of seeing EMU to completion. Crucial here was his perception that Germany might fail to meet the criteria.

Kohl's technique was to combine assertion of the principle of a firm timetable with the clear message that it was the responsibility of others—the Finance Ministry at home and the French, Italian, and Belgian governments —to take the necessary action. In this way Kohl put others, notably Waigel, under pressure to ensure that strict convergence was achieved. In March–April 1997 he took a more public tough line on his determination to meet the deadline following Germany's 3.8 per cent budget deficit in 1996 and the projection of the six leading economics research institutes that it would exceed 3 per cent in 1997, the key final year for assessment. 'The question is not whether EMU is coming, but what we can and must do to make it begin on time.' The interpretation of the budget deficit criterion as a maximum of 3.0 per cent of GDP was defined as Waigel's problem, not Kohl's. It was against this background that Waigel launched his proposal for a revaluation of the Bundesbank's gold reserves. Meeting the deadline was about maintaining Germany's reputation as a 'reliable partner' and Germany's 'special responsibility for completing monetary union'.

The principle of strict convergence came to focus on the fiscal criteria— maximum 3.0 per cent deficit and 60 per cent debt—especially the deficit criterion, and was subject to a particular German construction: that the requirement was 'three point zero' per cent. This requirement was not contained in the treaty, which in Art. 104c(2) refers rather to the ratio reaching 'a level that comes close to the reference value'. Leading voices warned against an excessively strict interpretation, notably Wolfgang Schäuble, head of the CDU/CSU parliamentary party, Klaus Kinkel, the Foreign Minister, and Welteke, then a member of the Bundesbank council and from 1999 Bundesbank president. Even the Federation of German Banks (Bundesverband deutscher Banken, BdB) argued against a 'book-keeping' approach to the criteria. They spoke of 'room for interpretation'. Waigel's interpretation of April 1997 that 'three does not mean three plus x' rested on three foundations. Ordo-liberal economists saw the strictest observance of this criterion as the essential safeguard for a 'stability community' in which convergence would be 'sustainable'. In addition, politicians like Edmund Stoiber, Bavaria's Prime Minister, argued that a stable currency had played a special role in

Germany's post-war democratic stabilization and identity and must not be placed in jeopardy. Stoiber maintained steady pressure on Waigel from within the Bavarian CSU.

The theme of a 'controlled delay' of one or more years became a standard argument of Ordo-liberals and was taken up most vocally by Stoiber, especially in summer 1997. The Bavarian CSU was preoccupied with the threat to its absolute majority in the State election in 1998 and the implications for its federal influence. It identified in the loss of the D-Mark a potential mobilizing issue for the extreme right. Hence Stoiber was keen to identify the CSU with staunch defence of German stability interests in EMU. Three point zero was a totem of stability. For Stoiber EMU was about the image of the governing competence of the established parties and the trust of ordinary Germans in the political establishment. Hence the criteria had to have precedence over the timetable.

In this context Waigel was a critical figure. He was both Finance Minister and chair of the CSU. As Finance Minister he was beleaguered by rising unemployment and deteriorating public finances, especially consequent on German unification and the attendant huge fiscal transfers. As chair of the CSU he was subject to huge pressures from Stoiber, who defeated him in the 1993 contest for the post of Bavarian Prime Minister. This position of weakness was, paradoxically, a source of strength to Waigel. He was indispensable to Kohl as a means of binding in the fickle CSU to the EMU process and hence a vital political ally. Waigel was also able to argue the need for concessions from EU partners to enable him to carry German public opinion.

But Waigel had to negotiate a very difficult political landscape in which he was tempted to tailor his message to different audiences. By a series of moves Waigel sought to take the wind out of the sails of those tempted to exploit a D-Mark patriotism. These moves focused on the basic principle of ensuring that the new single currency was 'at least as stable as the D-Mark'. Though central, this principle was never fully accepted by the large majority of Germans, who continued to be opposed to losing the D-Mark. Waigel's moves were also designed to bind the Bundesbank into the process by depriving it of key arguments for a 'controlled delay'. His strategy was to give credibility to the principle that the single currency would be 'at least as stable as the D-Mark' to get the Bundesbank on side in 1998 and to assuage German public opinion and contain domestic dissent.

- In agreement with Kohl, Waigel yielded in 1992 to the political demand of the SPD that the Bundestag and Bundesrat be given the further opportunity, after ratification of the Maastricht Treaty, to make their own political decision on whether the states proposed for stage three had met the strict convergence conditions.

- Again with Kohl, he secured Frankfurt as the site of the European Monetary Institute (EMI) and future European Central Bank at the Brussels European Council in October 1993.
- He gained a change of name from 'ECU' to 'euro' at the Madrid European Council in December 1995. This change dissociated the new currency from a unit that had depreciated in value and countered talk of exchanging the D-Mark for an 'Esperanto' currency.
- In 1995 he proposed the Stability Pact to put in place rules and sanctions to ensure that member-state governments pursued balanced budgets over the cycle, with a stability council to monitor compliance. This countered criticisms of the weakness of the existing convergence procedure and met the Bundesbank's clarification that by 'stronger political union' it meant tougher budget discipline.
- He adopted the theme of a 3.0 per cent budget deficit to demonstrate his toughness on the fiscal criteria.
- From 1996 he stressed the economic risks to growth and employment in Germany from a delay to stage three in the form of an overvalued D-Mark.
- He conceded an employment chapter in the Amsterdam Treaty in order to insure against the SPD's rejection of the treaty and to keep the SPD on side in the Bundestag and Bundesrat decision of 1998. At the same time he reassured Ordo-liberals by strict insistence on the principle of subsidiarity and national responsibility in employment policy.
- He engineering the additional 'Stability Declaration', approved by ECOFIN in May 1998, to persuade Bundestag deputies that Belgium and Italy were pledged to undertake additional efforts to tackle their debt problems.
- He took up the principle of subsidiarity in economic policy in response to Stoiber's argument in 1997–8 that EMU would strengthen competition for inward investment and lead to a more competitive regionalism in the EU.
- Along with Kohl, he ensured that the Bundesbank's candidate, Wim Duisenberg, was chosen as president of the ECB, with the Bundesbank's chief economist and 'stability' guru, Otmar Issing, as the ECB's chief economist.

The political threat was not just from the CSU but also from those in the SPD who, it was feared, might be tempted to launch a populist campaign against the euro. SPD regional leaders in the Baden-Württemberg and Hamburg elections of 1996 tested the theme of a delay. But in each case it was associated with serious electoral setbacks. Gerhard Schröder took up a 'structured delay' up to 2002 as late as December 1997 (*International Economy* 1997:

8–9). Schröder's strategy was to align himself with Tietmeyer's views and stress the risks to economic stability associated with a fixed timetable. In this way he sought to develop an image of economic competence vis-à-vis Kohl and the CDU/CSU and make himself an electable future Chancellor candidate.

This strategy of calling for a delay was strongly contested within the leadership of the SPD and neutralized by Lafontaine. By December 1996 Lafontaine as party chair was warning against delay, arguing that it would jeopardize convergence and produce crisis in the EU. He led the SPD to embrace EMU as a catalyst to speed domestic economic reform, in alliance with social democratic governments elsewhere in the EU, notably the French Socialists. EMU could be used to engineer an agenda change towards prioritizing coordinated European action for growth and employment, notably a European employment pact with binding objectives on member states. For others in the SPD leadership EMU was a matter of demonstrating the SPD's reliability as a party dedicated to European unification. Hence the SPD held back from mounting a populist campaign on the issue and voted with the government parties in the Bundestag in April 1998 to accept the eleven states as meeting the convergence criteria. But in May 1997 it had threatened to take into account the absence of an employment chapter in the forthcoming Amsterdam Treaty when the Bundestag and Bundesrat considered in 1998 whether the states chosen for stage three met the criteria. This threat, allied to the threat to block ratification of the Amsterdam Treaty, was designed to encourage Waigel to concede to French demands for an employment chapter at Amsterdam. It was, however, a questionably credible threat.

In consequence, Waigel had to play a tortuous political game in a climate of great uncertainty and subject to contingencies on both political and economic fronts and on domestic and European fronts. He did so in the context of a government strategy that rested deliberately on an ambiguous formula. The formula was that EMU would begin on time, with Germany on the starting line as both a reliable partner and in a 'flagship' role, provided that Germany met the criteria and that France was ready. The formula hid a mounting tension between aspiration to a 'flagship' role on economic stability and new doubts, first articulated in July 1993 and then again in 1996–7, about whether Germany could qualify by meeting its own tests. Above all, however, it expressed the strategy of avoiding a conflict between timetable and criteria.

Domestically, Waigel's three most difficult periods coincided with deteriorating economic conditions and political threats, notably from within his own party. The first stretched from Stoiber's letter to Kohl in September 1993 calling for a delay to EMU as much too ambitious, to the European Parliament elections of June 1994. Stoiber was preoccupied with heading off the extreme right in the 1994 European and Bavarian State elections. He was also alert to the negative signals from the ERM crisis of July 1993 about the prospects for EMU. The second period in early 1996 was associated with uncertainty about the SPD's position, given remarks by Schröder and by regional leaders in Baden-Württemberg and Hamburg, and also uncertainty about economic prospects, generating perceptions that the timetable was unrealistic. The third period lasted from Waigel's gold revaluation proposal in May 1997 through Stoiber's call for a controlled delay in summer 1997 into the late autumn when it was still unclear whether Germany would meet 3.0. As late as September 1997 senior CDU politicians believed that Kohl might be tempted to defer a decision on stage three till after the September 1998 elections.

At the European level, the main source of uncertainty was France. Kohl and Waigel were agreed that EMU did not make sense as a political and economic project unless France qualified. It was as much about strengthening the Franco-German relationship as making European unification irreversible. Hence the whole project was bound up with events and developments in France, which had domestic reverberations in Germany. The reverberations following the problems of the French franc in the ERM crises of 1992–3 were reflected in Stoiber's call for a delay in September 1993. The election of the 'unreliable' Jacques Chirac as President in May 1995 was followed by Waigel's Stability Pact proposal in November. The French strikes and demonstrations of November–December 1995 reinforced Kohl's determination that Germany must be blameless if EMU failed by showing that it had made every effort. The attachment of extra conditions to the transition to stage three by the new French government of Jospin in May 1997 required a forceful German response. This took the form of a defence of the Stability Pact against French amendments, the stringent application of the subsidiarity principle to the new employment chapter in the Amsterdam Treaty, and toughened resistance to a the idea of an 'economic government'. In 1996 the view in Bonn and among employer and industrial associations was that a small 'core group', without Italy, was the most realistic option. It was not till late 1997–8 that the view began to form that a larger group was practical.

Hence the overall impression was one of complex strategy in a context of uncertainty and contingency and of resort to an ambiguous political formula designed to reconcile contending domestic and European interests and responsibilities. Even as late as September 1997 it was not clear whether stage three would go ahead on time and, if so, with whom. Waigel stood at the epicentre of German policy and politics on EMU. That conflict between the timetable and the criteria was finally avoided owed much to his political skills, as well as to a benign configuration of economic data in 1997–8.

The Paradox of Bundesbank Power: Finding a New Role

After 1991 the Bundesbank retained impressive resources of power. But it had to manoeuvre in the narrower policy and political space left by the Maastricht commitment. In doing so it veered between taking up tough positions—for example, rejecting the Finance Minister's attempt to bring forward a revaluation of its gold reserves—and more accommodating positions—for example, in its advice of March 1998 about whether the states selected to form stage three met the convergence criteria. By 1999 it had to grapple with the issue of its own reform to adjust to the new operating conditions of EMU. Hence the 1990s witnessed tensions and conflicts between the Bundesbank and the Finance Ministry, as well as with the Federal Chancellor's Office and the Foreign Ministry, followed by new problems of defining the Bundesbank's role.

The resources of power available to the Bundesbank over EMU were formidable. The Bundesbank Law of 1957 required it to 'safeguard the currency'. Hence there was a clear legal basis for the Bundesbank to define its role as guardian of the stability foundations of EMU, ensuring that convergence was strict and sustainable. It had a clear, coherent institutional philosophy, grounded in Ordo-liberal economic theory. It had an enormous reputation as Europe's most successful central bank, grounded in its association with an excellent German record on price stability and with the D-Mark's position as a 'hard' currency and as the anchor of the ERM. The Bundesbank enjoyed the confidence of the global financial markets and was seen as the expert institution on these markets. Above all, the German public trusted it. On EMU matters, especially on ensuring that the euro was 'at least as stable as the D-Mark', the Bundesbank was seen as the authoritative actor by the German economic interest groups and banking associations. Hence, from the outset of EMU negotiations in 1988, the strategy of the federal government was to 'bind in' the Bundesbank at all key points. Failure to achieve its compliance, as over the revaluation of its gold reserves in 1997, was potentially very damaging.

But EMU also revealed the limitations of its power. Once EMU was agreed at Maastricht, the Bundesbank's role was defined as providing expert advice and criticism in a discreet rather than public manner. This role conception fitted its professional outlook. The law of 1957 enjoined the Bundesbank to respect the general economic policy of the federal government. In consequence it often found itself on the defensive. Its president was overruled over the Delors Committee in June 1988. A fixed, final date was agreed at Maastricht against Bundesbank views. In addition, at critical moments in the 1990s it was reminded that it had a duty of loyalty to the policies of the federal government and to the obligations entered into with the Maastricht Treaty.

At the level of the Chancellor and the Foreign Minister there was a view that the Bundesbank had a limited political and historical perspective. The argument was that EMU was ultimately situated in German external security interests and that a more activist approach to those interests was required in the post-cold war, post-German unification period. In particular, a distrust emerged towards Tietmeyer's motives in taking up an ultra-strict interpretation of the convergence criteria, in pressing the theme of an ambitious political union as a necessary accompaniment to EMU, and in his behaviour during the revaluation of gold reserves episode. These positions were seen within the Chancellor's Office and Foreign Ministry as an attempt to set high hurdles to stop EMU going forward. For Tietmeyer they were designed to ensure that, when launched, it would work in a sustainable manner.

The Maastricht Treaty made a difference to the Bundesbank's power by submitting it to EU treaty obligations to prepare stage three. Though stage two was essentially an 'empty shell' in that no monetary-policy responsibilities were ceded, the Bundesbank's own interest in actively shaping stage three meant that from 1994 it became thoroughly Europeanized. In addition, the ERM crises of 1992–3 administered a harsh lesson about the risk of the Bundesbank being held responsible for failure to take the European dimension more seriously in its monetary-policy decisions. Hence the Bundesbank opted for a more proactive approach on EMU. The effects were discernible in its internal structural working, notably the new European steering committee of October 1994. This committee represented a new Europeanization of its official apparatus 'from below', with the effect that Bundesbank directors were exposed to European issues in a new way. The effects were also noticeable in its policies: for example, its changed position on money market funds, its change to a two-year money-supply target in 1997, and its—imposed—responsibility for redenominating government debt from D-Mark to euro from 1997.

Stage two and participation in the EMI had important socialization effects, especially as the Bundesbank was able to have a disproportionate impact on negotiations there. Moreover, the numerous concessions gained by Waigel —and listed above—made the transition to stage three more amenable for the Bundesbank, or at least reduced its capacity to criticize. Another key factor was the absence of any serious ERM crises after 1995. These crises had—

notably in 1992–3—produced a more assertive behaviour by the Bundesbank on behalf of the primacy of its responsibility for domestic monetary stability. In their absence the Bundesbank lacked such opportunities.

Finally, the Bundesbank did not wish to be seen as disloyal to the elected government and as tarnished with the brush of sabotaging the next key step in European integration. It risked being seen as pursuing its own corporate interest in survival and protecting central banking jobs at the expense of Germany's higher political interests. Here the Bundesbank was influenced by its memory of how Kohl had dismissed its views on the terms of German unification in 1990. Unlike with German unification the Bundesbank could not claim that it had been marginalized over EMU.

In consequence, the Bundesbank's behaviour was a mixture of assertiveness and conciliation. Tietmeyer's presence as president guaranteed that it would act as the strong-willed advocate of German stability culture and Ordo-liberal values and arguments. Precisely because this role was facilitated by the federal government, and the Bundesbank's assertiveness directed outwards to the EU level rather than inwards against Bonn, the Bundesbank's room for manoeuvre in 1998 was limited. Hence its crucial report of March 1998 on whether the convergence criteria had been met proved accommodating. Another conditioning factor was loyalty to central bank solidarity within the European Monetary Institute. The Bundesbank had participated in agreeing the EMI's report on whether the convergence criteria had been fulfilled. It could not then be seen to act as an individual critic of its peers. Hence institutional factors are important in explaining why the Bundesbank was conciliatory in 1998.

The transition to stage three was the single most important challenge to the Bundesbank in its history. With the creation of the ECB it lost not just its monetary-policy responsibility but also its dominant monetary-policy role in Europe. Its president now made monetary policy as one of 17 members of the ECB's governing council. The Bundesbank council was responsible for acting in accordance with the guidelines and instructions of the ECB. Otherwise, it could only advise its president. The result was a three- rather than two-level system: ECB, Bundesbank, and State central banks. In consequence, the future functions and structure of the Bundesbank became a key domestic political issue. The rationale for a decentralized structure, with nine State central bank presidents in the Bundesbank council, and for individual responsibilities attached to the State central banks seemed no longer defensible. Hence the euro was associated with new concerns about the credibility and reputation of the Bundesbank within the ECB. It raised issues of identity, policy responsibilities, and structure.

The strategic objective of Ernst Welteke, the new president, was to strengthen his negotiating power within the ECB in the wake of the weakening of the Bundesbank by EMU and a changed operating context. The principle around which he sought to manufacture a new consensus was a shared interest in the future credibility and reputation of the Bundesbank within the ECB. This reputation was endangered by a slow, lowest-common-denominator reform of the Bundesbank, by public disputes over monetary policy, and by failure to establish the prime responsibility of the Bundesbank for the stability of the financial system. Accordingly, he developed his strategy in the form of two proposals. First, he advocated a centralized, one-level Bundesbank decision structure that would support a unified leadership role in European monetary policy. He argued that there was no longer a case for independent State central bank presidents in the central decision-making body of the Bundesbank. Unsurprisingly, the Bundesbank council was split on the issue, with many State central bank presidents bitterly opposed. State governments feared erosion of the federal principle, diminished political weight, and job losses. Welteke was concerned to insure himself against Bundesbank council members undermining his authority by offering independent public comments on ECB monetary policy or foreign-exchange market intervention. These comments led to criticisms from partners in the Euro-system. A centralized internal decision-making structure was also more consistent with the new orientation of monetary policy to Euro-Zone-wide data rather than micro-level regional data.

Second, Welteke sought full integration of responsibility for banking supervision in the Bundesbank based on its superior knowledge of market conditions. By doing so he wanted to create a German central bank model that others might emulate. The aim was to carve out new roles to compensate for lost ones, not just banking supervision but ultimately even integrated responsibility for financial market supervision. In addition, Welteke saw a new opportunity for the Bundesbank to give greater attention to Germany's needs as a financial centre including the competitiveness of the German banking system. This role remained, however, constrained by the principle of neutrality and by the overriding requirement to promote long-term financial stability. This proposal also met resistance. The BdB preferred a unified federal financial services authority independent of the Bundesbank.

However, Eichel's two proposals of January 2001 for reform of the structure of the Bundesbank and of financial supervision disappointed and surprised Welteke. He was offered a centralized leadership structure, with abolition of the Bundesbank council and just a directorate of six including the president and vice-president. But the responsibility for financial supervision—previously divided between three federal bodies for banking, insurance, and securities markets—was to be combined in a new federal authority for financial market supervision. This latter proposal reflected Eichel's desire to carve out a leadership role in dealing with the issue of integrated financial supervision within the Euro-Zone. But it had to be defended against the Bundesbank, which feared that its ability to ensure the stability of the financial system had been weakened. It also faced criticism from the ECB (2001b), which argued for a stronger role for national central banks in monitoring systemic risks, especially given the important issues of liquidity. It indicated that making financial supervision independent of the central banks endangered both the stability of the financial system and the reputation of the European System of Central Banks. By linking these two proposals Eichel was strengthening his image as a reformer by aligning himself with the idea of strengthening Germany as a financial centre. He sought to make it more difficult for Welteke to oppose without risking a delay to Bundesbank reform and associating the Bundesbank with damage to Germany as a financial centre. The reform was a difficult balancing act between strengthening the Bundesbank, creating a supervisory structure more favourable to the big commercial banks, and keeping intact the Bundesbank's responsibility for the stability of the financial system. But to ensure its passage the legislation had to gain the support of more than one-third of the votes in the Bundesrat.

Another change, parallel to the transition to the euro, that affected the power of the Bundesbank was the replacement of Tietmeyer by Welteke. In one respect this was a loss of power and status. Tietmeyer had an unrivalled 30-years' experience of international financial and monetary affairs. Welteke had been a regional politician and for five years a State central bank president. Hence he lacked Tietmeyer's reputation. On the other hand, Welteke had a less complex relationship to EMU, fully and unequivocally endorsed its political rationale, and had been critical of an overstrict interpretation of the convergence criteria. He was also personally and politically very close to Eichel, with whom he had worked very closely in Hesse. Values of social solidarity and justice were deeply rooted in his SPD background. Welteke was, in addition, knowledgeable through his regional contacts about Frankfurt as a financial centre and receptive to its needs. In essence, his appointment broke with recent practice. He was not a Bundesbank insider as Helmut Schlesinger had been. He was not an international star like Tietmeyer and Pöhl earlier. But, in the sensitive domestic political context of Bundesbank reform, Welteke enjoyed the confidence of Eichel and could bring a fresh perspective.

The Paradox of the German Model of 'Managed' Capitalism and EMU

The final paradox was that German politicians and officials were gradually forced to recognize that EMU 'Europeanized' the Bundesbank model but not the German model in its larger sense, that is, 'managed' capitalism. This issue especially preoccupied the Schröder government. It was reflected in the new emphasis on a dimension of social dialogue to EMU and on the critical role of coordinated wage bargaining for price stability. The problem of 'fit' with the German model derived from Europeanizing the steering function of the Bundesbank on economic stability without the supportive structure of 'implicit' coordination found in Germany (Gretschmann 1998: 53). The German political economy rested on an asymmetrical system of 'implicit' coordination, privileging the central bank as the authoritative 'signaller' but recognizing that a mechanism was required to ensure unit labour costs consistent with price stability (Dyson 1999a). This mechanism was provided by a model of 'managed' capitalism in which the state played an enabling role in encouraging cooperation within and among firms and between employers and labour. Unless the 'managed' capitalism model could be both re-dynamized at home and exported to the EU, the prospect was that EMU would undermine it at cost to treasured German values of consensus and social solidarity.

'Managed' capitalism had strong historical, cultural, and institutional roots. It endowed Model Germany with a reputation for corporate- and a macro-level responsibility in wage bargaining; for focusing on unit labour costs as a critical issue; for 'long-termism' in investment through reliance on bank rather than equity financing; for a stress on 'skill-upgrading'; for a collaborative approach to technology transfer; and for social and industrial peace through the negotiated management of change. This reputation focused on Germany as a successful manufacturing and exporting country, competing on the basis of product quality, reliability, and flexibility and characterized by high productivity. It also went along with a longer timescale of restructuring than was typical for states dedicated to primacy of 'shareholder' value.

Historically, 'managed' capitalism formed a continuum with the organized capitalism of cartels, cross-ownership, elite networking, self-regulation, and public-private pacts that characterized early German industrialization (Dyson 1992). It has fewer problems with mergers and the concentration of economic power than did post-war Ordo-liberalism. Culturally, it rested on a respect for the principle of consensus. This principle was deeply entrenched in both the political and the economic systems. Hence there was a 'goodness of fit' in domestic governance. Schröder was able to use consensus about tax reform in the Alliance for Jobs, notably the support of employers, to lever compliance from the CDU opposition. Institutionally, 'managed' capitalism was supported by the German system of corporate governance—especially co-determination and strong works councils—a domestic credit system that encouraged long-term banking finance of industry, the organization of labour-market policy and vocational training, and the management of welfare-state arrangements. Co-determination in corporate governance brought trade unions and bankers into sharing responsibility with employers as stakeholders in industry. In this way the concept of social partnership was deeply embedded in the German economy. From 1995 the vitality of the 'managed' capitalism model was manifested in the proliferation of employment pacts negotiated between individual firms and their works councils and trading off wage restraint for job creation.

Politically, the epicentres of this model were the SPD and the CDU in North-Rhine Westphalia. Within the North-Rhine Westphalian SPD Bodo Hombach, Klaus Gretschmann, and the Prime Minister, Wolfgang Clement, were key advocates of the 'managed' economy model. This model was adopted by Schröder, embodied in his political theme of the 'new centre' (neue Mitte) and the Alliance for Jobs, and demonstrated in the appointments of Hombach and Gretschmann to the Chancellery in 1998. It was also strongly represented in the Labour and Social Affairs Ministry and by the Economics Minister, Müller.

Ordo-liberalism lived in a relationship of antagonism with 'managed' capitalism. Ideologically, its insistence on open, competitive markets and on a wide distribution of ownership and economic decision making put them in conflict. Ordo-liberalism gave primacy to a clear long-term framework of rules for competition and a strong anti-trust policy. In contrast, 'managed' capitalism took an evolutionary view of competition, focused on the endogenous aspects of the economy, and stressed the importance of distancing services of general economic interest—like public savings banks—from the market. 'Managed' capitalism was seen by Ordo-liberals as a system for privileging labour-market 'insiders' at the expense of neglecting the unemployed. It was also viewed as threatening to shift blame for problems of growth and unemployment to the central bank, confusing responsibilities rather than clarifying them. There were also tensions on exchange-rate policy. Ordo-liberals favoured a strong euro as a means of exerting competitive discipline on the German economy. 'Managed' capitalists tended to be more pragmatic, seeing advantages from lower exchange-rate pressure for the peaceful negotiated management of change. On pragmatic grounds, some Ordo-liberals recognized that a cooperative approach to wages could induce greater macroeconomic responsibility and that consensus about change, by taking into account those affected, could strengthen the market economy. But pragmatism was much more likely to dispose them to identify in globalization, the single European market, the 'new' economy, and EMU forces that were reinvigorating the Ordo-liberal principle of open, free markets. Consensus might be too costly for an economy that required greater flexibility, especially in labour markets and wages. Globalization—its effects hastened by EMU— suggested to Ordo-liberals that the 'managed' capitalism model was outdated and destined to dissolve.

The Schröder government sought to rehabilitate 'managed' capitalism after it had been on the defensive since the failure of the trade-union inspired Alliance for Jobs in March 1996. The key initiatives were to establish a domestic Alliance for Jobs to seek cooperation on structural economic reforms and to extend this type of thinking to the EU level during the German EU presidency of early 1999. The main proposal agreed at the Cologne European Council was a Macroeconomic Dialogue as one of the three pillars of the European Employment Pact. The other two pillars built on the employment chapter of the Amsterdam Treaty and the procedure for structural reforms. The Macroeconomic Dialogue was designed to prevent macroeconomic conflicts between monetary, financial, and wage policies by encouraging cooperative behaviour. In so doing, German negotiators were at pains to seek out consensus with Ordo-liberalism. The Macroeconomic Dialogue was about supporting the ECB in pursuing its price stability objective and about achieving trust and reliability in behaviour. Above all, the social partners were drawn into EU-level consultation, but on the model of 'implicit' co-ordination and without challenging the privileged position of the ECB. The discourse of the Schröder government was one of pragmatic social engineering accommodated within an Ordo-liberal framework that ensured monetary policy leadership.

This very limited institution building at the EU level on the German 'managed' capitalism model had weaknesses. The ECB's monetary policy remained remote from the complex national, regional, and local realities of wage bargaining in a way that had not been so true before 1999. The social partners lacked the strength of EU-level organization to match the ECB that had existed at the national level in Germany. The comparison between this very limited institutional development and the forces of market competition unleashed both by EMU and by globalization suggested that these latter two forces were more likely to change Germany than Germany was to change EMU in a way that would protect the 'managed' capitalism model.

The question was whether the centrifugal forces outweighed the forces holding together the 'managed' capitalism model. One force was the exit of firms and workers from the traditional 'area-wide' wage agreements in favour of firm and plant-level bargaining. Here eastern Germany was a model for the rest of Germany (Padgett 1999). Another centrifugal force was the big private banks like Deutsche and Dresdner. Identifying new market opportunities with globalization and the euro, they pursued two strategies. The first was 'exit' from a retail-banking sector that was insufficiently competitive because of the privileged position of the public savings and the cooperative banks. They sought to carve out a new identity as international investment banks. The second was 'voice' in the form of seeking European Commission action against the privileged position of the savings and cooperative banks. The big private banks exhibited a diminished loyalty to the traditional features of the 'managed' capitalism model. This diminished loyalty was manifested in their advocacy of an end to capital-gains tax on disposal of bank shareholdings in German industry. In this way they sought to mobilize resources for their new corporate strategy.

By 2001 there were signs that the Schröder government was responsive to the commercial banks. It conceded the abolition of capital-gains tax on disposal of their shareholdings; it adopted the model of financial market supervision that they advocated rather than that promoted by the Bundesbank; and it provided them with new opportunities by proposing to encourage private pension funds to supplement the traditional 'pay-as-you-go' state system. These changes suggested that the dynamizing of 'managed' capitalism by the Schröder government might also be its unravelling. The paradox was that 'bottom-up' change from Germany to EMU was giving way to 'top-down' changes unleashed by the euro and globalization. German discomfort with this paradox was visible in the hostile reactions to the Vodafone takeover of Mannesmann in 2000; in the attempts of German companies to delist from the stock market and go private again; and in the government's threat to back out of the common position on takeover rules agreed by EU governments in June 2000.

The survival and effectiveness of the Alliance for Jobs became a litmus test for the continuing resilience of the 'managed' capitalism model. Its historical, institutional, cultural, and political foundations remained in place, though shaken. Schröder's government acted as one safeguard. But, at a deeper level, the institutional arrangements of co-determination and labour-market policy were more important. These arrangements were in tune with an economy whose leading firms remained committed to a strategy of pursuing product quality, reliability, and flexibility and hence were more rather than less dependent on skilled workers and a harmonious environment in the workplace (Silvia 1999; Thelen 2000).

What seemed to be happening was a redefinition of the scope of the 'managed' capitalism model (Dyson 2001). Global financial markets and the euro were weakening one of its pillars: the banking system and industrial financing. Another—'area-wide' wage bargaining—was under acute pressure from German unification and globalization pressures. In the changed circumstances of heightened competition through globalization, technological change, and the euro, the 'managed' capitalism model gained heightened legitimacy from its association with skilled employment, competitiveness through containment of unit labour costs, and vocational training. Hence its content shifted to the negotiation of employment pacts, tax reforms, and welfare-state reforms—notably a fall in social security contributions—involving trade-offs with wage restraint. Employer and trade-union organizations agreed to work within an inflation-plus-productivity wage formula and to pursue two-year rather than one-year wage deals in order to give more stability. The German state retained an essentially enabling role in the management of economic change but was redefining this role.

Consistent with the 'managed' capitalism model the Schröder government imposed new regulations on short-term labour contracts, gave greater rights to part-time workers, and proposed to extend the role of works councils to small and medium-sized firms. It did so in the face both of criticisms from the OECD that it was failing to tackle unemployment through liberalizing labour markets and of evidence from states like France that part-time and temporary working was the most important source of new jobs. The problem was that 'managed' capitalism's relevance and value to a high 'value-added' manufacturing economy competing on product quality, reliability, and flexibility was not so readily transferable to the parts of the economy that were most likely to create new employment, namely, a service sector of part-time and temporary working. German policy-makers remained loath to contemplate a 'low-wage' sector. Hence the Schröder government's record on job creation was worse than that of its equivalents in Denmark and the Netherlands.

Conclusion

The transition to stage three of EMU has been accompanied by major changes in Germany. At the level of discourse EMU has come to be invested with new meanings by Ordo-liberals, New Keynesians, and 'managed' capitalists. Each has defined EMU as posing a problem of 'goodness of fit' and requiring transformation rather than just accommodation by Germany. Where they differ is in their definition of this problem and the nature of the transformation. At the same time, following the departure of Lafontaine, the Schröder government has achieved a new measure of consensus about Germany and EMU. The result has been a shift in the centre of gravity of this consensus. But it remains a consensus that masks internal inconsistencies and tensions.

Structurally too there has been change. The Finance Ministry has been considerably strengthened while the Economics Ministry and the Bundesbank have been weakened. With the Europeanization of the Finance Ministry and the greater variety of views that it contains, it has taken on a more open character than under Waigel. By strengthening its European coordination function the Finance Ministry has gained greater leverage over structural economic reforms, notably as they affect employment. Eichel may lack the political power base of Lafontaine. But he leads a much more powerful ministry than Waigel and, unlike Lafontaine, he can count on Schröder's support. Less clear is the position of the Bundesbank. It faces a new problem of projecting a unified coherent image within the ECB consequent on its federalized structure. Structural reforms look likely to strengthen its power while functional reforms seem more likely to weaken it.

In programmatic terms EMU has had a powerful impact, notably within the SPD and within the federal government. In part, this is attributable to Lafontaine's impact as party chair in seeking to Europeanize SPD policy and use the ideas of other social democratic parties to open up debate and shift the domestic consensus in Germany. It also bears the marks of rethinking within the Chancellor's Office and the Finance Ministry. The programmatic impact has been associated with a new stress on benchmarking best practice, a technocratic methodology that eases problems of acceptance of structural reforms especially on the left and within the trade-unions. This technocratic outlook on reform was further strengthened by the Lisbon European Council's priority to a European knowledge and innovation society. EMU has been redefined as a technocratic project in a wider sense than just a monetary union of central bankers. In so doing a discourse has been created that expedites structural reforms by objectifying them. But, at the level of specific policies, there remains a reluctance to frame reforms as required by EMU. The preference remains for framing reform as done for good German reasons by reference to domestic political considerations and party principle. At the same time the new centrality of tax, labour-market, and welfare-state reforms is bound up with EMU, even if as a mediating variable for the effects of globalization.

These discursive, structural, and policy effects cannot, however, be disentangled from the factors of uncertainty and contingency and from how

German policy-makers have managed the paradoxes with which EMU faced them. The ability of Kohl and Waigel to manoeuvre their way through the economic and political, domestic and European complexities of the transition to stage three owed a great deal to benign economic circumstances. An upswing in the EU economy relieved national budget problems at the same time as financial crisis in the international economy showed the value of a prospective EMU in providing a shield against the worst effects. But it also demonstrated their strategic and tactical skills in making a series of timely concessions to keep EMU on track and contain domestic dissent. In the end, structure and agency conspired to make EMU possible for Germany. They did so, however, in a context of uncertainty and contingency that did not make the outcome a foregone conclusion.

Overall, there remains a 'goodness of fit' between Germany and EMU. This 'goodness of fit' does not mean that Germany has simply accommodated EMU without strain. There is accommodation to the extent that EMU embodies German ideas on economic stability and the Schröder government has attempted to export elements of 'managed' capitalism into euro economic governance. But the 'managed' capitalism model has not been fully exported. More importantly, EMU's effects are not what many German policy-makers anticipated. EMU is changing Germany fast and in complex ways. It is a force for transformation, but constructed in different ways. The Schröder government is the crucial test of the sustainability of 'managed' capitalism in this process of transition. Just how sustainable it proves to be will depend on improved German performance in economic growth and job creation within the Euro-Zone. By 2001 its performance, though improved, languished behind France and other Euro-Zone states with the exception of Italy.

A potential point of stress is between an elite consensus that stresses further steps to European political unification in order to give the euro a strong political foundation and domestic public opinion that is more hesitant about making sacrifices for Europe and more critical of Community institutions. The bedrock of German policy on EMU has been the assumption of a permissive consensus at the level of public opinion. The anxieties prompted by EU enlargement to the east, by the enduring burden of eastern Germany, and by unacceptably high unemployment there could prompt new tensions in elite-mass relations, entice a more populist politics on Europe, and make German policy less calculable. These threats remain contained by an institutional embedding of historical memories that support good neighbourliness as a German European policy goal, an embedding that has survived generational change with the Red-Green coalition.

8

The Italian State and the Euro:
Institutions, Discourse, and Policy Regimes

Claudio Radaelli

To examine EMU as Europeanization means to research its domestic effects, the mechanisms at work, and the temporal causal sequences (see Introduction). The nascent literature on Europeanization adds that the major domestic effects are at the level of policy rather than polity or politics (Radaelli 2000). But policy-level effects may produce major institutional change: a point raised by previous research on Italy and EMU (Dyson and Featherstone 1999; Giuliani 1999). The question is, therefore: to what extent has EMU changed the Italian institutions of economic policy?

The essential difference is between 'coping' with EMU and deeper transformation. Institutions can be flexible and accommodate extraordinary pressures without fundamental change in their logic of behaviour. The Italian political system is known for its coping mechanisms. Hence, following Fabbrini (1998), one could argue that Italian institutions have flexed like bamboo in the wind to accommodate the pressure to qualify for the single currency. According to the 'coping' argument, once this goal had been achieved institutions would soon revert to their original position. In contrast, paradigmatic change occurs when Europeanization changes the logic of political behaviour. To answer the question about the type of change is more than an issue of mere academic interest. European policy-makers and the business community wonder whether the Italian budgetary adjustment is relatively stable or the product of exceptional circumstances and hence ephemeral. Thus, the question of change has relevance for the debate about the sustainability of Italy's Euro-Zone membership.

I am grateful to the Social Sciences Methodology Centre of LUISS-Guido Carli University Rome for hospitality in May and June 2000. I wish to thank Andrew Baker, Bruno Dente, Kenneth Dyson, Maurizio Ferrera, Paul Furlong, Elisabetta Gualmini, Jean Leca, Sandro Momigliano, Lucia Quaglia, Vivien Schmidt, and James Walsh for their detailed comments and suggestions. The usual disclaimer applies.

This chapter seeks to shed light on the type of change under way in Italy by discussing the two rival hypotheses of 'simple coping strategies' and 'paradigmatic' change. The two rival hypotheses may be re-framed in terms of the debate between 'simple' and 'thick' learning. Simple learning is limited to coping mechanisms, whereas the thicker effects of EMU as Europeanization can be described as reflexive understanding (Dobuzinskis 1992), deutero-learning (Bateson 1973), or institutional development (Laird 1999). Specifically, Laird (1999) differentiates between learning and cognitive development. The former denotes a gradual, incremental process, whereas the latter denotes a discontinuous jump towards new ways of organizing knowledge.

How do institutions develop? Laird suggests three processes: political experience, robustness, and equilibration. Political experience is exemplified by the interactions between the core executive and other actors. Institutions become more robust by dint of advisory structures, improved technologies, and stronger bureaucratic structures. To what extent has EMU brought about 'institutional robustness' in the Italian Treasury and the presidency of the Council of Ministers? Institutions develop through equilibration when they face a crisis that does not fit any of the standard repertoires of action. Development, as opposed to simple learning, requires a discontinuity with the past. The rules and norms through which institutions learn are transformed and become institutionalized through experience. The question then becomes: to what extent have Italian institutions produced new norms, ideas, rules, and practices that have become embedded and therefore will outlive the individuals who promoted them (Laird 1999: 5)? The chapter tackles this issue by complementing the analysis of the run-up to the euro (1992–8) with more recent evidence.

There are two problems raised by the analysis of simple learning versus institutional development. One is that to cast the discussion of EMU as Europeanization in terms of 'thin' or 'thick' effects runs the risk of prejudging EMU's significance. The emphasis on *effects* should be accompanied by a contextualization of EMU (see Introduction) and by an explicit treatment of causality. It is difficult to assess the contribution of a single independent variable such as EMU. Thus in the Italian case the process of macroeconomic convergence with the criteria designed at Maastricht took place in the context of a threefold political crisis of authority, legitimacy, and distribution between centre and periphery (Bull and Rhodes 1997). EMU has to be contextualized in relation to the domestic political transition of the 1990s. At the same time, the process of Europeanization induced by EMU is a major component of this transition. One possible way out of this puzzle is to trace temporal sequences, as suggested in the Introduction. The historical analysis contained in this chapter will show when, why, and how actors responded to EMU and with what effects. Time is obviously a political resource in a process marked by convergence criteria and timetables. I will therefore describe when key decisions were made—time—the sequences of decisions—timing—and the rate of speed of change—tempo. Institutional development is a process, not a single episode in time.

The second problem is that institutions, strictly speaking, do not have cognitive capacities of their own. It is not appropriate to enter the debate between methodological individualism and the advocates of institutional thinking. But this chapter will try to connect institutional change and actor-centred analysis by looking at EMU as discursive construction. Discourse is fundamental both in giving shape to new rules, values, and practices and as a resource used by political actors to produce legitimacy for EMU-induced choices, such as the 'tax for Europe' and pension reform. Discourse will be considered in its dual role, that is, as a resource available to entrepreneurial actors—actor-centred analysis—and as a cognitive structure, that is, the insti-tutionalization of ideas about EMU and its implications for policy reforms. The aim is to avoid two common pitfalls: the reification of discourse and the elusiveness of some analyses of institutional thinking. Drawing upon Schmidt (2001) it is useful to distinguish between discourse formation at the level of elites—coordinative discourse—and the forms of political commun-ication directed to the mass public—communicative discourse.[1]

Building Institutional Capacity: The Early Attempts

Italy built up latent institutional capacity during the decade of unsuccessful economic management preceding the Treaty of Maastricht. These seeds of change provided a sort of imprinting. I do not argue that the politico-economic strategies of the 1990s were the product of past choices. Quite the opposite: institutional development requires dramatic innovation. But inno-vation does not take place in a vacuum. In zoology, imprinting designates 'the development in a young animal of a pattern of recognition and trust for its own species' (Concise Oxford Dictionary). Similarly, the individuation of economic strategies and the choice of trustworthy partners in the 1990s were

---

[1] Methodologically, I approached discourse analysis by covering a variety of sources, such as official speeches of politicians, parliamentary hearings, the surveys conducted for the Parliament's select committees (*indagini conoscitive*), and other institutional bodies, the quality press, the activity of think tanks, and, most importantly perhaps, a set of some 20 interviews with policy-makers and experts involved in the policy process in June 2000.

patterned by evolution in three areas: (1) the cognitive component of public policy, (2) rules, and (3) the policy style.

In terms of the cognitive structure of public policy, the 'sound finance' policy paradigm won the battle of ideas. The discourse of *risanamento* (fiscal adjustment) became a focal point in the debate on macroeconomic policy during the 1980s. A number of accurate diagnoses and therapies were elaborated (Sartor 1998). Thus, when Italy embarked on to the road to EMU in 1992 there was a consensus on what had to be done, at least in terms of the broad directions of economic policy. Italian policy-makers faced the tough road to the euro by drawing on shared beliefs and discourse about the necessary steps. An essential component of this process was the socialization of Italian elites in the process of making European monetary policy (Dyson and Featherstone 1999). The roots of EMU as Europeanization date back well before 1992.

As for the development of rules, innovations were introduced in monetary policy and in the budgetary process. Let us start with monetary policy. In 1981, the so-called divorce between the Bank of Italy and the Treasury inaugurated a season of increased autonomy of monetary policy (Epstein and Schor 1989). By 1992 the Bank of Italy was given full independence in terms of interest rates and the obligations to assist the Treasury were removed. Monetary policy was able to generate lower inflation and relative stability of the lira in the years that preceded the Treaty of Maastricht. Thus monetary adjustment achieved some initial results before fiscal adjustment began (Walsh 1999). Once some preliminary results in the fight against inflation were achieved, the correction of fiscal imbalances became the 'big issue' to be tackled.

The introduction of the first finance bill, inclusive of rules on the budget session in Parliament, in 1978 was an attempt to establish the institutional preconditions for fiscal adjustment (law no. 468–1978). The impact of these rules was modest, arguably because the law introduced a political process— the parliamentary session on budget—that the Prime Minister and the Treasury were not able to govern. The government made a more effective step towards the control of the budgetary policy process in 1988. Law no. 362–1988 introduced the finance and planning document (DPEF), which provided a framework for multi-annual planning to be discussed in late spring, well before the budget session of the autumn. It also imposed limitations on the role of Parliament. The DPEF should have acted as a political constraint in that the choices made in the finance bill would have to be compatible with the multi-annual path towards a balanced budget. However, the early impact was less than dramatic. The Treasury and the Prime Minister remained politically and organizationally weak, although law no. 400–1988 on the reorganization of the presidency of the Council of Ministers created the basis for a better organization of prime ministerial activity. Before 1992 the voice of ministers in charge of expenditure remained quite assertive. Although the parliamentary stage of the budget had been modified, the governmental stage of the budgetary process proceeded along the same old tracks (Verzichelli 1999).

The third component of the institutional imprint concerns the neo-corporatist policy style (Regini and Regalia 1997). In 1978 Italy witnessed the first neo-corporatist agreement in a political context dominated by economic and political crisis. The Minister of Labour, the three main national trade unions, and the national employers' associations signed a social pact in 1983. An attempt to institutionalize neo-corporatism in Italy with another pact in 1984 failed because of the divisions amongst the unions. Although social pacts were put on the back-burner up until the 1990s, this early experience in 1978–84 inaugurated a legacy, in the form of the persistence of neo-corporatist routines, symbols, and rituals (Gualmini 1997).

The Path to Convergence (1992–1998)

This section examines the changes in budgetary policy, discourse, and policy regimes in the period 1992–8. Table 8.1 contains essential information on the governments of the 1990s. Table 8.2 presents an overview of budgetary policy.

Once the Treaty of Maastricht was signed, the elite-level consensus on 'what had to be done' was high. Fiscal adjustment was perceived by the elites as a *scelta obbligata*, that is, a 'choice' with no degree of freedom, although there was debate on whether fiscal correction should be gradual or swift. Italy was due for general elections in April 1992. On 27 February 1992, during the electoral campaign, two economists, Mario Monti and Luigi Spaventa, made a public plea for an open political debate on convergence and how to distribute the cost of adjustment. However, the appeal was scarcely taken into account by the main political parties, which were involved in an electoral campaign characterized by new rules on preference voting, the rise of the Northern League, and the first investigations into political corruption (Pasquino 1993).

Giuliano Amato was chosen in June 1992 to lead the new government in a period of domestic political turmoil compounded by the uncertainty of the financial markets after the Danish referendum on EMU. Amato sought immediately the consensus of the social partners. On 31 July 1992 he revived the tradition of social pacts by agreeing with the main unions and the employers'

Table 8.1 Italian governments in the 1990s

Prime Minister	Period in office	Treasury minister	Budget minister
Amato	June 1992–April 1993	Barucci	Reviglio
Ciampi	April 1993–April 1994	Barucci	Spaventa
Berlusconi	May 1994–Dec. 1994	Dini	Pagliarini
Dini	Jan. 1995–Jan. 1996[a]	Dini	Masera
Prodi	May 1996–Oct. 1998	Ciampi	(*)
D'Alema I	Oct. 1998–Dec. 1999	Ciampi (until May 1999) Amato (May–Dec. 1999)	(*)
D'Alema II	Dec. 1999–April 2000	Amato	(*)
Amato	April 2000–June 2001	Visco	(*)
Berlusconi	June 2001–	Tremonti	(*)

[a] Dini resigned on 11 January 1996. Antonio Maccanico was appointed to form a new government, but he failed. The President of Republic, Scalfaro, dissolved Parliament on 16 February 1996. Elections took place on 21 April 1996 during the Italian presidency of the European Union.

(*) Treasury and Budget joined in a single Department.

Table 8.2 Italian budgetary policy in the 1990s

Year	Fiscal adjustment (Finance Bill) (billions of liras)	Fiscal adj. % of GDP	Overall balance % of GDP	Primary balance % of GDP	Debt % of GDP	Revenue % of GDP
1990	49,500	3.8	−11.1	−1.7	104.5	42.4
1991	61,500	4.3	−10.1	0.1	108.4	43.4
1992	93,000	6.2	−9.6	1.9	117.3	44.3
1993	48,000	3.1	−9.5	2.6	118.9	47.4
1994	55,000	3.4	−9.2	1.8	125.1	45.2
1995	32,500	1.8	−7.7	3.6	124.2	45.0
1996	16,000	0.9	−6.7	4.1	123.7	46.0
1997	78,500	4.0	−2.7	6.6	121.7	47.9
1998	25,000	1.2	−2.6	4.9	118.5	46.7

Sources: European Commission and Ministero del Tesoro

confederation of industry a package against inflation which included the abolition of the very icon of Italian industrial relations: wage indexation. Amato's search for trust and legitimacy beyond the Parliament reveals a typical feature of the style of Italian technocrats in government in the 1990s.

Fearing a legitimacy deficit, they sought the consensus of social partners. The choice for social pacts did not come out of the blue, however. The legacy of the social pacts of the 1980s left traces in an ongoing debate at the highest political levels, including the National Council for the Economy and Labour, a constitutional body where labour and capital had continued to probe the viability of concertation and incomes policy (Brunetta 1992).

The most urgent challenge for Amato was macroeconomic policy. A series of emergency measures in July 1992 did not go down well with EU partners and the financial markets. The real crisis came on 13 September 1992, when financial speculation against the lira forced the Italian currency out of the European Monetary System. Amato reacted to this event with an extraordinarily tough finance bill: the fiscal correction was 6.2 per cent of GDP.

Amato's finance bill was linked to two wider components of the government's strategy: the strengthening of the executive and discourse. He succeeded in persuading the Parliament to delegate power to the government in four crucial policy domains: pensions, the national health service, local government, and employment in the public sector. Amato's pension reform was not comprehensive, but it was incisive (Banca d'Italia 1993; 2000; Franco 2000). Some 200,000 pensioners protested in the streets, but the government was able to go ahead with the increase of the retirement age from 55 to 60 for females and from 60 to 65 for males in the private sector and with other substantial improvements. Public employment expenditure was pushed below the rate of inflation. The preconditions for privatization were put in place. Revenue was increased. Local governments gained more fiscal responsibility but the flow of resources from Rome was reduced.

The assertiveness of the Prime Minister was not a consequence of the Treaty of Maastricht. Amato was not empowered by EMU but by the financial crisis of the summer. However, this contingent factor operated in the wider framework of fiscal adjustment as discursive focal point, of monetary and budgetary rules, and of the neo-corporatist style that emerged in the previous decade. Empowerment requires legitimacy. Amato's discourse drew on different elements of legitimacy, such as the consensus of all 'responsible' social forces, the sense of emergency, and the humiliation of the Italians consequent on exclusion of the lira from the EMS. This discourse was effective in turning the focal point of *risanamento* into a crisis consciousness.

The Amato government was soon followed by a fully technocratic government—none of the ministers was a member of Parliament—headed by the former governor of the Bank of Italy, Carlo Azelio Ciampi. With Ciampi, the logic of change of industrial relations became clearer. Ciampi's social pact of 23 July 1993 produced a wider reform of representation and 'a stable architecture for incomes policy' (Regini and Regalia 1997: 214). The same expansion of scope can be found in administrative reform. With Amato, the main issue was to reduce costs, and expenditure on wages and salaries in the public sector was a natural target. Thanks to Minister Sabino Cassese, a world-class authority on public administration, the Ciampi government reasoned that an effective fiscal adjustment required, more than cuts, a permanent increase in the productivity of the public sector. Simplification and the rationalization of central administrative structures accompanied measures on public employees such as the freeze on hiring. Fiscal adjustment and administrative reform were thus melded in a single discourse.

With the elections of 1994, the balance switched from technocrats to politicians, although even Silvio Berlusconi could not do without the expertise of a Bank of Italy man, Lamberto Dini. The DPEF presented by the new Berlusconi government covered the crucial year of 1997—the decisive year for convergence—although at that time the situation was still one of uncertainty about the precise timing of the assessment of EMU applicants. The forecast for 1997 contained in the DPEF was not consistent with the Maastricht target for the deficit, although the scale of the fiscal correction for 1994–5 was substantial (see Table 8.2).

However, the main European problems for the Berlusconi government were not in the finance bill but in the political messages of Foreign Minister Antonio Martino, a member of the Eurosceptic 'Bruges group'. For the first time the discourse of the government was somewhat hesitant on EMU, with Martino arguing for a renegotiation of the Treaty of Maastricht. This position did not reassure EU partners about the determination of the Italians to join EMU, although Berlusconi distanced himself from Martino's positions and supported the idea of compliance with the convergence criteria.

Pension reform presented the most serious challenge. Berlusconi tried to break with the consensual policy style, but to no avail. Strikes and demonstrations, among the largest of the post-war era, put his pension reform plan under pressure. Although the plans of the unions and the government were not incompatible, Berlusconi was fiercely attacked because he tried to break the unwritten rule of the game, that is, the neo-corporatist style (Regini and Regalia 1997: 216). The truce of 1 December 1994 was perceived as Berlusconi's surrender. At that point Berlusconi's coalition had already entered its last month of life, with the Northern League willing to torpedo it. The vicissitudes of the Berlusconi government did not weaken the demand for concertation on the part of the unions. As Braun (1996: 212) observes, the unions 'used the conflict in the name of *concertazione*: they acted in defence of their right to decide reform'.

Lamberto Dini, formerly Treasury minister with Berlusconi, led a techno-cratic caretaker government with the support of the centre-left parties. He presented a series of measures in spring 1995 to respond to the international financial crisis and its reverberations on the lira and, later, a DPEF setting the 1997 budget deficit at 4.4 per cent. The European Council at Madrid on 15–16 December 1995 made clear that all EU states would be assessed 'as soon as possible in 1998' on the basis 'of the most recent and reliable effective data for 1997'. Time had shrunk for Italy: fiscal adjustment was to be completed in 1997, not in 1998. On 20 September 1995 a press release from the Bundestag reported that German Finance Minister, Theo Waigel, argued that the state of public finances in Italy, Belgium, and Spain would make it implausible for them to join EMU with the first group. The lira fell heavily. Even though Chancellor Helmut Kohl reassured the Italian government that no state had been already excluded from EMU, the debate on the appropriateness of the government's efforts became quite tense at home and abroad. Reportedly (Dastoli 1996: 176–7), Dini tried to persuade his EU partners, at an informal meeting of heads of state and government at Formentor on 22 September 1995, to consider postponing EMU in the event of a large number of states failing to converge on time. Dini was seeking to gain time for Italy. Never-theless, President Jacques Chirac and Kohl stood firm on the scenario of January 1 1999.

Politicians—for example, Romano Prodi and Giorgio La Malfa—business leaders—for example, Gianni Agnelli—and EU Commissioner Mario Monti made critical comments about the Dini government's economic policy. Monti warned that Italy was sending a message of self-exclusion: the death knell of Italian hope was in the figures presented by the government in the DPEF and the finance bill. The leader of the Bologna-based think tank Prometeia, Professor Paolo Onofri, who later became Prodi's chief economic adviser, argued that 'one can only express regret for a chance that was missed' (*Corriere della Sera* 1995a). The Bank of Italy warned against Italy's re-entry into the EMS in the absence of the preconditions for financial stability. The Budget Minister, Rainer Masera, expressed his belief that the lack of confidence on the part of the central bank could trigger undesirable reactions in the finan-cial markets (*Corriere della Sera* 1995b). The discourse at the level of domestic elites was fragmented and the sense of having lost the battle against time became acute. Dini's position was that only a political government, not a caretaker like him, could make firm commitments on the timing of Italy's EMU entry.

As for policy style, Dini sought and obtained legitimacy and support from the unions both in budgetary policy, on which the unions were consulted before the budget was discussed in Parliament, and on pension reform. He was rewarded by the unions' support for his budget and by a landmark agreement with the unions on pension reform in May 1995: an important victory as this had been an insurmountable obstacle for the Berlusconi government. However, the Dini deal did not solve all the problems. Indeed, afterwards the discourse on pensions was dominated by the issue of how to complete Dini's improvements with a definitive reform.

Together with the fiscal effort to join EMU, described below, pension reform was a major issue for the next government, headed by Romano Prodi. A high-profile committee of experts chaired by Onofri, Prodi's economic adviser, was established in January 1997. The Onofri Commission worked out a blueprint for a definitive reform but it did not make an impact in terms of political choices, for three reasons. First, the unions perceived the Onofri Commission as a change of style from consensual policy-making to technocracy. They felt marginalized by the decision of the government to entrust reform to a committee of experts. Second, the Onofri Commission launched a message of fairness across generations: 'less to the fathers and more to the young people'. For unions with a considerable portion of their membership made up of pensioners this was an unacceptable message, as it triggered a zero-sum game amongst unions' members. Third, the political difficulties increased during the summer of 1997 when the Northern League attacked the reform plan and asked its members to destroy their union membership cards in public. The unions became more rigid in their negotiation with the government. In the autumn, Prodi had to face the opposition of the party of Reconstructed Communism (*Rifondazione Comunista*) whose votes were indispensable for a majority in Parliament. Prodi was defeated in a crucial vote on the budget on 9 October 1997. Although the crisis was solved in a few days, Prodi had to walk a tightrope on pension reform. He managed to push through Parliament a limited package of reforms, including the elimination of seniority pensions.[2] But the 'definitive' reform of pensions remained on the agenda for the next governments.

On macroeconomic policy, the Prodi government—with Ciampi at the Treasury, Dini at the Foreign Office, and Vincenzo Visco in charge of tax policy—had to face the challenge of presenting the DPEF in its very early days. The DPEF of June 1996 confirmed the goals of the Dini government: the 3 per cent budget deficit target would not be reached in 1997.[3] This decision

---

[2] See Mira d'Ercole and Terribile (1998). Blue collar workers and 'equivalent' workers were not subject to new restrictive measures: an indicator of Rifondazione's blackmail power.

[3] The DPEF presented by Dini contained a 4.4% deficit target for 1997. Ciampi's DPEF (28 June 1996) did not change the framework proposed by Dini.

raised a wave of disillusionment among those who expected more decisive action from a government relatively free from political parties—Prodi was the leader of the 'olive-tree' coalition, not a party leader—with a clear pro-European attitude and operating in the immediate 'honeymoon' post-election stage. EU Commissioner Mario Monti warned the Italians that a late entry would be more costly in terms of the fiscal effort necessary to join EMU than an early one (*Corriere della Sera* 1996b). The Nobel prize-winning economist Franco Modigliani argued that there was a last opportunity for Italy to pitch for early entry to the Euro-Zone. He called this 'the possible miracle' (Modigliani, Baldassarri, and Castiglionesi 1996). He argued that a large fiscal correction undertaken as soon as possible in 1996 could enhance credibility, leading to a reduction of the spread between Italian interest rates and German rates. From the business community, FIAT chairman Cesare Romiti debunked the myth of the necessity of joining the Euro-Zone at any cost.[4] Once again, the coordinative discourse was fragmented.

However, the DPEF contained a paragraph (4.10) in which the government stated that, although an immediate diversion from Dini's path was impossible, the commitment to submit Italy's candidacy to enter EMU at the outset remained. The government, the DPEF argued, would check the possibility of speeding up the timing of compliance with the Maastricht criteria in autumn 1996, depending on the economic cycle and the situation in the financial markets. A series of parliamentary hearings in July 1996 confirmed the determination of Ciampi to intensify action. At the hearings, the governor of the Bank of Italy, Antonio Fazio, agreed with the timing and the scale of the fiscal correction envisaged by the DPEF, given the conditions of the Italian economy. He also added, somewhat prophetically:

I cannot exclude—indeed, I wish—that one could do more. But my conscience—as an economist and governor—tells me that to get to a correction of 3 per cent [from 6 per cent deficit in 1996 to 3 per cent in 1997] . . . is difficult. It is not impossible . . . The decision is political.[5]

Commissioner Monti stressed the role of paragraph 4.10 of the DPEF 'as point of potential development' in the context of a 'commitment towards convergence'.[6] In June Ciampi went public about his intentions to re-enter the EMS before the end of 1996 and to make full use of paragraph 4.10, although at that time it was difficult for him to pin down specific figures.[7]

---

[4] See especially his speech in front of thousand of young Catholics on 24 August 1996.
[5] Hearing of the governor of the bank of Italy Antonio Fazio, 9 July 1996: 110.
[6] Hearing of the EU Commissioner for the single market Mario Monti, 4 July 1996: 49.
[7] Hearing of Minister Carlo Azelio Ciampi, 20 June 1996: 10.

The strategy of the Prodi government from May to July 1996 was to accelerate the improvement of budget performance in the autumn and hopefully reach a value close to 3 per cent in 1997, perhaps something like 3.5 per cent. This, Ciampi and Prodi reasoned at the time, would insert Italy into the area of negotiation, especially in the event of Italy not being the only state with a deficit slightly above the 3 per cent criterion. The Italians would benefit from a 'political' interpretation of the 3 per cent threshold. Ciampi expressed his intention to intensify action, but until autumn 1996 he never spoke of a finance bill capable of reaching the 3 per cent target in 1997. Instead, he spoke against the 'exaggerations on parameters' and stressed 'convergent trends' as the main thrust of Maastricht (*Corriere della Sera* 1996d). This was fully consistent with Ciampi's statement of 30 April 1996: 'Our role in Europe does not hinge on arithmetic alone. Numbers are very important, of course. But in the final decisions—crucial both for Italy and Europe—political considerations will also play a role' (*Corriere della Sera* 1996a). Prodi reinforced the impression of not being willing to pursue the 3 per cent at any cost by telling the press that he wanted to bring Italy into EMU 'alive, not dead' (*Corriere della Sera* 1996c).

The fragility of this position was exposed by Waigel's bold statement in September 1996 that 'three per cent means three point zero', thus reducing the hope of a 'political' assessment of states just above the 3 per cent. Most importantly, the Italian position became extremely fragile at the bilateral meeting between the Spanish and Italian governments in Valencia on 23–4 September 1996. Spain was confident of achieving 3 per cent in 1997, and Prodi was left alone. The Spanish Prime Minister Aznar went so far as to accuse the Italians of seeking Spain's support 'to bend the criteria or the timetable' (*Financial Times* 1996). This was a serious diplomatic incident because the official press release from the Italian Prime Minister's Office denied that the EMU criteria and timetable were on the agenda of the meeting. Prodi denied that he changed his mind after Valencia (*La Repubblica* 1998; *Il Sole-24Ore* 1998). He argued that the Italian government had already decided to bid for an early EMU entry over the summer. Prodi refers to two letters to Kohl and Chirac, dated 6 September 1996, in which he expressed the firm intention of the Italian government 'to get to the EMU appointment on time'.[8] Be that as it may, the fact remains that Prodi introduced additional measures to strengthen the finance bill five days after Valencia. The measures announced,

---

[8] Indeed, as Spaventa and Chiorazzo (2000) observe, the letter was flawed in that Prodi argued that trust in Italy's EMU membership would cut the deficit through the dynamics of interest rates. But trust could not be asked for without a prior large fiscal correction.

inclusive of an extraordinary tax for Europe, were aimed at reducing the budget deficit to 3 per cent of GDP in 1997. The same man who had argued that it would not be a tragedy if Italy joined EMU somewhat belatedly stated emphatically 'either Italy is within EMU, or I shall resign' (*Corriere della Sera* 1996*f*). On 24 November 1996 the lira rejoined the ERM, thus securing an essential precondition for an early entry into EMU. Although a number of politicians in Germany and Holland, well-known US economists, and the international press were not entirely convinced, the financial markets trusted Prodi. Italy also benefited from tactical support from France, whose aim was to decrease the prospects of 'Germanization' of the Euro-Zone. Credibility reduced the spread between Italian and German interest rates. The interest rate bonus was crucial for the Italian deficit. In 1997 Italy achieved a deficit of 2.7 per cent. In 1998, it joined the Euro-Zone with ten other states.

How did Italy make it? The main factors were:

(1) The post-Valencia strategy, which, although far from perfect, produced the expected results. Clearly there were multiple equilibria in this process, based on self-confirming expectations. A shared belief in EU capitals and the financial markets that Italy was doing enough to qualify on time would yield low interest rates, thus reducing the cost of debt service, the major obstacle for the Italian budget, already at a high primary balance surplus (see Table 8.2). Negative expectations would produce the opposite effect, making qualification for EMU extremely difficult if not impossible.
(2) Domestic discourse and the political communication strategy of the Treasury.
(3) Policy style.
(4) The increased strength of the core executive due to organizational reforms, new policy technologies, and new rules.

Let us start with the political and economic strategy for 1997. In terms of politics, the cost of exclusion increased dramatically after Valencia. Until summer 1996 there was a strong expectation, especially in Germany, of a 'hard' group of currencies joining the euro in 1998, with the lira predestined to join later. The position of the Italians did not represent a problem until summer 1996: their own forecast put them out of the 'first wave' EMU group, and there was the expectation that Italy would be in good company within the 'second-wave' group. However, after Valencia the Italian government faced the certainty that Spain would join in 1998. At this point, it was difficult to accept a last-minute unilateral exclusion—as opposed to a coordinated exclusion based on mutual consensus—and leave the lira in a mini-group of 'second-wave' states, hostage to financial speculation. When in 1997 soft diplomatic pressures sought to persuade the Italians to remain temporarily out of EMU, it was too late. By that stage the Prodi government could not accept exclusion. The 'mission impossible' of qualifying on time had to be undertaken.

Let us now turn to the economic strategy. The journalistic debate has emphasized the 'budgetary fudges' of the Italians and ironic comments have been made about the temporary income surtax, known as the euro-tax.[9] However, state-of-the-art research shows that the compression of the deficit was not the result of Italian tricks (Spaventa and Chiorazzo 2000). True, the government took advantage, legitimately, of accounting revisions and postponed expenditure beyond the 1997 deadline. However, the fundamentals had presented a large primary surplus since 1992 (Table 8.2) and the finance bill for 1997 included more permanent revenue, as opposed to temporary measures, amounting to 1 per cent of GDP and a structural reduction of expenditure amounting to 1.4 per cent of GDP.[10] The major factor was, therefore, the international credibility of the Italian effort, which in turn secured a decline of interest payments. Credibility derived in large part from real measures to reduce the deficits and in minor but significant part from the personal reputation of people like Ciampi—see the section on discourse below.

The euro-tax was not a mere trick. Indeed, it played an essential role—more than 0.5 per cent of GDP—in getting the budget below the 3 per cent. Moreover, Spaventa and Chiorazzo (2000) put emphasis on the political message carried by the euro-tax. This brings us to the discussion of domestic discourse.

The communicative discourse reached a climax with the 'tax for Europe'. In a state with a high potential for tax revolts, the message of the euro-tax went down surprisingly well. Indeed, the tax became a symbol of the willingness not be excluded 'from Europe'. In the communicative discourse the tax became the 'price of the last ticket to Europe'. To highlight the issue of 'not being left out of Europe' was consistent with the long-term preferences of Italy's foreign policy (Sbragia 2001). The content of the message was, however, inherently false. Italy has been in Europe since day one of the Community-building process. The questions raised by the convergence process were all about EMU, not the EU! Further, there was full consensus about joining the EMU, the only open issue being timing. However, the

---

[9] See the references in Spaventa and Chiorazzo (2000). The surtax was temporary in that it was substantially repaid to the citizens in 1999.

[10] Data from F. Galimberti (1998). See also Spaventa and Chiorazzo (2000: esp. Table 6).

apocalyptic message 'either Europe or death' contributed to a successful dramatization of the Italian effort. The distortion of the language—EU instead of EMU—charged the discourse with passion and emotion. This 'crisis consciousness exercise' was combined with the reaction to the humiliation of Valencia, where Spain had sought to become the 'champion' of southern Europe in terms of EMU credentials. Prodi and Ciampi put their own reputations on the line by making the EMU target the key issue of the government.

The tone of the discourse used by the Prodi government does not represent an element of novelty. Indeed, it is consistent with the messages sent throughout the 1990s by Italian prime ministers and Treasury ministers. The communicative discourse was dramatized on several occasions: both the financial crisis of September 1992 and the danger of 'being left out' in 1996–7 were converted into political opportunities by telling Italians that they were facing a question of 'life or death', an apocalyptic message. A pro-European attitude was taken from granted; indeed, at the end of 1999, after almost a decade of budgetary stringency, Italy was the EU country with the highest percentage of supporters of the single currency (European Commission 2000*d*). The Europeanism of the Italians was a great asset in the communicative discourse, as shown by the message of the euro-tax, which went down well even though the Northern League stated that Italians 'will not pay'. The credibility of the domestic discourse was enhanced by an effective mechanism of blame avoidance: the disaster of public finance was explained in terms of the vices of the old party system.

There is also an interesting link between discourse and identity politics. The people who made the euro-dream possible for Italy used the external constraint of the convergence criteria to create enough tension, drama, and ultimately momentum for change. The path to EMU was turned into a manifestation of the politics of collective identity. Collective identity determines not only what 'we' are and where 'we' come from but also what can and cannot be achieved. Domestically, Italian policy-makers reacted bitterly to the scepticism of EU partners. They manifested surprise when at key junctures they discovered that their efforts were not considered sufficient. This was a component of the rhetoric stressing collective identity at home by drawing a bold line between 'us' and 'them'. The truth is that between 1992 and mid-1997 there were very few objective reasons to believe that Italy would join the euro in 1998. EU partners were simply inferring Italy's exclusion from Italy's economic choices and macroeconomic data. Dini, for example, was clearly not too bothered by the prospect of joining the euro a bit later. And Valencia was more a tactical mistake by the Italians than an example of Spanish *euro-machismo*. In this light, the reactions of the Italian policy-makers to the statements of EU partners cannot be justified on the basis of economic events. They have to be interpreted in the context of the politics of domestic identity.

What about the external dimension of discourse, that is, the messages sent to EU partners? The external communicative discourse was managed quite effectively notwithstanding the diffidence in some EU quarters and rumours circulated by the international press in Europe and the US with the purpose of weakening the Italian position. Ciampi exerted firm leadership in this process by becoming the only source of information from the Treasury. He spoke directly to his interlocutors, trying to avoid messages filtered by the newspapers. He embarked on a 'road-show' across different states with the aim of persuading the EU governments, the US Treasury, and the business community about the robustness of his economic policy. The role of financial markets was absolutely crucial through the effect on interest rates, and both Ciampi and Prodi arranged visits and meetings with international bankers and the main financial centres in Europe. Additionally, the Italian government arranged visits in Rome, including a Dutch delegation. This dense flow of information was very close to a protective net performing a function of reassurance and persuasion during decisive months. Policy credibility derived largely from economic fundamentals. However, an important part of credibility concerns individuals: and Ciampi put on the table his own international reputation.

Things went differently on the front of the domestic coordinative discourse. 'The policy of my government', Prodi said, 'has been always surrounded by scepticism. Certainly not by the people, but by the establishment' (*La Repubblica* 1998). Prodi argued that one of the main problems in meeting the 3 per cent target was to reassure the EU partners that the Italian effort was credible in the presence of different opinions at home. Many external observers, Prodi recollects, were always probing Italy's credibility by pointing out that the Bank of Italy was not reducing the rate of discount quickly or in large increments; and the Bank's governor was publicly critical of the government's choices.[11] The sceptical attitude of the Bank of Italy[12]

---

[11] See Prodi's interview with *La Repubblica* (1998). According to Prodi, the statements of the governor of the Bank of Italy 'sounded throughout Europe as opposition to our membership of the single currency'.

[12] The governor of the Bank of Italy, Antonio Fazio, argued on several occasions that it would be a mistake to join the euro without the necessary structural reforms: see for example his statements reported by the press on 25 September 1995 and 24 February 1996. On 10 October 1996 he said he did not believe that the budget for 1997 would secure the 3% target. On 13 February 1998, speaking at a hearing of the budget committee of the Chamber of Deputies, Fazio dampened the enthusiasm of the MPs by saying that EMU would be purgatory for Italy, certainly not heaven.

represented a potential problem in terms of credibility. And less credibility meant a more onerous burden of debt servicing and hence a problem with the overall budget balance, notwithstanding a high primary surplus. The distance of the main confederation of employers, Confindustria, compounded the problem. Prodi stated that 'I was not surprised: the scepticism of Confindustria in relation to the first Europe and then to the EMS is written in all history books' (*La Repubblica* 1998). Within Confindustria some members seemed to prefer a 'realistic' goal of delayed entry to be negotiated with EU partners. Other members were not against an early entry, but they had serious objections to the instruments used by the government. They thought that the macroeconomic measures of the Prodi government were not up to the job.

On balance, the communicative discourse was solid domestically and internationally, but the fragility of the domestic coordinative discourse represented a problem. Arguably, the distance between the core executive and some influential economists was due to the fact that Prodi and Ciampi took decisions in haste, as shown *inter alia* by the reaction to the Valencia meeting. Certainly, time was not on the government's side. This made a thorough debate on the economic choices simply impossible. In a sense, the Prodi government was self-referential. In addition, the determination to join the Euro-Zone at the outset was taken only in September 1996 and, by being partly based on the credibility bonus on interest rates, contained an objective element of uncertainty. Thus, the divergence of opinion between the core executive and some well-known economists was legitimate. Nevertheless, arguably, for Ciampi it was a major blow to read that most economists and think tanks thought that his finance bill would not do the trick.[13]

The relative distance between Prodi and Confindustria did not pre-empt a new season of neo-corporatist decision-making. The policy style remained consensual and, as in the previous experiences of the 1990s, slightly biased towards a closer dialogue with the unions. In September 1996 the government struck a deal with the main unions and the employers' organizations. The agreement was followed by laws that consolidated and introduced innovations, such as concertation-based policies for economic development at the local level—territorial pacts and area pacts—temporary work, and the termination of the public monopoly on placement services (Ferrera and Gualmini 1999).

The final element of Italy's successful rush to EMU concerns the strengthening of the core executive. The Prodi government ended the bifurcation

---

[13] A survey of sceptical opinions was presented by *Corriere della Sera* (1996e).

of economic policy between two departments, that is, Budget and Treasury. The two, jointly with the Treasury, were in charge of the process of budget formation within the executive. The previous reforms of the 1980s had sought to streamline the parliamentary stage of the budget-making process without provisions for the stage of budget formation within the executive. With law no. 94–1997 the structure and the process of budget formation were significantly improved (Felsen 2000; Vassallo 2000). By changing the structure of the budget—specifically by switching from bureaucratic concepts to economic concepts—the capability of the core executive to steer the administrative and governmental stages of the budget was increased. In sum, the new rules on the budget, together with the DPEF, allow the core executive to steer macroeconomic policy in the administrative, governmental, and parliamentary stages. Additionally, the reforms of the Prodi government brought about a reorganization of the Treasury (Vassallo 2000: 317–18), strengthened by the introduction of new technologies for a timely monitoring of the flow of public expenditure at the central and local level: an issue extremely relevant in 1997 when even small deviations could worry the financial markets and the EMU partners. Within the presidency of the Council of Ministers, the department for economic affairs was empowered by a new injection of some 35 highly qualified economists, most of them at the post-doctoral level.

These changes were partly the effect of the Prodi government's 'rush to the euro', but they were made possible by the political leadership of Ciampi and the administrative leadership of dedicated Treasury officials (Vassallo 2000: 313). On balance, the core executive has been empowered in the run-up to the euro. The executive—albeit often with slim, conflictual, and/or fragile majorities in Parliament and technocratic legitimacy rather than full democratic legitimacy—has brought its proposals to the attention of Parliament without major concessions to political parties on critical occasions. Political parties have, however, tried to influence and blackmail the government on other occasions.

In conclusion, Italy was able to reach the euro on time thanks to the synergy of three different policies: budgetary policy, incomes policy, and a restrictive, cautious monetary policy which delivered interest-rate reductions only *ex post facto* on the basis of 'good' fiscal behaviour. It would be wrong to see one of these elements without the others as they geared Italy towards convergence by acting simultaneously. The belief in 'stability' has been incorporated in all policies, most importantly in the social pacts. In this connection the agreement of 1993 was decisive in terms of accepting anti-inflationary stability as a public good. Ciampi (1996: 18–19) provides a vivid description of the link between social pacts, the confidence of financial markets, and the strategy of fiscal readjustment in his recollection of the days leading to the July 1993 pact:

Timing was essential. The financial markets trusted that negotiation [on the social pact against inflation]. They perceived its historical importance, that is, to eradicate the major cause of inflation from the mechanisms of price formation. The lack of an agreement would have stopped and inverted the tendency to decreasing interest rates . . . The important thing was to strike the deal at that very moment, at the beginning of summer 1993.

Two questions arise, namely, whether discourse and policy have changed *post*-1998 and whether the institutional effects of the *risanamento* are permanent or contingent. The next section will examine what happened to Italy within the Euro-Zone, leaving the issue of institutional change to the last section.

Living in the Euro-Zone: Policy and Discourse

Since the decision to accept Italy in the Euro-Zone the political situation has changed, with the resignation of the Prodi government, the establishment of two successive governments led by a traditional party leader, Massimo D'Alema, and, more recently, the return of the technocrat Giuliano Amato as Prime Minister (Table 8.1). Public opinion has remained pro-EMU, with 85 per cent of Italians in favour of the single currency, the highest percentage in the EU.[14]

In terms of public finance, the finance bills of the D'Alema and Amato governments have kept Italy on the tracks of the Stability and Growth Pact. However, fiscal discipline has to be kept under surveillance both in Rome and at the local level, especially in a state moving towards increasing fiscal responsibility of regions and local authorities. For this reason, the government introduced an internal stability pact with the finance bill for 1999. This is basically a rule imposing a reduction of the deficit on local governments. Its thrust is to make the process of institutional and fiscal decentralization compatible with the EU's Stability and Growth Pact. The experience with the internal stability pact has been mixed so far. The lack of effective sanctions limits the effectiveness of this new policy instrument. Additionally, at least in its original form, the domestic pact did not include incentives rewarding good fiscal behaviour.

---

[14] Data from European Commission (2000*d*), fieldwork conducted during October–November 1999.

Additionally, there are several technical problems (Balassone and Franco 1999). A limited step to improve the performance of the pact was taken with the finance bill for 2000 by rewarding good fiscal behaviour with a reduction on the interest rate on loans to local authorities. Thus there is at least one carrot but sticks are still missing. On balance, Italy is still experimenting with this instrument. The consistent devolution of administrative and fiscal powers to the regional and local governments makes the intention to streamline the pact a crucial task for economic policy in the near future.

The policy style has remained consensual. The fact that the centre-right was in opposition in 1999–2000 was another reason for the success of consensual policy-making (Levy 1999). The institutionalization of social pacts has proceeded with a pact signed by 32 organizations and the government in December 1998 and the proliferation of neo-corporatist practices at the local level. The philosophy of social pacts has changed slightly to include, in addition to the anti-inflationary component, measures of market flexibility and simplification and reduction of regulation. As Ferrera and Gualmini (1999) argue, the influence of the Dutch 'economic miracle' has been instrumental in redirecting the social pacts in these directions.

The major weakness in economic performance was the poor rate of growth.[15] This triggered a debate about the cost of the *risanamento*, whose main thrust is to ascertain whether the forms and timing of the fiscal corrections of the 1990s produced the perverse effect of slow economic growth. The most common critique is that the cost of fiscal adjustment was high because of excessive gradualism—Spaventa and Chiorazzo (2000) identify 14 corrections between 1990 and 1996—and the emphasis on revenue rather than structural reform of public expenditure. In order to minimize the negative impact on output, fiscal adjustment should be credible and perceived as permanent. In terms of its composition, a cut in the transfers to households and in public wages rather than a tax-biased adjustment is the best predictor of positive effects on growth and unemployment. When judged against these criteria, Italy seems to be bereft of the preconditions for the manifestation of non-Keynesian effects capable of producing growth in a context of severe and swift fiscal restrictions (Giavazzi, Jappelli, and Pagano 1998). The Banca d'Italia (2000: 32) has raised its voice against the centre-left governments of the second half of the 1990s by arguing that in this period 'fiscal adjustment should have focused on a more decisive curb of public expenditure, the

---

[15] The average rate of growth of the GDP in 1990–7 was 1.4% against an average of 2.1% for the other ten countries of the Euro-zone. Throughout the whole period, the Italian lag is 7 percentage points (Banca d'Italia).

relaunch of public investment, and the moderation of fiscal pressure and social contributions'.

The main elements of the Italian strategy were a relentless increase of tax pressure, a decrease of expenditure—through lower interest rates—on servicing the debt, the partial reform of pension regimes,[16] a lower number of public sector employees,[17] and a squeeze on the cost of local government.[18] Privatization accounted for 4.9 per cent of GDP throughout the 1990s, with a substantial increase towards the end of the decade (Banca d'Italia). The fiscal stance was eventually relaxed in 1998 when a fall in cyclically adjusted primary spending was more than compensated by a decrease of tax pressure. A comprehensive tax reform was implemented with the aim of modernizing the whole tax system. Administrative reform made substantial progress, although political attention has focused on the design of new laws rather than on the effective implementation of the innovations introduced since 1993 (Capano 2000).

There are at least a few elements of structural reform in the process of fiscal adjustment. On balance, Italy pursued a revenue-based strategy of fiscal adjustment, as did France, Portugal, Ireland, and Greece. The 'price' paid for adjustment is more or less in line with the European average (Spaventa and Chiorazzo 2000). The slow rate of growth of the Italian economy has more to do with a lack of competitiveness than with the process of *risanamento*. This observation leads us to the examination of the dominant issue in the post-1998 economic policy discourse, namely, competitiveness. Notwithstanding the reservations of economists about the concept of competitiveness when applied to states rather than economic agents (Krugman 1994), this theme has now seized the limelight in the debate on economic policy. The implications of a new cognitive focus on competitiveness are manifold, covering pensions, regulatory reform, and competition policy.

Let us start with pensions. The gradual pension reforms of the 1990s created the preconditions for the elimination of the explosive long-term expenditure trend. There is, however, a demographic trend that will raise expenditure in the medium term up to 15.6 per cent of the GDP in 2015. The debate on how to cope with the medium-term trend is hot. There is now a wide consensus

[16] The 1992 reform cancelled a quarter of prospective public-sector pension liabilities.

[17] Public employment in 1999 was almost five percentage points less than in 1992. The cost of public wages, which was above 9% of GDP in 1990, decreased to 7.5% in 1999 (Banca d'Italia). However, the Commission services calculate that the total of transfers to households and public wages—a strong predictor of non-Keynesian effects—did not vary during the consolidation period 1991–7 (European Commission 1999d: 20).

[18] Local government's expenditure was 14.7% of GDP at the beginning of the 1990s, 13.6% at the end of the decade (Banca d'Italia).

that sustainability in the long term requires further changes. The challenge for discourse is to recast pension reform in terms of fairness across generations, opportunity costs—a welfare state biased towards pensions prevents the development of adequate social protection in other areas—and competitiveness rather than narrow budgetary considerations.

As for supply-side factors, the focus on competitiveness has highlighted the importance of regulatory reforms beyond the process of privatization already under way. Unlike fiscal adjustment, regulatory reform is not driven by the imperative to curb the cost of running the state. It focuses on the impact of the state on the economy and the citizen. As such, the discourse on regulatory reform implies a shift from a limited conceptual framework—'getting public finances right'—to the more comprehensive framework of 'getting the relationship between the state, the economy, and the society right'. Politically, regulatory reform entails a shift from macroeconomics to the political economy of microeconomic change. To reform regulation means intervention in specific markets and attacking well-organized, entrenched interests by allocating concentrated costs and diffuse benefits. There is a vast programme of regulatory reform under way both in central government and in specific markets. Italy is certainly progressing fast on this front (Radaelli and Silva 1998), but the gap between it and the most competitive EU partners remains quite large.

The new discursive focal point provided by competitiveness has exposed the limitations of the traditional approach to industrial policy. In 1999–2000 laws and incentive schemes originally introduced by the government to boost the competitiveness of the Italian economy were renegotiated with EU Commissioner Mario Monti. At the elite level there is an acknowledgement that traditional incentives for the Italian south—the Mezzogiorno—should be abandoned in favour of policies which affect the 'environment' of economic activity. There is a new emphasis on 'immaterial capital' and the 'policy environment' in the discourse on the Mezzogiorno. Briefly, the Mezzogiorno is no longer 'framed' as a problem of economic engineering but rather as a challenge of social engineering, that is, using public policy to change the context wherein economic activity and specific policy instruments interact. A serious hurdle is making social engineering work if the relatively easier task of economic engineering has failed (OECD 2000; Salvati 2000). A suggestion formulated by Amato (Camera dei Deputati 1999) is to use the DPEF to set specific indicators for policies targeted on the environment—that is, the context—of economic activity.

This suggestion is indicative of a general demand for 'new Maastrichts', as Italians put it. Increasing attention is given to commitments and indicators that can induce a process of convergence on competition policy, liberalization, and regulatory reform. The DPEF has the potential to be converted from a tool setting deficit and inflation targets to a more consistent instrument of economic policy (Degni and Salvemini 2000). However, the design of indicators for 'context policies' is more difficult than the incorporation of the Maastricht criteria in the DPEF. Furthermore, although there is a trend towards the transformation of EMU into a stabilization state (see Introduction), the pressure for convergence in structural reform is based on a delicate mix of competition, emulation, and transfer of best practice: a process that does not lend itself to automatic parameter-based mechanisms Maastricht-style. In conclusion, the new focus on competitiveness has shed light on the new type of challenges facing Italy in the Euro-Zone. Whether Italy will tackle these challenges efficiently is a moot point.

Conclusion

What are the institutional effects of EMU as Europeanization? And what do the temporal causal sequences illustrated in this chapter say about the causality of EMU? It is to these questions that we now turn. As mentioned in the introduction, institutional development should be measured by looking at political experiences, 'physical maturation', the reaction to crises, and the evolution of discourse. To what extent has fiscal adjustment brought about the appropriate economic, political, and discursive conditions for institutional development?

In terms of economic conditions, Italy has a large primary balance. Incomes policy has been so far an effective weapon against inflation: a result consistent with the major achievement of the process of convergence, that is, the culture of macroeconomic stability. The budget and the mechanisms to govern it are more solid than in the past. However, structural reform goes well beyond the budget and will be decisive for Italy's performance within the Euro-Zone.

The most serious objections to the sustainability of convergence come from political scientists (Fabbrini 1998; 2000; Vassallo 2000; Verzichelli 1999). The argument is that convergence with the Euro-Zone has been possible thanks to exceptional circumstances such as the crisis of the political system and the external constraint of the Maastricht Treaty. The lack of fundamental institutional reforms, the argument concludes, does not bode well for the sustainability of Italy's membership of the Euro-Zone. This argument ignores the fact that the external pressure to converge is still alive and kicking, given the presence of (1) an independent European Central Bank in charge of monetary policy, (2) the Stability and Growth Pact, and (3) the increasing role of EMU as 'stabilization state' (Dyson 2000*b*). As for domestic policy, executive capacity increased throughout the 1990s, on the different indicators presented by Verzichelli (1999). The executive's control of Parliament has increased. The role of Parliament's budget committee has changed, from a distributive arena to a filter of political demands (Verzichelli 1999: 232). The Treasury has become more autonomous and more assertive in relation to the expenditure ministries. Moreover, the fusion of the two departments of Treasury and Budget under the roof of the Treasury and the quality of information and monitoring technologies available there make the 'core' of economic policy stronger. The power of traditional veto players—the Parliament, the expenditure ministries—has been reduced. The path to EMU has made the Treasury the main source of policy proposals in areas outside economic policy, notably pension policy. As Franco (2000: 25) observes, 'both the 1992 and 1995 [pension] reforms were developed by the Prime Minister's Office and the Ministry of Treasury, while the Ministry for Labour and Social Protection had a very modest role'. Finally, the reforms of the budgetary policy process enable the core executive to control all the stages of the process: within the executive, in Parliament, and in the administrative stage.

The government has been a reliable partner in concertation and neo-corporatist practices are well embedded in Italian institutions. Considering the fiasco of the Berlusconi government's pension reform in 1995, when it tried unsuccessfully to change the pension regime without concertation, it is not clear whether a future centre-right government could do without the social consensus of the unions. Paradoxically, neo-corporatist practices are perhaps *too* embedded in institutional behaviour. It is not at all certain that the challenge of competitiveness can be tackled by relying heavily on neo-corporatist practices. This challenge requires political leadership, a microeconomic approach, and the capacity to allocate losses to strong, concentrated, and pugnacious interests in a number of markets and professions where confederal trade unions are weak. These interests are protected by 'guilds' and 'independent unions' with a low propensity to accept the logic of competitiveness.[19] Concertation may be more suitable for macro-adjustment than for introducing flexibility sector by sector, although the EU endorsement of neo-corporatist practices and the prestige of the so-called Dutch model in Italy seem to bode well for the future of this instrument. On balance, the political conditions for institutional development are satisfied with the

---

[19] See Gualdo (2000) for a journalistic illustration of the 'untouchable' interests.

qualification that concertation—one of the great assets of the 1990s—may not perform so well at the microeconomic level.

However, the cognitive conditions are more problematic. The main achievement is the culture of macroeconomic stability. At the same time, the emphasis of the discourse has been on the costs of being out of Europe rather than the advantages of Euro-Zone membership. The dramatization of discourse in terms of 'being left out of Europe' has obfuscated essential questions of strategy, such as what Italy wants to gain from Euro-Zone membership. There has been an implicit equation between fiscal adjustment, results in terms of macroeconomic stability, and growth. However, the rate of growth in individual EMU countries depends on the competitiveness of the economy. The lack of a proper debate on the advantages to be achieved by dint of Euro-Zone membership has led the Italian discourse to a somewhat abrupt 'discovery' of the problem of competitiveness.

The *risanamento* has been presented to the Italians as a problem of finance bills and the DPEF, convergence criteria, and speed of adjustment. National identity was boosted 'in negative', that is, as a reaction to the—supposedly—evil intentions of those EU partners who wanted to leave Italy 'out of Europe'. In terms of communicative discourse, the Italian policy makers have been able to craft an effective discourse that secured legitimacy for hard economic choices such as the Euro-tax. However, they have not been cognitive leaders to the extent of having convinced their compatriots that the *risanamento* was an opportunity to modernize the state (Salvati 2000). Cognitive leadership is even more important within the Euro-Zone, where the challenge of competitiveness requires effective action, sector by sector, against entrenched pressure groups. The qualification for EMU and budgetary reasons was overwhelming cognitive drives in pension reform and changes in industrial relations. But now the discourse on reforms has to be de-linked from 'cash-trimming' considerations.

On the issue of causality, it is difficult to highlight a clear impact of EMU as independent variable. The episode after the meeting in Valencia is the best candidate to match this approach to causality. It is more useful to set EMU alongside other contextual changes, such as the crisis of the political system and the room of manoeuvre for technocratic politics offered by the Italian transition in the 1990s. The rush to the Euro-Zone provided a catalyst of energies and political capabilities which grew out of instruments, discourses, and practices of the 1980s. As intervening variable, EMU has impacted on the timing and tempo of fiscal adjustment. More generally, the socialization of Italian elites in the process of European monetary policy coordination, from the EMS to EMU, has produced a formidable process of cognitive convergence towards the paradigm of sound public finance and independent monetary policy (Dyson 2000b). Thus, if one does not approach causality in terms of short-term responses to EMU as cause and opts instead for a view of causality rooted in long-term processes of institutional change (Pierson 2000), the power of EMU in terms of institutional development appears greater. That institutional change was made possible in a context of severe political crisis is indicative of the resilience of the Italian state, in contrast to the stereotypical characterization of the Italian state as weak. Change is embedded in institutions and will probably outlive the individuals. It is simply inconceivable to imagine a future Treasury minister, from either of the two coalitions competing for power in Italy, managing the public purse without the culture of stability of the Euro-Zone.[20] This does not mean that Italy will be successful in the competitive race in the Euro-Zone: a race where the policy style and especially discourse may prove inadequate.

[20] The Minister for the Economy in the Berlusconi government, Professor Giulio Tremonti, confirmed the commitment to the stability pact in several interviews in May and June 2001.

9

The Netherlands and EMU: A Small Open Economy in Search of Prosperity

Amy Verdun

The coming of the euro to the Netherlands has not been, and is not likely to become, a very politicized event. As this chapter shows, the Netherlands has made gradual moves towards economic and monetary integration in Europe without considering it as having had a major impact on its identity or sovereignty. In fact, one could argue that obtaining the euro in the Netherlands is an indication of what is considered to be successful policy-making. The Netherlands is a small, open trading nation which is highly dependent on its neighbouring countries and on other EU member states. It has also considered this openness to be part of its collective national identity. Over decades its policies have been geared towards limiting the differences in monetary policy-making with its most important trading partner, Germany. In fact for many years De Nederlandsche Bank, the Dutch central bank, de facto copied German monetary policies. As such the creation of an Economic and Monetary Union (EMU), based on price stability, and the introduction of the euro can be seen as part of long-term policies of the Dutch authorities for improving trade and maintaining stability.

The Dutch have dealt with Europeanization in a very proactive manner. In the 1980s they were strong supporters of the completion of the single European market. They have also favoured progressive policies in a number of specific areas, such as environmental policies, social policy, and justice and home affairs. As far as policy implementation is concerned, they also have a

The research for this chapter was made possible by a major research grant from the Social Sciences and Humanities Research Council of Canada (SSHRC Grant: 410-99-0081). An earlier draft was presented at the workshop 'European States and the Euro', London, 14–15 September 2000, generously sponsored by the British Academy. The author wishes to thank the participants of the above workshop, in particular Kenneth Dyson and Erik Jones, for useful comments on an earlier draft. The usual disclaimer applies.

solid record. Europeanization was considered to be a strategy at the heart of the Dutch governmental policies of the Christian-Democratic/Liberal coalitions of the 1980s. When the Dutch government changed from being a centre-right coalition to one of Social Democrats and Liberals, there was no change in policies towards European integration. The same holds true for the approach to EMU. It was seen as yet another initiative to strengthen the general European integration process as well as the successful monetary policies pursued by the Dutch monetary authorities since the late 1970s. As will be discussed in more detail below, the Dutch have been strong supporters of European integration in general and also the economic and monetary integration process.

There is another interesting aspect of the Dutch economy. During the 1990s the Netherlands managed to restructure its economy with great success. It was sometimes called the 'Dutch miracle' (cf. Visser and Hemerijck 1997). In fact, some analysts have looked to the Netherlands as a 'model' for successful restructuring. The 'Polder model', as it is often called, attracts attention from academics, politicians, and the media. A clear definition of the term 'Polder model' is difficult to give as it seems to be used widely and loosely. Labohm and Wijnker (2000: 5) define it as follows: 'On an institutional level, the Polder Model includes a quasi-permanent dialogue between government and social partners (tripartitism), which is conducive to the creation of a climate in which both employers and trade unions trust each other and are prepared to strike deals that are beneficial to both parties in a long-term perspective.' They go on to explain what policy outcomes the Polder Model has produced: 'Within this institutional framework, it has been possible to foster wage moderation and gradual trimming of the welfare state, with positive effects on employment and social spending, thus contributing to the financial sustainability of the welfare state. Other positive effects include the reduction of public spending and budget deficits, as well as the gradual reduction of the public debt/GDP ratio'. Various commentators have wondered to what extent the Dutch model offers a successful formula for other states to adopt in order to deal with external constraints caused by globalization and Europeanization and, of course, EMU. Different states take on different roles in the overall interaction among the member states.

One could categorize the roles played by small states in the European integration process and subdivide them into four types: rogues, lone riders, active team players, and passive team players.[1] The Dutch have typically been

---

[1] These categories were inspired by comments Erik Jones made on an earlier version of this chapter.

in the third category. Where possible, they have indicated their willingness to collaborate and participate fully in the integration process. In the monetary sphere, the Dutch have closely aligned their policies to those of Germany. In fact, the Dutch often advocated policies that went even further than what the Germans were willing to bargain for. The EMU process for the Germans was about institutionalizing German practices in the EU institutional framework. They were often confronted with having to do a careful balancing act between being proactive and at the same time not appearing to be too dominant. In part this was caused by the specific historical time during which the EMU negotiations took place. Just after German reunification, the Germans wanted to show the other member states that they were aiming for a 'Europeanized Germany' rather than a 'Germanized Europe'. The Dutch, by contrast, did not have the same problem. It appears that they often expressed what the Germans were thinking without having to worry about what the others might be thinking about them.

This chapter examines how EMU has affected the Netherlands. In order to answer this question it will analyse the attitudes towards EMU and macroeconomic and monetary policy-making since 1969. The structure is as follows. The first section briefly discusses the Dutch view of EMU from the late 1960s and indicates how European economic and monetary integration served specific Dutch aims. The second section discusses the structural changes and retrenchment in the Netherlands from the early 1980s through the 1990s, leading to the Polder model. It assesses whether the Dutch model is equipped to deal with the constraints of EMU. It also examines whether and, if so, to what extent this process changed Dutch discourse about policy-making and attitudes to economic 'good governance'. The third section discusses Dutch policies towards EMU after the Maastricht Treaty, and reflects on how the Dutch have been an 'active team player' in the European integration process. The fourth section looks at Dutch attitudes towards EMU in the 1990s in the light of the earlier analysis. Attention is also given to opposition to EMU. The fifth section discusses some of the core questions of this volume: whether EMU has led to more Europeanization; whether there been a change in discourse in the Netherlands and, if so, to what extent this is due to EMU; and whether there been a change in identity due to EMU or to other factors. The final section draws conclusions about the way EMU has affected the Netherlands. It will also be argued that EMU was introduced in a period of ongoing restructuring of which EMU formed an integral part. EMU did not *cause* restructuring. Rather, the restructuring was perceived as necessary. The commitment to EMU meant that the need to restructure was made more urgent.

The Netherlands and Three Decades of Economic and Monetary Cooperation in Europe

The Netherlands is fully aware of its size and place in the larger world economy. Though its focus was initially geared more or less equally towards both the United States and Europe, its ties to other European countries have been gradually strengthened. With the collapse of the Bretton Woods system, the Dutch authorities refocused and upgraded the importance of securing exchange-rate stability in Europe (Rood 1990).

Throughout the late 1960s and 1970s the Dutch monetary authorities favoured close monetary cooperation with other EC member states. They made alliances with the Germans on policies for further economic and monetary integration. Like the Germans, the Dutch were keen to ensure that macroeconomic integration was well developed before moving towards deeper monetary integration.[2] Nevertheless, they favoured closer European cooperation in this area. They backed the exchange-rate agreements that were established to promote monetary and trade stability in Europe, such as the Snake and the exchange rate mechanism (ERM).

Throughout the 1970s, like many other states the Netherlands had to learn the hard way that high inflation can be devastating for a small open economy. After having been hit severely by the Arab oil embargo, the Dutch realised more than ever before that their economy was fully dependent on those of others. Both oil crises—1973 and 1979—had a major negative impact on the Dutch economy, the second being even worse than the first. Against this background, the Dutch monetary authorities chose to follow the policy of maintaining a 'hard guilder'. During the late 1970s the guilder still devalued against the D-Mark: 2 per cent in October 1976, in October 1978, in September 1989, and in March 1983). Since then there have been no more exchange-rate adjustments vis-à-vis the D-Mark.

In the late 1970s and early to mid-1980s the Dutch economy suffered from what became known as 'Dutch disease', which refers to the worsened competitiveness of the Dutch economy. André Szász (1988: 208–9) identifies four factors that caused the 'Dutch disease': first, the tradition of centralized wage bargaining; second, the political preference to increase wages rather than worry about profits; third, the rapidly increasing state expenditures made

---

[2] The Dutch and German governments both belonged to the 'economists' camp in the well-known debate between 'economists' and 'monetarists' in the 1960s and 1970s on how best to obtain further monetary integration.

possible by the high revenue from Dutch natural gas; and fourth, the rapid increase of general wages due to a number of automatic mechanisms. The decision to follow a strong currency policy put pressure on a number of these practices and offered a method to combat inflation.

For these reasons the Dutch authorities decided to follow German monetary policies and secure fixed exchange rates between the guilder and the D-Mark. This policy objective was maintained until the launch of the euro in 1999. By 1999 the Dutch exchange rate with the D-Mark had been the most stable of all ERM currencies over a period of two decades. The Dutch were among the first to decide to follow German monetary policies. In their case it should be seen as part of wider political and socio-economic factors supporting a restructuring of the Dutch economy (Jones 1998). The macroeconomic adjustments necessary to maintain these fixed exchange rates were spread over a longer period than was the case in a number of other ERM countries, notably Italy, Portugal, and Spain.

Structural Changes and Retrenchment in the Netherlands in the 1980s and 1990s

This section discusses to what extent the Dutch model is equipped to deal with the constraints of EMU. As we shall see, the Dutch welcomed these constraints.

After coming to terms with the economic decline of the 1970s, the Dutch government had the difficult task of dealing with the consequent economic problems. High wages, high public debt, lack of competitiveness, low economic growth, and high unemployment were among the many problems that the government faced. The governments of the 1980s chose to focus first on cutting expenditure. Thus, the 1980s could be characterized as one long period of *Bezuinigingen* (cuts in public expenditure). It started with the Van Agt government, which announced *Bestek '81* with as its main aim to reduce public expenditure.

In order to tackle unemployment, during the 1980s the three governments of Ruud Lubbers aimed at 'freezing' wages. Within the neo-corporatist structures of the Netherlands, representatives of trade unions, employers' organizations, and government bargained over labour conditions, wages, and public expenditure. In the 1970s they had only once succeeded in negotiating a collective agreement. A major breakthrough came in 1982 with the so-called 'Accord of Wassenaar '. For the first time since 1972 they reached a general agreement with recommendations on employment policy. After the

Accord of Wassenaar a number of important changes were made (Visser and Hemerijck 1997). The trade unions accepted that the overall profitability of Dutch industry had to improve in order to deal with unemployment. They accepted the employers' proposal that they should refrain from demanding a nominal wage increase in line with inflation. The employers, in turn, agreed to open discussions about reducing the working week for some jobs. Wassenaar also led to a change from a centralized, failing system of collective bargaining to a decentralized though highly coordinated system.

During the 1980s all kinds of automatic wage increases were abolished (Kapteyn 1993). In consequence, the overall wage level in the Netherlands compared with that in Germany declined considerably. The strategy of freezing wages appeared for most of the 1980s not to be very beneficial to employment. Reduction in unemployment subsequently moved higher on the agenda of the second Lubbers government in the second half of the 1980s. In this period the restructuring of the labour market followed some unconventional methods, not necessarily aimed at this result (de Beus 2001). The Dutch employment disability law was used to fund persons who were unable for medical reasons to continue their jobs. At one point as many as one million people out of a population of 15 million were on disability money and out of the labour force. By the 1990 it was clear that the employment laws needed to be changed in favour of flexibility, and that an end had to be made to using the disability law to place workers outside the workforce.

During the 1990s the use of temporary employment was 'rediscovered'. The labour market grew increasing more flexible, with jobs being done part-time, more temporary positions created, and an increasing number of women entering the labour market.[3] Meanwhile, the government continued on its path of reducing government expenditure, in particular to obtain lower public debt and to reduce the budgetary deficit to around 2 per cent of GDP. By the mid-1990s the Dutch economy had restructured itself in two important areas: employment law and government expenditure. Miraculously, by the mid-1990s the Dutch economy seemed to have come out of 15 years of hard restructuring to face the new reality of above-average economic growth, decreasing levels of unemployment, and a higher ratio of employed persons to the total population. The 'Dutch miracle' had emerged (Visser and Hemerijck 1997).[4] The Polder model was discovered by analysts as a guide to

---

[3] The percentage of female participation in the workforce increased from 34.7% in 1983 to 55.0% in 1996, compared with the EU average of 42.9% in 1983 and 48.4% in 1996 (Visser and Hemerijck 1997: 25).

[4] Over the period 1991–6 the Dutch economy did much better than the EU average on the important economic indicators. In annual growth of GDP the Dutch performance was 2.2% compared

how to deal with the constraints posed by Europeanization and globalization (Labohm and Wijnker 2000).

As a mode of governance the Polder model has the following character-istics. There is strong cooperation between the government, employers' organizations, and trade unions: neo-corporatist structures. These 'tripartite' bodies discuss employment issues and restructuring of the welfare state as well as issues relating to privatization and price setting. Wage moderation has been used to improve the competitiveness of the Dutch economy (Visser and Hemerijck 1997: 26–7; cf. Blanchard and Muet 1993). Jos de Beus (1999) identifies six features of the Polder model. The first feature is consensual decision-making. The second feature is the pragmatic application of social liberalism to deregulation of old markets and regulation of new markets. A third is the internal reorganization of the public sector by a policy mix of reduction of, and innovation in, public expenditure. The fourth is the re-gular renegotiation of forms of wage restraint and moderate wage inequality. The fifth feature is the use of unorthodox methods to reduce unemployment, such as part-time jobs, flexible jobs, and subsidized forms of job creation. The sixth and last feature is the continuity of public policies and arrangements beyond the four-year term of government.

It is noteworthy that the Dutch government was among the first in Western Europe to deregulate and privatize. Many large state-owned cor-porations were sold to the private sector. In numerous areas of traditional monopoly competitors entered the market. In the Dutch case marketization happened early but also in consultation with the tripartite bodies.

The Dutch Polder model has not always received unquestioned praise. Some critics argue that the Dutch system has considerable hidden unem-ployment. A large percentage of the Dutch workforce is at home on dis-ability payment, many of the 60–65-year-olds are on early retirement, and numerous new jobs are part-time. The Netherlands also traditionally has had one of the lowest percentages of female labour participation amongst EU member states. The new jobs for women and youth are often temporary and/or part-time and do not always offer the workers the full satisfaction that they seek (Jones 1998; OECD 1997b; Robinson 1988).

How does EMU fit into this picture? Let us look at the general policies of restructuring of Dutch governments. As part of the strategy of retrenchment in the 1980s, the Dutch decided that there were a number of policy areas that

with the EU average of 1.5%; private consumption 2.3% compared with 1.5%; investment 1.3% compared with minus 0.2%; total employment 1.5% compared with minus 0.5%; unemployment 6.2% compared with 11.1%; and employment/population ratio 64.2% instead of 60.6% (Visser and Hemerijck 1997: 11).

were *not* considered to offer an option for change. In these cases the Dutch government chose to allow external influence to affect the economy but to protect the policy regime. A key example was the status of the Dutch currency. As seen above, since the late 1970s the Dutch monetary authorities and social actors agreed that the Dutch economy needed a stable currency. Exchange rates needed to be stable in particular vis-à-vis the currency of its largest trading partner, that is, the D-Mark. This principle became the cornerstone of Dutch monetary policy. Thus, the Dutch central bank followed closely the interest-rate moves of the Bundesbank.

Another important area that was considered not an option for change was the image of the Netherlands as an open trading nation. With all the troubles of the 1980s, Dutch governments did not consider closing borders or putting up trade barriers. They favoured financial market liberalization and also fully supported the single European market. It was clear to the Dutch government, firms, and trade unions that the Dutch would have to be competitive to be successful. As in Germany, the Dutch realized that they needed to create a competitive framework for firms and adopt tax and other policies that create a favourable business environment.

Finally, the Dutch reconfirmed their 'pro-European' position. The Netherlands has traditionally been fully aware that its economic welfare is closely linked to that of its neighbours. Moreover, it is aware of the need to create an economic environment that promotes trade. The relaunch of the European integration project in the mid-1980s, and EMU in its wake, were fully supported by Dutch political parties, employers' organizations, trade unions, and monetary authorities. Even the convergence criteria of the Maastricht Treaty were not considered to be a major obstacle. They were seen as an expression of domestically established aims to restructure public debt and budgetary deficits. The Dutch government had accumulated considerable debt throughout the 1970s and 1980s, and the share of public expenditure used merely to service government debt was considerable. The convergence criteria were thus gratefully accepted as providing an additional external constraint to legitimize the need to reduce the Dutch budgetary deficit and public debt.

When EMU was relaunched in the late 1980s, it offered a package fully in line with the policy objectives and preferences of the Dutch government and the political elites. EMU aimed at opening markets, at having a more efficient payment system, and at reducing transaction costs through the introduction of a single currency. All these factors were fully compatible with the aims of the Dutch government and the self-image of Dutch employers and employees.

Throughout the 1990s the Dutch government continued the policies of the 1980s. The discourse used by the government still focused on reducing public debt and budgetary deficits and reducing unemployment. With the ERM crises of 1992–3 the Dutch monetary authorities were suddenly confronted with the possibility of the ERM collapsing all together and their endeavours threatened. However, the markets did not attack the Dutch guilder. In fact, it was the only currency that formally remained within the original 2.25 per cent band with the D-Mark when the ERM bands were eventually widened in August 1993.

By the middle of the 1990s the Dutch economy had gradually become the beneficiary of the work done in the previous 15 years. Unemployment came down, economic growth increased, the public debt declined, and the annual budgetary deficit was reduced to less than 2 per cent of GDP. The Dutch had done it!

The 1980s and 1990s were characterized by a strong public discourse about the role of government and the policies that were being pursued. During the 1980s the buzzwords were 'deregulation', 'privatization', 'reducing debts and deficits', and 'labour-market and welfare-state restructuring'. These object-ives proposed by Dutch governments were never really challenged by the opposition parties or the general population. As the final stage of EMU drew near, these issues did not change much. However, with the success of the Dutch model, the problems that the government was facing reduced. In the last five years of the 1990s the Dutch governments benefited from the improved economic conditions and the subsequent increase in wealth experienced by the entire population. Thus EMU did not impose the con-straints that other states, such as France or Italy, witnessed. The Dutch define 'good governance' in terms of whether the government is able to 'deliver' eco-nomic prosperity for all. With economic growth high for five years in a row, the Dutch were very happy with their governments and political confidence high.

The Creation of EMU: The Netherlands as an Active Player

The Dutch government of Lubbers held the rotating presidency of the EC at a key moment in the history of EMU: when the intergovernmental confer-ences preparing the Maastricht Treaty revisions were negotiated in the sec-ond half of 1991. They adopted a very proactive approach at the start of their presidency, launching an ambitious proposal for reforming the institutional structure of the EC towards a 'tree-like structure' (Dyson and Featherstone

1999; Moravcsik 1998). This proposal for political union went too far for many states, and the Dutch had to withdraw their proposal and return to the draft treaty of the previous Luxembourg presidency. With regard to the EMU negotiations they also made a provocative start. In late August the Dutch tabled a so-called 'technical paper', which toyed with the idea of introducing a 'two-speed Europe' (*Financial Times* 1991a). This proposal met with objections from the southern member states (Financial Times 1991b). The remainder of the autumn the Dutch worked very hard at getting a workable compromise that would satisfy all member states. The end result was the successful incorporation of EMU into the Treaty on European Union.

Though taken up in the Treaty, EMU was by no means completely settled in 1991. The interpretation of the convergence criteria would remain a hot political topic. Also, the Germans were concerned that once EMU was fully operational that some countries might return to their old practices of high levels of public borrowing and high levels of inflation. The Dutch were among the countries most sympathetic to these German concerns. In fact, they were often the ones to speak up about the concerns that the Germans had. As already touched upon above, the Dutch-German relationship had been carefully crafted throughout the 15 years prior to signing of the Treaty on European Union (Brouwer 1999). Also, the German government had to do a careful balancing act between being proactive on what it considered important and not seeming to be too dominant within the broader European context. It was the Dutch who often spoke out.

The issue of who would qualify to join the third stage of EMU was the topic of Dutch concern. When the ERM was under pressure, the idea of a 'two-speed' EMU was often discussed. On these occasions the Dutch were among those who thought that a two-speed EMU might be necessary if some or many states failed to meet the convergence criteria. They typically urged the need to stick to the timetable as much as possible (*Het Financieele Dagblad* 1993). Yet they did not want to compromise on the convergence criteria. The Dutch were often outspoken advocates of the German model, and dared to go public stating the importance of relying on the German experience in successful monetary policy-making. For example, to ensure low inflation, they advocated adopting money supply targets and monetary instruments similar to those in Germany rather than relying on inflation targeting as the British advocated (*Financial Times* 1995). On various occasions, when the performance of states like Italy, France, and other southern European states in meeting the convergence criteria was poor, the Dutch suggested going ahead with a smaller group. Thus Wim Duisenberg, then Dutch central-bank president, stated that an EMU without Italy was possible but it would be unthinkable without France. France should be able to join by 'a political judgment' (*Financial Times* 1995). On another occasion a Dutch official argued that the whole EMU project would lose credibility if Italy was allowed to join. In 1996, when the former French President Valéry Giscard d'Estaing suggested the idea of loosening the convergence criteria, the Dutch were again at the forefront, arguing that such an idea was unacceptable (*Algemeen Dagblad* 1996). By November 1996 prominent Dutch figures, like former central banker André Szász, advocated that EMU should start with a small group (*NRC Handelsblad* 1996). This view was supported in some banking circles.

Dutch Attitudes towards EMU 1989–2000

What were Dutch attitudes towards EMU when the Delors Report (1989) was first published? Did they change during the 1990s and, if so, how? In 1989 and 1990 this author conducted a study of perceptions of EMU in the Netherlands (Verdun 1990). The study examined the views of EMU held by the largest Dutch trade union confederation (FNV), the largest employers' organisation (VNO), the five major political parties—the Christian Democrats (CDA), the Social Democrats (PvdA), the right-wing Liberal Party (VVD), D'66, and Groenlinks—the Ministry of Finance, and the Dutch central bank. The conclusion was twofold. First, EMU had not been the subject of major discussion within these organizations, any more than it had caught the attention of the general public. It was simply considered to be a logical extension of existing policies: Dutch monetary policies; maintaining fixed exchange rates with Germany and other ERM currencies; being an open trading economy; and needing to restructure public expenditure, the welfare state, and the labour market (Rood 1990). It was viewed as logical and acceptable that monetary policy should be transferred to a European central bank. Dutch actors also realized that the restrictions on budgetary expenditure with EMU implied that the Dutch government would be less free in its choices about taxation and public expenditure. In addition, they recognized that there would be a dynamic effect from having EMU and from completing the single European market—the '1992 programme'. They understood that market pressures would be stronger and that some welfare-state provisions would have to be adjusted, some of them no longer being an option. Their main concern was the need for EMU to be firmly embedded in some kind of institutional framework that would be held accountable for the effects of EMU. Thus, they converged around the idea that 'political union', then being discussed in a separate IGC, would require further development so that issues of democracy, representation, and accountability could be dealt with. Dutch actors were, however, unclear about the implications for fiscal policy (De Grauwe *et al.* 1989; SER 1990)

In other words, the Dutch social partners, political parties, and monetary authorities had accepted EMU as part of a neo-liberal regime (also McNamara 1998; Crouch 2000: 20). Neo-liberal regime refers here to one in which (1) market forces are considered to be the key, (2) the government reduces its role in protecting citizens and companies from these market forces, (3) international pressures are accepted as factors with which a government has to deal rather than adopting protectionist policies, and (4) increasing interdependence will occur via Europeanization and globalization.

The Dutch parliament ratified the Treaty on European Union without any problems in November 1992. The media and public opinion were also quite positive towards EMU over this period as well as throughout the 1990s. Media reporting in the Netherlands tends to be supportive of European integration. Thus the Dutch case differs importantly from those of Britain and Denmark. Dutch support for the single currency, as indicated by *Eurobarometer* statistics throughout the 1990s, accounts for a majority of those polled.

In anticipation of the euro, the Dutch central bank started its own opinion polling in 1995 about acceptance of, and preparedness for, its introduction on the part the public and businesses. It polled four times a year. Its polls showed that business was substantially more favourable to the introduction of the euro than the public as a whole. Even so, overall public acceptance levels were at 60 per cent or higher throughout the period 1995–9. The percentage of people in favour of the introduction of the euro started with 60 per cent in 1995, climbed to 73 per cent in September 1996, and then declined to 62 per cent in September 1997. Thereafter, it rose steadily to 80 per cent in March 1999 (Prast and Stokman 1999: 4).

In October 1996 the PvdA issued a report 'De Strijd om de EMU' ('The Battle for EMU'), stating that the convergence criteria and the proposed Stability Pact were too stringent. According to this report, these stringent rules would lead to lower economic growth and higher unemployment (*Het Parool* 1996). However, and indicative of the state of Dutch opinion, the report did not lead to a major public debate on this topic.

Interestingly, after years of public support for European integration in general and economic and monetary cooperation in particular, a public debate suddenly emerged in 1997. There had already been some calls by a newly established action group, which claimed to represent small shop owners, for a boycott of the euro. In the view of its spokesperson, EMU would just cost money and would not guarantee a positive outcome. The group was particularly concerned about the lack of serious sanctions to constrain Greece and Italy (*Telegraaf* 1996). The real public debate opened on 13 February 1997, when a leading Dutch newspaper, *De Volkskrant*, published a declaration, signed by 70 Dutch economists, criticizing EMU: 'Met deze EMU kiest Europa de verkeerde weg' ('With this EMU Europe is choosing the wrong road') (Reuten, Vendrik, and Went 1998). The economists' main concern was that EMU would endanger the welfare state and the social welfare of European citizens. The fear was that, by having government expenditures as the only instrument to deal with economic shocks, it would not be possible to create an economically prosperous and equitable society. At the same time as the Dutch economists' declaration, a prominent Dutch liberal politician, Frits Bolkestein, also voiced criticism of the EMU project. The result was the first real public debate in the Netherlands on EMU.

However, the reaction of the Dutch Parliament and the government was lukewarm. Some parliamentarians, such as the Social Democrat Rick van der Ploeg, explained that Parliament did not take the criticism seriously, as the moment to discuss EMU had already passed some time ago. Hans Hoogervorst, a Liberal MP, said he thought that the advice of the 70 economists would lead to higher unemployment, rather than that EMU would do that, as they claimed. Parliamentarians also criticized the list of economists and noted that the 'real experts' were not amongst them (*De Volkskrant* 1997). A week later other politicians voiced the need to increase the amount of information to the public about the introduction of the euro (*NRC Handelsblad* 1997). By March 1997 the central banking community as well as the more prominent experts on EMU were expressing their surprise about the newly started debate on EMU.

Though the Dutch central bank opinion polling did not observe a decline in support, it is noteworthy that *Eurobarometer* data *did* show a decline in support for the euro by Dutch citizens in 1997. Whereas support in the spring of 1996 had been 66 per cent in favour and 26 per cent against, the numbers in support came down considerably in 1997 (European Commission 1996: 45). In the spring of 1997 those in favour dropped to 52 per cent, and those opposed rose to 42 per cent (European Commission 1997: 28). However, this dip in support was only temporary. The *Eurobarometer* figures for spring 2000 indicated that the Dutch were back to their earlier levels of support: 67 per cent in favour, and 27 per cent against (European Commission 2000f: 46).

These *Eurobarometer* figures suggest that the Dutch reduction in support for the euro in 1997 may have been caused by the new, more critical public debate on EMU. However, no systematic analysis has been made analyzing whether this debate had an impact on the general public attitude towards EMU.

Moreover, it is possible that other factors also had an effect on Dutch public opinion, such as the voting into power of left-wing governments in Britain and France; increasing expression of criticism of the EMU project throughout Europe and by the United States, and so forth. Finally, the two conflicting polls cast some doubt on whether there really was a downward trend in public support for EMU.

In any event, the debate in the Netherlands soon subsided, and after 1997 EMU was no longer debated in these terms. The media returned to its overall positive reporting of the European integration process. In 1999–2000 the Dutch seemed once again at ease with EMU. The debate about the EU moved on to discuss issues of accountability, legitimacy, and democracy.

At the start of the 1990s the Dutch government was still struggling with its economic performance. It felt strongly the negative effects of German stagflation, which had come about as a result of German reunification in 1990. However, by the middle of the 1990s it slowly became clear that the Dutch economy was finally benefiting from years of restructuring. With the improvement in the performance of the economy the Dutch government focused attention on reducing the public debt and the budgetary deficit. On the other convergence criteria the Dutch currency and monetary indicators already performed satisfactorily.

Once the 'Dutch miracle' became visible and the Polder model a talking point, economic policies of restructuring became much easier politically, and the reduction of budgetary deficits and public debt a less difficult process. Attitudes to EMU were no longer framed in the context of whether it might have a negative impact on the welfare state. With the Dutch economy performing so well, no one could make a serious claim that EMU or market forces were putting the Dutch model under pressure. With the Dutch better off than for many years, there was an overall sense of well-being in the country. The performance of the Dutch economy appeared even more spectacular against the background of the poor performance of its neighbouring states, in particular France and Germany.

EMU, Europeanization, and Changes in Discourse and Identity

It is now time to turn to some of the core questions raised in the introduction to this book. EMU has been at the core of the integration process during and after the 1990s. Has EMU led to more Europeanization? Or has Europeanization led to EMU? In the Dutch case one can argue that both happened. It seems that the process swings back and forth between the two like a pendulum (Wallace and Wallace 1996). In 1989, when EMU was put on the agenda, the Dutch accepted it as part of Europeanization and their over-all policies. Once EMU was accepted, it became part of the successful policies that one could look to in order to find evidence that Europeanization was happening.

Has EMU led to a change in discourse in the Netherlands? Again, the answer is not clear-cut. As has been argued above, the discourse in the Nether-lands at the end of the 1980s was already a neo-liberal one, with emphasis on restructuring and reducing debts and deficits. The Dutch had already kept inflation rates low, so the public debate did not emphasize so much the need for low inflation. However, with the coming of the EMU and the euro, the language extended to include more monetary policy-related keywords that were now heard more frequently. 'Low inflation', 'price stability', 'converg-ence criteria', and 'stability pact' were added to the words used throughout the 1980s. It appears that there was no regime shift but a specification of the words and concepts being adopted within the regime. In other words, the discourse had changed prior to EMU being put on the agenda. However, with the introduction of EMU the discourse was further strengthened and legitimized (Verdun 2000a).

EMU and Dutch identity is perhaps the most difficult topic to come to grips with. The Dutch see themselves as a trading nation and realize that they need to cater to this self-image and aim. EMU nicely fits this profile. With the rediscovered success of the Dutch economy, the Dutch started to appreciate that they were considered to be the 'winners' of the game that was being played in Europe. Most people realize that the introduction of the euro is to a certain extent an unknown quantity and that there will be winners and losers. What came out of the public debate in 1997 was this sense that the future was uncertain. However, with the Dutch economy doing well while their important and considerable larger and richer neighbours Germany and France were doing less well, the Dutch felt that Europeanization, globaliza-tion, and EMU had done their state and economy no harm. If anything, they have done well. It will be interesting to see whether the Dutch remain so positive once the economy cools down.

Conclusion: The Netherlands and EMU—Business as Usual

The Netherlands accepted EMU from the very first day it was initiated back in the late 1960s. EMU was considered to be in line with Dutch policies that focused on maintaining fixed exchange rates with Germany and other EU member states. The Dutch view themselves as a nation of traders who want their country to do well in an interdependent global world. European economic and monetary integration was accepted as a process that strengthened the realization of Dutch objectives.

The Dutch approach to EMU is firmly embedded in the Dutch approach to Europeanization. The construction of Europe is at the heart of Dutch policies and EMU is merely another stepping stone on the road to further integration. The Dutch have also remained confident that Europeanization in general, and EMU in particular, will not threaten the Dutch model of governance. On the contrary, the Dutch were more capable than most of maintaining their own model, performing well, and joining EMU without many problems at all. The Dutch case suggests that EMU was not a causal factor in restructuring the welfare state and the labour market. The pressures for reform preceded the plan to create EMU. The relaunching of the EMU project did, however, add another incentive to step up the process of restructuring, in particular of the public debt and the budgetary deficit. But it would be a serious misrepresentation to state that EMU had very much effect on the Dutch mode of governance.

It is difficult to judge how EMU as such affects Dutch society and identity. EMU is so firmly embedded in Dutch preferences and policy objectives that it is hard to draw the line between those and EMU per se. Moreover, the 'feel-good' factor in the Netherlands—a result of the economic growth and prosperity since the mid-1990s—makes the objective evaluation of what EMU does to the Netherlands very difficult. The Dutch are content with EMU and self-confident about their role within it, basically because they are doing well economically. Economic growth and job creation also mean that the Dutch government is not facing the most politically difficult redistributive questions.

Many critics of EMU stress that the euro and the specific policy regime chosen for economic and monetary integration in Europe involve a large number of risks. Various authors identify a lack of legitimacy of the EMU project (Crouch 2000b; Minkkinen and Patomäki 1997; Moss and Michie 1998; Patomäki 1997; Verdun and Christiansen 2000). Others focus on the fact that governments will be lacking tools to deal with economic shocks and social inequality (Boyer 2000; Pochet and Vanhercke 1998; Pochet 1998). Finally, there have been lively debates about how a fully symmetrical EMU might work, with both economic and monetary union and a *gouvernement économique*, as well as a more fully developed political union (Dyson 2000a; Dyson and Featherstone 1999; Verdun 1996; 1998a). During the IGCs of 1991 and in the course of the 1990s, the Dutch emphasized the need for further political integration. These debates consider what role there might be for national and

European governance and whether there might be a need for fiscal transfer payments to deal with any imbalances. Though in the background of such debates, the Dutch have shied away from seriously thinking about any of these matters. In contrast, EMU confirmed the belief of the Dutch government and people that neo-liberal policies, conducted within a framework of consensus governance—the Polder model—served them well in their aim of remaining a prosperous small trading nation. EMU also strengthened their overall commitment to Europe. Whether these Dutch perceptions of EMU will change in the near future remains to be seen.

PART III

Sectors, States, and EMU

Politics, Banks, and Financial Market Governance in the Euro-Zone

Michael Moran

Understanding the Euro-Zone is fraught with obvious difficulties. The historical novelty of the creation itself; the fact that as a recent creation its understanding presents special problems of historical interpretation; the very uncertainty of its continued existence at least as an entity connected by a single currency: all combine to present immense problems of understanding. Small wonder that, as Dyson has shown, those who study the process are soon entangled in complex questions of epistemology (Dyson 2000b). In the case of banking and finance this is further complicated by the way changes at the Euro-Zone level interact with at least three other levels: with the level of national systems of financial market governance; with the level of financial market governance in the wider 15-member European Union; and with the evolving global system. Banking politics in the Euro-Zone make little sense if not seen as embedded in these three systems, just as an examination of the national and the global would make no sense without the European. Indeed, the innocent image of 'levels' is misleading for it suggests systemic separation. But, in truth, all four are better conceived as having a symbiotic relationship: inextricably twined round each other, sometimes supporting, sometimes dragging down.

To this we must add a further complication. One obvious way of thinking about the money politics of the Euro-Zone is to work with a distinction between *monetary governance* and *financial market governance*. In these terms the single currency project amounts to a revolution in monetary governance,

I am grateful for comments offered on the original version of this chapter by participants in the preparatory conference for this volume held in London, September 2000. I owe particular debts to Iain Begg, Amy Verdun, and especially to Christopher Taylor, the discussant on the original paper. I also owe an immense debt to Kenneth Dyson for constant advice and encouragement, and for gentle, supportive, but insistent editorial criticism.

while financial market governance—essentially the regulation of competitive conditions and prudential control—remains a separate domain. Institutionally, indeed, this separation is commonly realized. Periodic crises of prudential supervision have progressively disentangled the role of prudential supervisors in particular. The response to crisis has been to try to create specialized supervisory institutions with clear lines of responsibility and accountability. But in practice the distinction between the two domains is difficult to maintain, as will be plain in the succeeding pages. It soon becomes obvious that the project to create a single currency has massive implications for what we conventionally call 'financial market governance'. Some of these are intended: part of the point of a single currency is to hasten the process of structural transformation and competition in markets, including banking markets. Some are more hidden in the implicit duties of institutions. If structural change is sufficiently brutal, then problems of systemic stability will inevitably be raised in banking markets. It is difficult to see the European Central Bank (ECB) not being activated in the role of prudential guardian (for some possible ways, Begg and Green 1996). I try to solve this problem in the succeeding pages by writing generally of *financial market governance*.

This simple realization shapes what follows. Understanding financial market governance in the Euro-Zone does indeed involve attending to institutions and cultural understandings which presently characterize the EMU system, notably the ECB and the attendant ideology of sound money which shapes its practices. But these institutions and culture are plainly inseparable from the 30-year history of financial market governance in Europe, from the way national systems of financial market governance developed in the same period, and from what is the single most important feature of financial market governance in the last generation: the way globalization has shaped both the character of trading and the character of institutions, national and global. In the interests of exposition within a confined space the discussion violates the complex relations that exist between all these elements by separating out three levels: the national, the European, and the global. It tries to explore all three and to examine the interactions between them. In essence, the assumption behind this procedure is that the national and the global are not be to considered 'settings' or 'backdrop' to the Euro-Zone but constitute part of its essential character. Insofar as this is given analytical substance in the chapter it is contained in the notion, outlined later, that the relations between the national, the European, and the global are *reflexive* in character. The substantive argument is that the creation of the Euro-Zone represents the triumph of a particular mode of financial market governance; that this mode both elevates the management of financial markets to the centre-piece of economic policy and insulates the development of policy from the institutions of liberal democracy; and that, in so doing, it represents the triumph of one long-term tendency in financial market governance in Europe and the defeat of another. This reinforces the argument made above: that, while separating *monetary* and *financial market governance* is indeed legitimate, in this particular case the governments of the two domains are inextricably mixed.

This observation also considerably complicates another central issue: that of causality. Disentangling the 'effects' of EMU from other effects, in theory manageable by maintaining the separation of monetary and financial market governance, in practice is immensely complicated. The complications are again summed up in the *reflexive* character of these processes; for reflexivity involves, precisely, the conscious action of human agents in appropriating, reappropriating, and learning for purposes of statecraft. As this argument also suggests, an additional important assumption underpins the chapter: that, while monetary union and all that surrounds it have an economic face, at heart what we are witnessing here is an attempt to reconstruct systems of government. Any appreciation of what the system of financial market governance amounts to in the present-day Euro-Zone therefore depends on getting some sense of the governing systems that preceded it. Thus, while the chapter tries to home in on the present-day Euro-Zone, it does this through an extended discussion of the global and national governmental settings of EMU. And underpinning that way of writing the chapter another, very crude assumption slowly reveals itself: that there is a high politics and a low politics of financial market governance in Europe. To put it simply—perhaps too simply—my argument is that high politics has pushed the system of government in one direction and low politics has pulled it in another.

These issues also raise analytical questions which are central to this whole volume concerning the complex issue of the relationship between *Europeanization, convergence*, and *divergence*: issues addressed separately by Dyson (2000b). In discussing issues of convergence and divergence Dyson works with the distinction between convergence of *processes, policies,* and *outcomes*. The most important focus in this chapter is on processes, on both the processes that produced EMU and the processes of financial market governance embedded in the new institutions. I return to this issue in the concluding section of the chapter.

Politics, Banks, and Democracy

All the national systems unified in the Euro-Zone and in the wider EU are, if only in a rough and ready way, species of liberal democracy. In some, liberal democratic institutions have deep historical and cultural roots; in others, they are constitutive of the national identities recreated after the catastrophe of fascism. By contrast, financial markets and institutions have long had an ambivalent, and in some instances hostile, relationship with democracy.

There are two sources of this latter state of affairs. First, many of the key governing institutions of the financial system were historically species of private-interest government that had established themselves, often, before the development of democratic politics. They existed apart from, and in some instances in hostility to, democratic institutions. In the Federal Republic of Germany, for instance, while the Bundesbank was integral to the character of the post-Nazi democratic regime, key institutions of regulation in the securities markets were in part the product of legislation dating from the Nazi era (see Moran 1989; 1992). More fundamentally, regulatory ideologies in financial markets functioned to exclude the characteristic actors of democracy—democratically elected politicians—from financial market governance. A good instance of this state of affairs is the government of the public trading of securities on stock exchanges. This characteristic institution of financial market governance was the self-governing corporation. While the exact legal form of exchanges varied according to constitutional traditions—a more or less private company in the UK, a public-law body in many continental European systems—what is remarkable are the similarities exhibited in both economic and political practices, regardless of the big differences between national forms of capitalism. It did not matter whether the capitalism was Rhineland or market capitalism: the market was self-governed. The supporting ideology characteristically pictured self-government as a technical necessity, arguing that effective government demanded the expertise and flexibility of the practitioner. Effective policing of the system depended heavily on the suppression of competition: on tight controls over entry, often exercised according to ascriptive criteria, and on controls over price and product competition among those allowed to enter markets.

The second source of the anti-democratic nature of the markets arose from the historical character of central banking. Modern central banking, fashioned around notions of the central bank as the ultimate guarantor of the stability of the banking system and the stability of currencies, developed within the elite of financial institutions. The key moments in its development —moments encompassing, for instance, the acceptance of the notion of the central bank as a prudential regulator and as a guarantor of systemic stability—were typically the product of critical moments in the history of elite financial institutions. Central banking also developed its own enclosed cross-national networks that were separate from, and often hostile to, democratic politics. In some important systems there was a close connection between the practice of central banking and the wider government of financial markets. But the governance of financial markets at national level not only had a tense relationship with democracy; it also had a tense relationship with capitalism, or at least with market competition. Governing financial markets characteristically involved suppressing competition: creating barriers to entry; segmenting markets; and erecting barriers to price and product competition, invoking in justification the demands of prudence and systemic stability.

In summary, the characteristic government of financial markets relied on: suppressing competition in markets; suppressing the kind of open political competition associated with democratic politics; and creating an enclosed, elitist world of financial market governance. A key to understanding the system of financial market governance that emerged in the Euro-Zone in the 1990s is the realization that, from the 1950s to the 1980s, financial market governance began to develop different characteristics in different centres. In particular, the governing experience of the two major financial centres in Europe, London and Frankfurt, diverged significantly.

London saw the systematic erosion of the three bulwarks of the system of financial market governance: the suppression of competition; the exclusion of democratic politics; and domination by an elitist policy community. The erosion of competitive restraints in the London markets is well documented. From the 1950s restrictions on product competition began to be undermined by the development of a whole new range of financial instruments. Indeed, instrument innovation became one of the key means by which competitive advantage was sought in markets. Other developments in the 1950s signalled a process of circumvention of the restrictions over market entry by the creation of new kinds of parallel markets in novel financial instruments. The key competitive developments in London—notably those associated with the rise of the Eurodollar markets—were, of course, the product of efforts to circumvent regulatory restraints in an even more important financial centre, New York. Deregulation of the American system, symbolized by the 'big bang' on the New York Stock Exchange in 1975, helped ignite deregulatory explosions in London. In fact the London 'big bang' took place in three sequences: the deregulation of banking following the reforms associated with competition and credit control in 1971; the abolition of exchange controls in 1979; and London's own special stock exchange 'big bang' in 1986 (Moran 1991). These reforms all attempted to dismantle or reduce price and entry controls, and controls over competition by product innovation, in a range of financial markets.

Many of these changes implied, and were in part caused by, the decline of systems that depended on control in enclosed, socially elitist worlds. The effect of traditional barriers to competition was to entrench the position of financial dynasties and to protect in many instances the power of family firms, often involving families that were in turn embedded in the wider British social elite. Governing through this kind of enclosed policy community became unsustainable because the policy community was transformed by competitive invasions into a much more diverse, unstable network.

This change in the social foundations of financial market governance was in turn connected to profound alterations that occurred in its relations with the institutions of democratic politics. Three should be highlighted.

First, the cultural autonomy of financial elites declined. In other words, the unthinking acquiescence which allowed financial market governance to be controlled by the financial elite began to disappear. Issues of financial governance—of prudence, honesty, and efficiency—began to turn up on the agenda of democratic politics.

Second, this change in cultural assumptions was part of a wider and much more significant regulatory transformation in the environment of financial market governance. This transformation abolished its character as private-interest government. Some of the change was directly connected to the competitive revolution: the single most important step change in the period, the Financial Services Act, was passed in 1986, the same year as the 'big bang' on the London Stock Exchange. But 1986 marked only one dramatic step in the decline of the regulatory autonomy of financial markets; and a decade and a half later the process has culminated in the new Financial Services Act which in 2000 established a single state agency, the Financial Services Authority.

The third big change, alongside the altered cultural assumptions and the reformation of the institutions of regulation, concerned the position of the central bank. London almost invented the idea of central banking as a mystical, delicate process that had to be protected from democracy. But from the 1950s to the 1980s there was a persistent pattern in the relations between the Bank of England and the central state. The Bank gradually ceased to look like and to think of itself as a City institution, and became integrated into the machinery of the core executive. The Bank lost much of its historic autonomy over its own internal affairs. And the Bank's authority, both in the core executive and in the City, ceased to rest on customary assumptions and became a product of formal authority on the one hand and its ability to function in the world of bureaucratic politics on the other. In short, the Bank ceased finally to be a private, secret institution and was integrated into the machinery of the democratic state.

In presenting this summary of changes in the government of the most important financial centre in Europe between the 1950s and 1980s I do not mean to suggest that the power of financial institutions in Britain declined. On the contrary: the very success of the competitive revolutions, by enormously expanding the financial services industries, magnified the importance of these industries as interests in the political system, especially in an era when manufacturing industries were in decline. Nor did the incorporation of the Bank of England into the core executive signify a decline in its influence. On the contrary again, it gave the Bank a legitimate voice in a much wider range of policy debates than was possible when it operated only from the seclusion of its private garden in the City. And in London, as in many other centres, changes in market structures and in ideological assumptions meant that by the 1980s the high statecraft of economic policy was increasingly preoccupied with managing key financial markets. Nevertheless, in London the totality of change meant that financial services industries were no longer separated from the democratic state. They were one set of interests among many, albeit an extraordinarily powerful set. The historical separation between financial market governance and democracy had been ended.

These changes in London helped prompt change in other European financial centres. The 'big bang' of 1986 was followed by a series of 'little big bangs' elsewhere and by a sustained debate in the other important European financial centre, Frankfurt, about how far it should go down what was commonly pictured as an Anglo-American regulatory road. But despite some institutional reform in the German securities markets and some deregulation of trading practices, the most important feature of German financial market governance was how far it escaped the secular incorporation into the democratic state that London experienced. At the centre of this was the position of the Bundesbank. Studies of the high politics of Bundesbank-federal government relations present a picture of a relationship which is far from the caricature image of Olympian detachment on the part of the central bank. The history since the Bundesbank law in 1957 is stormy, with lines of authority furiously contested at particular critical moments, notably those created by the high diplomacy of global economic management, by the high diplomacy of European monetary unification, and by the statecraft that produced German reunification (Kennedy 1991; Loedel 1999; Dyson and Featherstone 1999). But in the position of the Bundesbank there is nothing like the secular decline in separateness and autonomy experienced over a generation by the Bank of England. There are many reasons for this, and the precise weighting of those reasons need not detain us much here: the particular institutional, including constitutional, setting of the Bundesbank; the political skills of particular personalities; the internal culture of the Bundesbank, notably its ability to socialize incomers into its ideological world; even the often invoked, intangible character of a wider bourgeois culture haunted by memories of the cataclysm of inflation in the historic past.

The narratives which reconstruct the complex manoeuvring that produced the governing structure of the Euro-Zone make clear that it represents the victory of this German model: a victory notably in the governing structure of the new ECB (Dyson and Featherstone 1999). The fact that there was a 'road not taken'—that travelled by London over the last generation—is one of the many reasons why the British state finds living in the Euro-Zone an uncomfortable prospect. But that is to focus on the immediate workings of the high diplomacy that helped create the Euro-Zone. Just as important has been the shaping influence of what is usually summarized as 'globalization'.

Politics, Banks, and Globalization

What did globalization mean when applied to the financial services industries? In part the answer is straightforward and technical. It involved the global organization of trading in a number of linked markets: linked institutionally by ownership patterns; technically by the adaptation of the new communication technologies that allowed increasingly efficient and rapid communication from the 1950s onwards; economically by the development of common markets and common financial instruments. It is well known that all these features combined to produce systems of trading that transcended national political boundaries and often grew at an exponential rate.

Beyond these obvious technical features, globalization in financial services involved the same central feature as in any other economic sector. It involved an elaboration in the division of labour but on a more geographically extended scale. The consequence, critical for the process of financial market governance across Europe, was that it made competition between financial centres an overwhelming consideration in that process. The developing global system raised an obvious set of issues. What was to be the division of labour between established and newly emerging centres? What were to be the areas of specialization, and which centres were to be pre-eminent? It is easy to see why these issues soon convert into questions of financial market governance—and, indeed, soon involve states. In part, successful positioning in the global division of labour by an individual centre is a matter of issues external to the financial system. One of the main early pressures for regulatory reform in telecommunications, for instance, came from efforts to create telecommunication infrastructures capable of coping with the communication demands of global trading. But the most important sources of comparative advantage for a centre lie in regulatory matters: in the character of the legal system; the structure of accounting rules and institutions of accounting surveillance; the quality of supporting commercial services; and the immediate regulatory regime governing a particular market. Much of the early development of globalized markets centred around the revival of London as a financial centre in the 1950s, and much of that in turn had to do with the development of offshore Eurodollar markets, a development consciously fostered by the managers of London, notably the Bank of England. The example explains precisely why positioning in the global division of labour is so important to the governors of financial centres. Position as a leading financial centre confers status and importance on an institution like the central bank. In the case of London it helped maintain a position in the first rank of international financial regulators for the financial governors of an otherwise unimpressive, declining economic power.

But a second impulse was even more concrete. Financial services are a branch of service industries. As such, they are as important to an economy as any other leading sector. If, for example, it proves impossible to preserve a viable domestic car manufacturing industry, as was the case in Britain, it helps to substitute a booming financial services sector. This importance spreads well beyond the immediate metropolis and beyond the narrow field of financial market governance. Consider the case of London in the 1980s, when the 'big bang' and its associated changes stimulated a boom in the City. Financial markets in turn stimulate a range of other important commercial services with high added value, the most obvious being commercial law. And employment in turn spills over not only into demand in adjacent commercial markets but also into office and residential property markets. The boom in south-east Britain in the 1980s was closely connected to the City boom. In turn, the booming regional economy was one of the keys to British politics because it underpinned electoral support for the Conservative governments during the decade.

Some of the impact of globalization on the character of financial market governance in the Euro-Zone is unravelled in the next two sections of the chapter. But even this sketch allows us to see the connections in summary form: struggles between financial centres in Europe are part of the wider struggles set up by the elaboration of the global division of labour; and these struggles are entwined with the routines of financial market governance, with the high politics of monetary diplomacy, and with the electoral statecraft of national political elites.

Globalization, then, meant, in part, changes in the scale and range of market organization and, in part, a fresh twist in struggles over the division of labour. But, third, it meant the exercise of American structural power (Strange 1988). The sources of that structural power are various. The world financial-services revolution between the 1950s and the 1980s was an American creation and a response to American circumstances. American firms dominated markets and the innovation process in the revolution. Alongside the expansion of American banks and securities houses went the colonization by American institutions involved in ancillary commercial services, notably law and accounting. Underneath these institutional sources of structures of power was something less tangible: epistemic communities in financial services that were shaped by the weight and intellectual power of American regulatory analysis (see Braithwaite and Drahos 2000: 88–142).

So much for the *sources* of structural power. Its manifestations were various. Three are worth highlighting. First, the colonizing effect of American expansion meant that the preoccupations and interests of American institutions became embedded in the lobbying processes of European financial market governance, especially through influence over British participation in lobbying. Josselin's (1997: 169–70) study of the lobbying process over the EC Second Banking Directive shows British institutions and British lobbyists acting as the voice of the interests of American institutions. Second, American regulatory institutions were central to the refashioning of European regulatory standards in the 1980s and 1990s. Lütz's (1998) study of European Stock Exchange regulation in the 1980s and 1990s shows the US Securities and Exchange Commission using both the direct instrument of bilateral agreement with national authorities and pressure through the International Organization of Securities Commissions to diffuse American investor protection standards across European centres. Third, the particular preoccupations generated by the wider political setting of American financial market governance can be seen embedding themselves in the government of financial markets in Europe. The most obvious of these preoccupations arise from populist traditions of hostility to bankers and Wall Street, a hostility that by the 1980s had turned into a ferocious concern with investor and depositor protection. Reagan's administration was far more effective at jailing Wall Street financiers than was Roosevelt's. It can be seen, for instance, in the insistent spread of American standards of transparency and disclosure in dealings across a range of European national systems.

Crudely to summarize: globalization was not simply an important contextual influence on European financial market governance by the 1990s; its workings were inscribed into institutions, practices, and regulatory policies.

Politics, Banks, and Europeanization

In a world where the political setting of domestic financial market governance was evolving in different directions, and in a world of globalization,
what did 'Europeanization' add to financial market governance? 'Add' is a
treacherous word here for it suggests the existence of a distinctive set of
forces separate from the national and the global. But every time we look for
the impact of 'Europeanization' in financial market governance we find it
entangled with the national and the global. That is why here I settle for
describing it as 'reflexive'[1] in character: part of a process of adaptation,
mutual policy learning, opportunistic tactical manoeuvring, and strategic
bargaining. Still, it is a counsel of despair to say that all these things are mixed
up together. Some attempt has to be made at analytical separation. That is
what is attempted here. I identify three distinctive effects of 'Europeanization': on centre competition; on market competition; and on regulatory
reform.

Europeanizing Centre Competition

A major impact of the EU, particularly after its reinvention through the
Single Market project, was the intensification of competition between rival
financial centres in Europe. This competition took place at two levels, though
the two are often hard to separate. In the premier league, so to speak, was the
issue of whether there could exist a rival to London as *the* European world
financial centre. The most obvious rival was Frankfurt. At the second level
there was the question of what niches other financial capitals would fill.
In this connection, the most obvious rivalry was between Paris and Frankfurt.
It is obvious that these 'effects' of Europeanization made sense only when
embedded in the wider process of globalization.

Throughout the 1980s and early 1990s these questions were a major influence over the government of domestic financial systems. The effect could be
observed at two levels. The first concerned the analysis of what was needed
to reform institutions so as to position a financial centre most effectively. The
drift of policy favoured innovation in the creation of financial instruments
and in the creation of new financial structures. The 'successful' London
'big bang' after 1986 was a prototype. That in turn connected to the second
level: what was to be the source of such innovation, especially given systems
of financial market governance which typically entrenched interests that

---

[1] I borrow the term 'reflexiveness' from R. Rhodes (1997).

would be challenged by innovation? A subsidiary effect of centre competition was therefore to reshape domestic political alliances in financial market governance, as attempts were made in rival centres to create reform coalitions. In London the coalition encompassed the central bank, the big American banks, reformers in the state bureaucracy, and fragments of the ruling Conservative Party; in Paris state institutions were critical to coalition creation; in Germany the coalition was a Frankfurt coalition, organized around the Bundesbank, the government of Hesse, and the Frankfurt Stock Exchange. But, while the composition of reform coalitions differed across centres, there was a common effect. Organizing to promote the interests of rival financial centres everywhere drew state agencies more deeply into financial market governance, both as organizers of reform and as managers of new systems of regulation. The 1990s in European financial market governance was, among other things, a decade of reform in the legal framework across virtually every national system (Story and Walter 1997). I return to the significance of this in exploring the complexities of deregulation in financial market governance later.

Europeanizing Market Competition

The manifest purpose of, in particular, the move to complete the single European market was to open up previously protected national markets to Union-wide competition. For almost as long as the EU has existed this has produced a complex regulatory dance involving attempts to create the appropriate regulatory conditions for this competition across the different financial markets. By 1998, for instance, there were 15 directives covering banking alone (Pagouloulatos 1999). But a fundamental point about financial markets is that they are uniquely sensitive to regulatory conditions, since for the most part the things they trade are themselves regulatory creations: financial instruments. Thus, the search to open up markets to competition was inseparable from the attempt to construct a European-wide regulatory framework. This is not the place to retell the story of this effort but, in summary it has involved, especially in banking markets, the adaptation of the principles in the *Cassis de Dijon* judgment to create the notion of a 'passport'. In short, recognition by the regulatory standards and regulatory authorities of one member state is held to create an entitlement to enter the markets of all other member states (Moran 1994; Story and Walter 1997: 253–4.) Still, this summary characterization itself does not do justice to the complexities of regulatory change. If we look back at some of the landmark directives in banking alone, we can see 'passport'-creating measures—the Second Banking Directive,

1989; transparency-enforcing directives—the Bank Accounts Directive, 1986; and prudential-behaviour directives—the Own Funds Directive, 1993. Some are pretty plainly a direct manifestation of 'Europeanization'; some are a response to perceptions of fragility in the global banking system; some are about the diffusion of Anglo-American notions of transparency.

Europeanizing Regulation

Nothing exemplifies better the complexities of Europeanization itself as a concept than the history of the reform of regulatory processes and institutions in financial services. One common characterization of the connection between Europeanization and regulatory change tries to separate the national and the European by picturing a process of national deregulation and European reregulation. But that fails to communicate either the complexities of policy manoeuvring or the character of the relationship between policy changes at different levels. As is hinted at in the above passages, the most important effect of the EU has been to set up a complex chain reaction involving deregulation, reregulation, and regulatory reform. *Deregulation* has been genuinely achieved and involves two important areas. First, as the discussion of the 'passport' system shows, there has been extensive progress in dismantling national barriers to market entry: a process succeeded by significant structural change as institutions in markets set about creating defensive and offensive market alliances. Second, there has been genuine progress in dismantling prohibitions on instrument innovation: a central point since this kind of innovation is one of the main means of competition in financial markets.

But the paradoxes are embedded in the process of regulatory reform itself. If we look back at two decades of EC directives, it is striking how often these involve the prescription of standards. There are at least four mechanisms of transmission in this process of *reregulation*. First, there is the familiar regulatory game between different national regulatory systems as 'high-standard' regulators try to counter a potential 'Delaware' effect. Indeed the regulatory history of banking in the EU is a striking instance of success in counteracting the 'Delaware' effect. Second, there is a transmission process from the wider global attempts to manage sources of prudential failure and crisis in global markets: a particularly important effect in respect of banking regulation. Third, there is a process by which the wider structural power of American institutions is transmitted: partly through international bodies, partly through American presence at national level, and partly through American presence at the EU level. This is the best interpretation, for instance, of the spread of notions of investor protection and their manifestation in a widespread regulation, indeed criminalization, of insider dealing.

The fourth transmission mechanism brings us to the quintessence of reflexive Europeanization: it involves the process by which 'Europeanization' is invoked as a threat or opportunity by national reform coalitions as one means of prompting change. The reformed standards then become an element in struggles for EU-wide reform, and the reshaped European regulatory discourse is then invoked again in national struggles over reform.

The policy *process* by which Europeanization has been taking place reinforces its reflexive character. The policy networks in financial market governance in the EU impart a particular quality to the decision-making process. Even more than at the national level, they are conducted in an esoteric discourse which creates powerful barriers to participation by democratic political actors. This is decision making by technocracy in which a characteristic feature of regulatory struggle—the struggle to shape the most minute technical detail because the minutest technical detail can confer huge comparative advantage or disadvantage in markets—is the quintessence of the process. Some of the actors in this process 'specialize' at the EU level, but for the main part the composition of networks is fragmented and unstable and involves individuals in constant shifts of role from the national to the European, from the arena of financial market governance to the arena of financial market competition. These roles are constantly blurred: 'governing' is an aspect of seeking competitive advantage; 'competing' is an aspect of shaping and circumventing regulations.[2]

Politics, Banks, and EMU

The process by which monetary union was created has already been the subject of historical reconstructions which create rich narratives of a process spanning three decades (for one central institutional actor—the European Commission—for example, Jabko 1999). 'The road to EMU' involved complicated paths through both the high politics of monetary diplomacy and the kind of low politics of financial market governance which have so far dominated this chapter. In the 1990s, obviously, they mixed in particular the high diplomacy of European and global money management with one particularly

---

[2] For the possible stabilizing effect of the completion of monetary union on some of these networks, see below.

important domestic national struggle: that involving the (successful) attempt
to incorporate the Bundesbank into the project of creating the Euro-Zone.
That latter struggle, which is obviously central to the financial market governance of the Euro-Zone, has been detailed elsewhere, not least in Chapter
7, on Germany, in this volume, and there is no point in repeating that
narrative. Instead I here sketch four consequences of these struggles for financial market governance. A recurrent theme of this sketch is the paradoxical
nature of policy outcomes: the way the outcomes produced by the high
diplomacy that created the institutions of the Euro-Zone push financial
market governance—and indeed economic government in general—in a very
different direction from that produced by the low politics of regulation:
from, in other words, the complex brew of market struggles and reflexive
Europeanization.

Strengthening a Particular Model of Financial Market Governance

The existing narratives of the road to the Euro-Zone make clear the extent
to which the culture and institutions of German monetary governance
had to be surmounted or circumvented on that road. For a decade from the
late 1980s, in particular, a critical object of the project was to create a model
of monetary governance in Europe that would gain the support of the
Bundesbank. That object was perfectly understandable on grounds both of
democratic politics and of bureaucratic politics. The EMU project itself was
dictated by factors outside the realm of European financial market governance: by the complexities of Franco-German relations (Dyson 1999b); by the
wider imperatives of political unification; and by the ambition to create a
monetary weapon which could be effective in the high diplomacy of international monetary relations. In the realm of democratic politics these ambitions
involved the sacrifice of the single most important popular symbol of a
half-century of German economic success: the D-Mark. In the realm of
bureaucratic politics they involved the displacement of the Bundesbank:
an institution with a unique culture, sense of historical mission, not to mention unique powers in the economic government of the Federal Republic.
The culmination of these changes came, moreover, in a decade when self-
confidence in the robustness of the established German model was damaged
by a range of developments: by the economic stresses of reunification; by the
apparent incapacity of the institutions of economic government to respond
to many of the challenges of globalization; and by the strains placed upon
one of the building blocks of German success—the system of corporate
governance—by changes in financial markets themselves. Coopting German

support at the popular level, insofar as it was achieved, was inseparable from coopting the Bundesbank into the Euro-Zone project, and the price of cooption has been the 'Germanization' of the institutional structure of central banking in the Euro-Zone: the creation of an ECB whose geographical location is intended to symbolize continuity with the successful recent history of German central banking; the creation of a federal institutional structure that mirrors that of the Bundesbank; and the endowment of the institution with both control of policy instruments and a mission intended to replicate in the Euro-Zone the Bundesbank's historic success in creating a powerful and stable currency.

This is not intended to suggest that the ECB is simply the Bundesbank writ large. Apart from obvious differences in historical and institutional setting, we simply do not have enough evidence of operating practices to be at all certain about the practical reality of central banking in the Euro-Zone. Nor do we yet know how far the palsied condition of the new currency is acute or chronic. Nor can we know how institutional structures will convert into either operating practices or power relations. But this particular model of central banking is the result of a statecraft designed to create and sustain a coalition capable of bringing the Euro-Zone into existence. Put this way, the observation is just a truism. But what is striking is the way this statecraft has produced an institutional structure very different from the way the low politics of regulatory change have been breaking open traditionally enclosed · policy communities in financial market governance. The point is reinforced by a second impact on financial market governance of the creation of the Euro-Zone.

Strengthening a Policy Community

The low politics of financial market governance in Europe is an undemocratic world but it is a world of unstable networks: forming, reforming, opportunistically appropriating slogans and ideologies, adapting and readapting as actors' roles shift between market and negotiating table, between the European and the national; hence reflexiveness. Central banking in the Euro-Zone is developing a policy community dominated by central bankers themselves. It is a *community* rather than merely a *network* because, for all its internal differences, it is marked by a high level of normative cohesion. This policy community is powerfully insulated, by recent historical experience, by ideological understandings, and by operating practices, from the tumult and shouting of democratic politics. The recent historical experience refers to the intense diplomacy of the 1990s that produced the delicate institutional and policy compromises embedded in EMU. The ideological understandings refer in part to understandings derived from the Bundesbank legacy and in part to a revival of the traditional characteristic ideology of central banking. These understandings are centred at a 'common-sense' level on sound money and at a more technical level on constructions of the mission and responsibilities of the task of central banking. Operating practices refer to the developing procedures actually followed in key decision making by the new institution itself.

Just how bizarre these last can seem in a tradition of central banking which has been subjected for a generation to penetration by the norms of majoritarian democratic politics can be seen in the recent assault on the ECB by a member of the Monetary Policy Committee of the Bank of England:

The ECB will have to learn that independence, far from being inconsistent with openness and accountability, cannot, in a democratic society survive without these awkward customers. The attitude of the ECB is typical of a central banking tradition that was, until very recently, dominant across the world, which viewed central banking as a sacred and quasi-mystical creation, a cult whose priests perform the holy sacraments far from the prying eyes of the non-initiates. (Buiter 1999: 198)

Buiter's critique accepts monetary policy as the 'primary macroeconomic stabilization instrument' in the modern state and accepts central bank independence as a corollary (Buiter 1999: 182). A wider question, of course, is how far this policy community and its sustaining ideological understandings are sustainable in the face of three obvious countervailing pressures: the existence of national economies with very different structural features and locations in the global division of labour, and therefore with very different needs from monetary policy; uncertainty about whether there exists a Europe-wide popular cultural underpinning for the ideology of sound money; and the institutional disjunction between a central bank insulated from democratic politics and politicians pressured by the need to win elections within the confines of national democracies.

Strengthening the European Regulatory State

The creation of the ECB marks a potentially momentous step on the road to the creation of a European regulatory state, and for an obvious set of reasons. Majone's thesis (1996; 1999) that we are witnessing the creation of a regulatory state in Europe has thus far seemed highly implausible in the light of the most famous model of a regulatory state: that created in the United States. Regulations do not make a regulatory state; institutions do. The United States is a regulatory state because it has regulatory institutions. And thus far the institutional structure of the European regulatory state has been very under-developed. Institutions add a number of critical features: they develop and systematize surveillance capacity; they become centres of regulatory intellig-ence, centres alternative to the intelligence available to market actors; they become generators of regulatory ideologies; and they form the nuclei for the formation and the continuation of policy communities. Without institu-tional materialization there exist only regulations and unstable networks. Plainly in the ECB we are witnessing precisely such a potential institutional materialization of a regulatory state in the financial sector. The emphasis here should of course be on 'potential'. Much depends on the kind of organiza-tional culture the Bank develops, and at this early stage in its history it is difficult to discern a clear picture: imagine trying to forecast the historical role of the Federal Reserve in 1914.

Destabilizing Financial Market Governance

The culmination of the EMU project—the foundation of the institutions and the introduction of the new currency—destabilized both the high politics and the low politics of financial market governance. The most obvious instance of destabilization of high politics occurred in the most important centre that remained outside the Euro-Zone: London. In the low politics of financial market governance, EMU both intensified some struggles and changed the parameters of those struggles. The most obvious instance is provided by competition between financial centres. EMU has sharpened the question of which European centre will occupy pole position in the global system. But, as the current outbreak of merger mania between securities exchanges in different geographical centres shows, much of the struggle has shifted away from a straightforward competition between different geographical locations to a struggle between corporate actors for prime position in markets.

The Euro-Zone and the Democratic Deficit

In this chapter I have worked with a large number of simplifications to reduce the complexities of financial market governance in the Euro-Zone. Among the grosser of these are the separation between the national, the European, and the global, and the separation between a high and a low politics of finan-cial market governance. The fundamental purpose of these simplifications is to suggest that there is no single pattern to the politics of financial market governance in the Euro-Zone. Different systems of politics are producing very different, often conflicting outcomes. In particular, the diplomacy which created the institutions and ideology of EMU by the end of the 1990s had driven financial market governance in very different directions from that produced by the low politics of financial regulation. The latter was a chaotic, unstable world of bargaining where two powerful structural features were at work: America's structural power in the global system and London's pre-eminence as a financial capital. The two combined—especially given the Americanization of London as a financial capital—diffused distinctive ideologies of financial regulation. These ideologies in turn reflected the unique political environments of financial market governance in the United States and the United Kingdom: notably, the legacy of populist hostility to Wall Street in American culture and the incorporation, over a generation, of London's markets into the regulatory structure of the British state. The ramifications of these influences of course spread well beyond the direct sphere of financial market governance. The intimate connection between financial structures and corporate governance is helping reshape the latter in the search for enhanced shareholder value (Landoo 1999; Williams 2000; Jürgens, Naumann, and Rupp 2000; Moran 2001).

The preceding account raises critical issues for the future concerning the particular domains of financial markets, the character of regulation in the EU, and the complex matter of the connections between Europeanization, convergence, and divergence. Each is examined here.

Underlying the argument of this chapter has been the contention that financial market governance involves, among its many stresses and contradictions, a particularly powerful contradiction between the dominant political experience of some of the leading financial centres in the last three decades and the political experience represented by the governing structures created for the new euro currency. Political experience in turn is intimately connected with economic experience. The financial services revolution, conceived as a set of developments in market practices, was intimately connected to the changes in financial market governance. It both grew out of changes in the political environment of the markets and in turn reinforced those changes. The old world of cartelized markets went with an oligarchic political arrangement. The political consequences of the financial services revolution did not amount to the democratization of financial markets. But the revolution did represent an opening up of formerly enclosed financial communities to the gaze of many of the characteristic actors of democratic politics; and it openly politicized issues that had historically been discursively constructed as technical issues properly within the domain of financial oligarchies. Furthermore, because the government of financial markets and the government of currencies cannot be sealed off from each other, the political face of the financial services revolution inevitably impinged on the government of central banking.

This does not mean that the financial market governance of the Euro-Zone involved a rejection of the economic and political faces of the world financial services revolution. On the contrary: the history of the German model over the last couple of decades is a history of slow, often painful accommodation to an Anglo-American model of financial innovation. There is nothing in the early history of the ECB to suggest that it will change this course of accommodation. Nor is that surprising: the ECB is, after all, dominated by actors who have themselves been proponents of change. But it is to suggest that there is potentially a great contradiction embedded in the Euro-Zone project: a contradiction between the dominant recent political history of finance and the attempt to create, or perhaps re-create, a world of central banking insulated from democratic politics.

This of course begs an important question: what model of democracy is being invoked in this argument? And that question is also central to the issues of financial market governance and the regulatory state. The second issue for the future concerns the regulatory state. We noted above that the creation of the ECB amounts to a considerable step towards the creation of a regulatory state in the domain of financial market governance in the sense that it creates, precisely, an institution with control capacities, decision-making capacities, and regulation-making capacities. What foundations of legitimacy can be built for this governing arrangement? Much of the argument in this chapter has been about the history of exposure of financial institutions to the pressures of majoritarian democracy. Famously, Majone (1996: 286) has argued that a different, Madisonian model is needed for economic regulation. As Verdun (1998a) has shown, the mere fact of 'independence' need not itself be problematic (also Verdun and Christiansen 2000). But, measured by Madisonian standards, the checks and balances in the new institutional system appear to leave a large control and legitimacy deficit. The critical issue for the future of this part of the regulatory state, therefore, is how far a Madisonian model of democratic government can be developed in the sphere of financial market governance. The possibilities do not look promising, despite some attempts to rebut or refine Buiter's critique (Issing 1999; de Haan and Eijffinger 2000). The appropriation of the original Bundesbank model is a source of particular difficulty. The Bundesbank was obliged to operate within both a constitutional framework and a political culture which were vigorously democratic. The present institutional arrangement entrenches an oligarchy of central bankers in a wider EU system where there is a gaping democratic deficit: an entrenchment which attempts to reverse a generation-long penetration of financial market governance by democratic politics.

Finally, issues of convergence and divergence raise in their most acute form the analytical problems which underlie the discussion in this chapter, for questions of convergence and divergence necessarily raise the issue of the causal impact of the whole euro project. Two points are central. First, the wider history of financial market governance over the last three decades is one which has involved growing structural and regulatory similarity between the markets of leading European centres. 'Structural' and 'regulatory' here are shorthand for a variety of changes in both economic practices and governing practices. But 'convergence' is the wrong image to describe this change, for 'convergence' involves movement of different elements to a common point. Rather, growing similarity has involved diffusion, of an Anglo-American model of economic practice and government. It is central to the argument of this chapter that changes in market practices and in government are intertwined. At the level of market practice the foundation of the euro and the creation of its attendant institutional world involve no attempt to reverse this process of diffusion. If anything, the creation of a single currency zone has hastened diffusion. Nor is there any evidence that the ECB itself is hostile to continuing diffusion. Indeed, given the identities of the individual and institutional actors at the centre of the system, it would be surprising if they were. But this now raises the second central point. 'Monetary governance' and 'financial market governance' are inseparable. How the new world of European central banking will sit alongside this more open Anglo-American world is a critical, and unknowable, matter. Putting the question unkindly, it is unclear how far the attempt to revive the spirit of Montagu Norman can succeed in the twenty-first century.

II

The Euro and Labour Market and Wage Policies

Colin Crouch

When diverse systems are subjected to similar pressures, the result is not necessarily a convergence of policies, processes, and outcomes. If initial institutional configurations are very varied, exactly the opposite may sometimes occur. There are elements of such a situation in the way in which the labour-market institutions of different Euro-Zone states confront the apparently convergent pressures of the single European currency. For instance, it is unlikely that German trade unions and employers' associations, with their history of thickly structured neo-corporatist processes, will respond in anything like the same way as their French counterparts, who continue to find detailed interaction difficult. But there are also reasons for expecting change over time. In all countries where there is some effective resistance against the search for pure neo-liberal solutions to labour-market problems, the introduction of the single currency and its associated ECB is likely to produce some pressure for a convergent search for 'concertative' or neo-corporatist policies and processes. However, since in the first instance these are national-level responses they may generate a new diversity of actual outcomes as the aim of the national strategies will be directed at the interests of national, not European, interests. But, again, one can at the same time identify both interests in and some limited capacities for true European convergence around a very restricted but important agenda. This chapter analyses the reasons for this paradoxical set of possibilities.

The Industrial Relations Implications of the Loss of Devaluation

There are five different major kinds of strategy that can be used at a national political level to respond to uncompetitiveness in labour markets, whether the problem is of wage levels, non-wage labour costs, or inefficiencies in the operation of the markets:

(1) deflation;
(2) deregulation of the labour market by eliminating limitations on employers' capacity to exploit labour resources and by reducing the role of organizations in the labour market;
(3) reduction of direct non-wage labour costs imposed by government by reducing taxation in general and/or employment-based taxes in particular, usually involving welfare-state reform;
(4) neo-corporatist action to improve the operation of labour markets through collective agreements among employers' organizations, trade unions and —but not necessarily—the government; and
(5) devaluation of the currency.

There can be mixes of these strategies, though some elements of them are mutually incompatible. For example, if a deregulation strategy involves eliminating or reducing the role of labour-market organizations, it cannot be combined with a strategy of neo-corporatist action.

Deflation is not only unpopular but by itself may not necessarily lead to any long-term improvement. It operates by temporarily reducing wages pressure, by forcing the least efficient firms and workers out of the market and by leading less efficient firms to keep their place in the market by improving their labour efficiency. However, these efficiency gains might last only until a reflation begins, and meanwhile unemployment is created. The original Keynesian policy model assumed an economy sufficiently sensitive to government steering for a minor and containable deflation to provide adequate market signals to prevent inflation. But the post-war development of labour-market institutions developed a series of protective mechanisms against shocks which reduced this sensitivity. For such signals to induce serious labour-market reform they would then need to exist alongside mechanisms associated with a neo-corporatist strategy.

A strategy of neo-corporatist action is available only where labour-market organizations are capable of centrally coordinated action and are under pressure to do so without externalizing costs which have to be borne in making adjustments. Such systems operated effectively from the 1950s to the 1970s in a number of countries, mainly in northern Europe (Crouch 1993: Chs 6, 7). However, during the 1980s they began to function less and less well, except perhaps in Austria and Norway. This strategy imposes considerable strain on the centralized actors, who must impose reform and restraint on different levels of their organizations and on their individual members if problems of uncompetitiveness are to be addressed. This became particularly difficult during the 1980s and 1990s as the structure of the labour force changed. The manufacturing and public-service components, in which workers' organizations in particular had their main strength, were declining relatively and absolutely, and were providing a decreasingly strong base from which to try to coordinate a whole economy (Crouch 1999a: Ch. 4). Meanwhile, within manufacturing itself an increasing number of firms were seeking decentralization of wage-setting to individual plants.

Strategies of deregulation and of reduction of direct non-wage labour costs, particularly the former, constitute the main planks of the neo-liberal approach to labour-market problems. This approach became a global orthodoxy during the two decades after the oil shocks of the 1970s, following the collapse of confidence in Keynesian demand management and, later, in the capacities of neo-corporatist systems. The strategy of reducing non-wage labour costs largely takes the form of welfare-state reform and is discussed in detail in Chapter 12. Neo-liberal strategies potentially involve considerable conflict with workers and their organizations and possibly with certain welfare-state recipients. In particular, workers' employment security and employment rights are considerably reduced by deregulation.

Under fixed exchange-rate regimes, the devaluation strategy is also likely to be problematic. Under floating exchange rates it can, however, take the form of a non-decision as a currency is allowed to sink gently downwards. A devaluation improves competitiveness by reducing the prices of exported goods and services and by imposing a decline in living standards of the domestic workforce to the extent that they buy imported goods and services. Such an approach avoids actually tackling the sources of the competitiveness problem—unless of course it had resulted from an earlier exogenously produced upward revaluation of the currency—and therefore avoids confronting difficult domestic issues. If the gentle decline produces a speculative panic or if the foreign-exchange markets suspect that a government is having deliberate and frequent recourse to permitting the currency to sink, then its value may start to decline uncontrollably, leading to further panic and an inflationary threat through rapidly rising import prices.

Achievement of European monetary union has removed the devaluation option from the list of policies available to governments, thereby changing the array of alternatives. Given that participation in the new currency was limited to those states that had reduced their public spending deficits and national debts to specified levels, there was an immediate shift to the negative deflation option. Given the decline that had taken place in the viability of the option of neo-corporatist action in previous years, there was also an

overall shift in the potential bias of policy towards deregulation and reduction of direct non-wage labour costs. This was in any case overtly encouraged
by the adoption of strategies of deregulation and welfare reform by EU governments (Visser 1998).

In the straightforward scenario envisaged by neoclassical economics (for
example, Gros and Hefeker 1999) and some influential neo-liberal parts of the
European Commission, member-state governments, and employer opinion,
the competitive pressures imposed by the single currency will strengthen
existing pressures. The result will be a trend towards the dominance of strategies of deregulation and reduction of direct non-wage labour costs, the
dismantling of all non-market labour institutions, and thus convergence on
a hypothetical Anglo-American model. Convergent pressures will produce
convergent policies and convergent outcomes. One may doubt whether the
pressure is pure market pressure; it often seems to be a conscious imitation of
Anglo-American policies, which is not the same thing. One may also doubt
to what extent the Anglo-American world really resembles the models of
the economics textbooks. However, to some extent the expectations of the
neo-liberals are certainly being fulfilled, and a convergence of the expected
kind is taking place. My purpose here will be to consider reasons why it will
not be the whole story because there is plenty of material in the economic
literature to show why it will be part of it. The emphasis of the following
discussion needs to be seen in that context.

In particular, there is evidence that the strategy of negotiated coordination
policies has not only not been fully exhausted but in a number of states
actually gains a new lease of life under monetary union. There is a triple paradox here. Not only does such coordination stage a recovery within a policy
regime generally designed to engineer a shift to neo-liberalism, but what
is strengthened is also an essentially national response within a process of
Europeanization. But, then again, these national moves exist in a potential
positive-sum relationship with limited moves to coordination at a European
level. More precisely, one can envisage three possible stages in the development of industrial relations within the Euro-Zone, corresponding to short-,
medium-, and long-term perspectives.

The Short Term: Euro-devaluation

During the pre-euro period, as national economies were required to conform
to the entry criteria, a clear and powerful deflationary, neo-liberal logic was
played out. Pre-Keynesian approaches to public spending, budget deficits,

and public debt were enforced in order to minimize inflation. One objective, and outcome, was to shift virtually all costs of adjustment on to labour and the welfare state (de Villé 1996; Freyssinet 1996; Pochet and Turloot 1996). The interests of capital were not touched as this was being progressively deregulated and globalized. It will long remain a matter of debate whether the introduction of the single currency was used to facilitate and justify the imposition of a neo-liberal regime. In an alternative view this regime was needed in order to make the new currency credible among financial markets which were themselves dominated by neo-liberal doctrines. Meanwhile, most European economic growth rates lagged behind US ones, and the US Federal Reserve Bank was able to adopt a far more relaxed stance towards inflation than its European counterparts as these prepared the legacy that they would hand over to the ECB. This further increased the gap between US and European growth rates.

The single currency therefore started its career with a weakness that had in part been caused by the conditions of its establishment. Money flowed from the Old Continent to the USA as European investors sought access to the higher growth rates, a process intensified further by the coincidental soaring of US new technology stocks. The euro dropped in value, and the ECB had to protect its level by keeping interest rates higher than would have been justified if the goal had been European recovery alone. At times the policy seemed self-defeating as it only kept European growth even further behind that of the USA and therefore perpetuated the main problem.

However, for European exporters and collective bargaining actors this very weakness provided a helpful breathing space, providing a Euro-Zone-wide devaluation against most of the rest of the world and in particular the US dollar and sterling areas. The strategy of devaluation, far from being excluded by monetary union, became the most dominant one in evidence, but at the European rather than a national level. Because the devaluation was not planned or deliberate, it was less vulnerable to retaliatory measures than earlier national devaluation strategies. It was not, of course, a competitive devaluation which adjusted the prices of any one Euro-Zone state against another. Rather, it provided a useful and solidary overall increase in competitiveness for the whole Euro-Zone against its major external trading partners without producing conflict between member states as had the national devaluations which were previously possible under the previous European Exchange Rate Mechanism (ERM).

This devaluation has been important in different countries in very different ways. Southern European countries had feared that their less efficient economies would suffer in competition with Germany if they no longer had currencies that could slip down against the D-Mark. Germans, on the other hand, feared that their prices would be kept at the uncompetitively high levels enforced on them by the upward revaluations of the D-Mark that had taken place in the years between the ERM crises of 1992–3 and the introduction of the euro. In the event, both sides have had their mutual intra-European competition eased by the improvement in their global competitiveness.

This advantage of weakness enjoyed by the euro bears considerable resemblance to the first quarter-century of the history of the D-Mark itself, a period which laid the foundations of that currency's strength. The D-Mark eventually acquired an extraordinary record for stability and for being a 'hard' currency, which came to mean a currency that was slightly overvalued in terms of purchasing power parities (PPP). The result was a deflationary effect on prices and wages in the exposed sector of the economy and therefore a tough regime for domestic producers as opposed to importers. This was not, however, the situation in the initial decades of the 'economic miracle'. For a lengthy period the D-Mark was systematically undervalued. This resulted from the circumstances of its origin as the newborn currency of a nation and economy wrecked by war, and carrying a prior record of massive monetary instability. At that moment the Bretton Woods regime of virtually fixed exchange rates had been established. Although the D-Mark was repeatedly revalued upwards during the period of that regime until its collapse in the early 1970s, the revaluations were always running behind the D-Mark's continuously rising PPP value. It was only after the collapse of Bretton Woods and the regime of floating exchange rates that the D-Mark acquired the true attributes of a hard currency.[1] Soon afterwards began the various experiments with Snakes and exchange rate mechanisms within western Europe designed to contain currency movements and prevent the D-Mark rising too rapidly in relation to the currencies of its main trading partners.

The central lesson is that the institutions of German society had their opportunity to learn how to cope with a highly autonomous central bank during an unusual period of a currency that was strong while being undervalued (Crouch 1994; Streeck 1994). This considerably reduced pressures on domestic producers and in fact served as a useful de facto protection against imports at the expense of domestic consumer interests, while the German economy moved out of its earlier protectionism into a true free-trading position.

---

[1] These had been the attributes of the Swiss franc for a much longer period, but it is notable that this economy had previously been strongly protectionist, and in the post-war period developed its extraordinary characteristics of a high—at times over 30%—proportion of the labour force being immigrants on temporary residence permits based on employment.

The newborn euro lacked the environment of fixed exchange rates of Bretton Woods which had protected the infant D-Mark and had to survive in a deregulated and computerized global financial market. As occurred several times during the 1990s, this market can inflict enormous damage on even major currencies like the yen or the pound sterling if it lacks confidence in them. In these conditions it is difficult for a currency to remain, like the young D-Mark, 'stably weak', which is what would in fact constitute the ideal condition for European economic recovery. On the other hand, the very size of the monetary resources of the Euro-Zone exempt the currency from the kinds of speculative pressure that used to produce crises of weak national currencies. It floated down rather than collapsed.

This situation will eventually change. Gradually the factors that kept the euro low will decline in importance. There were already signs of this in early 2001 as US high-tech stocks inevitably passed a peak and US growth rates started to slip behind those of a number of Euro-Zone economies. The new European currency will slowly rise in value, eventually probably becoming overvalued in PPP terms. The breathing space will be over. Will it have been used to set appropriate labour-market reforms in place in order to achieve competitiveness through other means, or will governments and labour-market organizations have used it only for respite from policy pressure? The answer is unlikely to be solely the latter, at least in some states. The effects of an export-led recovery of the kind induced by devaluations may well be limited to manufacturing and the relatively small number of internationally traded services, neither of which create large amounts of employment. European manufacturing sectors which have survived globalization—a force operating anyway, quite apart from the single currency—are those which have achieved considerable improvements in labour productivity, while exported services create most of their new employment in the country where they are being sold. Employment creation today is increasingly within untraded sectors. The current European economic recovery is in itself not doing much to reduce unemployment. The pressure to improve labour market efficiency therefore continues. However, the main reason for thinking that the breathing space is not being entirely wasted is the evidence already accumulating of elements of what I call the medium-term perspective.

The Medium Term: Social Pacts for Labour-market Reform

Current economic orthodoxy assumes that pursuit of policies of deregulation, and possibly also of reducing direct non-wage labour costs, is more feasible than those of neo-corporatist action. But the a priori assumptions on which this judgement is based overlook the reality of the choice confronting decision-makers in some national contexts. If, in fact, certain forms of neo-corporatist strategy remain viable, they might be used to provide a kind of functional equivalent of devaluation, bargaining partners at national level using a capacity to achieve restraint in order to ensure that their labour costs do not threaten competitiveness.[2]

A useful starting point for understanding this dynamic and its relationship to neo-liberal strategies is the inverted U-curve proposed by Calmfors and Driffill (1988) for analysing labour-market policies (for a more detailed version of this argument see Crouch 2000a). The vertical axis of their graph measures the real wage; the horizontal axis measures the degree of coordination of economies. According to the authors, two *opposite* conditions will be associated with the containment of real wages. The first requires purely free, self-clearing labour markets where no organizational forces can interfere at all—zero centralization. The second involves a complete centralization of bargaining by the organizations of capital and labour, which represent a whole national economy and therefore have the ability and incentive to fix wage levels in a non-inflationary way (Olson 1982). This latter condition implies a tough and thoroughgoing form of policies associated with neo-corporatist strategy. These alternatives form the opposite poles of the U-curve.

The intriguing aspect of the Calmfors-Driffill thesis is its specification of two opposed extreme conditions for labour-market stability: complete decentralization—market determination—or complete centralization. They represent the two main rival options stipulated at the outset of this chapter once devaluation is removed from account and deflation seen as an excessively negative strategy to work by itself. Given that extreme conditions are more difficult to sustain than intermediate compromises, interesting questions are raised about what must be the very frequent cases of economies unable to sustain either extreme and landing in the middle of the U-curve. In the case of centralized, or neo-corporatist, labour markets a decline from the optimal position would mean that, while interests remained organized —that is, there were significant trade unions and employers' associations— their capacity for coordination and therefore the containment of labour costs was being lost. This describes what happened to most examples of

---

[2] In some national contexts devaluation should more accurately be seen as a functional equivalent of neo-corporatist coordination, rather than vice versa. In this case disappearance of the devaluation option through introduction of the single currency only increases the burden on social partners to show restraint over labour-cost increases.

this type of system, mainly the Nordic countries, in the 1980s, subsequently undermining confidence in neo-corporatist strategies.

In the case of the other extreme—pure, unorganized labour markets— slippage takes the form of the growth of organization in the labour market, leading to the same outcome as a deteriorated neo-corporatism: labour markets that are organized but uncoordinated.

The general policy lesson is that, once slippage has started, the actors in a system face a choice. If they wish to avoid inflation they must move to one or other of the poles. An attempt to move to the neo-corporatist pole involves the construction of elaborate institutions. While they are being built, they might take an organizational form that is as yet incapable of coordination, keeping them in the worst-case mid-point of the inverted U curve. An attempt to move to the uncoordinated or neo-liberal pole requires the deconstruction of labour market institutions. This is likely to be a slow and conflictual process, again involving some time being spent in the worst-case mid-point.

The preferred solution to the dilemma of the dominant neo-liberal economic policy community, including Calmfors and Driffill, is clear. Labour markets must be thoroughly deregulated and de-organized so that countries can congregate around the free-market pole, achieving simultaneous low inflation and low unemployment. This solution is at the cost of a drastic weakening of labour protection, the virtual disappearance of trade unions— possibly also employers' organizations—and almost certainly a major increase in inequality: strategies of deregulation and reduction of direct non-wage labour costs. The OECD *Jobs Study* (1994: 20–2), which set the subsequent pattern for labour-market policy throughout the advanced capitalist world, explicitly addressed the question of paths from the mid-point of the Calmfors-Driffill U-curve. It argued that achieving the level of economic centralization necessary to secure non-inflationary stability through the neo-corporatist option could take place only under very special conditions. These conditions were highly unlikely to obtain in the decentralized, rapidly changing economies of the contemporary period, and attempts to reach this pole of the U were therefore virtually certain to fail. Therefore, it followed, even those states that once achieved good records of centralization must undertake the difficult and extremely radical task of dismantling labour-market institutions and regulation so that they can move to the free-market pole.

The OECD did not consider the serious possibility that a state might embark on a strategy of dismantling its labour market institutions, only to find it can go no further towards maximum performance at the market-clearing pole than it could at the centralization pole. It would have to be willing seriously to interfere with trade unions' rights to exist and ignore electoral demands for some forms of labour-market security. In democratic societies with complex institutional structures it cannot be assumed that the logic of neo-liberal economic theory can be automatically implemented. This is a highly germane argument for most western European economies, where unions are important and wage determination heavily institutionalized.

There is a further problem with the neo-liberal argument which is particularly relevant to the question of the relationships between the ECB and labour markets. As Hall and Franzese (1998) and Traxler (1999) point out, the rational expectations theories, on which neo-liberal policy arguments depend heavily, assume a capacity of individuals to respond in a highly accurate and well-informed way to the signals given to the labour market by a central bank's monetary stance. However, apart from a small number of expensively and professionally advised wealthy individuals and institutions, the mass of individual persons is in no position at all to make such calculations. The rational expectations model becomes realistic for ordinary employees only if we assume that they belong to organizations, like trade unions, which have a professional capacity to interpret these complex signals for them and to act strategically on their behalf in relation to them. Ironically, the model that justifies the move to the free-market pole of the EU is a realistic representation of human behaviour only under conditions of organized labour markets which contradict other assumptions of the model.

In such a context the opposite policy recommendation—the revival of national neo-corporatism—needs to be reconsidered for states within EMU (for similar arguments, see Boyer 1993; 1999; Marsden 1992; Pochet 1999; Visser 1998). But are there any prospects for a revival of mechanisms of this kind? We need to examine both the incentives and the organizational capacities of the main actors involved. For national trade unions it is very bad news indeed if the single currency regime continues as it inevitably started: severely deflationary, monetarist, and neo-liberal. They therefore have a strong incentive to demonstrate that it is after all possible to assert some basic moderating influence on the labour market through neo-corporatist mechanisms. The situation confronting employers is less clear-cut. They will share unions' aversion to perpetual deflationary policies, but may prefer an attempt to achieve completely unregulated labour markets to a revival of corporatism and its concomitant need for dialogue with organized labour. However, if the past record of coordination has been reasonably successful and uncostly, and if unions are relatively strongly entrenched, employers may prefer this path to one of complete deregulation that could be reached only after prolonged conflict. If unions in such a context make the running in re-establishing corporatist arrangements, employers may not be opposed.

While these arguments are most easily seen in relation to the avoidance of inflation, they may be transferred to other ways of containing labour costs and therefore to the entire labour-market reform agenda. Of course, this agenda is shaped very differently when it is tackled through collective bargaining and other constitutional forms than when it is imposed more or less un-ilaterally, as in many sectors of the UK during the 1980s and 1990s. Unions must be expected to steer negotiations away from forms of flexibility and cost reduction which are troublesome to their members, and towards more Schumpeterian, enterprising innovations (Fritsche *et al.* 1999: 83). Which form of agenda-setting ends up more efficient cannot be determined a priori.

Governments too have good reasons to avoid deflation and may baulk at the social conflict likely to be engendered by a major deregulation struggle. Also, however Europeanized or globalized economies become, and however much governments may welcome such moves, they remain trapped within their nation-states and their national electorates. National electoral politics remains the most potent and vibrant form of political activity within the EU. The more that developments like the single currency, the single market, or, on global scale, the rules of the World Trade Organization eliminate major areas of national autonomy, the more politicians responsible to national electorates must be expected to turn to those forms of action which remain legally available to them. In several states deals with social partners remain high on the list of such possibilities.

A fundamental condition of any form of coordination is that it must not merely interfere with, or try to prevent, the working out of demand and sup-ply pressures. This is especially true of government-imposed incomes policies which have often been temporary alternatives to voluntary cooperation among social partners. Often incomes policies have simply dammed up pay claims until the policy is removed, creating an inflationary pressure that may well be more intense than the problem that the policy was originally trying to resolve. The stream of market forces will insist on flowing. Indefinite damming leads only to disaster, but the course of a stream may be intelli-gently diverted. Markets must flow; but they might be able to flow through more than one potential channel; and some channels might give outcome mixes that are preferable, both to other available 'artificial' ones and to the so-called 'natural' one that would dominate were organized actors to do nothing at all. Coordination institutions must therefore be mechanisms for diverting the channel. They must correspond to, rather than simply attempt to impede, some kind of market force.

The minimum conditions for the success of a labour-market policy of this kind are less onerous than the full centralization by encompassing organizations that the Calmfors-Driffill model and the OECD's interpretation of it seem to require. Soskice (1990) has argued that what was required was that those involved in wage setting had means of *coordinating* their action. A variety of mechanisms short of, or different from, centralization of bargaining might achieve this coordination. One possibility, which has been historically important, is where branch-level unions and employers in the export sector within a small open economy and free-trade regime perceive the obvious inability of their national political system to manipulate prices on the world market. This perception forces recognition of the need for wages to be internationally competitive (Crouch 1993: Ch. 7; Katzenstein 1985).

Another significant context is where labour-market actors with a capacity for coordination face a strong and autonomous central bank, which has obvious direct relevance for our current concern. Given that, at least at sectoral level, German collective bargaining was organized in an essentially neo-corporatist way, the actors within this system were able to anticipate the actions of the Bundesbank. Knowing that it would refuse to accommodate inflationary actions but would respond to them by depressing the whole economy, the bargaining partners had a strong incentive to reach deals that would not lead it to do this. They therefore built moderation into their own behaviour (Hall and Franzese 1998; Kloten, Ketterer, and Vollmer 1985; Streeck 1994). It is important to recognize—and it emerges clearly from Streeck's (1994) analysis—that the strength of the German system lay in the *combination* of a highly corporatist labour market and a central bank that stood beyond the reach of organized interests. Its strength did not derive from any power of the corporatist actors to influence the Bundesbank's behaviour. This is true a fortiori of the Austrian and Dutch cases, whose currencies had for some years been tied to the D-Mark, which lay beyond the reach of their national political communities. These collective bargaining systems had to accommodate themselves to the German central bank, with no hope at all of influencing its behaviour.

Neo-corporatism and the Bundesbank, far from being mutually contradictory, played complementary roles. Organizations within the former, knowing that the latter could not be brought within their influence, adjusted to its requirements. Without the Bundesbank's guaranteed autonomy, it is likely that such a heavily organized economy as Germany's would have slipped, as the old Bismarckian one did, into protectionism. Full 'encompassingness' or bargaining centralization was not required to give the social partners a sufficient incentive to act in a *marktkonform*—'consistent with the market'—manner). The labour-market actors simply needed to have enough organizational capacity to reach, and impose on their members, agreements which recognized that a powerful third party, outside the framework of negotiation, would behave in certain predictable ways unless they cooperated.

A recent extended study of collective bargaining institutions in relation to central banks and economic performance by Thorben Iversen (1999) reaches similar conclusions with a somewhat different argument. An independent central bank will operate most effectively alongside central collective bargaining institutions when these latter seek a minimal objective of overall labour-cost containment rather than elaborate redistributive goals. This is because the effectiveness of containment depends on extensive coverage of the labour force, while the more extensive the coverage is the more difficult it will be to achieve consensus on overall distribution.[3] Even more than in the above argument, Iversen is demonstrating that the tight conditions for centralized control over labour costs of the Calmfors-Driffill centralization model are not just unnecessary but actually negative. The principal condition for effective action in an institutionalized system of wage- and other labour-cost setting is both a capacity and a strong incentive on the part of central bargainers to exercise some degree of overall, aggregate coordination.

These arguments have clear salience for possible alternatives to straightforward neo-liberalism within the European single currency and its guardian ECB. Under what circumstances will the existence of such an independent central bank at the European level facilitate either national or Euro-Zone-wide efforts at coordination?

The General Revival of Coordination Strategies

As noted, the prevailing neo-liberal ideological climate discourages coordination, regarding it as market interference. Further, in a global economy, particularly one with highly mobile finance capital, firms are less tied to individual national economies, and agreements and regulations that stabilize competition among firms at national level achieve nothing for them internationally. Furthermore, the highly competitive international climate requires individuals firms to do everything they can to protect and increase their market share. This makes them resentful of any external constraints whether from

---

[3] The long period of effective centralization alongside egalitarian redistribution achieved in the first post-war decades by Scandinavian unions was, according to Iversen (1999: Ch. 3), feasible because the expansionary Keynesian policies possible at that time did not require central bank independence, and monetary policy could accommodate many of the strains coming through the bargaining system.

governments, collective agreements, or their own membership associations. It also induces them to seek autonomy to shape their personnel policies, without external interference, as part of the competitive strategy. Finally, the complex occupational structure of the post-industrial economy no longer gives such a dominant role to the organized manual workers in manufacturing industry, whose self-discipline made the previous coordinated systems possible.

It is therefore remarkable that, in a number of states, there have recently been attempts by governments and/or social partner organizations to revive and reshape the coordination capacity of the collective bargaining system. It must be noted at the outset that the pressures producing these responses extend considerably further than the introduction of the European single currency, and indeed include some states not immediately involved in that development. It becomes important at a number of points to note how the single currency is often an example of certain wider, more general pressures associated with globalization and indeed certain internal changes within societies.

Schmitter and Grote (1997) make good use of the analogy of the labour of Sisyphus[4] to analyse these alternating characteristics of neo-corporatist policy-making. Something about labour markets in many European states seems to destine their major participants to keep returning to the task of constructing neo-corporatist agreements even though, just as the tiring work seems almost complete, something goes wrong and it crashes again. The impossibility of the opposite task of achieving pure free labour markets may well explain the refusal of neo-corporatist policy attempts to obey predictions of their final demise.

The conclusions of Schmitter and Grote are corroborated by Pochet (1999) and also by Traxler (1996) in an analysis which, admittedly stopping at 1990, takes a statistical rather than, like Schmitter and Grote, a narrative approach. Traxler concludes that a *polarization* of cases is taking place rather than a convergence on neo-corporatism, pluralism, or disorganization. This occurs, he argues, because industrial relations systems tend to be embedded in past practices and develop in ways consistent with past trajectories. In a typology related to but different from that adopted here, he distinguishes between 'inclusive' and 'exclusive' patterns of collective bargaining. The former are characterized by multi-employer bargaining with arrangements for extending the scope of bargains to all firms in either a sector or a whole country; this

---

[4] The figure in Greek mythology who was destined for ever to push a huge boulder up a steep cliff, only to see it roll back to the bottom as he neared the top, requiring him to start all over again.

is clearly a heavily organized and coordinated form. The latter are character-ized by single-employer bargaining with no arrangements for extension; this is a disorganized form. Distinguishing statistically between these forms he is able to allocate states as follows. In the former category he puts Austria, Australia, Belgium, Denmark, Finland, France, Germany, the Netherlands, New Zealand, Norway, Portugal, Spain, Sweden, and Switzerland. In the latter fall Canada, Britain, Japan, and the USA.

Traxler did not include Greece, Ireland, or Italy because of difficulties with data. In more recent work (Traxler 1997) he adds Ireland and Italy and considers the simpler question of whether or not multi-employer collective bargaining predominates within a state, the existence of such non-localized bargaining being a refutation of theories of disorganization. States divide, as in the bargaining extension analysis, with Italy being added to the multi-employer group while Ireland had neither form predominant.

While Traxler stresses institutional continuity, this is not the same as rigidity. It is a question of how institutions respond to a need to adapt by changing in ways sympathetic to their existing structure. There has in fact been considerable change in recent years in industrial relations systems as various reform programmes have been introduced by social partners and, in some cases, governments (Hassel 1999). As Iversen (1999) shows, these reforms have nowhere reproduced, or even tried to reproduce, the tight coordination once achieved by Scandinavian corporatist institutions. The decentralization of labour questions to the individual firm and failing power of associations have to be accepted. Coordination attempts have to be reshaped in the light of this, which means they restrict themselves to certain minimal tasks of labour-cost containment, which firms and individual unions are prepared to accept as limited restrictions on their freedom made necessary by some widely accepted common objectives.

In further work Traxler and Kittel (1998) consider the empirical record of an array of different forms of collective bargaining. They find that two have been most effective: both the classic Scandinavian type and the 'pattern' bargaining model whereby a leading union and employers' association in the exposed sector of the economy effectively set the pattern for the rest, as exemplified by the metal-working industries in Austria and Germany. If the more central-ized 'Scandinavian' type fails in its governance capacity but retains its degree of centralization, it becomes the least effective available system, a situation that is likely to provoke direct state intervention (Traxler 1999). Given the declining capacity of strong centralization, Traxler's thesis and empirical evid-ence produce very similar conclusions about the advantages of minimum coordinating capacity to those of Iversen (1999).

In order to distinguish these new approaches within the general neo-liberal scene, one needs first to see the difference between what Traxler (1995) had earlier called 'disorganized' and 'organized' decentralization. In the former category come those states where decentralization to the firm level took the form of a *collapse* of wider organized structures. Britain is the clearest example. Under organized decentralization, in contrast, the shift away from centralized bargaining was *managed* by employers' associations and trade unions. They wanted both to reap the benefits of sensitivity to the individual company and to retain a capacity to act more generally if need arose. Organized decentralization might be seen as a type of neo-corporatism in that representative organizations are accepting a restraining role over their members, but it is a rather new form of it.

A further motive for governments and perhaps employers preferring a policy of incorporating labour-market organizations in reform plans rather than trying to destroy them in order to produce deregulated markets appears in those states—the great majority of western European cases—where the agreement of social partner organizations is required for welfare-policy reform (Ebbinghaus and Hassel 1999; Crouch 1999b). They are able or likely to agree to such reforms only if they are fully included in general social dialogue processes. In these cases a strategy of neo-corporatism becomes a precondition for a strategy of reducing direct non-wage labour costs, rather than the latter being an alternative to it.

In some other states a real capacity to make deals at a central level is lacking, but governments and the social partners, especially the unions, have good reasons for trying to demonstrate some capacity for coordinated action or at least for forming so-called social pacts. This situation occurs mainly in states with major problems of national integration or where governments lack legitimacy among at least some groups in the population. Spain and Italy are examples; so might be post-unification Germany; and others can be found in central and eastern Europe. These pacts are largely outside the range of labour-market policy as such. Government, or perhaps the whole state system, seeks a wider legitimacy within the population. The unions, as representatives of part of that population, can help provide this legitimacy. Meanwhile, unions today are themselves constantly seeking legitimization to avoid the marginalization and exclusion which is otherwise likely to be their fate within neo-liberal orthodoxy. Being associated with government can help give them this legitimacy. Governments and unions therefore exchange the same thing—legitimacy—but the exchange can be politically very important for both. The absence of a predominantly economic component to these pacts is both a weakness and a strength. It is a weakness because it means that they might not be able to achieve anything practical within the labour market. It is a strength because, not being dependent on labour-market success for survival, they may then become a useful platform from which labour-market reform measures may be launched.

The discussion so far has dealt with a number of challenges and opportunities faced by contemporary labour-market organizations. As anticipated, those posed by creation of the single European currency can then be seen within this wider context of globalization and economic change, and not as something unique. This becomes clearer if we examine the conditions of some of the leading examples of recent major institutional change.

Following a period of prolonged inflationary crisis during the 1970s and early 1980s, Denmark seemed to be leaving the 'Scandinavian model' and joining the then high-inflation, high-conflict model of Britain. Employers eventually agreed with the unions that they had no option but to reform a heavily institutionalized system rather than marginalize it, as was the eventual British solution (Due, Madsen, and Strøby 1994; Iversen 1999: Ch. 5). They were particularly constrained in this direction by being in an exceptionally open economy made up primarily of small, locally rooted enterprises. On what one might call Iversen-Traxler lines, the reformed system conceded considerable autonomy over collective bargaining to individual firms and to individual economic sectors. Central national associations retained only the right to intervene in the case of severe inflationary crisis: a very basic, minimal form of coordination. It is notable, however, that firms were willing to recognize the continuing potential legitimacy of such intervention.

These reforms were not carried out in relation to EMU, and indeed Denmark remains outside the Euro-Zone. Its economy remains, however, heavily tied to capacity to export to the rest of Europe and the world, and the Danish krona has long had to shadow the D-Mark. The general issue of wage competitiveness and very limited ability to devalue are already very important in this economy and would not be dramatically changed by euro entry. And the kind of institutional solution found is similar to that which Iversen (1999) identifies as suited to organized labour markets confronted by an independent central bank.

The Netherlands, in contrast, is a core member of the single currency. Again, however, the guilder was long before that firmly tied to the D-Mark, and the need to export to the rest of Europe and beyond has long been paramount. By the 1980s the once effective labour-market institutions of the Dutch economy were ceasing to function other than to accumulate cost burdens. In particular, the system of financing social insurance and for allocating social benefits was considered to be reducing competitiveness (Visser and Hemerijck 1997). The emergence of these concerns predated preparation for the single currency but was directed generally at issues of labour-market costs. Government threatened to act unilaterally, along the lines that Traxler (1999) predicts, if the social partners did not cooperate with it on reform. The overall agenda of reform was ambitious, covering major Dutch problems of low labour-force participation rates and high non-wage labour costs resulting from the existing system of social insurance contributions (Visser and Hemerijck 1997).

The resulting prolonged and detailed negotiations produced some distinctive policies. Dutch labour markets have undergone a negotiated deregulation, with new rights often being won by labour in exchange for conceding flexibility. For example, both part-timers and temporary agency-workers have acquired clear statutory rights. There have been clear gains in competitiveness as labour markets have become more flexible and labour-force participation has grown, reducing the dependency ratio. In the event the reforms are proving helpful to the Dutch economy in the context of the single currency and in particular in relations with its powerful neighbour and trading partner, Germany.

Irish labour-market strategists seemed to develop both a capacity and a desire for a more coordinated collective bargaining system as the country adjusted generally away from its historical links to Britain towards continental Europe during the 1980s and 1990s and as Britain moved away from European developments despite its formal membership of the EU (Hardiman 2000). Ireland was receiving a major boost to its long-retarded economy as a result of the Common Agricultural Policy. It also began to attract major inward investment from US as well as European corporations. Initially with lower wages than Britain as well as better links with Europe, while sharing the English language, Ireland was particularly attractive to US firms seeking a European base. Without coordination in the labour market there were severe risks of major inflation as the country moved into the most extraordinary period of economic growth in its history. Government took an active part in this and persuaded the social partners to use the existing, well-recognized Irish wage round as a basis for 'pattern' bargaining rather than for leapfrogging. By 2000 the inflationary potentialities of the newly prosperous economy were beginning to defeat the mechanisms established. However, some remarkable institution-building had been accomplished. The country's entry into the single currency was among the factors in the background of these innovations, but, as with the Danish and Dutch cases, more general processes of Europeanization and globalization were prominent too.

Changes in Italy can be more closely related to the euro. Here, as in the Netherlands, the issues concerned non-wage labour costs through the social insurance system and low labour-force participation rates, as well as the inflationary potential of highly organized but ungovernable and contestative collective bargaining (Regini and Regalia 1996; Regini 1997). The frequent paralysis of Italian political and other institutions both hindered and eventually helped the process of industrial relations reform. Partly because of these institutional deficits, both Italian elites and ordinary citizens are more likely than their counterparts in other countries to welcome European rather than national solutions to problems. The EU often plays the part of Hobbes's Leviathan in the virtual state of nature of Italian politics. Employers, trade unions, and general public could therefore be called upon to make sacrifices 'for Europe' which they might not have been willing to make for the sake of priorities set by purely national actors.

The country started with particularly poor prospects of becoming a founder member of the Euro-Zone, so far was it from meeting the various criteria. In particular the pension system had to be reformed, since it was allowing relatively young and capable workers to leave the labour force, reducing participation rates and imposing heavy social insurance costs on those who remained in work and on employers. In the tense years of preparation for the euro entry criteria it was possible for government to exact compromises on these issues from employers' associations and, in particular, the unions. Once euro entry had been achieved, the consensus became much weaker and it became more difficult to make further progress, which indicates the political and symbolic importance of the euro in the Italian debate.

Limited coordination exercises therefore seem feasible for certain kinds of industrial relations system, given political will among government and the social partners to construct appropriate institutions and make them work. The requirements for effective operation are considerably weaker than those for the classic neo-corporatist centralization of post-war Scandinavia. Given that, following Iversen (1999), this kind of limited coordination seems particularly well suited to the coexistence of organized labour markets and independent central banks, it seems particularly likely to be attempted in Euro-Zone economies.

The Long Term: Europe-wide Collective Bargaining?

These national stories are all examples of what M. Rhodes (1998) calls 'competitive corporatism', a resurgence of national action. This raises two interesting questions. First, it seems ironic that a major Europeanizing initiative like the single currency might intensify rather than reduce nationalist action. Second, it raises the major fear of European trade unions: that national capacity for coordination could lead to a competitive downward wage spiral which would eventually reduce the consumption capacities of European populations, leading to economic recession (see many of the contributions to Jacoby (*sic*) and Pochet 1996; Jacobi 1996; Pochet and Turloot 1996; Busch 1996; Freyssinet 1996; de Villé 1996). Already, within the ERM Austrian and Dutch collective bargainers had learned how to solve the problem that their national currencies were tied to the D-Mark while their economies were never quite as productive as the German one, by ensuring that their wage rises remained slightly below German levels. By the mid-1990s, faced with both their own emerging internal economic difficulties and the prospect of the single currency, German bargainers began to show signs of trying to pitch their own pay changes at levels lower than those of their competitors (Fritsche *et al.* 1999). The prospect of downward competitive bargaining became real as collective bargainers seemed to be developing a capacity to use wage restraint as an alternative to devaluation. Should not a single European currency be reducing rather than increasing such responses and instead producing a single European industrial relations system?

At present very little collective bargaining is conducted at a transnational level within Europe, let alone at a European level. Unions and, in particular, employers' associations are extremely weak and certainly incapable of exercising authority over their national affiliates for anything like the degree of coordination necessary for neo-corporatist collective bargaining. Few of the main actors at national level have much incentive to change this situation and empower a European level. Governments are often reluctant to relinquish what we have seen to be a useful issue area for retaining autonomy when so much else is being Europeanized or globalized. Employers and their associations are particularly reluctant to accept a European level. Individual transnational firms have it well within their own managerial power to organize whatever cross-national coordination or, more often, isolation they like. To concede a bipartite or tripartite European level would involve losing a valuable instrument of power and control.

National and local union officials may similarly want to hold on to their autonomy and retain a capacity to respond to their members' concerns. However, unions and workers have more to fear from downward wage competition than the other partners, and there have been important initiatives. Given the difficulty and remote possibility of actually bargaining at the European level, these initiatives mainly concern far more limited objectives.

Most significant has been the Doorn Agreement: a joint approach to collective bargaining in the metal-working industry in Belgium, the Netherlands, and the neighbouring *Länder* of Germany (Golbach and Schulten 2000; Erne forthcoming). The lead has been taken by the German union, IG Metall, afraid that weaker bargaining by its Belgian and Dutch counterparts will undercut its members' wages within the standardized prices of the Euro-Zone. But the Belgian and Dutch unions have seen advantages in accepting a degree of coordination, especially since the German unions have recently shown their own capacity to engage in downward competition.

IG Metall, probably the world's most significant individual union, is trying to sponsor a number of similar agreements through its regional offices in all of Germany's border regions. This means developing relations with colleagues working within a variety of different industrial relations systems, from Scandinavia to central Europe and from Italy to France and Britain (Golbach and Schulten 2000). More generally, the European Metalworkers Federation (EMF), of which IG Metall is the most powerful member, has been seeking to achieve some minimal European coordination throughout the sector (Golbach and Schulten 2000). More generally still, towards the end of 2000 the European Trade Union Confederation (ETUC) launched a similar attempt across as many sectors as possible.

The return of German unions to an inflation plus productivity wage target in 2000 and their increasingly leading role in cross-border activity suggest some progress within what had seemed to be the deadlocked character of the post-unification German industrial relations system. Major advance on a 'Dutch' agenda of labour-market regulation and social insurance reform seems to continue to elude the Alliance for Jobs (*Bündnis für Arbeit*), the attempt at redesigning the German social contract (Streeck 1999). However, on German unionism's favoured and familiar territory of wage bargaining consistent with the needs of export sectors and macroeconomic desiderata, the system seems to be recovering its capacities.

The aim of these initiatives is very simple and minimal: to assert a basic wage rise target, for all unions, of compensation for local inflation rates plus a component matching local productivity growth. Such a goal embodies a number of policies. First, as Traxler (1999) has pointed out, it in no way seeks a European level of substantive collective bargaining but a procedural norm for coordinating a mass of separate bargains. It is therefore not ambitious and makes minimal requirements of member unions, whose capacity for Europe-wide action remains extremely weak. On the other hand, it does require some capacity for articulation among employers' and workers' organizations, that is, some ability to organize the division of labour between different bargaining levels (Crouch 1993; Freyssinet 1996). Second, by asserting a goal of inflation plus productivity it seeks to stop the lurch towards downward competition, the logic of which had been constantly to reduce the wage share by accepting rises below the productivity gain level. Third, however, in sectors and countries with tight labour markets such a norm embodies an important level of wage restraint. Fourth, by specifying local inflation and firm-level productivity rather than Europe-wide figures, the strategy recognizes the need for local adaptability. In particular, unions do not lose any incentive to improve the productivity of their members' labour through changes in working practices or labour regulation.

Problems of a Minimal Coordination Strategy

How successful this strategy will be remains to be seen. Theoretically it is strongly based, corresponding to both Iversen's (1999) and Traxler's (1999) criteria of minimal procedural coordination objectives as the optimal strategy for unions confronting an independent central bank. Also, unions, and often also employers, in both the most and the least efficient economies within and around the Euro-Zone have an incentive to participate. The formula inhibits downward competition while recognizing the different capacities of different economies to afford rises of a certain level. It very specifically does not seek an equalization of wages across the Euro-Zone or even within particular sectors at the European level. It therefore more closely resembles the Austro-German form of 'pattern' bargaining identified by Iversen and by Traxler as more likely to be successful under contemporary conditions than the more ambitiously redistributive Scandinavian systems of the 1960s and 1970s. There remains a potential Prisoner's Dilemma trust problem. But within what is becoming the highly interactive world of European trade unionism and employers' associations, with a clear path of reiteration of the basic game and with clearly publicized actions, most of the conditions which make the Prisoner's Dilemma soluble are present.

Two major problems faced by such a policy of limited coordination are:

- the difficulty of applying both the productivity criterion and the incentive of regulating trade competition to many services sectors; and
- the existence of national-level bargainers who are either too weak or too lacking in coordinative capacity to be able to implement the guidelines.

The first issue becomes increasingly important as services account for an ever larger proportion of employment. Of course, many services are traded, and

increasingly so, and ways are increasingly being found of applying productivity measures to work in these sectors. But the differential with most sectors
of manufacturing remains. Particularly important is the non-traded character
of nearly all public-service activity, while the public services remain among
the most important points of trade-union strength. A growing incompatibility between the bargaining interests of export-oriented manufacturing and
public services, and the declining hegemony of the former within national
union confederations, were at the heart of the crisis of many neo-corporatist
national systems during the 1980s (Crouch 1993: Ch. 7). Interestingly, the
export sector in the shape of the EMF continues to occupy a leading role
within the ETUC. The capacity of this sector to have a general influence will
probably depend on how far national social pacts have reconstructed themselves on the lines discussed above. Particularly where governments are party
to or strongly involved in these pacts, it can be expected that formulas are
found for binding in public services.

The second issue includes two different situations: first, where unions are
simply too weak to exercise much leverage. Here wages are likely to decline
in real terms according to the logic of downward competition, which uncoordinated employers facing weak unions are unlikely to resist. This is not
competitive corporatism because the unions are too weak for corporatism to be
effective. It is simply the competitive market. These forces will mainly affect
low-paid sectors in poorer states and will remain outside the reach of any
coordination. The situation becomes most problematic if it includes France,
a core country of the Euro-Zone but one with weak and very divided unions.
French *government* continues, despite the deregulation of recent years, to play
an important role in the management of what passes for a collective bargaining, partly through its capacity to extend agreements signed by employers'
associations and unions throughout the sector concerned, and partly by
its manipulation of the influential minimum-wage system, the SMIG.
Traxler (1999) identified this kind of government-led wages policy in both
France and Belgium as an only moderately effective kind of coordination.[5]
The movement of French wages in relation to those in Germany and its
associated economies will remain a major point to watch as the single
currency matures.

Second, there is the possibility of unions that are strong but incapable of
articulation and coordination. Within Europe this situation formerly applied
mainly to the British and Irish cases (Crouch 1993: Chs 6, 7). Since the 1980s
the latter country has moved towards a more coordinated system, as noted

[5] See also the discussion of alternative possibilities and their relative feasibility in Boyer (1999).

above, while British unions have become much weaker, though they remain formidable at points of labour shortage. While Britain remains outside the Euro-Zone and its currency continues to fluctuate unchecked against the euro, questions of the bargaining system will not be central. Eventual entry would, however, raise some interesting challenges.

Parallel with these developments in bargaining, the space of European social dialogue, though thinly populated, is not empty. First, the European Commission itself is in a situation closely resembling that of governments with low legitimacy: building links with social partners as well as other non-nation-state institutions like regions, localities, and individual enterprises. This strategy can be a way of embedding a legitimacy for itself within the populations of Europe beyond the reach of individual national governments. In exchange, trade unions, though far less so employers, have a strong incentive to seek a role at the European level in order to ensure that they are not bypassed. In most industries we therefore find an increasingly active union presence in Brussels.

While employers are more reluctant to accept the growth of this level, for reasons already listed, they often need to lobby the Commission for both employment and trade or technical issues. If they can approach either the Commission or the European Parliament with the support of their respective trade unions on a cross-Europe basis, their powers of persuasion and of securing political consensus are that much enhanced. The degree of low-level bipartite industrial relations activity at the EU level has increased very considerably, particularly since the initiation of the single market process, which greatly extended the range of industries in whose trade and technical issues the Commission was involved. Only very rarely do these relations extend to actual bargaining, but they are increasingly embracing what one might call the *Vorberg* of bargaining: joint memorandums, meetings with mutually agreed agenda, and so on (Dubbins 2001).

It is interesting to note that the metal-working industry, which is at the centre of European bargaining coordination, is one of those where Brussels-level industrial relations are most *weakly* developed. This fact points to a major difference between employer and union preferences. Virtually all the running in bargaining coordination is being made by the unions. Employers' associations are capable of responding to this and reaching agreements, but their official position often remains that of preferring a complete deregulation of labour markets. The demands placed on Europe-level interaction between the social partners by these union bargaining initiatives are minimal, and it is not necessary for employers to take up a position on them. Where such a position is necessary, as for Brussels-level social dialogue, they tend to refuse it when unions are powerful within the sector, hence the poorly developed state of metal-working social dialogue.

Some very complex games are being played out in the new European economic and monetary space. Cross-national, let alone Europe-wide, organizations are very weak. However, they are growing and European integration is the major factor impelling their growth. It is a mistake to write off Brussels social dialogue activity as a mere talking shop, as it can provide the framework—at least among unions and among employers' organizations, and sometimes between the two sides—within which European interaction develops among essentially nationally organized actors. This can be important for the capacity to transcend prisoner's dilemmas as described above.

Conclusions

It is not the conclusion of this chapter that neo-corporatist wage bargaining institutions are likely to be established at the level of the new single European currency. Rather, it is precisely in the capacity for labour-market institutions to adapt at *national*, and possibly lower geographical, levels that there are grounds for believing that wage-determination systems in *some* states might be able to pay a part in facilitating adjustment to the euro. To the extent that these systems remain among the mechanisms of economic steering left at national level following recent developments in European integration, the general neo-liberal move to the single currency might paradoxically give rise to new institutions for coordinating labour markets.

Perhaps the most striking conclusion of this analysis, however, is that, contrary to first impressions, the paradoxical renationalization of industrial relations systems which seems to be provoked by the single currency can coexist positively with, rather than undermine, a potential growth of Europe-wide coordination. Procedural coordination at the European level can both offset tendencies for downward competition embodied in competitive national corporatism and make use of the greater capacity for coordination made possible by those stronger national institutions. It is difficult to see this through the virtually axiomatic assumption of most British European debate that the nation-state and the EU exist in a zero-sum relationship: that is, if a power is 'gained by Brussels' it must be 'lost to London'. If the axiom is suspended, it becomes possible to perceive some possibilities of mutual reinforcement of national and European institutions, certainly within the industrial relations arena.

It is the unions, whose normal work is made particularly difficult by intensified competition, who will be the ones to make the running. They have the strongest *relative* preference for neo-corporatism in the choice between it and either deflation or deregulation. Therefore they are likely to seek this goal wherever the basic institutional design makes it feasible, though this should not be interpreted as some kind of new union 'power'. Their power is only that, as the ones who most need a particular outcome, they will be the ones most willing to make sacrifices to achieve it. And the outcome they seek is mainly negative: avoidance of high unemployment, the right to bargain, and measures of employment security. This logic of the situation and power balance in the new economy explain why the objectives of recent and prospective future revivals of neo-corporatism are not only very limited—for example, they exclude any attempts at income redistribution—but will usually embody an attempt at reaching neo-liberal goals through the means of corporatist consensus.

In other words, one of the consequences of pursuing a neo-corporatist strategy is to achieve the goals of deregulation and reduction of direct non-wage labour costs with less pain and more compromises than if these paths are pursued without social dialogue. For example, the recent Dutch agreements involve relaxing forms of labour protection and reducing the generosity of welfare states (Visser and Hemerijck 1997). However, by participating in discussions about these agreements unions acquire the chance to make the move to neo-liberalism selective and discretionary, avoiding the wholesale dismantling of social protection that might otherwise occur. A comparison between the Netherlands and Britain is particularly instructive in this regard.

As already noted, there is little prospect that these new initiatives will be used to establish ambitious redistributive social projects of the social democratic kind pioneered by Scandinavian labour-market institutions during the Keynesian period. This is what Streeck (1998) has called the new 'peace formula' between capital and labour, based on sharing risks and responsibilities in a precarious environment. It is primarily defensive, though it does not exclude innovation and the development of new models of employment relations. It may possibly produce new syntheses between workers' desire for security and the economy's need for flexibility by embodying both in forms different from those which are taken for granted in most policy discussion.

Some social learning is also taking place. Most of the new institutions acknowledge that most wage-fixing today takes place at company level; the organized sectoral or national actors merely retain the capacity to exercise a general moderating touch at moments of crisis. In effect, they turn themselves into functional equivalents of devaluation. This is a painful role as it involves internalizing within the social partner organizations the stress and conflicts that devaluation manages to dump on trading partner nations. It is because European monetary union has made devaluation impossible that it provides a strong incentive to these organizations to be willing to take on the thankless task of neo-corporatist restraint.

Monetary union is most accurately seen here as reinforcing certain tendencies already induced by globalization and sectoral change. All economies have already found that the globalization of financial markets in particular has intensified competition and produced difficulty in using exchange-rate manipulation as an economic policy tool. If anything, the single currency and associated strengthening of European institutions are more likely to facilitate some stabilization of economic life in the face of globalization than an exacerbation of its effects. Similarly, at both national and European levels the single currency is providing some new incentives for reconstructing social pacts after the decline of employment in manufacturing had unsettled the base of those established in the middle of the twentieth century.

Why EMU Is—or May Be—
Good for European Welfare States

Martin Rhodes

It is frequently assumed that EMU will contribute to the erosion of European welfare states—a process which is already well-advanced, according to some, because of 'globalization'—and their convergence on a residual, 'Anglo-American' model. By contrast, this chapter argues, first, that neither EMU nor the single market has had particularly adverse consequences for welfare states to date. While economists have successfully identified a clear 'Maastricht effect' in terms of a fiscal policy behavioural shift in the 1990s, with convergence discipline replacing concern with output or employment, it is much harder to attribute key causal responsibility to EMU for the nature of welfare reform. However, it has certainly been a key determinant of timing and a major influence on decision-making, exerting, a largely positive impact on the capacity of governments and social partners for reforms required even in a non-EMU world. Second, this chapter also argues that, while the jury is still out on the future impact of the EMU and its Stability and Growth Pact, EMU may have further positive effects in contributing to a new architecture for a coordinated European welfare policy.

The argument follows four steps. In the first, the chapter contests the assumption that EMU is a 'neo-liberal project', arguing that there is no necessary or logical incompatibility between a single currency and 'sound money policy' and the preservation of large, redistributive welfare states. In the second, the chapter considers what we know so far about welfare state adaptation under the single market and EMU convergence. Although there has clearly been an adverse, deflationary effect on employment rates and some welfare cuts linked to deficit and debt reduction, there is no evidence of a 'race to the bottom' in social standards nor of convergence among still vastly different social systems. Step three considers the prospects for welfare states under monetary union and the constraints of the Stability and Growth

Pact. Key issues for the future of welfare under EMU include the impact of symmetric and asymmetric shocks, the purported need for social and regional transfers, and the adjustment capacity of national economies. Although many believe that European states lack such capacity in the absence of a fiscal federation, in reality the EMU entry process has already helped improve the performance of economic governance mechanisms in the most vulnerable member states. Step four considers the development of a new coordinating capacity at the EU level regarding the interplay between broad macroeconomic objectives and social and employment policies. Although we are currently in a period of institutional experimentation, recent developments indicate the emergence of a new architecture for pan-European 'steering' across these policy domains.

Is EMU a Neo-liberal Project?

Much of the political economy and political science literature on EMU divides between what Boyer (2000) calls 'the European dream of Keynesianism at the Continental level' and a 'European nightmare of free markets and the balkanization of societies'. In the first view EMU provides a strong impulse towards greater coordination, in which various economic and political actors create a new and sophisticated architecture of checks and balances, leading to a fully integrated and ultimately federal Europe. Within this structure the national legacies of institutional frameworks can be preserved, if not strengthened. The more common, Euro-pessimist nightmare scenario, by contrast, is one of uncontrolled, Darwinian neo-liberalism, with erosion of the tax base and a 'race to the bottom' in social standards. Competitive wage and social cost reductions combine with productivity wars to produce a convergence of industrial relations and welfare states on the 'Anglo-American model', a frequently used synonym for residual social policy and deregulated labour markets (for example, Crouch 1994; Leander and Guzzini 1997; Gill 1998; Teague 1998). Although both views expressed in such summary form are caricatures rather than plausible scenarios, the argument in this chapter is closer to the first in stressing that political choices remain possible, including those which will help sustain European welfare systems and the values that underpin them. European member states retain the capacity to build on their traditional welfare-state foundations and adapt them positively to changing economic times.

A number of important arguments can be made against the simple equation between the single market and EMU and a neo-liberal project for welfare.

The first concerns the impact of the single market, the second the purported links between EMU and globalization, and the third the incompatibility of EMU with social democracy and welfare states. As for the single market, obviously this is a 'marketizing' programme: it breaks down the barriers to the flow of capital, products, and people. But does 'more market' across the EU mean 'less welfare' in its member states? This is indeed a common assumption. For some time it was generally accepted that in the absence of a 'European welfare state' the juxtaposition of jurisdictions with different welfare states and labour costs—some generous, in the north, others meagre, as in the south—would generate a competitive 'race to the bottom'. This was supposed to operate through social dumping and social devaluation, both involving a process of regulatory arbitrage by firms. While social dumping would involve the shift of firms from high- to low-cost countries—for example, from Germany to Portugal or Spain—social devaluation would occur as competitive pressures forced large welfare states to retrench. In fact, there have been only limited examples of firm migration to lower labour-cost countries, and little evidence in the EU that welfare states are becoming 'competitive' —that is, purposefully downgrading social protection—in their desire to attract mobile capital.

There are several reasons for this. First, there is no necessary correlation between the size of welfare states and the competitiveness of their companies in export markets. The costs paid by firms and workers for welfare are often compensated for by high rates of productivity and labour costs are usually among the least important elements in location choices of companies. So far there is no evidence of an EU equivalent of the US 'Delaware effect', whereby the permissive corporate regulatory regime of the State of Delaware attracts a disproportionate share of large company incorporation and has arguably— though this is contested—eroded standards of corporate regulation (Barnard 2000; Andersen, Haldrup, and Sørensen 2000). 'Cheap' welfare states in Europe are not exploiting their low costs vis-à-vis neighbouring countries. In recent years, there has actually been a 'race to the top', with Portugal, for example, expanding the scale of its welfare state substantially rather than consolidating its status as a low-cost jurisdiction (see Figs. 12.1 and 12.3). As a recent cross-national study of social dumping admits, 'in contrast to the idea of a race to the bottom, almost all countries examined . . . continued to increase the level of social spending at a faster rate than economic growth so that their social expenditure ratios kept growing' (Alber and Standing 2000: 107). In reality, even if governments believe that they have to cut welfare to make their economies competitive, welfare retrenchment and its effects are exceedingly difficult to calculate, programme and achieve in line with budgetary, let alone competition objectives (Scharpf 1997; see Pierson 2001).

Tax competition in the EU, a supposedly major factor in the 'downward' convergence of welfare states, has also failed to operate as predicted. As the European Commission (2000b: 67) demonstrates—confirming other analyses, including those from the OECD—there is no evidence that tax competition has reduced the tax burden on capital 'which has remained broadly stable over the past three decades'. Rates of direct corporation tax have been lowered, it is true, but tax breaks have been steadily removed and the corporate tax base has been widened in most countries. The mechanisms whereby competitive pressures translate into deregulatory policy are also complex and much less direct than often supposed. While increased capital mobility in theory places downward pressures on tax rates, such pressures are countered by the fact that investors take many other factors into account when making investment decisions. At the same time, the high degree of complexity in modern economies makes it impossible for states to act 'rationally' in calculating the real gains of engaging in such a competitive cost game (Dehejia and Genschel 1999; Basinger and Hallerberg 2000). More generally, financial market actors are much less concerned with the nature and size of welfare states or in the composition of their funding and spending than is generally supposed. As Mosely (2000: 748–9) demonstrates, while they may have concerns about certain macroeconomic trends, such as the movement towards or away from certain levels of debt and 'risk', the inflation rate and the current account, bond market participants, for example, pay much less attention to the micro-management of the economy.

A second assumption concerns the nature of EMU itself. EMU is often linked with globalization as a vector or reinforcing framework driving forward the spread of neo-liberal ideas. Thus, although the Werner Committee first set out a plan for monetary union in 1970, the fact that EMU succeeded only some 25 years later is usually explained by the dramatic surge in short-term capital movements in the late 1970s, triggering the launch of the EMS in 1978 (for example, Boyer 2000) or by the spread of neo-liberal ideas and 'sound money' ideology in the 1980s. Others argue that capital mobility and the spread of neo-liberal ideology go hand in hand (for example, McNamara 1998). But it is also worth noting that another factor was critical in pushing governments towards a hard currency policy and ultimately EMU: the inability of governments to control domestic distributive conflict, especially in the wake of the oil-price shocks of the 1970s. The effect was to change the minds of European social democrats about how best to achieve wage and price stability, while also converting Europe's central bankers from soft Keynesians to hard-currency advocates.[1] This suggests that the brute reality of domestic economic management in hard times was at least as decisive in driving a shift in the policy regime as the arrival of a 'neo-liberal paradigm' or spread of a 'sound money ideology' (Notermans 1999).

A third, and closely related, assumption is that large welfare states or social democracy are incompatible with EMU. But as Notermans (2000b) argues, pessimism about the compatibility of strong welfare states and the social democratic project with EMU is misguided in two respects. First, microeconomic regulation and protectionism plus a large public sector—typical of most post-war European welfare states—are not necessary elements of a social democratic polity. Rather, the hallmark of successful social democracy has been its capacity to combine redistributive politics, growth-oriented macroeconomic strategies, and non-inflationary wage and price setting. When it has failed to make the latter two compatible, then its tenure in government is threatened, and the first objective—egalitarian policies—has also come under threat. This is what happened in the 1970s, allowing a shift towards monetarism and a move, albeit only minimal in most European states, away from redistributive welfarism.

Also, while it is true that the Stability and Growth Pact is not conducive to Keynesian counter-cyclical management, as Notermans (2000b) and others have argued, there was no such thing as 'the Keynesian welfare state' strictly speaking during the so-called 'golden age'. Keynesian counter-cyclical management played no key role in European states during the long post-war boom and, when it was attempted in the 1970s, failed abysmally. In addition, there is nothing in EMU and the Stability Pact as such that stops EU governments having large welfare states and public sectors or prevents them from pursuing egalitarian policies if they so choose. The key requirement is that the expenditure involved is balanced by revenue and the policies legitimized by public support (Glyn 1998; Mosely 2000). European nations remain faced with the difficult choices and trade-offs that they have always had to deal with, and which several—Italy, Belgium, and the Netherlands—have managed appallingly badly in the past. If you want to have a large and sustainable welfare state, you have to be able to pay for it. If you want to have price and wage stability, you need to institutionalize or enforce it.

Finally, there is the argument that even if EMU and globalization have not damaged welfare states to date, their future under the Growth and Stability

---

[1] Wim Duisenberg is an excellent example. Far from being the tough, natural neo-liberal as whom he is sometimes portrayed—for example, McNamara 1999—he was in fact converted very reluctantly from committed Keynesianism to no less committed monetarism by the crisis of the Dutch economy in the late 1970s and 1980s (see Marshall 1999 for an entertaining account).

Pact and an accentuated globalization process is bleak. This issue is discussed in greater detail below. For now, suffice to say that the new macro regime in Europe can help welfare-state sustainability in a number of ways. First, the creation of the euro can be understood as an attempt to deal with the Mundell-Fleming impossibility theorem: that you cannot have complete capital mobility, a fixed exchange rate, and an autonomous monetary policy simultaneously. As Erik Jones (forthcoming) argues, EMU can be conceived as an 'alternative form of embedded liberalism' since it embodies a similar choice to that made by the architects of the post-war order when limiting capital markets in order to preserve domestic monetary autonomy while also promoting free trade. With EMU 'the architects of Europe have chosen to eliminate national currencies in order to preserve access to international capital markets while laying the basis for a common market'. Entry into EMU eliminates the exposure of individual states to foreign exchange markets, so compared with the 1950s and 1960s 'all that has changed is the source of flexibility and the nature of the constraint' (Jones forthcoming). Already in the mid-1990s being in line for EMU entry meant greater credibility with the markets for the most indebted member states. The consequent reduction in interest-rate premiums played no small role in facilitating their budgetary adjustment (Chapter 8) and the leeway that was provided helped avoid swingeing cuts in welfare. Thus if there is any truth to the argument that globalization is depriving governments of their autonomy in welfare policies, EMU should therefore moderate rather than reinforce its effects.

Second, as argued in greater detail below, EMU can also contribute to welfare sustainability by helping encourage wage moderation through social pacts and new incomes policy arrangements (Rhodes 1998; 2001*b*; Schulten and Stueckler 2000; Chapter 11). Social democrats are thus provided with the kind of externally-constrained domestic stability that they have been unable to resurrect in the last two decades by other means while also gaining an institutional stabilizer for fiscal policy, allowing policy-makers to make sometimes long-overdue reforms in public finances and welfare programmes. At the same time, adherence to the Stability and Growth Pact will make relaxed monetary policies more likely, while providing for flexible interpretations in the case of 'exceptional circumstances' or 'severe downturns' (Notermans 2000*b*). A strict fiscal policy helps to bring down interest rates, which, over time will stimulate the economy, reduce the public debt burden, and strengthen the confidence of consumers and potential investors in the economy. This has already happened in some of the most chronically indebted European states, of which Italy is the prime example. There, EMU has been critical in allowing a more rational and controlled management of the public accounts, in part by placing expensive welfare programmes, most notably pensions, on a firmer footing (Ferrera and Gualmini 2000).

The last point concerns the welfare state itself and the nature of reform. Many observers assume that any changes to welfare programmes amount to retrenchment, are inherently bad, and must be neo-liberal in inspiration. Some reforms can indeed be understood as neo-liberal if their motive is to sacrifice social justice and equity to ill-specified and unnecessary objectives of 'competitiveness'. But many reforms in continental states have been unavoidable either because of economic management mistakes, coupled with an escalation in costs, or because welfare sustainability requires the search for a new equilibrium between revenue and spending as well as innovation in programme design (Ferrera and Rhodes 2000). We have to recognise that most of the ambitious social programmes introduced during the so-called *trentes glorieuses*—or 'golden age'—of the welfare state have come to full maturation in the last decade or so: they work 'in high gear' and apply to the vast majority of the population. The metaphor of 'growth to limits' is quite appropriate here. Rising health care costs and pensions provisions have contributed massively to welfare budgets and fiscal strains, and pension sustainability is the number one social and budgetary policy issue that many European states have to face (Davis 1997; Marshall and Butterworth 2000). These extended government commitments produce persistent budgetary pressures and a marked loss of policy flexibility, making even marginal change inherently difficult. Neither EMU nor 'globalization' is responsible for the core policy dilemmas and difficult choices facing these large welfare states. Nevertheless, as this chapter argues, EMU has certainly influenced the timing and character of many of the reforms introduced to deal with these problems.

EMU Convergence and Welfare State Reform in the 1990s

There are two principal points to be made about the relationship between EMU and welfare states. The first is to consider what has happened. Has welfare been cut back or have programmes become less generous? The second is to look behind the aggregate figures and consider how different countries have gone about reforming, and why. What were the motives? What was the link, if any, between EMU pressures and other reform imperatives?

As for the first point, aggregate statistics reveal remarkable continuity in levels and distribution of spending and across various types of benefits in the Euro-Zone states (although mentioned in passing, Greece—which is joined

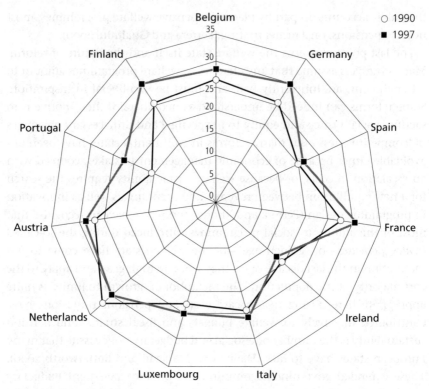

Fig. 12.1 Expenditure on social protection in the EMU countries as a percentage of GDP

Source: Eurostat (2000a: theme 3, Table 1)

the EMU in January 2000—is generally excluded from the following analysis). The most important institutional changes have been greater managerialism; attempts to make certain benefits, especially unemployment support, more 'incentive compatible'; a marginal degree of privatization, mainly in health; some decentralization; and attempts to control budgetary expansion. In terms of programme design, a consensus has emerged around the need to modify the funding of welfare by shifting the burden of costs, for example, away from payroll taxes to general taxation; removing tax wedges and eliminating poverty traps; introducing wage subsidies in various forms and 'in-work' benefits; the 'activation' of so-called 'passive' benefits; and the revision of employment rules (Therborn 1997; M. Rhodes 2001a). Meanwhile, although income inequalities increased somewhat in Europe in the 1990s—but only marginally compared with Britain—this has mainly been due to population ageing, higher unemployment, and more single-parent families, which have

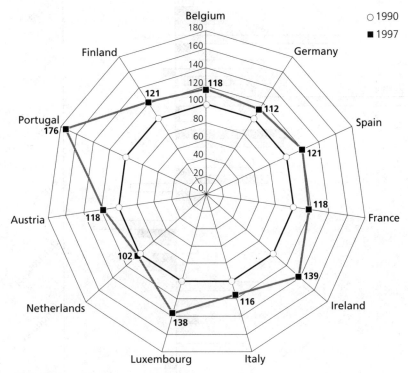

Fig. 12.2 Social protection expenditure per capita at constant prices, 1990 and 1997

Source: Eurostat (2000*a*: theme 3, Table 2)

all pushed existing programmes into 'higher gear', rather than neo-liberal retrenchment (European Commission 1999*a*; 2000*a*).

From the figures we can observe the following. First, if we look at general spending, there has been a downward trend in spending on social protection as a proportion of GDP since 1993. But this had nothing to do with radical retrenchment. It was, rather, related to rising GDP and a decline in spending on unemployment benefits as employment increased. Between 1990 and 1997, social spending as a share of GDP actually increased in all eleven original EMU member states, except Ireland and the Netherlands (see Fig. 12.1). Moreover, it came against a background of a real increase in social spending each year between 1990 and 1993 of 4.1 per cent a year. Spending trends at constant prices for the EU15 show that, over the period 1990–7, total benefits increased from index 1990 = 100 to 120, that is, a near 20 per cent increase in real terms. The most important increases were in pensions, housing, and social exclusion and family/child benefits (see Fig. 12.2). Figures 12.3 and 12.4 demonstrate the trend for welfare spending to rise and for the distribution of

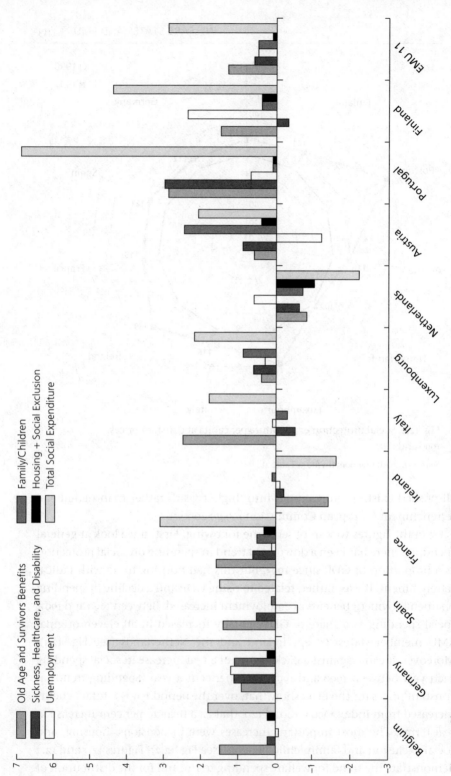

Fig. 12.3 Change in social protection expenditures as a percentage of GDP, 1990–1997

Source: Author's calculations based on Eurostat (2000a: theme 3, Table 2)

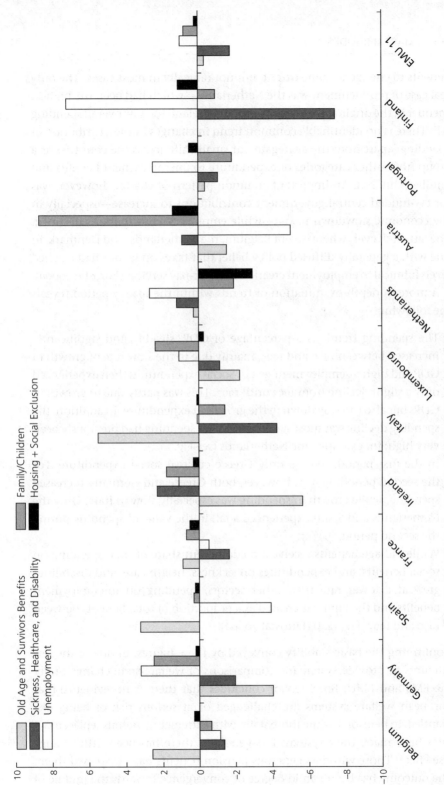

Fig. 12.4 Changes in social spending by function as a percentage of total social expenditure, 1990–1997

Source: Author's calculations based on Eurostat (2000a: theme 3, Table 5/99)

Legend:
- Old Age and Survivors Benefits
- Sickness, Healthcare, and Disability
- Unemployment
- Family/Children
- Housing + Social Exclusion

Categories: Belgium, Germany, Spain, France, Ireland, Italy, Luxembourg, Netherlands, Austria, Portugal, Finland, EMU 11 benefits to change to some extent, but not radically in most cases. The only real case of retrenchment was the Netherlands—which had been the highest spender in the original EMU group—though Ireland too saw overall spending fall. There is no identifiable common trend in changes in the distribution of spending, apart from the aggregate but small shift across the countries as a group from other categories of expenditure to unemployment benefits and families/children. An important common pattern of change, however, was for tax-funded central government contributions to increase—especially in the economic slowdown 1990–3—while employers' contributions declined. The latter fell everywhere except Belgium, the Netherlands, and Denmark, in line with a generally diffused policy belief that taxes on labour had reached levels inimical to employment creation in lower-pay services (Eurostat 2000a).

A more in-depth examination of trends within the 1990–7 period reveals the following:

- The spending trend, as a percentage of GDP, steadily and significantly increased between 1990 and 1993, mainly due to the slow rate of growth of GDP and high unemployment levels. Social expenditures then experienced only a slight decline from 1993 until 1997. This was partly due to growth in GDPs but also to a slowdown in the growth of expenditure. In addition, the spending decline was most significant where spending had previously been very high: for example, the Netherlands (see Fig. 12.3).
- In the first period, 1990–3, only Greece cut real social expenditure. For the second period, 1993–7, however, both Greece and Germany increased spending, while growth in spending was especially slow in Italy. Only the Netherlands and Spain experienced a fall in the value of spending during the second period, 1993–7.
- While old-age benefits receive a predominant share of total spending on social benefits, and expenditures on sickness, health care, and disabilities grew at a lower rate than other sectors, spending on unemployment benefits and the family increased as a proportion of total benefits between 1990 and 1997 (Fig. 12.4) (Eurostat 2000a).

Confirming the basic stability conveyed by these figures, in one of the few attempts to provide systematic comparisons of welfare-state change under the EMS and EMU, Boeri (2000) concludes that there is no evidence that European welfare systems are challenged or at serious risk of being dismantled. In pensions, while those states with extremely generous replacement rates have made their systems less generous, there has been little change elsewhere. Those with less generous pension benefits have increased them. The outcome has been a mild degree of convergence towards the middle of the distribution range. As for unemployment benefit generosity, there was a very slight decrease in the D-Mark zone countries. But other eventual EMU members—Finland, Ireland, Portugal, and Spain—revealed no common trend, with some increasing and others reducing benefit levels. As for social assistance—that is, cash transfers—there has actually been a 'race to the top', with the top of the distribution itself shifting upwards. The only area in which there was a common downward trend in the EMU-11 countries was in employment protection. But this has generally been due more to the pro-liferation of new types of contract—temporary, part-time—than a radical change in the protection of permanently employed workers.

How can we explain this stability in the face of a remarkable series of changes in the European economy? Welfare retrenchment on a larger scale has been avoided because lower spending on interest payments, facilitated by the reduction of deficits, debts, and interest rates, plus higher taxes and privatisation have allowed budgetary consolidation without savage cuts even in the most indebted member states. An upturn in the economic cycle in the second half of the 1990s also helped, in particular by reducing expenditure on unemployment related benefits and transfers. While lower interest rates pro-vided a conducive environment for balanced adjustment, so too did the fact that as many as seven stabilization plans in 1994–8 produced so-called non-Keynesian effects—that is, a virtuous result linking the reduction of public deficits and debt with the stimulation of aggregate demand (Zaghini 1999). It is also important to recognise that during the Maastricht 'retrenchment period', most states—except those that, like Italy, combined high debts and high inflation—engaged in a combination of fiscal restriction and monetary expansion which allowed gradual and publicly acceptable processes of reform. For the EMU group as a whole, a period of revenue-based consolidation in 1992–3 was followed by expenditure-based adjustment in 1994–7. This 'switch-ing strategy' was most striking in the cases of Belgium, Germany, the Nether-lands, and Spain. France, Ireland, and Portugal pursued mainly revenue-based retrenchment, with an especially large reliance on new taxes in Italy and Greece. Meanwhile only Denmark, Finland, and Sweden engaged in a fully-fledged strategy of spending reduction (European Commission 2000b). Over the period 1995–2000, much of the expenditure reduction was carried out in areas other than social policy (Fig. 12.5). This has produced a clear conver-gence across EMU members in terms of *non-welfare* spending to around 20 per cent of GDP, while differences remain striking, and outright retrenchment minimal in welfare-linked expenditure.

Understanding the relationship between EMU and other factors behind reform is a complex undertaking. In general, though, for those states that had

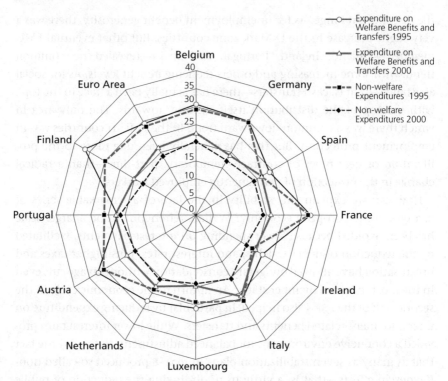

Fig. 12.5 Welfare and non-welfare expenditures as a percentage of GDP, 1995 and 2000

Source: Author's calculations based on statistical annex of European Commission (2000*b*)

not already initiated reform in response to economic problems, recession, and the inadequate performance of their systems EMU has facilitated long over-due reform by helping cut through opposition and creating a new consensus on the modalities and substance of change. The EMU states can be broken into three groups with regard to the relationship between EMU and welfare reform and the presence of other reform impulses (see Vanhercke 1999; Pakaslahti 1997; 1998; Ferrera, Hemerijck, and Rhodes 2000).

France, Germany, Belgium, and *Austria* made important changes to their social protection systems while also launching plans to reduce social spending. But the driving force came from problems of an economic nature, the resolution of which was accelerated by EMU convergence. The welfare problems facing these states stem partly from the way in which social insurance and employment benefits interact. Until recently, high rates of unemployment and associated levels of welfare spending have been linked to generous insurance-based cash benefits, high earnings replacement ratios, and long benefit durations, and 'passive' insurance benefits with limited conditionality: for example, active job search, availability for job offers, and training requirements. Meanwhile, high social charges and wage floors have blocked the expansion of private service jobs. Because of fiscal overload there has been little scope for expanding public-service employment. In response, a complex reform agenda in these systems has centred on: containing the expansion of social insurance; rationalizing social spending by trimming pensions and 'passive' benefits; improving and updating family policy; introducing 'active' incentives in cash benefits; and reducing the incidence of social charges (Ferrera, Hemerijck and Rhodes 2000: 47–53).

These changes were linked in many cases more or less explicitly to Maastricht adjustment. In Austria an expenditure-based consolidation strategy involving unemployment, pensions, and health care helped reduce social contributions and other revenue, while in Belgium cuts in social contributions to promote employment were matched by increases in other forms of taxation. Wage indexation changes helped cut public spending. In France, a combination of cuts and spending increases reduced cyclically adjusted social security spending by almost 1 per cent in 1993–7, but actual social spending did not fall. Thereafter transfers began to expand. In Germany, as part of a 'social pact' linked to unification, there were cuts in unemployment and related transfers plus increases in indirect taxes and social security contributions. But social transfers increased until 1996, falling only moderately thereafter, and the German strategy became more revenue-based, with higher taxes taking up the slack (von Hagen, Hallett, and Strauch 2001).

Portugal, Spain, and *Italy* were generally highly cautious in their introduction of social reforms and followed a dual strategy of protecting their social programmes, while using other means to get into shape for EMU. These countries' welfare states suffer from a different set of problems from those of their northern neighbours, with institutional and financial underdevelopment linked to internal imbalances. Their social transfer systems display both peaks of generosity—at least in terms of legal formulae—for certain occupational groups and serious gaps of protection for others. These are essentially 'pensioner states', but while in the early 1990s the 'standard pension'—in terms of replacement rates—in the three systems was markedly higher than the EU average, the minimum non-contributory pension was well *below* the average. Unemployment benefits were virtually non-existent. These states have thus been trying to rationalize their systems while also 'catching up' with the rest of Europe. Reforms have centred on ironing out benefit formulae for privileged occupational groups, upgrading minimum benefits, introducing and consolidating safety nets, remedying deficiencies in family benefits and services, and reorganising health systems.

But the southern European states have showed no inclination towards a 'social devaluation' strategy based on low protection standards. Restrictive reforms have been undertaken primarily for budgetary and 'equity' reasons. In Italy, key reforms have reduced transfers to regional governments and made pensions more sustainable, while social transfers and health spending have been restrained. But higher taxes—some *una tantum*, or exceptional and short-term—and sharp reductions in interest payments have helped prevent swingeing cuts. Also benefiting from interest-rate reductions and exploiting changes to taxes and the tax administration, Portugal has actually expanded its welfare system quite markedly while also reforming pensions. Spain also compensated for welfare expansion in the early 1990s by adjusting taxes upwards and enjoying the fruits of lower interest payments

Because of the need to respond to recession early on, *Finland, the Netherlands,* and *Ireland* had already made important changes to their social systems before the convergence criteria began to bite. In the Dutch case, with the twin oil-price shocks and rising unemployment across western Europe in the 1970s, part of the response was an early engagement in hard currency and tough budgetary policies, linked to a revival of concertation and coordinated wage bargaining. This provided the basis for far-reaching, and negotiated, reforms of the benefit systems and labour market. The result, despite persistent shortcomings, has become something of a model for other states, especially in its combination of flexible jobs and strengthened social entitlements for employees. This meant that the state's fiscal position was already in good shape. But a 'Maastricht effect' was observable in the revenue and spending reforms thereafter, with health reform, tougher disability and employment schemes, and social security benefit restrictions helping reduce primary expenditure from 46 per cent to 40 per cent of GDP from 1992 to 1998.

Finland, like the other Scandinavian states, experienced an economic crisis that was largely created by government policy. As Huber and Stephens (2001) explain, Finland and Sweden deregulated financial markets with a distinct lack of caution in the 1980s, producing a sequence of boom and bust. GDP fell for three consecutive years—in Finland by as much as 8 per cent in 1991—budgetary balances worsened dramatically, and unemployment levels rose alarmingly. Social expenditure in 1993 reached 36.9 per cent of GDP in Sweden and 34.8 per cent in Finland. As a result, throughout the past decade the Nordic states have been grappling with pressures for cost-containment and labour-market reorganization, especially with a view to generating more demand for private-sector employment. In Finland, the high tax and social security burden could be tackled with renewed vigour once the EMU commitment was made. But, in fact, the adjustment process was largely underpinned by a decline in cyclically adjusted spending and revenue, especially from social security contributions, as economic conditions improved and high unemployment levels fell.

Ireland entered the Maastricht process with a high level of debt but reduced it from 92 per cent to 43 per cent of GDP over 1990–9. As one of the more important examples of a concerted adjustment process involving unions and employers, the Irish convergence programme was also geared to improving the supply and demand for labour, with a reduction in social security contributions, targeted at new and low-paid employment creation, alongside a broadening of the tax base to increase revenue. A critical contribution to Ireland's deficit reduction came from wage moderation—which helped reduce the public-sector pay bill—and a decline of transfer payments in line with rising employment. Although Ireland differs from most other EU countries in that it has experienced a decline in 'welfare effort'—that is, the proportion of welfare spending in GDP—the real value of social security payments and spending on social services has increased (see Figs. 12.1–12.3). This latter, solidaristic commitment, underpinned by the terms of the Irish social pact, distances Ireland from the British experience and places it much closer to the priorities of the 'European social model' (Ó Riain and O'Connell 2000: 324–34).

In conclusion, EMU has been an important contributing factor in European welfare reforms in the 1990s. The causal link can be made between the convergence imperative and the timing of certain key policy initiatives. But, as argued above, EMU as such did not generate the need for such changes. Difficult reforms to health care, pensions systems, and social transfers would have been necessary in any case in most of these states, and had long been on the agenda if not already on the statute books. EMU has been a catalyst and a spur for reform in states already experiencing the problems of a poorly-managed 'growth to limits' in their large and still—especially in France, Germany, and Scandinavia—highly redistributive welfare states. In many cases, these were problems accumulated from the crises of the 1970s or, as in the case of pensions and health, involved long-term liabilities that threatened further, and in some cases acute, budgetary imbalances in the coming decades (European Commission 2000b: 44). In this respect, it can be argued that the main effect of Maastricht to date has been to improve rather than undermine the long-term sustainability of these systems: first, by encouraging, and helping legitimize, pre-emptive budgetary strategies, creating greater room for manoeuvre once the impact of ageing becomes more acute; and second, by drawing the attention of policy-makers to the need for reform to pensions and health-care systems and tackling the demographic problem head on (Artis and Buti 2000).

Living with EMU: The Third Phase and After

The policy conclusions are therefore far from pessimistic. First, there is no inevitability about the emergence and victory of a *pensée unique* or convergence on neo-liberal values and solutions. The European states are certainly not immune to pressures for change. But, by contrast with the liberal welfare states—Britain, New Zealand, the US—welfare-state restructuring to date in Scandinavia and continental Europe has avoided radical retrenchment and preserved much greater degrees of cross-class solidarity, trust, and confidence. What happens next? There are two sets of issues here. The first concerns the implications of the Stability and Growth Pact, the second the capacity of Europe's social and employment systems to cope with external shocks.

Many have argued that the coming period will see unprecedented turbulence in European social systems as the constraints of living in EMU really begin to bite. Geoffrey Underhill (Chapter 1), for example, argues that the consequences of the new 'stability culture' of EMU for social and corporate systems are likely to be profound. It is certainly true that, while satisfying the entry conditions, many states are far from the Stability and Growth Pact's objective of fiscal positions 'close to balance or in surplus' over the medium term. For only then can the requirement of fiscal discipline be squared with the need to let automatic stabilizers—for example, allowing fiscal deficits to increase during recessions—operate freely inside EMU (Artis and Winkler 1998). In the meantime, the strains of slow down in European growth rates will be felt. On the other hand, the additional budgetary adjustment now required is more modest than that achieved to meet the initial 3 per cent convergence target.

It can of course be argued that Europe has already been suffering the consequences of a monetary straitjacket that does not fit. As Steinherr (2000) points out, a decline in growth occurred in both the US and Europe after 1988, but interest rates were increased in Europe to reach their highest level in 25 years in 1992, with zero growth that year and negative growth the next. Fiscal policy was arguably overly restrictive in the EU and, together with monetary policy, squeezed aggregate demand. Since the 1970s, investment in the EU as a share of overall GDP has declined dramatically, from 25 per cent to 18 per cent. In 1998, partly linked to the fact that public investment was halved in the 1990s from 4 per cent to 2 per cent of GDP, it fell due to EMU-driven fiscal consolidation. However, low interest rates, the upswing in the economic cycle, and the external demand stimulus provided by the weakness of the euro since its inception have begun to change this situation. Meanwhile a move towards the 'close-to-balance' position in an environment of price stability over the next couple of years, in line with Stability Pact objectives, should help the ECB avoid an over-restrictive monetary stance and prevent Europe falling into a new deflationary trap (see Buti, Franco, and Onenga 1998: 89). I return to this point in the final section below.

Moreover, although it is of course difficult to assess how history would have differed in the absence of economic and monetary integration, recent research on the counterfactual has shown that few benefits would have come from being outside the ERM in the 1990s. Quite apart from the costs of 'non-membership' in the form of delayed reform in states with acute budgetary imbalances and blocked reform agendas, life may have been much more difficult outside than in. Gordon (1999) compares the performance of those states outside the ERM after the 1992 ERM breakdown—Finland, Italy, Portugal, Spain, Sweden, and Britain—with those inside—Austria, Belgium, France, the Netherlands. The analysis shows that some 80 per cent of the extra nominal GDP growth enjoyed by those outside was 'chewed up' by extra inflation—which was especially acute in Italy, Portugal, and Spain—leaving only 20 per cent to spill over into real GDP. Further, with regard to the fiscal constraints required by sound budgetary positions, research by Buti, Franco, and Onenga (1998) demonstrates that there are no free lunches to be gained from the greater fiscal laxity that may have been permitted in a non-EMU world. High public finance imbalances in the past have frequently hampered the use of budgets for stabilization purposes by forcing tighter fiscal stances, and these have frequently translated into outright retrenchment policies, especially during periods of prolonged recession.

There is a further reason why the EMU fixed-exchange-rate regime may not just be compatible with welfare-state sustainability but may indeed enhance it. Rather than posing a threat to domestic economic management, EMU may have provided European states with an optimal institutional arrangement for avoiding one of the main causes of their welfare state crisis in the 1970s and 1980s: their inability to control the wage-push component of inflation (Notermans 2000b). EMU should allow governments to pursue a growth-oriented macroeconomic policy without also producing uncontrollable wages and price spirals. For much of the 1980s there was a strong tendency towards the decentralization of collective wage bargaining, suggesting that national incomes policies would give way to less disciplined combinations of sectoral and company bargaining. More recently, however, we observe a remarkable resurgence of corporatist forms of social pacts and policy concertation in a number of states, all of which, to one degree or another, have involved incomes coordination (M. Rhodes 1998; 2001*b*). Thus, the shift to a hard-currency regime in Denmark and the Netherlands during the early 1980s brought the social partners closer together, while the completion of the single market and the EMU entrance exam provided the key impetus for concertation or social pacts in Ireland, Italy, Portugal, and Spain. It seems that one of the unanticipated effects of EMU has been to help rekindle the urge to find cooperative, positive-sum solutions to the predicament of adjustment, among which initiatives to make taxation and social protection more 'employment-friendly' have figured prominently (see Chapter 11).

However, according to many commentators there may still be serious problems in store for the Euroland economies because of critical flaws in the EMU system. These include:

- limitations on member-state fiscal autonomy due to an absence of European coordination;
- the very weak mobility of labour amongst the member states;
- the absence of a federal system of social security or other mechanisms of cross-national solidarity; and
- the presence of different legal systems, cultures, and social and political structures within EMU.

The consequence, it is feared, will be a high degree of vulnerability to symmetric and asymmetric shocks and, in the worst-case scenario, a collapse of EMU—and even the EU—if a new fiscal constitution is not put in place (for example, Chapter 3).

Although the literature has been replete with nightmare scenarios, there is actually little consensus among economists about the actual degree of vulnerability to external shocks. As for limitations on fiscal autonomy, if the ambitions of the Stability and Growth Pact are achieved, as already discussed there should be more scope for automatic stabilizers to operate and for fiscal intervention to correct regional disparities and employment problems in the event, say, of an adverse terms-of-trade shock. A new constitutional settlement is not required for these mechanisms to work. As for weak labour mobility, much hinges on whether EMU fosters greater regional specialization or greater diversification—the so-called Krugman-Frankel/Rose debate. If greater diversification occurs rather than a greater concentration of economic activity, then the low responsiveness of European migration to regional disparities in per capita income and unemployment rates will be much less of a problem (Bentivogli and Pagano 1999). Pench, Sestito, and Frontini (1999: 17–18) argue that better financial integration and the absence of exchange-rate risk may favour a process of asset diversification, which may itself provide an automatic, market-driven shock-absorbing mechanism. In any case, the best available evidence suggests that radical changes in the current distribution of activity are extremely unlikely, for processes of specialization and diversification/concentration are very slow in the EU and far from unidirectional. According to Midelfart-Knarvit *et al.* (2000), during the 14 years to 1997 there was very little change in specialization patterns, although the overall trend was for the structures of the EU economies to become more dissimilar. The completion of the single market programme appears to have had no marked effect on location and specialization patterns. Against the predictions of both old and new trade theory, any concentration trends apparent in some sectors are being counteracted by dispersion in others. Major adjustment costs are unlikely to be triggered by this process.

As for the oft-decried absence of a European fiscal federation, recent research suggests that the potential benefits of providing inter-regional insurance by creating such a federation are actually too small to compensate for the many problems associated with its design and implementation. Fatás (1998) estimates that even if a Europe-wide fiscal system managed to reduce the volatility of disposable income by 30 per cent, it would be providing less than 10 per cent insurance. The other two-thirds would occur in the form of inter-temporal stabilization via countercyclical budgets, a tool that is already available to European states and will still be available in the future. Other economists—for example, Artis and Zhang (1999)—stress that greater synchronization of the business cycle across Europe and the growth of inter-regional private market insurance mechanisms will reduce the likelihood that EMU will generate unsustainable disturbances to the socio-economic fabric of the continent.

Finally, it has been argued that different legal systems, cultures, and social and political structures in Europe will undermine the smooth functioning of EMU, while the uneven capacity of national systems to manage social conflict will exacerbate the impact of asymmetric external shocks. De Grauwe and Skudelny (1999), for example, suggest that differences in social conflicts and bureaucratic inefficiency have important consequences for economic growth after the same terms-of-trade shock. The southern states are expected to suffer more from a negative shock than their northern neighbours, mainly because of their weaker bureaucracies and a poor capacity for conflict resolution. Others—for example, Martin (1998: 20)—argue that EMU is likely to generate a more general collapse of traditional mechanisms of wage solidarity and a 'deflationary vicious circle of labour cost dumping, or competitive internal depreciations'. In this argument, the fragmentation of wage bargaining is intimately linked to the sustainability—or, rather, unsustainability—of distinct national welfare systems. At worst, argues Martin (1998: 20), EMU may turn out to be part and parcel of the neo-liberal project of eliminating the obstacles to labour-market flexibility posed by trade-union and social-policy institutions. The Americanization of European industrial relations would be 'one of its principal intended consequences'.

Both sets of arguments need to be considered together, despite the fact that the literature on fiscal adjustment and decision-making is generally not connected to that on social conflict resolution. In practice they have been linked and it is in the relationship between the two that those EU member states most prone to social conflict and bureaucratic inefficiency have most radically innovated. The De Grauwe/Skudelny and Martin arguments can be countered with evidence that the 1990s have seen many states develop greater fiscal decision-making authority as well as new mechanisms of conflict resolution. The southern states, especially Italy and Portugal, are cases in point of systems whose adjustment to EMU inflation and budget criteria were heavily assisted by a set of reforms that strengthened the power of finance ministers and secured concerted incomes and social policy reform. In Italy, the centralization of power around the finance minister coincided with a series of incomes policy deals that helped take inflation out of the Italian labour market. Belgium is another state at the tail end of the convergence league which none the less managed to qualify. Fiscal contracts and the coordination and monitoring of budgetary policy by the Belgian High Council of Finance in the 1990s were accompanied by a new confidence in wage concertation from 1998. This followed several years in which the government was forced by lack of agreement among the social partners to impose a statutory wage norm. In both the Italian and the Belgian cases, the greater consistency in, and credibility of, government policy, linked to the external stick of EMU, helped underpin contractual relations with employers and unions and produce convergence on the deficit and inflation criteria (for budgetary policy see Hallerberg 1999 and von Hagen, Hallett, and Strauch 2001: 47–55; on incomes policy, M. Rhodes 1998; 2001b; and Chapter 11).

Parallel developments have occurred elsewhere in Europe. Ireland, Sweden, Spain, and Austria all improved budgetary policy-making while maintaining or renewing their systems of social dialogue and/or wage coordination. Italy, Austria, Belgium, and Spain have all introduced forms of internal stability pact, improving the domestic coordination of budgetary policy with sub-national authorities. These institutional innovations render EMU members much more capable of responding to asymmetric shocks than hitherto.

Chapter 11 provides a full account of the 'social pact' dimension of these changes. But it is worth mentioning briefly here how these mechanisms for social conflict management have developed as a result of both a new external constraint—the Maastricht convergence criteria—and the resolution of what we can refer to as 'flexibility struggles' in the member states. In addition to its impact on budgetary policy, the realization of EMU and the creation of the single market have placed new pressures on wage-cost competition and made competitive devaluation impossible. Meanwhile, employers in all systems are searching for greater company and plant-level flexibility in three areas: internal, or functional, flexibility in the work place; external, or numerical, flexibility vis-à-vis the wider labour market; and greater pay flexibility at local levels. Furthermore, cost competitiveness and monetary stability, as well as 'credibility' with international financial markets, require a means of preventing wage drift and the emergence of new inflationary pressures. This has focused the attention of most if not all governments on revitalizing incomes policies, a critical component of many of these new national bargains. If these can be linked to reforms of social and employment protection systems, then a consensus-based recalibration of welfare states in line with both efficiency and equity demands may also be achieved.

As argued below, these developments will also improve the potential for some form of coordinated fiscal policy as well as the creation of a collective EU capacity for avoiding symmetric—e.g. pan-EMU demand or cost—shocks (see Soskice 1999). Much will depend on flexible but concerted national wage determination systems and mechanisms for avoiding or absorbing broader distributive conflict. In this respect Germany and France, not to mention Britain, remain distinctive in their lack of *explicit* national coordinating systems or pacts. But Britain is the true 'outlier' following years of determined marginalization of the trade unions from all realms of policy. France and Germany are cases in which a problematic search for national-level social dialogue has been launched but has stalled. In France the absence of a national pact should not detract from the importance of social partner agreement in any major area of reform to the social protection system. Although the state is seeking to weaken the role of the social partners in certain parts of the system—in health care, family, and poverty policies—there are plans to increase it in unemployment insurance and pensions. Within firms, there is a vigorous dialogue on reforms linked to the 35-hour week, while employers have been trying to implement a 'social constitution' to underpin concerted reform (Palier 2000). Nevertheless, the failure to institutionalise the 1997 Wage and

Employment Conference has deprived France of the benefits of a more centralized mechanism of wage bargaining. In Germany, an implicit social pact in the early 1990s helped facilitate the unification process and, more recently, the negotiation of a national employment policy has achieved some, albeit limited, success. Unlike the UK, and in contrast to France in the wage-setting arena, this remains a highly coordinated economy, a key pillar of which has been continued employer commitment to a sectoral bargaining system for wages and an employer-led training system (see for example Wood 2001). This pillar, plus pragmatic regional pacts in a number of *Länder*—a trend also apparent in another of the EU's federal systems, Spain—have provided functional equivalents to the national deals being struck in less coordinated social and employment systems. But the fact remains that a national agreement on social and employment policy reform sought by the Schröder government— the *Bündnis für Arbeit*—is proving very difficult to achieve.

Making Welfare Sustainable: The Search for a Coordinated European Response

The analysis in the second and third sections focused on the domestic circumstances of the EMU states. The central claim was that welfare states are not under threat in terms of their core functions, or core beliefs; and, if anything, national governance mechanisms have been strengthened by the EMU process, helping provide a new sustainability for expensive welfare programmes rather than eroding their purpose and operation. But this does not rule out the need for innovation in pan-European coordination between the new monetary policy system and national fiscal systems, in which social and employment systems are protected from the dangers of 'negative spillovers' (see Chapter 1) and a potential constitutional quandary (predicted in Chapter 3).

In fact, steps were well under way by 2000 to initiate change in two directions at the EU level: finding a new role for the EU in coordinating welfare policies and systems to help safeguard the European social model; and putting in place a new mechanism for coordinating macroeconomic management with social and employment policies. The remainder of this chapter builds on these recent developments to illustrate how a new architecture for welfare policy is steadily being put in place. Apart from helping defend and even improve the quality of European welfare provision, and further embedding what Faist (2001) calls 'nested citizenship'—forms of citizenship which function in complementary ways at regional, state, and supranational levels —if successful, this process will also provide the basis for a form of fiscal coordination that will enhance EMU resistance to both symmetric and asymmetric shocks.

First, regarding the coordination of welfare systems against the background of new challenges to social cohesion, there has been a quest for a new synthesis in EU social policy, reconciling flexibility and security in labour markets with solidarity and sustainability in broader welfare programmes. In so doing, an implicit objective has been the conciliation of efficiency imperatives with social justice. Although not using such language, the special meeting of the European Council in Lisbon on 23–4 March 2000 did emphasize the need to create an 'active welfare state' through a 'positive strategy which combines competitiveness with social cohesion'. The Commission's Broad Economic Policy Guidelines, published shortly before the Lisbon Summit, present a rather clearer recipe for reform. Alongside stability-oriented macroeconomic policies, sound and sustainable public finances, and ensuring efficient product—that is, goods and services—markets, the emphasis in the social and employment sphere is very much on:

- reducing the tax burden on low-wage labour;
- encouraging real wages to increase in line with labour productivity;
- facilitating access to training;
- reforming tax and benefit systems to ensure appropriate incentives and rewards for participation in active working life; and
- negotiating a modernization of labour markets including flexible working hours and a review of tight job-protection legislation and high severance payments (Ferrera, Hemerijck, and Rhodes 2000).

The Broad Economic Policy Guidelines have become an umbrella for strategic planning, with a greater involvement of Council ministerial groupings other than ECOFIN to encourage a better management of policy interdependencies. This is designed to ensure that social policy does not become subordinate to finance ministers but rather assumes a parallel importance to economic affairs. How all this will evolve in practice remains unclear. Following the Lisbon Summit, social protection is being considered by the Commission in ideal terms as the third side of a policy triangle together with macroeconomic and employment policy. The European Council now meets every spring to address economic and social questions. Member states have to prepare each year a document illustrating their own social policy agenda, with indicators and targets; and this, it is hoped, will contribute to greater continuity and coherence in Council deliberations.

These innovations seek to streamline and bring together three existing European 'processes' or channels for innovation in policy coordination: the Cologne process on macroeconomic policies, the Cardiff process on structural policies, and the Luxembourg process, based on the new strategy for employment set out in the Treaty of Amsterdam. The latter has put in place and coordinates 'national employment plans' (NAPs) and seeks a convergence of policy priorities and to a lesser extent procedures across member states. In order to help avoid the creation of complex and opaque procedures, as well as overlaps between the various processes themselves, the Macro-Economic Dialogue put in place in Cologne in 1999 began to address the issue of policy interdependencies within EMU. It specifically promotes relations between European employer and union representatives, the Commission, ministers of finance and employment, the European Central Bank, and governors of national central banks, focusing on the interconnections between wages, monetary, budgetary, and fiscal policies (Goetschy 2000).

As far as European welfare policies are concerned, an attempt is now being made to use the experience of the Luxembourg process and the NAPs in moves towards an 'open method of coordination' (Lönnroth 2000). The aim is to fix guidelines for social policy, combined with specific timetables for achieving short-, medium-, and long-term goals; establish quantitative and qualitative indicators and benchmarks tailored to the needs of different member states and sectors; translate European guidelines into national and regional policies by setting targets and measures; use periodic monitoring, evaluation, and peer reviews to promote 'mutual learning'; and to benchmark best practices on managing change. In effect, this is the Luxembourg process 'writ large' for the modernization of the welfare state and the European Commission is to work alongside governments, companies, social partners, and non-governmental organizations to put it in place. But making it work requires further progress on a number of related fronts.

To make sure there is a real improvement in policy integration, rather than the subordination of social and employment policy to financial concerns, a broad and incisive rationalization of the overall institutional framework for open coordination would have to occur. One solution would be to use the Cologne process, and especially the Broad Economic Policy Guidelines, as a sort of 'umbrella' framework under which two distinct but interconnected tracks would run:

- a first track for the coordination of national social policies, prioritizing both procedures and desirable outcomes in terms of broad objectives, for example, in poverty reduction programmes, active labour-market spending, and effective policy mixes; and

- a second track for coordinating fiscal policies, both to encourage convergence on key priorities across member states and also to prevent them from being locked into inflationary or deflationary responses to external or internal supply or demand shocks (Soskice 1999).

Track one has already been initiated since the Lisbon summit of March 2000. A number of rather specific targets have been identified for enhancing education and training systems. Social exclusion and the 'eradication of poverty' have been indicated as top priorities for public policy at all levels, with a commitment to set specific targets and to monitor their achievement through 'soft' coordination procedures. A High-Level Working Party on Social Protection has been given a broad mandate to investigate the future evolution of social protection. Its special brief covers social exclusion and the sustainability of pension systems. It is already clear from its first report where the emphasis for future policy will lie. In social protection, the extent to which activation measures are provided as an integral part of minimum income schemes will receive close attention; while in pensions there will be a stress on 'active ageing'—extending the retirement age—alongside an examination of the implications of second- and third-tier pensions. Track two is less developed, but the new Macro-Economic Dialogue does respond to criticism that fiscal and monetary policy coordination under EMU has not been as intense as it was hitherto within the member states themselves (Bini Smaghi and Casini 2000). More problematic is the relationship between the stability-oriented monetary policy, budgetary policies, and wage policy. But, as argued in Chapter 11, the strengthening of national incomes policies and broader social pacts induced by EMU can also assist procedural coordination at the European level.

These innovations are potentially far-reaching in their implications, both for the architecture of European policy-making and the future of European welfare states. Social protection issues will move much closer to the centre of European policy, and their interdependencies with other areas of employment and macroeconomic policy making will be explicitly acknowledged. As in the past, questions of national sovereignty will inevitably be raised, but this is unavoidable as action on the broad employment policy front logically spills over into related areas of social security and taxation policy where member-state autonomy is still jealously guarded.

As for the 'open method of coordination', there is also a logic in the extension of the Luxembourg process from labour-market issues strictly defined to other dimensions of the welfare state. The new focus on benchmarking and the definition of qualitative and quantitative indicators for cross-national coordination, coupled with deadlines for the achievement of short-, medium- and long-term objectives, provide in theory the basis for an EMU-style approach to European welfare-state convergence. There are enormous problems in store in terms of policy design, actor coordination, and monitoring reform across highly diverse systems, not to mention the legitimacy of a process that seeks explicitly to penetrate previously protected national policy domains. Its success will depend critically on the preservation and strengthening of the processes already in place in many member states, which, frequently involving social partner concertation, seek to tackle the complex interdependencies between social protection, employment, and broader economic policies. A new coordinated policy for EU fiscal policy can function and be made legitimate only by linking together strengthened national decision-making structures and social dialogues.

As for the nature of welfare reform itself, there is of course a risk that national conflict over the direction of change, for example in pensions systems, will transfer to the supranational arena, creating the prospect of new policy blockages and joint decision traps. But a stable system of multi-level and multi-actor interaction may also help 'depoliticize' the issues at stake, shielding them from national political cycles and encouraging a problem-solving style in their management. As with the EMU process, governments may be able to use a coordinated European strategy to legitimize difficult choices by appealing to the existence of a European 'community of fate'. Like EMU, this process will develop through a combination of altered incentive structures—perhaps linked to a redeployment of the European structural funds—and the constraints of compliance with EU-wide objectives which will increasingly be set by qualified majority votes. At the same time—as has also occurred during the transition to EMU in a range of areas ranging from budgetary policy to employment policy—a process of learning will result from participation in these multi-level processes.

Conclusion

The title of this chapter hedges its bets by suggesting that there may be circumstances in which EMU may *not* be 'good' for European welfare states. I have argued against the Euro-pessimism of those who equate EMU with a neo-liberal project in which a downward adjustment in welfare is driven by deregulatory competition among EU member states. Most European welfare states entered a period of 'crisis' in the 1970s and 1980s linked to rising unemployment and declining rates of growth, while demographic, demand, and cost pressures all pushed up welfare spending. Many states did engage in cost-containment and retrenchment as a response to these pressures before the 1990s, and under EMU budgetary constraints increased their efforts to contain programme growth. But in most EU states the real value of benefits and levels of spending were maintained if not increased. As Pierson (2001) argues, only the liberal welfare states, in Europe represented by Britain and Ireland, have engaged in clear strategies of 'recommodification'—tightening eligibility, cutting benefits, removing entitlements—while cost containment has been rather linked to a rationalization or updating of welfare programmes in the Nordic Social Democratic and Continental Conservative welfare regimes. Therein lies the paradox that those states making the weakest effort to protect their citizens have also engaged in the most draconian anti-welfare reforms. For the most problematic cases—the heavily indebted states in the Continental cluster—EMU became part of the solution for enhancing welfare-state sustainability rather than a force for destruction.

If the essence of the European social model can be embodied in pan-European policy-making, and if the sustainability of national systems can be reinforced by a combination of supranational steering and subsidiary national bargains, then, as I have also argued, the possibility that the new stability-biased macroeconomic regime will also be welfare-enhancing will be increased. One should never make predictions—especially about the future. But the history of European integration has witnessed the steady emergence and evolution of such new supranational spaces before that, over time, have enabled actors to overcome their political differences and cooperate. In so doing they have also created a set of understandings, both formal and informal, that have allowed that cooperation, in one way or another, to continue to expand (Stone Sweet, Fligstein, and Sandholtz 1999). This is precisely what we are now witnessing in the area of social and employment policy where the defence of national sovereignty has traditionally been fierce.

In taking this generally positive tone, I am arguing that the EU and its member states together retain the capacity and resources for a positive adjustment of their welfare systems to new cost and demand pressures, one that avoids direct and zero-sum trade-offs between equity and efficiency. Of course, they will not necessarily achieve it. One can imagine a scenario in which a neo-liberal project *is* elaborated by European and national elites that seeks deliberately to unravel the complex social bargains and commitments that underpin welfare societies and social citizenship, or indeed one in which they are allowed to erode by neglect. This is why EMU *may* be good for European welfare states. But, at least so far, EMU has had a largely positive impact on European welfare states and their future sustainability.

Conclusions: European States and Euro Economic Governance

Kenneth Dyson

The issue of strengthening economic policy coordination within the Euro-Zone is one of the most politically problematic and sensitive legacies of EMU. Its implications go beyond detailed changes to structures, procedures, and practices at the EU level to touch on contentious questions of sovereignty, identity, and legitimacy. These problems and sensitivities were highlighted by the frosty reception from the Euro Group to the European Commission proposals of February 2001 about strengthening economic policy coordination (European Commission 2001a). They were also evident in the criticisms of ECOFIN's formal recommendation, proposed by the Commission, criticizing the budgetary policies of the Irish government as inconsistent with the Broad Economic Policy Guidelines of the EU. Likewise, central bankers were opposed to the idea of the Euro Group's president Didier Reynders that it should 'oversee' broad economic policy coordination, sharing responsibilities with the ECB as its political 'counterpart' (Cottrell 2001).

Why Coordination? Its Politically Contested Nature

The politically contested nature of coordination was in part bound up with earlier failure to anticipate the problems of euro economic governance and in part with the difficulties of 'learning by doing'. It was also related to the reluctance of some 'ins', notably Germany, to make life more difficult for 'outs' like Britain in manoeuvring their electorates to endorse EMU entry.

The first version of this chapter was delivered to the Workshop on Euro Economic Governance organized by the Forward Studies Unit of the European Commission and the Robert Schuman Centre for Advanced Studies in Florence on 19 February 2001.

In addition, economic policy coordination was caught up in a contest about institutional empowerment and disempowerment, vertically—between national governments and the Commission—and horizontally—between the ECB and the Euro Group, with the Commission finding it difficult to make friends in either camp. The Commission was frustrated in its attempts to build a supranational coalition to support macroeconomic policy coordination. Its efforts were made more difficult by the contested economics of how to practise policy coordination, for instance in relation to the Irish case (see Alesina *et al.* 2001).

The evolution of economic policy coordination within an emerging euro economic governance is caught up in a paradox. The case for improved macroeconomic coordination is widely accepted, not least by ECOFIN and the European Council. It rests on the importance both of taking account of policy externalities and of the improved visibility of policies for the credibility of EMU as a 'community of stability'. Externalities take two forms (Bayer 1999). First, because of regional spill-over effects, the total effect of a domestic policy may exceed its effects for the state concerned. This argument provides the rationale for the Broad Economic Policy Guidelines and the procedure of mutual surveillance. Second, there are institutional spill-over effects, notably from the coexistence of a single monetary policy with decentralized fiscal and supply-side policies at the domestic level. This argument underpins the Stability and Growth Pact and the procedure for reviewing and monitoring national stability programmes. The Pact is designed to prevent one or more states from running budgetary policies that are inappropriate for the stability policy of the Euro-Zone as a whole. It ensures continuing pressure for long-term budget consolidation and averts the possibility of an early clash between the ECB and the national fiscal authorities. Such a clash would be costly to the credibility of the ECB and would impact on all states in the form of higher interest rates. The problem is that the effects of a policy may depend on other policies that are outside its control. Hence attention has to be paid to the 'policy-mix' issue by coordinating monetary with fiscal and with supply-side policies. Coordination is required in order to safeguard a stability-oriented macroeconomic policy and avoid the damaging effects from volatility on output and inflation. Moreover, questions of coordination arise from the increasing importance of supply-side policies for wages, product markets, and labour markets once devaluation and interest-rate adjustment are abandoned as instruments to tackle asymmetric economic disturbance.

The question of the form of coordination has been answered by a combination of supranational coordination and 'hard' coordination on the demand side—embodying the logic of the model of implicit coordination—and by the 'open' method of coordination in relation to the supply-side. The reasons for this complex answer are to be found in ideational, institutional, and political factors at the EU and the domestic levels that shape and constrain how coordination develops. The 'sound' money and finance paradigm defines the key problem as the credibility of EMU as a 'community of stability' and implies the primacy and special quality of the ECB's monetary policy. The political contest about coordination takes place within this ideational framework.

In addition to this macro constraint at the level of economic paradigm, presided over by the ECB, national institutional diversity in forms of capitalism and welfare-state and educational provision makes flexibility desirable in designing policy coordination for supply-side policies. Any mechanism of coordination has to be adapted to the complex, multiple domestic veto points on change. This diversity in the expression of vital national interests also means that legitimacy is better safeguarded in a form of coordination based on the premise that employment and welfare-state policies will continue to be made at the national level. Hence both arguments of principle and pragmatic arguments point to 'soft', 'bottom-up', or 'open' economic policy coordination as most appropriate on the supply side (Hodson and Maher 2001). This mode of integration eschews common policy instruments in favour of setting EU-level guidelines, establishing benchmarks as a means of spreading of best practice, setting targets, and peer review and surveillance. With respect to euro economic governance the key question is whether the 'open' method of coordination represents a new mode of integration or a transitional mechanism pending the formal transfer of policy competence to the EU level (cf. Wallace and Wallace 2000: 33–4; Hodson and Maher 2001).

What Kind of Coordination? The Political Exposure of the Commission

Since 1 January 1999 economic policy coordination has been gradually strengthened but in a manner—based on mutual surveillance and peer review, without sanctions—that indicates its character as 'soft' rather than 'hard' law (Louis 2001b). In the Euro Group and in ECOFIN there was a discernible consensus behind modest measures to improve economic policy coordination, short of inserting an element of compulsion and formally institutionalizing coordination in the Euro Group. In June 1999 under the German EU presidency the Cologne European Council introduced the Macro-Economic

Dialogue. Its role was to expedite the exchange of information between the ECB, national governments, the social partners—employers and trade unions —and the European Commission with the objective of an optimal policy mix consistent with the aims laid down in the Maastricht and Amsterdam treaties. The Helsinki European Council of December 1999 adopted an ECOFIN report that called for a strengthening of coordination arrangements in stage three of EMU. The Broad Economic Policy Guidelines had been improved by extending their scope to embrace structural policies, by their clearer formulation, by their application on a state-by-state basis, and by reports on their implementation. The Lisbon European Council of March 2000 added a new dimension: an explicit role for the European Commission as a forum for expediting policy transfer in improving economic policy performance, especially in competitiveness and innovation, through 'benchmarking' best practice. An innovation here was the production of an annual synthesis report covering, in particular, the interactions between macroeconomic policy and structural policies. A new 'open coordination' process, experimented with in employment policy after the Luxembourg European Council in 1997, was codified in the Lisbon conclusions.

In addition, under the French EU presidency, in summer 2000 the Euro Group's work as an informal forum for dialogue was strengthened. The range of topics was widened to include structural reforms, for example to labour markets and to deal with demographic problems affecting pensions. There was also a better organization of meetings and higher visibility, notably through a press conference after each meeting. Economic policy coordination within the Euro-Zone remains centred on the consensus principle within this informal body. But, contrary to the recommendations from Jacquet and Pisani-Ferry (2000), the Euro Group was not in process of being transformed into a 'Council of Economic Policy' with the right to take binding decisions.

Two factors shaped and constrained the kind of economic policy coordination that emerged. One was the intellectual ascendancy of a model of implicit policy coordination. This model ruled out formal, *ex ante* coordination of fiscal and monetary policies and favoured decentralized, market-led adjustment through competition of policies. It was promoted by the ECB, the Bundesbank, and leading monetary economists. The other was the issue of who benefits in institutional terms from strengthened coordination of any type, for instance of microeconomic structural policies. Suspicion of the ambitions and opportunism of the European Commission in making proposals in this area was augmented by a sense of Commission arrogance in presuming to tell the Irish government what kind of fiscal policy it should have. What was striking in February 2001 was the willingness of EU governments that had accepted the Commission recommendation on Ireland to let the Commission take the political heat. This episode underlined the problems of trying to strengthen coordination and the political vulnerability of the Commission as the guardian of coordination. It showed just how exposed the Commission was to 'scapegoating' as European states passed responsibility for policy problems and failures to it rather than shouldered collective responsibility.

The issue of the kind of coordination went to the heart of the question of the relationship between European states and euro economic governance. At the macro-structural level the discourse about coordination revealed the ascendancy of a 'sound' money and finance paradigm that privileged the ECB and the problem of the credibility of its policies. The result was the model of implicit policy coordination (Remsperger 1999). According to this model, responsibility for individual policies was assigned to different actors. Coordination worked best when each actor concentrated on effectively discharging its own responsibility by pursuing appropriate and prudent policies: the ECB for price stability, the national governments for long-term fiscal sustainability by maintaining a cyclically adjusted balanced budget, the social partners for employment. There was a sub-text: that governments and the social partners were more vulnerable to policy failures consequent on short-term political incentives; that they were not always well-intentioned policy-makers. In consequence, the prime casualty of any mechanisms for explicit, *ex ante* policy coordination would be price stability and the credibility of the ECB.

The model of implicit policy coordination had a number of implications for the design of euro economic governance. It rejected anything beyond informal dialogue in the Euro Group and in the Macro-Economic Dialogue to improve the exchange of information. Formal meetings between the ECB and governments and social partners were either unnecessary or harmful (Alesina *et al.* 2001). They would provide an official forum in which national governments as fiscal authorities could put pressure on the ECB, with costs to the credibility of monetary policy and the euro. Such pressure was likely because governments were motivated by short-term opportunistic goals related to domestic electoral cycles and by ideology (Alesina, Roubini, and Cohen 1997). In that case explicit policy coordination between fiscal and monetary authorities can only be harmful. It would also lead to a confusion of responsibilities (Remsperger 1999). Finally and not least, a formal role for the Euro Group and more explicit coordination would highlight the lack of political will and capability to enforce agreed policies. The result would be a deepening credibility problem with markets and legitimacy problem with national electorates.

Against this background that stressed the pitfalls of formal economic policy coordination, the European Commission found itself in a very difficult situation in playing the central role in this area assigned to it in the Treaty. Especially problematic was its attempt to strengthen simultaneously the Euro Group and its own role within the Euro Group. Many of its ideas found a ready acceptance. The Commission sought to strengthen coordination by producing a common assessment of the economic situation in the Euro-Zone and suggesting and seeking out agreement on appropriate economic policy responses. Above all, it stressed its commitment to consensus rather than coercion and to working through peer-group pressure. Its objective, which was to better establish the idea that domestic policies should be analysed and assessed in the light of the economic situation of the Euro-Zone as a whole, also gained support in ECOFIN and the Euro Group. On this basis the Commission decided to present a twice-yearly report appraising the policy mix in the Euro-Zone, designed to improve the preparation and evaluation of the national stability programmes (European Commission 2001a).

Much more controversial were the procedural changes proposed to effect these objectives. The Commission suggested an alteration in the timing of the submission of stability programmes so that they were available before the finalization of domestic budget laws. More generally, it sought to enforce the provision in Art. 103 (1) that 'member states shall regard their economic policies as a matter of common concern and shall coordinate them within the Council'. It did so by proposing the principle that member states must give advance notice of economic policy measures to other members of the Euro-Zone and to the Commission. These proposals brought it into conflict with member states.

Other proposals from the Commission roused the suspicions of the ECB. Indicative of the objective of strengthening the European perspective in assessing domestic policies were the proposals to: (1) establish a Euro Group working party within the Economic and Financial Committee, (2) increase the frequency of Euro Group meetings, and (3) institute regular meetings between the ECB President, the President of the Euro Group, and the representative of the Commission in the ECB governing council. Though the ideas of 'reinforced dialogue' and of a more efficient functioning of euro economic governance found a ready political acceptance, anything that smacked of Commission empowerment, more detailed intervention in national budgetary processes, and a formalization of the Euro Group aroused opposition.

The dominant definition of a politically acceptable economic policy coordination was conditioned by an interrelated complex of ideational, institutional, and political factors. Ideationally, the model of implicit policy coordination was consistent with the notion of EMU as a 'community of stability'. This notion had been written into the Treaty and found institutional expression in an ECB-centric form of euro economic governance (Dyson 2000a). Ideas about appropriate kinds of coordination were shaped and constrained by the primacy attached to the problem of establishing the credibility of the ECB's monetary policy. In this context references by the Commission (European Commission 2001a: 6) to 'ex ante' coordination proved counterproductive. Institutionally, the larger member states, the EMU 'outs', and the ECB distrusted the motives of the Commission in pursuing an agenda of strengthened coordination.

Beyond the Stability and Growth Pact and the Lisbon process there was political resistance to a stronger role for the Commission in coordinating fiscal and structural policies through new rules of conduct. These rules were presented as helping the Euro Group to deal more effectively with economic shocks and to better adjust budget policies according to the phase of the economic cycle. But they were seen as too interventionist. Underlying this resistance was a perception that the Commission lacked both the political legitimacy and the technical knowledge and skills to intervene in such a manner. Politically, states like Germany were unwilling to make life more difficult for a British government which in principle favoured entry into the Euro-Zone but had first to clear the hurdle of a referendum. A language of rolling back national sovereignty over fiscal and structural policies would make that electoral task impossible. Against this ideational, institutional, and political background the Commission's reference (European Commission 2001a: 6) to the possibility of using the reinforced cooperation procedure laid down in the Treaty of Nice to formalize coordination instruments found little support. It offended against the two principles defended by the Bundesbank: the informality of the Euro Group and the independence of the ECB (Stark 2001).

The way in which economic policy coordination is developing illustrates the structural power of the 'sound' money and finance paradigm and the ECB-centric nature of euro economic governance in shaping and constraining debate (Dyson 2000a). Euro economic governance is based around the model of implicit policy coordination in relation to monetary, fiscal, and structural supply-side policies. Outside the privileged area of monetary policy, 'negative' coordination has triumphed over 'positive' coordination. 'Positive' coordination would mean a commitment by states to establish common policies or undertake common actions designed to reach a Pareto-optimal outcome. An example might be a stabilization fund as an insurance against asymmetric economic shocks (Italiener and Vanheukelen 1993; MacDougall *et al.* 1977). In contrast, 'negative' coordination is about multilateral surveill-ance and peer pressure to monitor the compliance of states in using their own policy instruments, whether fiscal policy or wage policy, in accordance with commitments. Examples of such commitments are the Stability and Growth Pact and the Broad Economic Policy Guidelines. They involve a commitment not to undertake certain policies or measures. 'Negative' coordination can be 'hard' when sanctions exist to reinforce peer group pressure—for example in the Stability and Growth Pact—or 'soft'—for example in the case of the Broad Economic Policy Guidelines or employment and structural policies. In the absence of a crisis and paradigm change it is unlikely that euro economic governance will make a qualitative leap to 'positive' coordination.

The Commission finds economic policy coordination a deeply sensitive and difficult area. Economically, it faces pressure to ensure adequate co-ordination to take account of externalities, improve the visibility of policies, and enhance EMU's credibility. But it must do so in the context of a model of implicit coordination. Legally, the Treaty imposes self-restraint on the devel-opment of economic policy coordination in the form both of a 'community of stability' and of the drafting of EMU as a project for the Community as a whole rather than as just an affair of the 'ins'. Hence the 'outs' act as brake, and moreover one that can be used by 'ins' who are reluctant about strengthened coordination. Under Treaty law it would be very difficult to use the reinforced cooperation procedure, after the Nice Treaty, to transform the Euro Group into a formal decision-making body. One of the cardinal prin-ciples of reinforced cooperation is respect for the single institutional frame-work (Louis 2001*b*). Politically, the Commission is confronted by member states many of which are deeply suspicious of its motives. They also fear the effects of a system of euro economic governance that is 'harder' and more interventionist in fiscal, employment, and structural policies on both their own legitimacy and that of the EU.

Consistently with the model of implicit coordination, it seems sensible to exchange information and improve knowledge about each other's positions and to attempt to agree a common model of how the Euro-Zone economy is working. Coordination as reinforced dialogue can even be more decision-oriented. It can include the search not just for a common understanding of the nature of economic disturbances and shocks but also for how they might be responded to in an optimal manner. In these ways economic policy co-ordination can contribute to the credibility of EMU by curbing policy-induced shocks. But reinforced dialogue finds its limits in the different responsibilit-ies of the parties to the dialogue—they may remain committed to different objectives—and in the problems of enforcement—they may renege in the face of the pressures to which they are exposed. In going beyond these limits coordination would risk the credibility of EMU. The result is an emerging system of euro economic governance that walks a political tightrope, leaving the European Commission very exposed and vulnerable to scapegoating by member states.

Euro Economic Governance and Domestic Institutions and Processes

The prospects for closer economic policy coordination are intimately bound up with the complex, multifaceted relationship between an emerging euro economic governance and domestic institutions and processes. This relationship is defined by the five factors set out below.

1. *The contrast between the historical novelty of euro economic governance and the deeply entrenched nature of domestic beliefs about how economic policies should be managed.* These beliefs are embedded in domestic institutions, creating 'path-shaping' effects on the scope for developing euro economic governance. The result is an overall bias both against conferring more powers to Community institutions in economic policy coordination and against a 'hardening' of coordination and in favour of the 'open' coordination method emerging as a policy mode in its own right.

2. *The enormous complexity of, and contrasts between, the domestic institutions and processes with which euro economic governance interacts.* There are at least three distinct models of capitalist organization: market or liberal capitalism, British-style; state-centric capitalism, French-style; and 'organized' or 'co-ordinated' capitalism, Danish-, Dutch-, and German-style (Iversen, Pontusson and Soskice 2000; Schmidt forthcoming). Each projects different views on to the European level about how euro economic governance should be organized. British policy-makers tend to see EMU as creating an economic logic that requires European politicians to embrace coordination through market-led adjustment. French policy-makers are prone to stress the role of interventionist states in shaping markets through stronger, formal economic policy coordination. Danish, Dutch, and German policy-makers are more likely to highlight the role of the social partners in euro economic governance, not least to coordinate wage, welfare-state, and labour-market policies with macroeconomic policy. Underpinning these contrasting views are different normative and causal beliefs about how euro economic governance should and does operate. The result is a lack of agreement about the problems of, and prospects for, euro economic governance and a lack of convergence around appropriate domestic processes for managing economic adjustment.

3. *The important differences in size, economic structure, level of economic development, as well as political preferences among member states.* In terms of externalities the economic policies of some states, most notably Germany, have greater impact than others, like Ireland (Sapir and Sekkat 2001). Germany accounts for over 30 per cent of the Euro-Zone's GDP. Hence prima facie there is a greater need to coordinate German policies than Irish policies —a factor underpinning criticisms of the Commission for rebuking the Irish government in February 2001. However, the size and weight of Germany means that its economy plays a disproportionately large role in the ECB's calculation of appropriate interest rate policy. Hence there is less likelihood of a clash with Germany than with smaller, peripheral economies. The result is potential for inbuilt clashes with these smaller states, which have to deal with a greater discrepancy between ECB interest rate policy and the needs of their economies. Differences in economic structure and level of development suggest that common exogenous shocks could have asymmetric effects. In addition, contrasting political preferences, consequent on the different ideological character of governments and on different electoral calendars, suggest the prospect of policy-induced shocks. The overall result of these differences is a vulnerability of the Euro-Zone to economic shocks and a difficulty in putting in place mechanisms and common policy instruments of euro economic governance to deal with them. More likely is a reliance on encouraging market-based adjustment through structural reforms, especially to labour markets, combined with fiscal constraints. Another mechanism of adjustment is through temporary inflation differentials, that is, wage increases (Alesina *et al.* 2001). This mechanism is appropriate when domestic overheating is caused primarily by external demand. In that case an appropriate solution is an increase in the relative price of the goods of the state concerned. Inflation differentials are, in other words, not always bad.

4. *The qualities of judgement, political will, and capability shown by European leaders in manoeuvring within structural constraints and using exigencies to the advantage of the Euro-Zone.* The boundaries within which euro economic governance operates will be shaped by whether political leaders remain informed by the historical memories that drove the European integration process and whether they bring a sense of strategic vision to the political development of Europe. The passing of the political generation of Helmut Kohl and François Mitterrand has been associated with a more pragmatic, hard-nosed calculation of interests. This matters because developing euro economic governance is not a stand-alone project. It requires strong political fundamentals in the sense of a closer political union and solidarity. Indirectly, it is important for euro economic governance that significant political

progress is made in EU home affairs and justice policies, in EU foreign, security, and defence policies, and in strengthening the Community institutions to cope with an historic enlargement process to east-central Europe.

5. *The implications of EU enlargement with potentially eight or more new members by 2010.* The candidates from east-central Europe are much poorer than the EU average and at lower levels of both economic and institutional development, for instance in financial markets. Full 'catch up' in terms of GDP per capita will take decades. On the other hand, these new members are likely to replicate the economic dynamism of Ireland and Portugal and to meet the budget criteria for EMU entry (Gros 2001). More problematic will be their ability to meet either the inflation criterion or the exchange-rate stability criterion specified in the Maastricht Treaty for entering stage three of EMU. It might be judged that an inflation differential was appropriate in their case because of the so-called Balassa-Samuelson effect. In this view, higher inflation can be an equilibrium phenomenon reflecting the adjustment of relative prices naturally associated with potential for faster growth. Such an effect is not allowed for in the Treaty, creating some difficulties. The result of a possible expansion of Euro-Zone membership to between 18 and 20 by 2010 will be a 'numbers game' problem, especially in the ECB governing council which would become simply too large to operate by the consensus principle. Hence Treaty revision will be needed to change its composition, introducing the principle of rotation of voting rights for ECB national central bank governors. At any one time some would not be able to vote.

For these reasons the development of euro economic governance is likely to be mired in political controversy. Political science and public policy analysis can help tease out a few basic underlying patterns in the way that euro economic governance interacts with domestic institutions and processes. But these patterns are by no means coherent, and euro economic governance is beset with paradoxes. What emerges is the difficulty of building a common European model and a common economic culture; the provisionality of any judgements about the likely outcomes of the complex interactions between euro economic governance and domestic institutions and processes; and the tentativeness of proposals for improving this interaction.

Contextualizing Euro Economic Governance

To add to the complications, euro economic governance as a source of change cannot be considered in isolation from other sources of domestic institutional and political change. One thinks here of globalization, the 'post-Fordist' economy or 'new' economy, and demographic developments, notably the effects of an ageing population. To these can be added domestic political crises of authority, legitimacy, and distribution. We can adapt Schmitter (1999: 297) to argue that the net effect of EMU 'seems to be to complement (and, probably, to enhance) trends that were already affecting domestic democracies'. EMU alters nothing, for instance, about the underlying sources of employment growth. But, critically, it affects the timing, tempo, rhythm, and sequencing of domestic reforms. In this sense it features more as an intervening than as an independent variable in explaining domestic policy and political changes. As Moran argues in Chapter 10, EMU as Europeanization needs to be understood reflexively and that means taking into account other levels—global and sub-national—as well as the interactions between different sectors.

EMU's effects are paradoxical. On the one hand it sharpens competitive pressures by accelerating financial market integration and capital mobility, by lowering transaction costs, and by focusing attention on developing mechanisms to reduce domestic unit labour costs. In these ways it mirrors the effects of globalization, as Moran (Chapter 10) and Underhill (Chapter 1) argue. The result is changes in the logic of behaviour of market players, notably the corporate multinationals that see themselves as possessing a credible exit threat with which to promote a competitive deregulation. Political acceptance of this logic was apparent in tax rule changes in Germany, agreed in 2000, that encourage divestiture of shareholdings by banks and insurance companies. In this respect 'shareholder' capitalism seems to be making faster strides at the expense of 'organized' capitalism and EMU contributing to a neo-liberal agenda.

On the other hand globalization and EMU contain a different logic, especially for small and medium-sized firms and family-owned firms that lack a credible exit threat and also for many multinationals. As part of more complex production chains, these firms become more dependent on the quality of skills and reliability of their employees and more vulnerable to industrial conflict (Thelen 2000). Where their strategy is to compete on quality and reliability, they will have a self-interest in developing and sustaining neo-corporatist forms of coordination.

EMU's effects were important in another way. As Crouch argues in Chapter 11, domestic economies were given a breathing space by the combination of the greater insulation from financial market pressure—consequent on the monetary resources and the lower trade dependency of the euro economy—and the devaluation of the euro since its launch. In this sense, as French

Finance Minister Laurent Fabius (2001) stressed, EMU functions as a shield against globalization, giving the European economy a greater degree of autonomy and capacity to influence global developments. The question is whether this breathing space is being used constructively to put in place the conditions for robust and sustainable growth in Europe by modernizing public administration and especially labour markets and welfare states. As Crouch (Chapter 11) and Rhodes (Chapter 12) suggest, EMU offers an opportunity to renew the European social model with its idea of economic and social rights and of a safety net.

Additionally, it is important to reiterate that the effects of EMU on domestic political and policy changes did not begin on 1 January 1999. The ERM was in effect a long apprenticeship for the domestic elites in acquiring the appropriate skills for living within the constraints of ever-closer economic and monetary union. Though historical starting points and timing differed significantly, as the country-specific chapters demonstrate, euro economic governance could build on a context of domestic political victories in putting in place 'sound' money and finance policies. Domestic institutions had flexed themselves to accommodate these values, albeit often under great pressure. The interesting question was whether, in the absence of ongoing external pressure, they would spring back to older behaviour patterns. Presumably, the rationale of euro economic governance is to keep that pressure in place and to extend the pressure points to include those aspects of labour-market, vocational education, welfare-state, taxation, and product market policies that are critical to strengthening competitiveness. As Radaelli (Chapter 8) stresses, we should not underestimate the role of institutional learning and development, of a change in the logic of behaviour of domestic elites.

Finally, the development of euro economic governance has been accompanied by a trend to neo-corporatism across the EU during the 1990s, involving new forms of collaboration between employers and trade unions in joint negotiation of improved competitiveness. It was not observable in all states, being typical of 'organized' rather than market capitalist states. Moreover, its timing, scope, organizational forms, levels, and impacts varied. As a starting point it is important to be clear that it was not a return to forms of centralized wage coordination that were characteristic of the 1970s—especially Scandinavian models—and discussed at that time as 'neo-corporatism'. Neo-corporatism '90s-style differed in agenda—more attention to competitiveness, especially unit labour costs—and represented a general shift to more decentralized and flexible forms of domestic coordination, principally to deal with the challenges of globalization. However, against the background of diverse types of capitalist organization and the decentralized and flexible forms that domestic neo-corporatism takes, the prospects for centralized EU-level coordination involving employers and trade unions are non-existent. Any neo-corporatist coordination at the EU level is likely to be minimalist.

Euro Economic Governance as a Process of Europeanization

To what extent is euro economic governance 'Europeanizing' domestic institutions and processes? With what effects? In addressing these questions one needs to be alert to two qualifications: EMU's effects need to be contextualized; and the theme of Europeanization biases analysis towards 'top-down' effects.

EMU as Europeanization refers to a process leading to domestic change in one or both of two ways, triggered by a misfit between European-level changes and domestic institutions, processes, and policies (Börzel and Risse 2000). First, it alters the structure of opportunities and constraints at the domestic level, empowering some actors over others. Second, it produces domestic change through a socialization and collective learning process, leading to the internalization of new ideas and identities. These two views of how the process operates reflect the distinction between what March and Olsen (1998) call the 'logic of consequentialism' and the 'logic of appropriateness'. The French and Italian case studies have shown how these two logics have operated in a complementary, mutually supportive way to help overcome multiple domestic veto points to change. The result has been the diffusion and institutionalization of 'sound' money and finance beliefs. Domestic rules and procedures have been put in place to support a powerful new role for the EU in macroeconomic stabilization. Less clear is whether 'soft' economic policy coordination in growth and employment policies will have similar domestic policy effects. 'Benchmarking' is designed to foster cognitive learning about what is appropriate policy behaviour. But it lacks the direct domestic empowerment that comes from binding decisions backed by the threat of EU-level sanctions.

Policy convergence is one possible effect of EMU as Europeanization. But it can also produce divergence in terms of policy processes and outcomes. At best, it is leading to 'clustered' convergence (Kitschelt *et al.* 1999*b*; Börzel and Risse 2000; Iversen, Pontusson, and Soskice 2000). States like Denmark, Germany, the Netherlands, and Sweden are converging around a 'managed' capitalism model with respect to wage bargaining, macroeconomic management, and the organization of the welfare state. Britain offers a different pole of convergence around market capitalism.

Crouch and Rhodes stress how EMU leads to 'competitive' corporatism at the domestic level as employers and trade unions, perhaps with government, seek a substitute for devaluation by agreed measures to drive down domestic costs. EMU is important in increasing pressures for convergence, notably around notions of 'best' performance in economic stability, employment, and growth. Such a notion has been established in monetary policy: the German model has been exported to the European level rather than designing monetary policy by averaging out the different monetary policy regimes of member states. The Stability and Growth Pact has put in place a notion of 'best' policy in relation to long-term budget consolidation. But this leaves open questions about whether and how best to adapt fiscal policy to the economic cycle and about the 'best' design of automatic stabilizers in terms of the amount of stabilization that they deliver and whether it is targeted on the appropriate components of demand (Alesina *et al.* 2001). In employment and growth policies the notion of 'best' remains even more contested. This contest reflects the different political preferences embedded in domestic institutional arrangements for labour markets and welfare states. Hence, overall, EMU does not appear to be producing a convergence in domestic economic policy processes. In consequence, divergence or 'clustered' convergence is likely to figure as a major effect of EMU on domestic economic policies and policy outcomes for growth and employment.

The top-down bias of the Europeanization perspective is, however, only part of the story. The narrative is incomplete without stressing two important aspects of the 'bottom-up' process affecting euro economic governance and its potential as a force shaping domestic change:

(1) how the configuration of domestic institutions, processes, and policy legacies constrains the development of euro economic governance; and
(2) how the outcomes of EMU feed back into the processes of designing and adapting euro economic governance.

The constraints appear powerful. A crucial constraint is the deeply embedded historical association between taxation and structures of representative government. These structures are in place at the domestic level, where powerful entrenched interests work to maintain what is seen as a key constitutional requirement against erosion by any putative system of euro economic tax governance. To this constraint at the level of political legitimacy can be added the legacy of complex and diverse tax systems at the domestic level which make tax harmonization particularly difficult. EMU is, if anything, a trigger for increased tax competition as a means of creating national, regional, and local advantage especially by peripheral economies that seek to attract inward investment. Similar processes are observable in labour-market and welfare-state policies aimed at an optimal combination of competitiveness and social solidarity. What is judged 'optimal' differs with the legacy of very different labour-market regimes and welfare-state regimes within the EU. Again, EMU has sparked an intensification of domestic initiatives, notably in the form of a 'competitive' corporatism. A cursory examination of these constraints suggests that it is all too easy to overstate just how powerful a force euro economic governance can be in the development of domestic political systems compared with the 'path-shaping' and 'path-constraining' power of domestic institutional traditions.

A survey of how EMU outcomes feed back into euro economic governance suggests potential for cleavage and conflict based on differences of size, levels of economic development, and economic structure. In particular, asymmetric effects of common shocks, and potentially policy-induced shocks, are likely to test the limits of a system lacking common economic policy instruments like a fiscal transfer mechanism for stabilization. The result will be pressures for euro economic governance to develop greater flexibility in macroeconomic policy to accommodate these differences. Problems will also arise in relation to the implementation of the Stability and Growth Pact and to the multilateral surveillance procedure—Ireland is a test case. Just how these pressures and problems affect euro economic governance will depend on two factors: (1) the judiciousness of Community institutions in making policy recommendations that are economically sensible and politically enforceable, and (2) whether domestic elites possess the political capability and will to abide by loyalty to the overall requirements of the Euro-Zone.

What emerges is a more complex picture of the interactions between euro economic governance and domestic institutions and processes than the Europeanization literature accommodates. It suggests an ongoing process of patient and difficult negotiation. On the one hand Community institutions will need to respect domestic autonomy and variety in dealing with asymmetric shocks and the asymmetric effects of common shocks. On the other hand the maintenance of the credibility of the Euro-Zone requires a capacity to curb policy-induced shocks. This involves a process of coordination that is adapted to walking a tightrope between political legitimacy and market credibility

What more precisely can we learn from political science about the scope for developing euro economic governance? In the conclusions that follow a set of propositions about states and the euro will be developed.

Closeness of Fit: The Differential Impact of Euro Economic Governance and Cognitive Leadership

'Closeness of fit' or compatibility shapes the nature of the relationship between euro economic governance and domestic institutions and processes (see Börzel and Risse 2000; Héritier, Knill, and Mingers 1996). Quite simply, at a macro-institutional level some types of national political system are more compatible with the way in which euro economic governance is evolving than others. The degree of 'closeness of fit' shapes how domestic institutions and processes respond and whether a necessary condition—namely, 'misfit' —is in place to trigger change.

Four types of response can be identified (Radaelli 2000). Where there is compatibility, states are likely to *accommodate* euro economic governance and adapt smoothly to its requirements. They are not being challenged to modify their essential structures or behaviour. Examples are the Netherlands, Denmark, and Germany. Where such compatibility is lacking, adaptational pressures are created. Domestic elites face a choice, a choice that is likely to be affected by prevailing public sentiments towards European integration. They may choose *inertia* and resist taking decisions. Here the British Labour government might be seen as an example, though 'prepare and decide' might be presented as a form of decision. Over the longer term, however, inertia threatens to produce crisis in relations with the EU and might prove difficult to sustain. Another option is *retrenchment*. In this case policy becomes less European. This option is not currently being exercised, though it seems likely that it would be adopted by a British Conservative government.

The final and most interesting option is *transformation*. Here domestic elites are convinced of the pressing need for, and viability of, policy change in order to bring about a greater 'closeness of fit'. However, transformation requires more than just adaptational pressure from a 'misfit'. It requires a domestic leadership with the will and capacity to overcome potential veto points (Börzel and Risse 2000). Euro economic governance is more likely to empower domestic change agents where domestic rules and procedures offer them opportunities to act and where these agents can draw on a political culture that supports European integration. In such circumstances, as in Italy in the 1990s, elites can dramatize the euro as a domestic policy issue.

These four options are by no means mutually exclusive. For instance, France displays a complex combination of accommodation, transformation, and inertia. Germany appears the classic case of accommodation but has also displayed inertia in certain key areas like labour-market reforms. For Greece and Italy the option of transformation has been very much in evidence along with inertia.

'Closeness of fit' also has implications for cognitive leadership in developing euro economic governance. The higher the degree of institutional compatibility, the greater is the prospect for a state to play a leading role in the development of euro economic governance. Germany's domestic system of 'semi-sovereign' economic governance is most compatible with that at the European level. Hence Germany can be expected to play the leading role in how euro economic governance develops. It is likely to have support from states with similar domestic systems like the Netherlands and even, outside the Euro-Zone, Denmark. Such states have a greater potential to exercise cognitive leadership, defining the parameters within which euro economic governance develops. For German policy-makers these parameters are provided by the two principles of the informality of the Euro Group and the independence of the ECB.

A Paradox: Strengthening Society against the State, Strengthening the State against Society

Euro economic governance rests on a paradox. Its institutional embodiment of a 'sound' money and finance paradigm represents an attempt to enforce responsibility on states. Its rules and practices seek to protect society from a state that is prepared to debase the value of money in order to satisfy short-term political interests of political elites. Paradoxically, this aim requires the strengthening of the state against society. The paradox is resolved in the notion of 'self-binding' states that, through EMU, are imposing rules on themselves that discipline their own behaviour.

This combination of self-binding and strengthening the state against society puts euro economic governance within an established characteristic of European integration. Euro economic governance empowers some domestic actors—senior finance ministry officials, central bankers, monetary economists, governing parties—and disempowers others—parliaments, opposition parties, interest groups including trade unions. A powerful edifice of economic theory, notably the theory of the political business cycle and the credibility theory of inflation, has provided a form of technocratic legitimization for this process (Dyson 1994). The power of these theories derives from their compatibility with the principles underpinning the structural power of global financial markets and from the prediction of policy failure if they are not respected. Policy performance remains a key factor in the process of legitimizing euro economic governance.

At the same time euro economic governance has to come to grips with two overriding political realities. First, redistributions of domestic power are by their nature political. The very fact of their empowerment exposes what technocrats propose and do to public gaze and scrutiny. In the context of prevailing liberal democratic theories, issues of accountability and transparency are bound to be critical. They are tests that euro economic governance must meet if it is to prove compatible with democratic legitimization. At the same time these tests are contested (see Dyson 2000a: Ch. 7). However, in the early stages the requirements of consolidating euro economic governance by developing the confidence of the financial markets will take priority over the quality of democratic legitimization. Delivering good policy performance will come before explaining that performance.

Second, there are serious democratic risks of alienation from the political process if the core of economic policy is seen to be remote from, and unaffected by, processes of electoral competition. These risks are exacerbated when EMU is seen as essentially a neo-liberal project rolling back welfare states and employment rights and emasculating the flexibility of domestic politics in these policy areas. The legitimacy of euro economic governance depends, accordingly, on two interrelated processes for broadening political support: by reinforcement of, and acting as catalyst for, domestic institutional developments; and by developing the European institutional arena.

In the context of public sentiments across the EU that strongly support welfare-state provision and employment rights, the legitimacy of euro economic governance depends on developing the theme of social solidarity. This approach involves *supporting* existing trends to neo-corporatist forms of action in some states, like Germany, and acting as a *catalyst* for neo-corporatism in other states where it has been historically weaker or appears an alien device. It also requires the development of new forms of procedural coordination at the European level in relation to labour-market, welfare-state, and structural reform policies (see below).

Strengthening the democratic legitimacy of euro economic governance requires European institutional developments that open up opportunities for participation in economic policy dialogue beyond finance ministries and central banks to the key 'stakeholders' in civil society. The Cologne process based around the Macroeconomic Dialogue is a move in this direction, associating employer and trade-union representatives with information exchange about the development of the EU economy and about appropriate policy mix. Indeed, the term 'governance' draws attention away from the notion of intergovernmental arrangements for economic policy coordination to the role of key actors representing civil society in this process. It is particularly important to associate domestic actors who have strong backing from public sentiments but who may feel disadvantaged or threatened by the effects of EMU.

The Cologne process might be developed by neo-corporatist forms within euro economic governance aimed at achieving a basic procedural coordination in employment, wage, welfare-state, and structural reform policies. This development would not imply formal, ex-ante coordination of monetary policy with these other policies. After all, neo-corporatist action in the—asymmetrical—framework of central bank independence is long established in Germany, Austria, the Netherlands, and Denmark. In these states it has functioned to ensure that wage policy is made consistent with the requirements of macroeconomic stabilization (Iversen 1999).

It is, of course, possible, indeed likely, that this form of development in euro economic governance would increase the institutional incompatibility for Britain and make inertia and retrenchment more likely in this case. Britain does not, after all, fit into the more prevalent forms of 'managed', consensus-based capitalism to be found across the EU. In order not to make Britain's euro entry more difficult states like Germany may have a political interest in not pressing ahead with this kind of development in euro economic governance.

The Reactivation of Domestic Policies and Processes

EMU is stimulating a reactivation of structural reform, employment, and welfare-state policies and of neo-corporatist processes to promote greater competitiveness. The catalyst has been the loss of devaluation—which is available only to the Euro-Zone as a whole—as a policy tool. Wage restraint is an alternative tool which in terms of the practical management of political costs is seen in most states as more attractively handled by negotiated change than by imposed deflation or by imposed 'pure' market policies. The incentive for employers to enter into and sustain neo-corporatist arrangements has been their association with high productivity performance, notably in manufacturing. Employers have become more dependent for high-quality, flexible, and reliable production on skilled workers and social peace in the more competitive environment associated with globalization and the euro (Thelen 2000). For trade unions the incentive is influence over the terms of economic adjustment. Hence there is considerable institutional self-interest in sustaining forms of social partnership. These processes demonstrate a striking resilience in the face of globalization and the euro.

'Competitive' corporatism is not, however, synonymous with efforts to return to negotiated centralized wage bargaining. In Germany, Ireland, Italy, the Netherlands, and Spain it has been about more decentralized and flexible arrangements for containing unit labour costs through negotiating basic wage formulas and linking wage bargaining to labour-market flexibility and reduction of direct non-wage labour costs. The spread of 'competitive' corporatism in the 1990s, which can be traced back to the Dutch Wassenaar Accord of 1982, was by no means attributable solely or even primarily to EMU. But, as Radaelli shows in the Italian case, the pressures of qualifying for EMU were an important catalyst, affecting the timing and tempo of this domestic development. Problems of competitiveness within the Euro-Zone underlined the value of neo-corporatist arrangements, especially for states and firms committed to competing on the basis of product reliability and quality.

Euro economic governance takes place within a prevailing context both of convergence of domestic processes of managing economic adjustment around neo-corporatism and of adjustment in the ways in which 'coordinated' economies are managed (Iversen, Pontusson, and Soskice 2000). This convergence appears to present both threat and opportunity. On the one hand EMU is intensifying domestic activism in taxation, employment, welfare-state, and structural policies. The competitive nature of domestic neo-corporatism induces a new sense of collective danger from a 'race to the bottom', notably in taxation, wages, and welfare-state provision: the so-called Delaware effect. Thus the European Commission has attached itself to a policy narrative of 'harmful' tax competition to justify EU tax harmonization (Radaelli 1999). However, empirical evidence since the 1960s does not lend support to these fears with respect to the average tax rate, which has risen as rates in the periphery converge upwards, or welfare-state expenditure (Chapter 12; Baldwin and Krugman 2000). More positively, convergence of domestic processes of managing economic adjustment might make it easier to envisage—and achieve—a greater measure of coordination at the European level.

Institutional Diversity, Procedural Coordination, and Benchmarking

How euro economic governance develops will be shaped by the constraints imposed by domestic institutional diversity on the way in which labour markets, welfare states, tax regimes, and financial markets are managed. This diversity is documented in this volume, notably by Crouch on labour markets, Rhodes on welfare states, McKay on fiscal regimes, and Moran on financial markets. There may be strong and strengthening pressures for convergence from such factors as EMU, globalization, the 'new' economy, and demographic developments. But different institutional mechanisms militate against convergence of domestic policy contents and outcomes.

In this context of national institutional diversity, euro economic governance is more likely to develop by concentrating on the development of procedural coordination at the European level than by pursuing detailed coordination of the contents of labour-market, welfare-state, and fiscal policies. This form of coordination does not involve setting substantive targets for wages or employment policy spending. Procedural coordination focuses on setting a wage formula—which can lead to different targets and outcomes at sectoral and firm levels—or gaining agreement on how employment policy is to be organized. Methodologically, it is consistent with using benchmarking as a tool for promoting policy change and the 'open' coordination process.

This focus on procedural coordination stems from the recognition that economic policy-making will involve a mass of separate domestic bargains in such areas as wages, labour markets, welfare-state policy, and taxation, as well as within these areas. An example of such an approach would be development and monitoring of a basic wage norm of compensation for local inflation rates plus a component matching of local productivity growth. Applied to fiscal policy, it would involve agreed basic norms about national budget processes. These norms might include a firm commitment to numerical budget targets and to measures to strengthen the hand of the finance ministry as the representative of the collective interest in the efficiency of public finances (von Hagen and Harden 1994). There might be a norm relating to basic pension provision. More ambitiously still, each member states could be encouraged to establish an official poverty line as a way of focusing public debate and political action around the idea of a European social model (Dyson 2000a: 230).

Benchmarking is a potentially powerful tool of policy coordination. Its power is not primarily as a tool of convergence in domestic policy processes and outcomes. More importantly, it serves to alter forms of discourse: in short, the way in which policy change is argued at the domestic level (Dyson 2000a: 5). Benchmarking strengthens the technocratic element in policy discourse, redefining how domestic actors see economic policy problems by 'objectifying' the case for change. It has two major functions. First, benchmarking identifies how particular policy measures are linked to improved and superior performance in other contexts, for example part-time employment and short-term contracts to lower unemployment. In doing so it creates a case to answer for those resisting these measures. Second, and more important, benchmarking highlights the balance of political forces that support these policy measures in other states. Where these measures have been supported there by economic and ideological interests with which one identifies, it becomes much more difficult to deny a logic for change. An example is the way in which, in the 1990s, Danish and Dutch Social Democratic-led governments and trade unions embraced liberalization of labour markets and achieved significant reductions in unemployment. Faced with such knowledge generated by benchmarking it becomes more difficult for the German Social Democratic Party and trade unions to justify rejecting these policy reforms. Hence the power of benchmarking lies in changing forms of domestic political and policy argument. As far as convergence is concerned, it is likely to be more important within particular types of capitalism than across them. Benchmarking is more conducive to 'clustered' convergence, with British policies shaped more by US comparisons, while Germany, the Netherlands, Denmark, and Sweden refer much more to each other, and France seeks to retain a more *sui generis* character.

Benchmarking provides a tool for linking the strengthening of euro economic governance to the production and use of a technology of economic statistics that redefines how domestic actors define their interests and reform their identities. Following Michel Foucault, euro economic governance does not rest on the exercise of sovereign and disciplinary powers, with the accretion of coercive powers at the European level. In an ad hoc, experimental, and contingent way it generates new knowledge about the European economy and how it functions, recording that knowledge in economic statistics. In reinforcing the technocratic element in domestic debate, benchmarking is not about importing across the EU a particular set of economic policies that represent best practice. It is about questioning and challenging the basis for resisting change, for instance to labour markets, and in this way overcoming domestic veto points like trade union power. But, as the chapters in this book demonstrate, legitimizing domestic change still requires two essential elements: framing it as about 'saving' the domestic model; and the deliberate attempt to create a crisis consciousness to impress on reluctant elites and publics the importance of reforms.

The Time Dimension and the Coordination of Electoral Cycles

EMU highlights important and complex issues about the management of political time. Many of the difficulties in euro economic governance stem from differences in the temporal dimensions of EU and domestic politics. These difficulties take two forms. First, with the increased economic inter-dependence consequent on EMU domestic electoral cycles are likely to have stronger macroeconomic spillover effects on other states. This effect is especi-ally significant from the German electoral cycle (Sapir and Sekkat 2001). As German federal elections approach, fiscal policy tends to relax, according to the 'opportunistic' politics model; while electoral victory for the political left also leads to a more relaxed budgetary stance, according to the 'partisan' politics model. These 'opportunistic'—election-winning—and 'partisan'—ideological—models explain a similar impact of domestic elections on output growth in all states (Alesina and Roubini 1992; Alesina, Roubini, and Cohen 1997). EMU is likely to increase spillover effects, raising issues of coordination. Second, political considerations relating to the management of domestic electoral cycles make for difficulties in coordinating structural reforms, for instance to pensions or labour markets. Just as governments facing an election may prefer to defer reforms that might alienate public opinion, so other states may fear that by not acting together, for example over utilities reform, those that reform may be disadvantaged by relaxing market entry without reciprocity. Hence there are potentially high macroeconomic costs from a lack of electoral coordination inside Europe.

These 'bottom-up' effects from domestic political timing are comple-mented by 'top-down' effects from EMU on domestic political time manage-ment. As we noted earlier, EMU has been more important in affecting the timing, sequencing, and tempo of domestic policy change than in introduc-ing a new agenda separate from that produced by such factors as globalization, the 'new' economy, and demographics. This time effect operates on different levels and in different ways (Schedler and Santiso 1998: 6). Euro economic governance can define a specific timetable for domestic policy change by fixing specific 'time rules', for example, to meet a deadline for entry, to imple-ment a convergence programme. These rules can be used strategically to manipulate the timing, tempo, sequencing, and rhythm of domestic reforms. As in the Italian case, domestic policy reformers can use these time horizons as a resource to overcome opposition and push through 'overdue' changes, especially by dramatizing the urgency of reform and the consequences of not reforming. Not least, euro economic governance can generate a new form of 'time discourse' at the domestic level, affecting perceptions of what is judged to be 'good' or 'bad' timing, the 'right' or 'wrong' tempo of change, and the 'correct' or 'incorrect' sequencing of reforms.

Differences in time rules affect attitudes to the timing, tempo, sequencing, and rhythm of reforms. Precisely because the ECB is liberated from the time rules of electoral politics, it can afford to adopt a longer-term time horizon for its own monetary-policy decisions and to press the case for accelerating the pace of domestic structural reforms on member states. In contrast, the EU Council presidency thinks in terms of what practically can be done in a six-month period. It must operate within the complexity and constraints of domestic time rules relating to elections and, for treaty changes, referendums. These rules affect attitudes towards the time dimension of EU-level structural reforms. Domestic complications are added by different time rules for presidential and for Assembly elections in France—the subject of reform in 2001—and by the 16 State elections as well as the federal elections in any four-year period in Germany. The result is variability in the timing and tempo of domestic structural, labour-market, and welfare-state reforms, not least difficulty in synchronizing reforms across the EU. For instance, the Kohl government elected in 1994 deferred major domestic reforms till after the 1996 State elections. It then found itself in timing problems because it was in the last two years of the federal legislative period. Similarly, the Schröder government put labour-market reforms on the back burner once it found itself in the last two years of its first federal legislative period. This problem also affects fiscal consolidation, for instance in France—a key reason for bringing forward Assembly elections to 1997.

There is some evidence that domestic actors are beginning to problematize the issue of time rules in order to expedite reforms, notably in France. The problems of the federal system for economic reform in Germany, and especially of federalism's increasingly competitive nature, are increasingly recognized. But discussions about electoral coordination are defined in domestic rather than European terms. It is a discussion that the European Commission and ECB can welcome. But they can provide no more than background intellectual support: namely, that domestic time rules matter for the effectiveness of the system of euro economic governance and that greater coordination of these rules inside Europe would assist macroeconomic stabilization.

Is EMU a Neo-Liberal Project?

The most politically promising line of advance for developing euro economic governance is to concentrate on the negotiation of basic norms of procedural coordination. The challenge is to do so within the logic of a dominant model of implicit policy coordination, which rules out formal *ex ante* coordination of macroeconomic policy and requires prioritizing the independence of the ECB. Acceptance of this powerful constraint does not mean that EMU implies a logic of market capitalism and the triumph of neo-liberal ideology. On the contrary: political success in sustaining price stability has been a key precondition for effective social democratic economic policies in Europe (Notermans 2000a; also Iversen 1999). In this respect EMU could better secure social democratic values in Europe by locking in price stability and encouraging more decentralized and flexible forms of collaboration in wage setting and labour-market policy.

The three key variables in determining whether the outcome is more neo-liberal or more social democratic are: (1) the strategies of firms, (2) the organizational configuration of employer organizations and their interests, and (3) the way in which governments define the problems of globalization, the 'new' economy, and EMU. Neo-corporatist forms are most likely to be sustained when three conditions are present (see Iversen, Pontusson, and Soskice 2000). First, firms focus on product flexibility, quality, and reliability rather than competing on costs and the threat of exit. Second, officials in strong employer organizations define an interest in collaborating with trade unions in collective area-wide wage bargaining in order to shield plants from distributional conflicts and allow them to concentrate on production issues. Third, governments prioritize skill-upgrading through training and retraining over deregulated labour markets as the means to improved productivity and lower unit labour costs. These conditions are well-established within the Euro-Zone.

The Role of the European Commission

In developing a role as guardian of coordination through euro economic governance, the European Commission faces an old problem. This problem is whether to pursue an active or a passive interpretation of this role. In active mode the Commission would develop and articulate a particular policy narrative that would help direct and legitimize the development of euro economic governance. This narrative might take the form of pushing the politico-economic case, cast in suitably technocratic terms, for the increased importance of developing shared norms about how to deal more effectively with the risks associated with a more competitive European economy and with the breadth and speed of technological change. By identifying these risks and focusing political attention on how to manage them without creating extreme winners and losers, the Commission could mobilize political support across Europe, not least in the many applicant states. A key part of this narrative might be improvements to government social insurance, notably to deal with pensions. More problematic is the attempt to devise a policy narrative around 'a race to the bottom' in taxation and social spending (see Chapter 12).

In passive mode the Commission would present itself as basically a forum for policy transfer, diffusing policy knowledge and expediting learning about best policy practices in structural, taxation, labour market, and welfare-state reforms. In a less ambitious manner it would organize the process of exchange of knowledge, facilitating networking and policy learning by domestic actors. But it would draw back from being an intellectual driving force—in the Delors manner—in developing euro economic governance. The Commission would concentrate on organizing procedural coordination through benchmarking.

From 1996 the Commission sought to use a policy narrative of 'the discouragement of harmful tax competition' as an instrument for focusing action, if only by a more self-critical approach by states in developing tax proposals. By this means it aimed to redefine taxation as a potential aspect of euro economic governance. But this type of narrative had its limits in the lack of substantial evidence of a 'race to the bottom' in taxation or of a retreat of welfare states in the face of competitive deregulation. As we saw above, the thesis of globalization and EMU as capital mobility creating a neo-liberal logic is questionable in the face of other strategies of firms and policies of governments to deal with these phenomena.

There are also powerful reasons for expecting a passive interpretation of the Commission's role to prevail. First, after Jacques Delors—indeed earlier—the political position of the Commission weakened. This weakness was reinforced by the resignation of the Santer Commission in 1999. Second, its scope for cognitive leadership is tightly constrained by the model of implicit macroeconomic policy coordination in EMU. Furthermore, the Lisbon European Council of March 2000 consolidated the political basis for a passive role with the so-called 'open' or 'soft' coordination method for supply-side reforms. A greater measure of political support for, and self-confidence within, the Commission is arguably the key precondition for assuming a more activist role identity in euro economic governance. But with a dominant paradigm of implicit macroeconomic policy coordination it would not be sufficient.

In the absence of this political support and self-confidence, euro economic governance is likely to be more strongly conditioned by the 'policy pushing' role of the ECB and to remain fundamentally 'ECB-centric' (Dyson 2000a). Hence much depends on how the ECB develops its own role conception. This role conception may be inward-looking, focused on protecting its prerogatives, and inspired by a fusion of institutional self-interest with a 'depoliticized' ideology of Ordo-liberalism. Alternatively, it may evolve in a more outward-looking way, focusing more on the economic and political value of macroeconomic coordination at the European level both as a way of mobilizing support for its mission and as a means of integrating wage policy into macroeconomic stabilization. A key feature of the strategy of the European Commission must be to encourage a more enlightened conception of institutional self-interest on the part of the ECB as guardian of its role in promoting a consensual 'win-win' approach to euro economic governance. The Cologne process and the Lisbon 'follow-ups' should be important in facilitating this strategy.

Finally, the Commission can employ techniques that it has used to great effect in the past. These techniques relate to the management of the temporal dimension of euro economic governance. Central here is the activity of persuading member states to precommit to action by agreeing time horizons for domestic reforms. Once these horizons are in place, domestic reformers can use time as a resource to increase tempo and effect sequencing of change. More challengingly, because much more sensitive, the Commission might engineer a process of collective reflection about how a complexity of different domestic time rules, principally relating to elections, affects the processes of economic reform in Europe and aggravates economic policy coordination. Reform of domestic time rules to generate a more coordinated sequencing of elections inside the EU might do more to improve euro economic governance than any other proposal.

Conclusion: Convergence around Anglo-American Capitalism?

It is generally agreed that EMU is having profound effects on European states and that, as a consequence, they are becoming more alike. The truth is, as so often, more complex. Profound changes are linked to EMU. But these changes often preceded EMU and made it possible in the first place. EMU reinforced a commitment to an economic policy philosophy of 'sound' money and finance whose origins were outside this framework—notably in the growing structural power of global financial markets. It was, however, sometimes vitally important in influencing the timing and tempo of this philosophical conversion, for instance in Greece, Italy, and Spain. Meeting the requirements of the Stability and Growth Pact on fiscal discipline has had major practical implications for these states. European states have also

become more alike, most strikingly as a consequence of the institutionalization of 'sound' money and finance at the EU level. They share a commitment
to price stability and to upholding a stability culture in economic affairs. But
there is no evidence that EMU is functioning as a mechanism of convergence
around an Anglo-American model of neo-liberal market capitalism. The
processes of change under way in labour-market policy and welfare-state
policy are more accurately characterized as about the redefinition of the European social model. This model stresses 'security in change' and emphasizes
the state's role in assisting processes of economic adjustment by minimizing the risks that individuals must bear. EMU does not appear to be eroding
the European social model in favour of neo-liberalism.

Before returning to these questions, it is helpful to remind ourselves of the
complex and wide-ranging nature of the EMU process. The 'big' story of EMU
culminating in the Maastricht Treaty of 1993 was the institutionalization of
monetary union. But since 1995–7 the 'big' story has shifted to the two other
pillars. Their development keeps the so-called 'outs' still actively involved
in EMU as participants. As the EU faces up to asymmetric economic shocks,
the centre of political gravity will be fiscal coordination and economic policy
and employment policy coordination. As a variable promoting domestic policy
and political changes, EMU is itself changing.

In studying the effects of EMU, this book has also stressed a temporal
perspective. EMU did not begin on 1 January 1999, and the critical junctures
associated with it varied from state to state. But, however different the timing
and tempo of its effects in individual cases, the ECB was able to start its
institutional life in a setting of political culture that was highly supportive. In
particular, the major costs of monetary and fiscal convergence had already
been managed by individual states before 1999, notably in lost output and
employment during the 1990s. For these reasons, supplemented by the lengthy
period of careful technical preparations, the final stage of EMU was able to
start remarkably smoothly.

The complex and wide-ranging effects of EMU will take some time to fully
exhibit themselves. Most potently, states are under pressure to be politically
inventive. They have lost two policy instruments that have traditionally
been associated with their sovereignty over economic policy. Neither interest
rates nor devaluation are available to those states that have joined monetary
union. Hence they have to consider how to devise new instruments to
smooth processes of adjustment to economic shocks. This major change in
the policy environment has shifted attention to the institutions of collective
bargaining to promote greater flexibility at work and to reforms of the welfare
state and educational systems for the purpose of supporting employability.

The result has not been retreat and dismantlement of collective bargaining and welfare-state provision. A major development since the early 1990s has been the negotiation of 'social pacts' at the national level. On the whole— Britain is very much an exception—state elites have preferred to negotiate with employers and trade unions. This preference for negotiating economic change has in turn directed political attention to what can be learnt from states like Denmark and the Netherlands. These states gave up de facto their sovereignty over monetary policy in the early 1980s and have used negotiated change by consensus as the main instrument for promoting economic adjustment. For this reason, at the level of economic policy practices Denmark and the Netherlands have proved more important than Germany as a source of lesson-drawing in a post-EMU European Union.

In debate about EMU much attention has been given to the 'top-down' effects of EMU. EMU puts states under new pressures, and not just because their repertoire of policy instruments is radically changed and 'sound' money and finances more firmly institutionalized than before. Economic behaviour of consumers and of firms will also change. Firms will be operating in a single European market without the transaction costs of exchange-rate variability. They will also be offered new opportunities by the integrated financial markets spurred by a single currency, the first signs of which are to be seen in the explosive growth of the euro-bond market. The result will be major corporate restructuring to anticipate and cope with new pressures of competitiveness. These pressures will be enhanced by the effects of the new transparency of prices and costs that will come with a single currency. Consumers and firms, armed with this information, are likely to seek out new ways of reducing costs and paying lower prices. The result will be new political pressures on European governments, notably over taxation questions. The combination of Internet technology with a new price and cost transparency will empower European consumers to seek out advantages by shopping around the Euro-Zone. Hence 'top-down' effects will draw states into much closer webs of interdependence in managing tax and regulatory policies.

In practice, the Euro-Zone will exhibit a complex interplay between these 'top-down' effects and 'bottom-up' effects. Individual states 'construct' EMU in different ways. For the Danish elites the stress has been on the essential compatibility of EMU's 'sound' policy values with the welfare state. Their difficulty in persuading Danish public opinion to support EMU entry in the referendum of September 2000 had much to do with residual doubts about this argument. For the French elites EMU has been seen as a shield behind which to develop new forms of intervention in social and employment policies. For British elites EMU was a neo-liberal project for making welfare states and labour markets more compatible with the Anglo-American values of market capitalism. Behind these different constructions of EMU, the influence of contrasting national economic structures was discernible. British views were strongly conditioned by the structural power of the financial institutions of the City. In Germany, the Netherlands, and Denmark the institutional power of employer and trade-union officials was more important in shaping attitudes. French views displayed the continuing role and self-interests of the *grand corps*. There was no sign of national traditions being torn up by the roots. EMU was being framed in different ways at domestic level to make it credible, comprehensible, and legitimate.

'Convergence' is a term that has been applied too readily to characterize what is at work in the relationship between EMU and European states. It is more helpful to discriminate between pressures for convergence and other aspects. There are indeed powerful pressures for convergence, from financial markets as well as from EMU. Their effect is seen most clearly in the political ascendancy of ideas of 'sound' money and finance and the relatively easy way in which the ECB has been able to bed down as a new and powerful institution. But convergence is in other respects much more limited. There is some convergence of domestic policy processes. Finance ministries have been empowered by EMU to extend the scope and grip of their influence on domestic policies. They must, however, deal with powerful entrenched policy communities, for instance in welfare-state institutions that often involve traditions of self-management and also in often very autonomous systems of collective bargaining.

It is also difficult to identify convergence of policies and of policy outputs around a neo-liberal, market capitalism model. This type of convergence is most apparent in financial market regulation where a shift in the direction of the Anglo-American model is discernible. The combination of the 'sound' money and finance values of EMU with an ascendant Anglo-American model of financial markets can be seen as the most powerful catalyst for a convergence around neo-liberalism. EMU then emerges as part of a process by which the model of shareholder value comes to reign supreme across Europe and efforts to manage capitalism, whether of the Schröder or Jospin type, come unstitched.

This conclusion ignores three aspects of EMU. First, EMU provides relatively small European states with a more powerful shield against currency volatility than they have known since the collapse of the Bretton Woods system. Second, in so far as EMU stimulates a more competitive environment, the effects are not simply or solely felt in a greater regulatory and tax rivalry to drive down business costs. They are also discernible in a higher premium on capacity to deliver product quality, reliability, and flexibility. This capacity means a heightened dependency of businesses on skilled employees. Hence EMU is compatible with more rather than less attention to the social dimension. Finally, the achievement of a 'sound' monetary and fiscal position through EMU is perfectly compatible with the continuation of high welfare-state spending and more active labour-market policies. Over the longer term the combination of security with change may prove to be a more sustainable and less costly model for coping with the vagaries and volatility of competitive markets than opponents of the European social model have recognized.

References

Abromeit, H. (1998). *Legitimising Politics in a Non State Polity*. New York: Berghahn Books.

Aeschimann, E. and Riché, P. (1996). *La guerre de sept ans: histoire secrète du franc fort, 1989–1996*. Paris: Calmann-Lévy.

Alber, J. and Standing, G. (2000). 'Social Dumping, Catch-up or Convergence? Europe in a Comparative Global Context'. *Journal of European Social Policy*, 10/2: 99–119.

Alesina, A. and Roubini, N. (1992). 'Political Cycles in OECD Economies'. *Review of Economic Studies*, 59: 663–88.

—— and Cohen, G. (1997). *Political Cycles and the Macroeconomy*. Cambridge, MA: MIT Press.

——, Blanchard, O., Gali, J., Giavazzi, F., and Uhlig, H. (2001). *Defining a Macroeconomic Framework for the Euro Area* (Monitoring the European Central Bank 3). London: Centre for Economic Policy Research (30 March).

Algemeen Dagblad (1996). 'Duisenberg: Geen twijfel aan invoering Europese munt', 26 January.

Allsopp, C. and Vines, D. (1996). 'Fiscal Policy and EMU'. *National Institute Economic Review*, 158: 91–107.

Alphandéry, E. (2000). *La réforme obligée sous le soleil de l'Euro*. Paris: Grasset.

Andersen, B. N. (2000). 'Danmark og Euroen'. Speech to the British Import Union, 18 January. http://www.nationalbanken.dk/nb/nb.nsf/alldocs/Ftaler

Andersen, S. (1994). *Hoffmeyer*. Copenhagen: Børsens Forlag.

Andersen, T., Haldrup, N., and Sørensen, J. (2000). 'EU Labour Markets: Effects of Greater Product Market Integration'. *Economic Policy*, 15/30: 107–33.

Arestis, P. and Sawyer, M. (1999). *The Economy and Monetary Union: Current and Future Prospects* (Working Paper No. 288). Annandale-on-Hudson, NY: Jerome Levy Economics Institute, Bard College.

Arthuis, J. (1998). *Dans les coulisses de Bercy, le cinquième pouvoir*. Paris: Albin Michel.

Artis, M. (1992). 'The Maastricht Road to Monetary Union'. *Journal of Common Market Studies*, 33: 299–309.

—— and Buti, M. (2000). ' "Close-to-Balance or in Surplus": A Policy-Maker's Guide to the Implementation of the Stability and Growth Pact'. *Journal of Common Market Studies*, 38: 563–91.

—— and Zhang, W. (1999). 'Further Evidence on the International Business Cycle and the ERM: Is there a European Business Cycle?'. *Oxford Economic Papers*, 51: 120–32.

—— and Winkler, B. (1998). 'The Stability Pact: Safeguarding the Credibility of the European Central Bank'. *National Institute Economic Review*, 163: 87–98.

Ayral, M. (1975). 'Essai de classification des groupes et comités'. *Revue du Marché Commun*, 18: 330–42.

Baimbridge, M., Burkitt, B., and Whyman, P. (eds) (2000). *The Impact of the Euro: Debating Britain's Future*. London: Macmillan.

Baker, A. (1999). 'Nébuleuse and the "Internationalization of the State" in the UK? The Case of HM Treasury and the Bank of England'. *Review of International Political Economy*, 6: 79–100.

Baker, D., Gamble, A., and Ludlam, S. (1994). 'The Parliamentary Siege of Maastricht: Conservative Divisions and British Ratification'. *Parliamentary Affairs*, 47/1: 37–60.

—— —— and Seawright, D. (1998). *Mapping Changes in British Parliamentarians' Attitudes to European Integration* (ESRC R000222397). Swindon: Economic and Social Research Council.

Bakker, A. F. P. (1996). *The Liberalization of Capital Movements in Europe: The Monetary Committee and Financial Integration 1958–1994*. Dordrecht: Kluwer Academic Publishers.

Balassone, F. and D. Franco (1999). 'Fiscal Federalism and the Stability and Growth Pact: A Difficult Union'. Paper presented to the conference on 'I controlli di gesione delle Amministrazioni Pubbliche', Perugia, 2–3 December.

Baldwin, R. and Krugman, P. (2000). *Agglomeration, Integration and Tax Harmonization* (CEPR Discussion Paper No. 2630). London: Centre for Economic Policy Research, November.

Balleix-Banerjee, C. (1999). *La France et la Banque Centrale Européenne*. Paris: PUF.

Banca d'Italia (various years). *Relazione Generale*. Rome: Bank of Italy.

Banchoff, T. (1999). 'The Force of an Idea: Globalization and the German Social Market Economy'. Paper presented to the annual meeting of the American Political Science Association, Atlanta, September.

Bank for International Settlements (BIS) (2000). *70th Annual Report*. Basel: BIS (5 June).

Barnard, C. (2000). 'Social Dumping and the Race to the Bottom: Some Lessons for the European Union from Delaware?'. *European Law Review*, 25: 57–78.

Basinger, S. and Hallerberg, M. (2000). 'Remodeling the Competition for Capital: How Domestic Politics Erases the Race-to-the-Bottom'. Paper presented at the Annual Meeting of the American Political Science Association, Washington DC, 31 August–3 September.

Bateson, G. (1973). *Steps to an Ecology of Mind*. St Albans: Paladin.

Baumann, H. and Lang, H. (2000). 'Austrian Report', in J.-V. Louis (ed.), *Euro Spectator: Implementing the Euro. National Reports: Austrian Report/Belgian Report* (EUI Working Paper LAW No. 2000/5). San Domenico: European University Institute.

Bayer, K. (1999). 'Perspectives on Future Policy Co-ordination under EMU'. *Empirica*, 26: 271–9.

Bayoumi, T. and Eichengreen, B. (1992). 'Shocking Aspects of European Monetary Integration', in F. Torres and F. Giavazzi (eds), *Adjustment and Growth in the European Monetary Union*. Cambridge: Cambridge University Press.

—— and Masson, P. R. (1995). 'Fiscal Flows in the United States and Canada: Lessons for Monetary Union in Europe'. *European Economic Review*, 39: 253–74.

——, Eichengreen, B. and von Hagen, J. (1997). 'European Monetary Unification'. *Open Economies Review*, 8: 71–91.

Beetham, D. and Lord, C. (1998). *Legitimacy and the European Union*. London: Longman.

Begg, D., Wyplosz, C., Von Hagen, J., and Zimmermann, K. (eds) (1998). *EMU: Prospects And Challenges For The Euro*. Oxford: Blackwells.

Begg, I. and Green, D. (1996). 'Banking Supervision in Europe and Economic and Monetary Union'. *Journal of European Public Policy*, 3: 381–401.

Bentivogli, C. and Pagano, P. (1999). 'Regional Disparities and Labour Mobility: the Euro-11 versus the USA'. *Labour*, 13: 737–60.

Berger, S. and Dore, R. (1996). *National Diversity and Global Capitalism*. Ithaca, NY: Cornell University Press.

Berlingske Tidende (2000). 28 July.

Biangi, M. (1998). 'The Implementation of the Amsterdam Treaty with Regard to Employment: Co-ordination or Convergence?'. *International Journal of Comparative Labour Law and Industrial Relations*, 14: 325–36.

Bini Smaghi, L. and Casini, C. (2000). 'Monetary and Fiscal Policy Co-operation: Institutions and Procedures in EMU'. *Journal of Common Market Studies*, 38: 375–91.

Bird, R. (1986). *Federal Finance in Comparative Perspective*. Toronto: Canadian Tax Foundation.

Blair, T. and Schröder, G. (1999). 'The Third Way/Die Neue Mitte', in B. Hombach, *The Politics of the New Centre*. Cambridge: Polity.

Blanchard, O. and Muet, P. (1993). 'Competitiveness through Disinflation: An Assessment of the French Macroeconomic Strategy'. *Economic Policy*, 16: 11–56.

Blom-Hansen, J. (2000). 'Still Corporatism in Scandinavia? A Survey of Recent Empirical Findings'. *Scandinavian Political Studies*, 23/2: 157–81.

Boeri, T. (2000). *Social Europe: Dramatic Visions and Real Complexity* (CEPR Discussion Paper No. 2371). London: Centre for Economic Policy Research.

Boissonnat, J. (1998). *La révolution de 1999. L'Europe avec l'Euro*. Paris: Sand.

Børsen (2000). 'Bodil Nyboe takes stand on EMU-membership', 19 January.

Börzel, T. (1999). 'Towards Convergence in Europe? Institutional Adaptation to Europeanization in Germany and Spain'. *Journal of Common Market Studies*, 39: 573–96.

—— and Risse, T. (2000). *When Europe Hits Home: Europeanization and Domestic Change* (EUI Working Paper RSC No. 2000/56). San Domenico: European University Institute.

Boyer, R. (1993). 'D'une série de National Labour Standards à un European Monetary Standard?'. *Recherches Économiques de Louvain*, 59/1/2: 119–53.

—— (1998). 'An Essay on the Political and Institutional Deficits of the Euro: The Unanticipated Fallout of the European Monetary Union'. *Couverture Orange CEPREMAP*. No. 9813. Paris, August.

—— (1999). *Le gouvernement économique de la zone euro*. Paris: Commissariat Général du Plan.

—— (2000). 'The Unanticipated Fallout of European Monetary Union: The Political and Institutional Deficits of the Euro', in C. Crouch (ed.), *After the Euro: Shaping Institutions for Governance in the Wake of European Monetary Union*. Oxford: Oxford University Press.

Braithwaite, J. and Drahos, P. (2000). *Global Business Regulation*. Cambridge: Cambridge University Press.

Braun, M. (1996). 'The Confederated Trade Unions and the Dini Government: The Grand Return to Neo-Corporatism?', in M. Caciagli and D. Kertzer (eds), *Italian Politics: The Stalled Transition*. Boulder, CO: Westview Press.

Brouwer, H. (1999). 'Toekomstige Samenwerking in de Europese Unie', in *De Weg naar de Europese Unie*. Amsterdam: Duitsland Instituut.

Brunetta, R. (ed.) (1992). *Retribuzione, Costo del Lavoro, Livelli della Contrattazione*. Milan: ETAS Libri.

Buiter, W. (1999). 'Alice in Euroland'. *Journal of Common Market Studies*, 37: 181–210.

Buksti, J. and Lund, T. (1999). 'Another Currency Union'. *Berlingske Tidende*, 15 January.

Bull, M. and M. Rhodes (eds) (1997). *Crisis and Transition in Italian Politics*. London: Frank Cass.

Bulmer, S. (1994). 'The Governance of the European Union, A New Institutional Approach'. *Journal of Public Policy*, 4: 351–80.

Bundesministerium der Finanzen (2000). *Arbeitsplätze Schaffen–Zukunftsfähigkeit Gewinnen. Jahreswirtschaftsbericht 2000 der Bundesregierung*. Berlin.

Bundesministerium für Wirtschaft (1997). *Reformen für Beschäftigung. Jahreswirtschaftsbericht der Bundesregierung*. Bonn.

—— (1998). *Den Aufschwung Voranbringen–Arbeitsplätze Schaffen. Jahreswirtschaftsbericht 1998 der Bundesregierung*. Bonn.

Busch, K. (1996). 'The European Economic and Monetary Union and the Dangers of Wage and Social Dumping', in O. Jacoby (*sic*) and P. Pochet (eds), *A Common Currency Area: A Fragmented Area for Wages?* Düsseldorf: Hans Böckler Stiftung.

Buti, M., Franco, D., and Onenga, H. (1998). 'Fiscal Discipline and Flexibility in EMU: The Implementation of the Stability and Growth Pact'. *Oxford Review of Economic Policy*, 14/3: 81–97.

—— and Sapir, A. (1998). *Economic Policy in EMU*. Oxford: Oxford University Press.

Butler, D. and Kitzinger, U. (1975). *The 1975 Referendum*. London: Macmillan.

Calmfors, L. and Driffill, D. (1988). 'Bargaining Structure, Corporatism and Macro-Economic Performance'. *Economic Policy*, 6: 14–61.

Cambadélis, J.-C. (1999). *L'avenir de la gauche plurielle*. Paris: Plon.

Camera dei Deputati (1999). *Il Mezzogiorno nella politica generale del dopo-Euro: Rapporto Amato*. Rome: Servizio studi della Camera, Osservatorio sulla legislazione (16 February).

Cameron, D. R. (1995). 'Transnational Relations and the Development of European Economic and Monetary Union', in T. Risse-Kappen (ed.), *Bringing Transnational Relations Back In*. Cambridge: Cambridge University Press.

Campbell, J. (1998). 'Institutional Analysis and the Role of Ideas in Political Economy'. *Theory and Society*, 27: 377–409.

Capano, G. (2000). 'Le politiche amministrative: dall'improbabile riforma alla riforma permanente?', in G. Di Palma, S. Fabbrini, and G. Freddi (eds), *Condannata al successo? L'Italia nell'Europa integrata*. Bologna: Il Mulino.

CEPS (Centre for European Policy Studies) (2000). *The Future of Tax Policy in the EU: From 'Harmful' Tax Competition to EU Corporate Tax Reform*. Brussels: CEPS.

Cerny, P. (1997). 'Paradoxes of the Competition State: The Dynamics of Political Globalization'. *Government and Opposition*, 32: 251–74.

Christensen, J. and Ersbøll, N. (2000). 'The Referendum Institution Up for Debate'. *Politiken*, 31 January.

Christiansen, P. and Rommertvedt, H. (1999). 'From Corporatism to Lobbyism? Parliaments, Executives, and Organized Interests in Denmark and Norway'. *Scandinavian Political Studies*, 22/3: 195–220.

—— and Sidenius, N. (1995). 'Korporatisme på retur?'. *Politica*, 27: 436–49.

—— (1999). 'Venner for altid? Samspillet mellem centraladministration og interesseorganisationer', in J. Blom-Hansen and C. Daubjerg (eds), *Magtens organisering. Stat og interesseorganisationer i Danmark*. Aarhus: Forlaget Systime.

Ciampi, C. (1996). *Un metodo per governare*. Bologna: Il Mulino.

Ciavarini Azzi, G. (1985). 'Les experts nationaux, Chevaux de Troie ou partenaires indispensables?', in J. Jamar and W. Wessels (eds), *Community Bureaucracy at the Crossroads*. Bruges: De Tempel.

Coates, D. (2000). *Models of Capitalism*. Cambridge: Polity.

Cobham, D. and Zis, G. (eds) (1999). *From EMS to EMU: 1979 to 1999 and Beyond*. London: Macmillan.

Cohen, B. (1993). 'The Triad and the Unholy Trinity: Lessons for the Pacific Rim', in R. Higgott, R. Leaver, and J. Ravenhill (eds), *Pacific Economic Relations in the 1990s: Co-operation or Conflict*. Sydney: Allen and Unwin.

—— (1996). 'Phoenix Rising: The Resurrection of Global Finance'. *World Politics*, 48: 268–96.

—— (1998). *The Geography of Money*. Ithaca, NY: Cornell University Press.

Cole, A. and Drake, H. (2000). 'The Europeanization of the French Polity: Continuity, Change and Adaptation'. *Journal of European Public Policy*, 7: 26–43.

Collignon, S. (1999). 'Unemployment, Wage Developments and the Economic Policy Mix in Europe'. *Empirica*, 26: 259–69.

Collin, F. (1981). *Grondlijnen voor een monetair beleid*. Lannoo/Tielt/Bussum: Universitaire Pers Leuven.

Commissariat Général du Plan (1999). *Le gouvernement économique de la zone euro* (Rapport du groupe de réflexion présidé par Robert Boyer). Paris: La Documentation française.

Conseil d'analyse économique (1998). *Coordination européenne des politiques économiques* (Report to the Council for Economic Analysis, Prime Minister's Office). Paris: La Documentation française.

Corbey, D. (1993). *Stilstand is Vooruitgang. De Dialectiek van het Europese Integratieproces*. Assen/Maastricht: Van Gorcum.

Corriere della Sera (1995a). 30 September.

—— (1995b). 9 November.

—— (1996a). 1 May.

—— (1996b). 28 June.

—— (1996c). 5 July.

—— (1996d). 26 August.

—— (1996e). 29 October.

—— (1996f). 21 November.

Corry, D. (1996). *Restating the Case for EMU: Reflections from the Left*. London: Institute for Public Policy Research.

Cottrell, A. (2001). 'Brussels Spouts Ideas on EMU Reform'. *Global Economic and Strategy Research*. London: UBS Warburg (21 February).

Council of the EU (1997a). 'Council Regulation (EC) No. 1466/97 of 7 July 1997 on the Strengthening of the Surveillance of Budgetary Positions and the Surveillance and Coordination of Economic Policies'. *Official Journal*, L 209, 2 August: 1–5.

—— (1997b). 'Council Regulation (EC) No. 1467/97 of 7 July 1997 on Speeding up and Clarifying the Implementation of the Excessive Deficit Procedure'. *Official Journal*, L 209, 2 August: 6–11.

Council of the European Union (1999). 'Economic Policy Co-ordination: Review of Instruments and Experience in Stage 3 of EMU. Report by the ECOFIN Council to the European Council in Helsinki'. Press Release: Brussels, 29 November, Nr 13123/1/99.

—— (2000). 'Council Recommendation of 19 June 2000 on the Broad Guidelines of the Economic Policies of the Member States and the Community'. *Official Journal*, L 210, 21 August 1–40.

—— (2001). '2329th Council meeting–ECOFIN'. Press Release: Brussels, 12 February, No. 5696/01.

Cowles, M. G., Caporaso, J., and Risse, T. (2001). *Transforming Europe*. Ithaca: Cornell University Press.

Crockett, A. (2001). 'Monetary Policy and Financial Stability'. Speech by Andrew Crockett, General Manager, Bank for International Settlements, 4th Annual Hong Kong Monetary Authority Distinguished Lecture, Hong Kong, 13 February, in *BIS Review*, 13/2001, February, available at http://www.bis.org/review/r010216b.pdf.

Crouch, C. (1993). *Industrial Relations and European State Traditions*. Oxford: Oxford University Press.

—— (1994). 'Incomes Policies, Institutions and Markets: An Overview of Recent Developments', in R. Dore, R. Boyer and Z. Mars (eds), *The Return to Incomes Policy*. London: Pinter.

—— (1999a). *Social Change in Western Europe*. Oxford: Oxford University Press.

—— (1999b). 'Employment, Industrial Relations and Social Policy: New Life in an Old Connection'. *Social Policy and Administration*, 33: 437–57.

—— (2000a). 'National Wage Determination and European Monetary Union', in C. Crouch (ed.), *After the Euro: Shaping Institutions for Governance in the Wake of European Monetary Union*. Oxford: Oxford University Press.

—— (ed.) (2000b). *After the Euro: Shaping Institutions for Governance in the Wake of European Monetary Union*. Oxford: Oxford University Press.

—— and Streeck, W. (eds) (1997). *Political Economy of Modern Capitalism: Mapping Convergence and Diversity*. London: Sage.

Currie, D. (1997). *The Pros and Cons of EMU*. London: HM Treasury.

Dahl, R. (1964). *A Preface to Democratic Theory*. Chicago: University of Chicago Press.

Danmarks Nationalbank (1986). *Oversigt over informationsmateriale fra Nationalbanken*. Copenhagen: Danmarks Nationalbank.

Dastoli, P. (1996). 'The Stone Guest: Italy on the Threshold of European Monetary Union', in M. Caciagli and D. Kertzer (eds), *Italian Politics: The Stalled Transition*. Boulder, CO: Westview.

Davis, P. E. (1997). *Can Pensions Systems Cope? Population Ageing and Retirement Income Provision in the European Union*. London: The Royal Institute of International Affairs.

de Beus, J. (1999). 'Eternal Well-Being or How the Dutch Left Bids the Twentieth-Century Farewell' (unpublished manuscript). Amsterdam: University of Amsterdam.

—— (2000a). 'Quasi-National European Identity and European Democracy'. *Law and Philosophy*, 20/1: 1–29.

—— (2000b). 'Are Third Way Social Democrats Friends or Enemies of European Integration?—A Tocquevillean Tale on the Politics of Consensus'. Paper presented at the mini-workshop 'Social Democracy and Economic Management: Can the Primacy of the Political Be Regained?', Florence, European University Institute, 31 May.

—— (2001). 'The Netherlands Case', in G. Ross and A. Martin (eds), *EMU and the European Model of Society*. Oslo: ARENA.

Degni, M. and G. Salvemini (2000). 'L'evoluzione del processo di bilancio dalla legge 468/1978 alla recente riforma'. Paper presented to the 18th national conference on public accounting. Teramo, Italy: 12–13 May.

De Grauwe, P. (1994). *The Economics of Monetary Integration*. Oxford: Oxford University Press.

—— (2000a). 'Discussion', in A. Hallet, M. Hutchison, and E. Jensen (eds), *Fiscal Aspects of European Monetary Integration*. Cambridge: Cambridge University Press.

—— (2000b). *The Economics of Monetary Integration*. Oxford: Oxford University Press.

—— and Skudelny, F. (1999). *Social Conflict and Growth in Euroland* (CEPR Discussion Paper, No. 2186). London: Centre for Economic Policy Research.

—— Knoestler, A., Kolodziejak, A., Muijzers A., van der Ploeg, F., and Rijnvos, C. J. (1989). *De Europese Monetaire Integratie: Vier Visies*. Wetenschappelijke Raad voor het Regeringsbeleid. The Hague: SDU.

De Haan, J. and Eijffinger, C. W. (2000). 'The Democratic Accountability of the European Central Bank: A Comment on Two Fairy Tales'. *Journal of Common Market Studies*, 38: 393–407.

Dehejia, V. and Genschel, E. (1999). 'Tax Competition in the European Union'. *Politics and Society*, 27: 403–30.

Delors Report (1989). *Report on Economic and Monetary Union in the European Community*. (Committee for the Study of Economic and Monetary Union). Luxembourg: Office for Official Publications of the EC (April).

De Nederlandsche Bank (1973). *Report for the Year 1972*. Amsterdam: De Nederlandsche Bank.

—— (1974). *Report for the Year 1973*. Amsterdam: De Nederlandsche Bank.

Desportes, G. and Mauduit, L. (1999). *La Gauche imaginaire et le nouveau capitalisme*. Paris: Grasset.

Deutsche Bundesbank (1990). 'Eine Stellungnahme zur Errichtung einer Wirtschafts- und Währungsunion in Europa'. *Monatsberichte der deutschen Bundesbank*, 42/ October: 41–5.

—— (2001). 'Recent Institutional Developments in Economic and Monetary Co-operation'. *Monthly Report*, January: 15–33.

de Villé, P. (1996). 'Collective Bargaining, Wage Policies and European Monetary Integration', in O. Jacoby (sic) and P. Pochet (eds), *A Common Currency Area: A Fragmented Area for Wages?* Düsseldorf: Hans Böckler Stiftung.

De Volkskrant (1996). 'Wijffels wil Italië buiten EMU houden', 7 December.

—— (1997). 'Overeenstemming tussen zeventig economen ruikt naar onraad', 15 February.

DiMaggio, P. and Powell, W. (eds) (1991). *The New Institutionalism in Organisation Analysis*. Chicago: The University of Chicago Press.

Dobuzinskis, L. (1992). 'Modernist and Postmodernist Metaphors of the Policy Process: Control and Stability vs. Chaos and Reflective Understanding'. *Policy Sciences*, 25: 355–80.

DØR (1985). *Dansk Økonomi*. Copenhagen: Det Økonomiske Råds Formandskab (September).

—— (1994). *Dansk Økonomi*. Copenhagen: Det Økonomiske Råds Formandskab (December).

Dore, R., Boyer, R., and Mars, Z. (eds) (1994). *The Return to Incomes Policy*. London: Pinter.

Dornbusch, R., Favero, C., and Giavazzi, F. (1998). 'A Red Letter Day?' (Discussion Paper No. 1804). London: Centre for Economic Policy Research.

Dubbins, S. (2001). 'The Growth of European Industrial Relations' (Ph.D. thesis). Florence: European University Institute.

Duckenfield, M. (1999). 'The *Goldkrieg*: Revaluing the Bundesbank's Reserves and the Politics of EMU'. *German Politics*, 8/1: 106–30.

Due, J., Madsen, J., and Strøby, J. (1994). *The Survival of the Danish Model*. Copenhagen: DJØF.

Dyson, K. (ed.) (1992). *The Politics of German Regulation*. Aldershot: Dartmouth.

—— (1994). *Elusive Union: The Process of Economic and Monetary Union in Europe*. London and New York: Longman.

—— (1997). 'La France, l'union économique et monétaire et la construction européenne: Renforcer l'exécutif, transformer l'État'. *Politiques et Management Public*, 15/3: 57–77.

—— (1999a). 'German Economic Policy after 50 Years', in P. Merkl (ed.), *The Federal Republic of Germany at 50*. London: Macmillan.

—— (1999b). 'The Franco-German Relationship and Economic and Monetary Union'. *West European Politics*, 22: 25–44.

—— (1999c). 'Economic and Monetary Union in Europe: A Transformation of Governance', in B. Kohler-Koch and R. Eising (eds), *The Transformation of Governance in the European Union*. London and New York: Routledge.

—— (1999d). 'EMU, Political Discourse and the Fifth French Republic: Historical Institutionalism, Path Dependency and "Craftsmen" of Discourse'. *Modern and Contemporary France*, 7/2: 179–96.

—— (2000a). *The Politics of the Euro-Zone: Stability or Breakdown?* Oxford: Oxford University Press.

—— (2000b). 'EMU as Europeanization: Convergence, Diversity and Contingency'. *Journal of Common Market Studies*, 38: 645–66.

—— (2000c). 'Europeanization, Whitehall Culture and the Treasury as Institutional Veto Player: A Constructivist Approach to Economic and Monetary Union'. *Public Administration*, 78: 897–914.

—— (2001). 'The German Model Revisited: From Schmidt to Schröder'. *German Politics*, 10/2: 135–54.

—— and Featherstone, K. (1999). *The Road to Maastricht: Negotiating Economic and Monetary Union*. Oxford: Oxford University Press.

—— and Michaelopoulos, G. (1994). *Reinventing the French State: Construction européenne and the Development of French Policies on EMU*. Bradford: Department of European Studies, European Briefing Unit, University of Bradford:.

—— (1995). 'Strapped to the Mast: EC Central Bankers Between Global Financial Markets and Regional Integration'. *Journal of European Public Policy*, 2: 465–87.

—— — (1998). 'Strapped to the Mast: EU Central Bankers between Global Financial Markets and Regional Integration', in W. Coleman and G. Underhill (eds), *Regionalism and Global Economic Integration: Europe, Asia and the Americas*. London: Routledge.

Ebbinghaus, B. and Hassel, A. (1999). *Striking Deals: Concertation in the Reform of Continental European Welfare States* (MPIfG Discussion Paper 99/3). Cologne: Max-Planck-Institut für Gesellschaftsforschung.

ECB (European Central Bank) (2000a). 'The Two Pillars of the ECB's Monetary Policy Strategy'. *European Central Bank Monthly Bulletin*, 11: 37–48.

—— (2000b). 'The ECB Announces Joint Intervention in Exchange Markets' (ECB Press Release). 22 September.

—— (2000c). 'ECB Confirms Intervention in Exchange Markets' (ECB Press Release). 3 November.

—— (2000d). 'Introductory Statement' (ECB Press Conference, Monetary Policy Decisions). Frankfurt, 5 October.

—— (2001a). 'Transcript of Questions and Answers/WF Duisenberg and P Noyer' (ECB Press Conference, Monetary Policy Decisions). Frankfurt, 1 February.

—— (2001b). 'The Role of National Central Banks in Prudential Supervision'. Paper, 16 February.

Economist (2000). 2 September: 129.

Economist Intelligence Unit (1992–2000). *Country Report, France*. London: EIU.

Eichengreen, B. (1994). 'Fiscal Policy and EMU', in B. Eichengreen, J. Frieden, and J. von Hagen (eds), *The Political Economy of European Monetary Integration*. Berlin: Springer.

—— (1997). *European Monetary Unification: Theory, Practice, and Analysis*. Cambridge, MA and London: MIT Press.

—— and Wyplosz, C. (1998). 'The Stability Pact: More Than a Minor Nuisance?', in D. Begg, J. von Hagen, C. Wyplosz, and K. F. Zimmerman (eds), *EMU: Prospects and Challenges for the Euro*. Oxford: Blackwell.

Eijffinger, S. and de Haan, J. (2000). *European Monetary and Fiscal Policy*. Oxford: Oxford University Press.

Epstein, G. (1992). 'Political Economy and Comparative Central Banking'. *Review of Radical Political Economics*, 24/1: 1–30.

Epstein, G. and Schor, J. (1989). 'Divorce of the Bank of Italy and the Treasury', in P. Lange and M. Regini (eds), *State, Market and Social Regulation: New Perspectives on Italy*. Cambridge: Cambridge University Press.

Erne, R. (forthcoming). 'Organized Labour: An Actor of European Union Democratization?' (Ph.D thesis). Florence: European University Institute.

Esch, J. van and Mangé, E. (1980). *Documenten over de Economische en Monetaire Unie 1974–1980*. Deventer: Kluwer.

Esmark, A., Frankel, C., Højbjerg, E., Pedersen, D., and Pedersen, O. K. (2001). *Broen fra Slotsholmen til Bruxelles—EU og den centrale forvaltning i Danmark*. København: Jurist-og Økonomforbundets Forlag.

Euro Spectator Series (2000). *Euro Spectator: Implementing the Euro* (ed. J.-V. Louis) (EUI Working Papers LAW No. 2000/4–9). San Domenico: European University Institute.

European Commission (1990). 'One Market, One Money'. *European Economy*, 44 (October).

—— (1992). 'Briefing Note: the Maastricht Agreement' (ISEC/B25/92). 29 September.

—— (1996). *Eurobarometer 45*. Brussels.

—— (1997). *Eurobarometer 47*. Brussels.

—— (1999*a*). 'Report on Social Protection in Europe 1999'. Brussels COM (2000) 163 final.

—— (1999*b*). *Employment in Europe 1999*. Luxembourg: European Communities.

—— (1999*c*). *Treaty of Amsterdam: What Has Changed in Europe?* Luxembourg: Office for Official Publications of the European Communities.

—— (1999*d*). 'Italy's Slow Growth in the 1990s'. *European Economy* (special issue, No. 5).

—— (2000*a*). *Communication from the Commission: Social Trends: Prospects and Challenges*. Brussels COM (2000) 82 final.

—— (2000*b*). *Public Finances in EMU-2000* (Report for the Directorate-General for Economic and Financial Affairs). Brussels.

—— (2000*c*). D-G For Economic and Financial Affairs, *European Economy*, 70.

—— (2000*d*). *Eurobarometer 52*. Brussels.

—— (2000*e*). *Report on the Implementation of the 1999 Broad Economic Policy Guidelines*. ECOFIN/200/00-EN, Brussels, 14 March.

—— (2000*f*). *Eurobarometer 53*. Brussels.

—— (2001*a*). *Communication from the Commission: Strengthening Economic Policy Co-ordination within the Euro Area*. COM(2001) 82 final, Brussels, 7 February.

—— (2001*b*). *Eurobarometer 54*. Brussels.

European Council (1992). *Treaty on European Union*. Luxembourg: Office for Official Publications of the European Communities, 7 February.

—— (1997). 'Resolution of the European Council on the Stability and Growth Pact Amsterdam' (17 June). *Official Journal*, C 236, 2 August: 1–2.

—— (2000). 'New Impetus for an Economic and Social Europe'. Presidency Conclusions: Nice European Council Meeting, 7–9 December, at http.www.europa.eu.int/council/oft/conclu/dec2000_en.htm.

Eurostat (2000*a*). *Statistics in Focus: Social Protection in Europe*. Luxembourg: Eurostat.

—— (2000*b*). *Yearbook 2000: A Statistical Eye on Europe* (data 1988–98). http://www.europa.eu.int/comm/eurostat

—— (2000c). 'EU External Trade in 1999'. *Statistics in Focus*, Theme 6–10.

—— (2001a). Euro-Indicators News Release. No. 19, 19 February.

—— (2001b). Euro-Indicators News Release. No. 30, 14 March.

Fabbrini, S. (1998). 'Due anni di governo Prodi: un primo bilancio istituzionale'. *Il Mulino*, 47/378: 657–72.

—— (2000). 'Parlamento, governo e capo del governo: quali cambiamenti?', in G. di Palma, G. Freddi, and S. Fabbrini (eds), *Condannata al successo? L'Italia nell'Europa integrata*. Bologna: Il Mulino.

Fabius, L. (2001). Franco-British Symposium Speech, Paris, 19 January.

Faist, T. (2001). 'Social Citizenship in the European Union: Nested Citizenship'. *Journal of Common Market Studies*, 39: 37–58.

Falkner, G. (2000). 'Policy Networks in a Multi-Level System: Convergence Towards Moderate Diversity?'. *West European Politics*, 23/4: 94–120.

Fatás, A. (1998). 'Does EMU Need a Fiscal Federation?'. *Economic Policy*, 26/April: 165–203.

Featherstone, K. (2001). *Three Dimensions of Europeanization: Institutional, Strategic and Cognitive*. Bradford: Department of European Studies, University of Bradford.

Feldstein, M. (1997). 'The Political Economy of the European Economic and Monetary Union: Political Sources of an Economic Liability'. *Journal of Economic Perspectives*, 11: 23–42.

—— (2000). 'The European Central Bank and the Euro: The First Year' (NBER Working Paper No. 7517). Cambridge, MA: National Bureau of Economic Research (February).

Felsen, D. (2000). 'Changes to the Italian Budgetary Regime: The Reforms of Law No. 94–1997', in D. Hine and S. Vassallo (eds), *Italian Politics: The Return of Politics*. New York and Oxford: Berghahn.

Ferrera, M. and Gualmini, E. (1999). *Salvati dall'Europa?*. Bologna: Il Mulino.

—— (2000). 'Reforms Guided by Consensus: The Welfare State in the Italian Transition'. *West European Politics*, 23/2: 187–208.

—— and Rhodes, M. (2000). 'Building a Sustainable Welfare State'. *West European Politics*, 23/2: 257–82.

——, Hemerijck, A., and Rhodes, M. (2000). *The Future of Social Europe: Recasting Work and Welfare in the New Economy*. Lisbon: Celta Editor.

Financial Times (1991a). 'The Horse Is Back Before the Cart', 13 September.

—— (1991b). 'Three-point Consensus Ends Two-speed Europe', 23 September.

—— (1995). 'Dutch push German line on EMU policy', 9 November.

—— (1996). 30 September 1996.

—— (1998). 'Tax: Reforms Essential to Fund True Harmony?': 3.

—— (2001a). 24 January 2001.

—— (2001b). 25 January.

—— (2001c). 'Japan's Sharp Reminder', 9 March.

—— (2000d). 'Fears of Slowdown', 12 April.

Fitoussi, J.-P. (1992). *La désinflation compétitive, le mark et les politiques budgétaires en Europe*. Paris: OFCE and Éditions du Seuil.

—— (1995). *Le Débat interdit*. Paris: Éditions du Seuil.

Fitoussi, J.-P. Atkinson, A., Blanchard, O., Flemming, J., Mahnvaud, E., Phelps, E. and Solow, R. (1993). *Competitive Disinflation: The Mark and Budgetary Politics in Europe.* Oxford: Oxford University Press.

Flassbeck, H. and Spiecker, F. (2000). *Löhne und Arbeitslosigkeit im internationalen Vergleich* (Eine Studie für die Hans-Boeckler-Stiftung und den Bundesvorstand des DGB). Berlin, June.

Fligstein, N. and McNichol, J. (1998). 'The Institutional Terrain of the European Union', in W. Sandholtz, and A. Stone Sweet (eds), *European Integration and Supranational Governance.* New York: Oxford University Press.

Forrester, V. (1996). *L'horreur économique.* Paris: Fayard.

Franco, D. (2000). 'Italy: A Never-Ending Pension Reform'. Paper delivered to the NBER-Kiel Institute conference on Coping with the Pension Crisis: Where Does Europe Stand?, Berlin, 20–1 March.

Franklin, M., Marsh, M., and McLaren, L. (1994). 'Uncorking the Bottle: Popular Opposition to Unification in the Wake of Maastricht'. *Journal of Common Market Studies*, 32: 455–72.

Freyssinet, J. (1996). 'The Impact of the EMU on Pay Policy and Collective Bargaining', in O. Jacoby (*sic*) and P. Pochet (eds), *A Common Currency Area: A Fragmented Area for Wages?* Düsseldorf: Hans Böckler Stiftung.

Frieden, J., Gros, D., and Jones, E. (eds) (1998). *The New Political Economy of EMU.* Lanham: Rowman and Littlefield.

Fritsche, U., Horn, G., Scheremet, W., and Zwiener, R. (1999). 'Is There a Need for a Co-ordinated European Wage and Labour Market Policy?', in G. Huemer, M. Mesch, and F. Traxler (eds), *The Role of Employers Associations and Trade Unions in EMU: Institutional Requirements for European Economic Policies.* Aldershot: Ashgate.

Funabashi, Y. (1988). *Managing the Dollar: From the Plaza to the Louvre.* Washington, DC: Institute for International Economics.

Fyns Stifttidende (1999). 'Danish job are best secured with the common currency', 29 November.

Galimberti, F. (1998). 'La vera storia del miracolo 3 per cento'. *Il Sole-24Ore*, 12 May.

Gamble, A. and Kelly, G. (2000). 'The British Labour Party and Monetary Union'. *West European Politics*, 23/1: 1–25.

—— and Payne, A. (eds) (1996). *Regionalism and World Order.* London: Macmillan.

Garret, G. (1998). *Partisan Politics in a Global Economy.* Cambridge: Cambridge University Press.

George, S. (1994). *An Awkward Partner.* Oxford: Oxford University Press.

Germain, R. (1999). 'In Search of Political Economy: Understanding European Monetary Union'. *Review of International Political Economy*, 6: 390–8.

German Constitutional Court (1995). 'Judgement of October 12, 1993 on the Maastricht Treaty', in A. Oppenheimer (ed.), *The Relationship between European Community Law and National Law: The Cases.* Cambridge: Cambridge University Press.

Giavazzi, F., Jappelli, T. and Pagano, M. (1998). 'Searching for non-Keynesian Effects of Fiscal Policy' (IGIER Discussion Paper). Milan: Bocconi University (September).

Gilbert, E. and Helleiner, E. (eds) (1999). *Nation-States and Money: The Past, Present and Future of National Currencies.* London: Routledge.

Gill, S. (1995). 'Globalization, Market Civilization and Disciplinary Neoliberalism'. *Millennium: Journal of International Studies*, 24: 399–423.

—— (1998). 'European Governance and New Constitutionalism: Economic and Monetary Union and Alternatives to Disciplinary Neoliberalism in Europe'. *New Political Economy*, 3/1: 5–26.

Giordano, F. and Persaud, S. (1998). *The Political Economy of Monetary Union: Towards the Euro*. London: Routledge.

Giuliani, M. (1999). 'Europeanization and Italy'. Paper presented to the sixth biennial conference of the European Community Studies Association, Pittsburgh, 2–5 June.

Glyn, A. (1998). 'Internal and External Constraints on Egalitarian Policies', in D. Baker, G. Epstein, and R. Pollin (eds), *Globalization and Progressive Economic Policy*. Cambridge: Cambridge University Press.

Goetschy, J. (2000). 'European Union and National Social Pacts: Employment and Social Protection put to the Test of Joint Regulation', in G. Fajertag and P. Pochet (eds), *Social Pacts in Europe: New Dynamics*. Brussels: European Trade Union Institute.

Goetz, K. (2000). 'Europeanizing the National Executive? Western and Eastern Style'. Paper delivered at the 30th Annual Conference of the University Association for Contemporary European Studies, Budapest, 6–8 April.

Golbach, J. and Schulten, T. (2000). 'Cross-Border Collective Bargaining Networks in Europe'. *European Journal of Industrial Relations*, 6/2: 161–80.

Goodman, J. B. (1992). *Monetary Sovereignty: The Politics of Central Banking in Western Europe*. Ithaca, NY: Cornell University Press.

Gordon, R. (1999). *The Aftermath of the 1992 ERM Breakup: Was There a Macroeconomic Free Lunch?* (CEPR Discussion Paper No. 2217). London: Centre for Economic Policy Research.

Gourevitch, P. (1978). 'The Second Image Reversed: The International Sources of Domestic Politics', *international Organization*, 32: 881–911.

Green Cowles, M., Caporaso, J., and Risse, T. (eds) (2001). *Transforming Europe: Europeanization and Domestic Change*. Ithaca, NY: Cornell University Press.

Gretschmann, K. (1998). *Der Euro. Eine Währung für Europa*. Vienna: Renner Institut.

Gros, D. (1995). *Excessive Deficits and Debts* (CEPS Paper 65). Brussels: Centre for European Policy Studies.

—— (2001). 'Health not Wealth'. Workshop on Euro Economic Governance, organized by the Forward Studies Unit of the European Commission and the Robert Schuman Centre. Florence: 19 February.

—— and Hefeker, C. (1999). 'Les coûts de main-d'oeuvre et la politique salariale dans l'UEM'. Document de travail. Série Affaires économiques. Luxembourg: European Parliament.

—— and Steinherr, A. (1994). 'In Favour of EMU: A Manifesto of European Economists', in A. Steinherr (ed.), *Thirty Years of European Monetary Integration: From the Werner Plan to EMU*. London: Longman.

Gualdo, A. (2000). *Guai a chi li tocca*. Milan: Mondadori.

Gualmini, E. (1997). *Le rendite del neo-corporativismo. Politiche pubbliche e contrattazione privata nella regolazione del mercato del lavoro italiano e tedesco*. Rubbettino: Soveria Mannelli (Catanzaro, Italy).

Guyomarch, A., Machin, H., and Ritchie, E. (1998). *France in the European Union*. Basingstoke: Macmillan.

Haahr, J. H. (1993). *Looking to Europe*. Aarhus: Aarhus University Press.

Haas, P. (1992). 'Introduction: Epistemic Communities and International Policy Co-ordination', in*ternational Organization*, 46/1: 1–35.

Hägele, S. and Wessels, W. (2000). 'Euro-Gruppe und Wirtschafts- und Finanzausschuss', in W. Weidenfeld and W. Wessels (eds), *Jahrbuch der Europäischen Integration 1999/2000*. Bonn: Europa-Union Verlag.

Hall, P. (1993). 'Policy Paradigms, Social Learning and the State: The Case of Economic Policy-Making in Britain'. *Comparative Politics*, 25: 275–96.

—— and Franzese, R. (1998). 'Mixed Signals: Central Bank Independence, Co-ordinated Wage-Bargaining, and European Monetary Union'. *International Organization*, 52: 505–35.

—— and Soskice, D. (eds) (2001). *Varieties of Capitalism*. Oxford: Oxford University Press.

Hallerberg, M. (1999). 'The Importance of Domestic Political Institutions: Why and How Belgium and Italy Qualified for EMU'. Paper presented to the Annual Meeting of the American Political Science Association, Atlanta, Georgia, September.

Hanny, B. and Wessels, W. (1998). 'The Monetary Committee of the European Communities: A Significant though not Typical Case', in M. Van Schendelen (ed.), *EU Committees as Influential Policymakers*. Aldershot: Ashgate.

—— (1999). 'Wirtschafts- und Finanzausschuss und Euro-11–Gruppe', in W. Weidenfeld and W. Wessels (eds), *Jahrbuch der Europäischen Integration 1998/99*. Bonn: Europa-Union Verlag.

Hardiman, N. (2000). 'Social Partnership, Wage Bargaining, and Growth', in B. Nolan, P. O'Connell, and C. Whelan (eds), *Bust to Boom? The Irish Experience of Growth and Inequality*. Dublin: Institute of Public Administration.

Hardis, A. (2000). 'The Contract' (Interview with Ivar Nørgaard). *Weekendavisen*, 28 April–4 May.

Hassel, A. (1999). *Bündnisse für Arbeit: Nationale Handlungsfähigkeit im Europâischen Regimewettbewerb* (MPIfG Discussion Paper 99/5). Cologne: Max-Planck-Institut für Gesellschaftsforschung.

Haverland, M. (2000). 'National Adaptation to European Integration: The Importance of Institutional Veto Points'. *Journal of Public Policy*, 20: 83–103.

Hay, C. (2000a). 'Globalization, Regionalization and the Persistence of National Variation: The Contingent Convergence of Contemporary Capitalism'. *Review of International Studies*, 26/4.

—— (2000b). 'What Place for Ideas in the Structure-Agency Debate? Globalization as a 'Process Without a Subject'. Paper delivered to a conference on Ideational Institutionalism: Perspectives on European Politics, University of Birmingham, 2–4 June.

—— and Rosamond, B. (2000). 'Globalization, European Integration and the Discursive Construction of Economic Imperatives'. Paper delivered at the International Political Science Association, 18th World Congress of Political Science, Quebec City, 1–5 August.

Hazareesingh, S. (1994). *Political Traditions in Modern France*. Oxford: Oxford University Press.

Healey, D. (1990). *The Time of My Life*. New York: Norton.

Held, D. (1991). 'Editor's Introduction', in D. Held (ed.), *Political Theory Today*. Oxford: Polity Press.

——, McGrew, A., Perraton, J., and Goldblatt, D. (1999). *Global Transformations: Politics, Economics and Culture*. Cambridge: Polity Press.

Helleiner, E. (1994). *States and the Re-emergence of Global Finance: From Bretton Woods to the 1990s*. Ithaca, NY: Cornell University Press.

Hellermann, J. (2000). 'Die Europäische Wirtschafts- und Währungsunion als Stabilitätsgemeinschaft und der nationale Stabilitätspakt in der bundesstaatlichen Solidargemeinschaft'. *Europarecht*, 1: 24–41.

Hemerijck, A. (1995). 'Corporatist Immobility in the Netherlands', in C. Crouch and F. Traxler (eds), *Organized Industrial Relations in Europe: What Future?* Aldershot: Avebury.

Henning, C. Randall (1994). *Currencies and Politics in the United States, Germany, and Japan*. Washington, DC: Institute for International Economics.

Héritier, A. and Knill, C. (2000). *Differential Responses to European Policies: A Comparison*. Bonn: Preprints aus der Max-Planck-Projektgruppe Recht der Gemeinschaftsgüter, 2000/7.

—— and Mingers, S. (1996). *Ringing the Changes in Europe. Regulatory Competition and the Redefinition of the State: Britain, France, Germany*. Berlin and New York: De Gruyter.

Het Financieele Dagblad (1993). 'Lubbers wil niet af van EMU-tijdpad'. 26 November.

Het Parool (1996). 'PvdA-rapport: EMU-normen te streng'. 16 October.

Hirschman, A. (1970). *Exit, Voice and Loyalty: Responses to Declines in Firms, Organizations and States*. Oxford: Harvard University Press.

Hirst, P. and Thompson, G. (1996). *Globalization in Question*. Cambridge: Polity Press.

Hodson, D. and Maher, I. (2001). ' "Soft" Economic Policy Co-ordination'. *Journal of Common Market Studies*, 39/4: [PAGES].

Hoeller, P., Louppe, M.-O., and Vergriette, P. (1996). *Fiscal Relations Within the European Community* (OECD Economics Department Working Paper, 163). Paris: OECD.

Hoffmeyer, E. (1980). 'How We Approach the Abyss'. *Berlingske Tidende*, 10 January.

Hogg, S. and Hill, J. (1995). *Too Close to Call*. London: Little Brown.

Hollingsworth, J. and Boyer, R. (eds) (1997). *Contemporary Capitalism: The Embeddedness of Institutions*. Cambridge: Cambridge University Press.

Holmes, M. (ed.) (1996). *The Eurosceptic Reader*. London: Macmillan.

Hombach, B. (1998). *Aufbruch: Die Politik der neuen Mitte*. Düsseldorf: Econ Verlag.

Hooge, L. (ed.) (1996). *Cohesion Policy and European Integration*. Oxford: Oxford University Press.

Hörburger, H. (1998). 'Die soziale und beschäftigungspolitische Dimension der EU nach Amsterdam', in M. Jopp, A. Maurer, and O. Schmuck (eds), *Die Europäische Union nach Amsterdam. Analysen und Stellungnahmen zum neuen EU-Vertrag*. Bonn: Europa-Union Verlag.

Howarth, D. (1998). 'European Employment Policy and Lowest Common Denominator Politics'. Paper presented at the annual UACES conference, Leicester, January.

Howarth, D. (1999a). 'French Aversion to Independent Monetary Authority and the Development of French Policy on the EMU Project'. Paper presented at the biannual European Community Studies Association conference, Pittsburgh, Pennsylvania, June.

—— (1999b). 'Planning the Juppé Plan: A Case Study of Co-ordination in the French Core Executive'. Paper presented at the annual Political Studies Association Conference, Nottingham, April.

—— (2000). 'France', in J. Lodge (ed.), The 1999 European Parliamentary Elections. London: Routledge.

—— (2001). The French Road to European Monetary Union. Basingstoke: Palgrave.

Howell, D. (2000). The Edge of Now. London: Macmillan.

Huber, E. and Stephens, J. (2001). 'Welfare State and Production Regimes in the Era of Retrenchment', in P. Pierson (ed.), The New Politics of the Welfare State. Oxford: Oxford University Press.

Huemer, G., Mesch, M., and Traxler, F. (eds) (1999). The Role of Employers Associations and Trade Unions in EMU: Institutional Requirements for European Economic Policies. Aldershot: Ashgate.

Hutchison, M. M. and Kletzer, K. M. (1995). 'Fiscal Convergence Criteria, Factor Mobility and Credibility in Transition to Monetary Union in Europe', in B. Eichengreen and J. Frieden (eds), The Political Economy of European Monetary Integration. Oxford: Westview.

Il Sole-24Ore (1998). 30 December.

Inglehart, R. (1971). 'Public Opinion and Regional Integration', in L. Lindberg and S. Scheingold (eds), Regional Integration, Theory and Research. Cambridge, MA: Harvard University Press.

International Economy (1997). 'The Dark Side of EMU?' (Interview with Gerhard Schröder). November/December: 6–9.

Ipsen, H. (1994). 'Zehn Glossen zum Maastricht-Urteil'. Europarecht, 1: 1–21.

Irish Independent (2001). 27 January.

Issing, O. (1999). 'The Eurosystem: Transparent and Accountable or "Wilhelm in Euroland"'. Journal of Common Market Studies, 37: 503–19.

Italiener, A. and Vanheukelen, M. (1993). 'Proposals for Community Stabilization Mechanisms: Some Historical Applications'. European Economy, 5: 493–510.

Iversen, T. (1996). 'Power, Flexibility, and the Breakdown of Centralized Wage Bargaining—Denmark and Sweden in Comparative Perspective'. Comparative Politics, 28: 399–436.

—— (1999). Contested Economic Institutions: The Politics of Macroeconomics and Wage Bargaining in Advanced Democracies. Cambridge: Cambridge University Press.

Iversen, T. and Thygesen, N. (1998). 'Denmark: From External to Internal Adjustment', in E. Jones, J. Frieden, and F. Torres (eds), Joining Europe's Monetary Club—The Challenges for Smaller Member States. New York: St Martin's Press.

——, Pontusson, J., and Soskice, D. (eds) (2000). Unions, Employers and Central Banks: Macroeconomic Co-ordination and Institutional Change in Social Market Economies. Cambridge: Cambridge University Press.

Jabko, N. (1999). 'In the Name of the Market: how the European Commission Paved the Way for Monetary Union'. Journal of European Public Policy, 6: 475–95.

Jacobi, O. (1996). 'EMU—a Quantum Leap', in O. Jacoby (sic) and P. Pochet (eds), *A Common Currency Area: A Fragmented Area for Wages?* Düsseldorf: Hans Böckler Stiftung.

Jacoby, O. (sic) and Pochet, P. (eds) (1996). *A Common Currency Area: A Fragmented Area for Wages?* Düsseldorf: Hans Böckler Stiftung.

Jacquet, P. (1998). 'L'Union monétaire et la coordination des politiques macroéconomiques', in Conseil d'Analyse économique (ed.), *Coordination européenne des politiques économiques*. Paris: La Documentation Française.

—— and Pisani-Ferry, J. (2000). 'La coordination des politiques économiques dans la zone euro: bilan et propositions', in Conseil d'Analyse économique (ed.), *Report 27: European Issues*. http://www.premier-ministre.gouv.fr/GB/PM/CAE/ REPORT27.HTM on 11 November.

Jones, E. (1998). 'The Netherlands: Top of the Class', in E. Jones, J. Frieden, and F. Torres (eds) (1998), *Joining Europe's Monetary Club: The Challenges for Smaller Member States*. New York: St Martin's Press.

—— (forthcoming). 'The European Monetary Union as a Response to Globalization', in Leslie Armijo (ed.), *Debating the Global Financial Architecture*. New York: SUNY Press (forthcoming).

——, Frieden, J., and Torres, F. (eds) (1998). *Joining Europe's Monetary Club: The Challenges for Smaller Member States*. New York: St Martin's Press.

Jospin, L. (1999). *Modern Socialism*. London: Fabian Society.

—— (2001). Intervention sur 'L'avenir de l'Europe élargie'. Paris, 28 May. http://www.premier-ministre.gouv.fr/fr/p.cfm

Josselin, D. (1997). *Money Politics in the New Europe: Britain, France and the Single Financial Market*. Basingstoke: Macmillan.

Jürgens, U., Naumann, K., and Rupp, J. (2000). 'Shareholder Value in an Adverse Environment: The German Case'. *Economy and Society*, 29: 54–79.

Kaltenthaler, K. (1998). 'Central Bank Independence and the Commitment to Monetary Stability: The Case of the German Bundesbank'. *German Politics*, 7/2: 102–27.

Kapteyn, P. (1993). *Markt Zonder Staat*. Bussum: Coutinho.

Kassim, H., Peters, B., and Wright, V. (2000). *The National Co-ordination of EU Policy: The Domestic Level*. Oxford: Oxford University Press.

Katzenstein, P. (1985). *Small States and World Markets*. Ithaca, NY: Cornell University Press.

Keen, M. and Smith, S. (1996). 'The Future of Value Added Tax in the European Union'. *Economic Policy*, 23: 375–420.

Kenen, P. (1995). *Economic and Monetary Union in Europe: Moving Beyond Maastricht*. Cambridge: Cambridge University Press.

Kennedy, E. (1991). *The Bundesbank: Germany's Central Bank in the International Monetary System*. London: Royal Institute of International Affairs/Pinter.

Kitschelt, H., Lange, P., Marks, G., and Stephens, J. (1999a). 'Conclusion: Convergence and Divergence in Advanced Capitalist Democracies', in H. Kitschelt et al. (eds), *Continuity and Change in Contemporary Capitalism*. Cambridge: Cambridge University Press.

—— (eds) (1999b). *Continuity and Change in Contemporary Capitalism*. Cambridge: Cambridge University Press.

Kloten, N., Ketterer, K.-H., and Vollmer, R. (1985). 'West Germany's Stabilization Performance', in L. Lindberg and C. Maier (eds), *The Politics of Inflation and Economic Stagnation*. Washington, DC: The Brookings Institution.

Knill, C. and Lehmkuhl, D. (1999). 'How Europe Matters: Different Mechanisms of Europeanization'. *European Integration Online Papers*, 3/7. http://eipo.or.at/

Knudsen, T. (2000). 'How Informal Can You Be? The Case of Denmark', in B. Guy Peters, R. Rhodes, and V. Wright (eds), *Administering the Summit—Administration of the Core Executive in Developed Countries*. London: Macmillan.

Köhler, H. (1992). 'Stabilität oder mehr Inflation? Gespräch mit Horst Köhler'. *Der Spiegel*, 15: 41–52.

—— (1998). *Aufgaben auf dem Weg in die Europäische Währungsunion*. Bonn: Friedrich-Ebert-Stiftung.

Kohler-Koch, B. (1998). 'Die Europäisierung nationaler Demokratien: Verschleiß eines europäischen Kulturerbes?', in M. Greven (ed.), *Demokratie—eine Kultur des Westens?*. Opladen: Leske und Budrich.

—— (1999). 'The Evolution and Transformation of European Governance', in B. Kohler-Koch and R. Eising (eds), *The Transformation of Governance in the European Union*. London and New York: Routledge.

—— (2000). 'Europeanization: Concepts and Empirical Evidence'. Paper for the international workshop on Europeanization. Bradford: University of Bradford, 5–6 May.

—— and Eising, R. (eds) (1999). *The Transformation of Governance in the European Union*. London: Routledge.

Kristensen, Henrik Dam (1999). 'Closed Dors'. *Aktuelt*, 8 November.

—— (2000). 'The Danes Will Come to Love the Euro'. *Aktuelt*, 17 January.

Krogh, T. (1999). 'The Odd Country in Europe' (Interview with Ritt Bjerregaard). *Politiken*, 28 November.

Krugman P. (1993). 'Lessons from Massachusetts for EMU', in F. Torres and F. Giavazzi (eds), *Adjustment and Growth in European Monetary Union*. Cambridge: Cambridge University Press.

—— (1994). 'Competitiveness: A Dangerous Obsession'. *Foreign Affairs*, 73/2: 28–44.

Labohm, H. and Wijnker, C. (eds) (2000). *The Netherlands' Polder Model: Does It Offer Any Clues for the Solution of Europe's Socio-economic Flaws?* (Monetaire Monografieën 17, DNB Seminars). Amsterdam: De Nederlandsche Bank.

Ladrech, R. (1994). 'Europeanization of Domestic Politics and Institutions: The Case of France'. *Journal of Common Market Studies*, 32/1: 69–88.

Lafontaine, O. (1999). *Das Herz Schlägt Links*. Düsseldorf: Econ Verlag.

—— and Müller, C. (1998). *Keine Angst vor der Globalisierung*. Bonn: Dietz Verlag.

Laird, F. (1999). 'Rethinking Learning'. *Policy Currents*, 9/3–4: 3–7.

Lamfalussy, A. (2000). *The Euro-Zone: A New Economic Entity?*. Paris: L.G.D.J. Montchrestien.

Landoo, K. (1999). 'A European Perspective on Corporate Governance'. *Journal of Common Market Studies*, 37: 269–94.

La Repubblica (1998). 30 December.

Lawson, N. (1992). *The View from No. 11*. London: Bantam.

Leander, A. and Guzzini, S. (1997). 'European Economic and Monetary Union and the Crisis of European Social Contracts', in P. Minkkinen and H. Patomaki (eds), *The Politics of Economic and Monetary Union.* Dordrecht: Kluwer Academic Publishers.

Le Monde (1991). 17 January.

—— (1992). 4 September.

—— (1996*a*). 22 November.

—— (1996*b*). 29 November.

—— (1997). 2 April.

—— (2000). 9 September.

Levitt, M. and Lord, C. (2000). *The Political Economy of Monetary Union.* London: Macmillan.

Levy, J. (1999). 'Vice into Virtue? Progressive Politics and Welfare Reform in Continental Europe'. *Politics and Society*, 27: 239–73.

Libération (1992). 4 September.

—— (1999). 13 January.

Lijphart, A. (1999). *Patterns of Democracy: Government Forms and Performance in Thirty-Six Countries.* New Haven and London: Yale University Press.

Linder, W. (1998). *Swiss Democracy.* London: Macmillan.

Linsenmann, I. and Müller, T. (2000). 'German Report', in J.-V. Louis (ed.), *Euro Spectator: Implementing the Euro. National Reports: French Report/German Report* (EUI Working Paper LAW No. 2000/6). San Domenico: European University Institute.

Linz, J. and Stepan, A. (1996). *Problems of Democratic Transition and Consolidation: Southern Europe, South America and Post-Communist Europe.* Baltimore: Johns Hopkins University Press.

LO (Landsorganisationen) (1999). *Beskæftigelse og Fælles Mønt.* Copenhagen.

Loedel, P. (1999). *Deutsche Mark Politics: Germany in the European Monetary System.* London: Lynne Reiner.

Lönnroth, J. (2000). 'The European Employment Strategy, A Model for Open Coordination: and the Role of the Social Partners'. Paper presented at the SALTSA/ Swedish National Institute for Working Life Conference on Legal Dimensions of the European Employment Strategy, Brussels, 9–10 October.

Loriaux, M. (1991). *France After Hegemony.* Ithaca, NY: Cornell University Press.

Louis, J.-V. (ed.) (1989). *Vers un Système Européen de Banques Centrales. Projet de Dispostions Organiques* (Rapport du groupe présidé par Jean-Victor Louis). Brussels: Institute d'Études européennes. University of Brussels.

—— (2000). 'The Institutional Framework of Economic Policy Co-ordination'. Paper presented at the Symposium of Jean Monnet Chairs, The Intergovernmental Conference 2000 and Beyond, Brussels, 6–7 July.

—— (2001*a*). *The European Union and the Euro: Economic, Institutional and International Aspects* (4th ECSA-World Conference, Brussels, 17–18 September). Brussels: European Commission.

—— (2001*b*). 'Which Economic Governance in the Euro-Zone?', Workshop on Euro Economic Governance, organized by the Forward Studies Unit of the European Commission and the Robert Schuman Centre, Florence, 19 February.

Luhmann, N. (1981). *Politische Theorie im Wohlfahrtsstaat.* München Wien: Olzog.

Lütz, S. (1998). 'The Revival of the Nation-State? Stock Exchange Regulation in an Era of Globalized Financial Markets'. *Journal of European Public Policy*, 5: 153–68.

Lykketoft, Mogens (2000). 'I Have Become Much Wiser'. *Politiken*, 16 January.

Lyngesen, Hanne (2000). 'No Alternative to a Danish "Yes" '. *Information*, 10 February.

MacDougall, D. *et al.* (1977). *Report of the Study Group on the Role of Public Finance in European Integration*, Vols 1 and 2. Brussels: Commission of the European Communities.

McKay, D. (1999a). 'The Political Sustainability of European Monetary Union'. *British Journal of Political Science*, 29: 519–41.

—— (1999b). *Federalism and European Union: A Political Economy Perspective*. Oxford: Oxford University Press.

—— (2001). *Designing Europe: Institutional Adaptation and the Federal Experience*. Oxford: Oxford University Press.

McKinnon, R. I. (1997). 'EMU as a Device for Collective Fiscal Responsibility'. *American Economic Review: Papers and Proceedings*, 87: 227–9.

McNamara, K. (1998). *The Currency of Ideas: Monetary Politics in the European Union*. Ithaca, NY, and London: Cornell University Press.

—— (1999). 'Consensus and Constraint: Ideas and Capital Mobility in European Monetary Integration'. *Journal of Common Market Studies*, 37: 455–76.

Madsen, M. (1996). 'Fanget mellem økonomi og politik. Socialdemokratiets EF-historie', in G. Callesen, S. Christensen and H. Grelle (eds), *Udfordring og omstilling—Bidrag til socialdemokratiets historie 1971–1996*. Copenhagen: Forlaget Fremad.

Majone, G. (1996). *Regulating Europe*. London: Routledge.

—— (1999). 'The Regulatory State and its Legitimacy Problems'. *West European Politics*, 22: 1–34.

Major, J. (1999). *The Autobiography*. London: HarperCollins.

Mamou, Y. (1987). *Une machine de pouvoir: La direction du Trésor*. Paris: Éditions La Découverte.

March, J. and Olsen, J. (1998). 'The Institutional Dynamics of International Political Orders'. *International Organization*, 52: 943–69.

Marcussen, M. (1998a). *Central Bankers, the Ideational Life-Cycle and the Social Construction of EMU* (EUI Working Papers, RSC no. 98/33). Florence: European University Institute.

—— (1998b). 'Ideas and Elites: Danish Macro-Economic Policy-Discourse in the EMU-Process' (Ph.D. thesis, ISP No. 226). Aalborg: Institute for Development and Planning, Aalborg University.

—— (1999). 'The Dynamics of EMU Ideas'. *Co-operation and Conflict*, 34: 383–411.

—— (2000a). *Ideas and Elites: The Social Construction of Economic and Monetary Union*. Aalborg: Aalborg University Press.

—— (2000b). 'Internationalisering, idéer og Iidentiteter', in T. Knudsen (ed.), *Regering og embedsmænd—om magt og demokrati i staten*. Aarhus: Systime.

—— (2000c). '"ØMU"en som politisk projekt'. *Økonomi and Politik*, 73/2: 47–59.

—— and Zølner, M. (2001). 'The Danish EMU Referendum 2000: Business as Usual'. *Government and Opposition*, 36, 3: 379–402.

Marian, M. (1999). 'Lionel Jospin, le socialisme et la réforme'. *Esprit*, March–April:. 112–21.

Marks, G., Hooghe, E. and Blank, K. (1996). 'European Integration from the 1980s: State-Centric vs. Multi-Level Governance'. *Journal of Common Market Studies*, 34: 341–78.

——, Scharpf, F., Schmitter, P., and Streeck, W. (1996). *Governance in the European Union*. London: Sage.

Marquand, D. (1997). 'The Politics of Monetary Union', in D. Marquand (ed.), *The New Reckoning*. Cambridge: Polity.

Marsden, D. (1992). 'Incomes Policy for Europe? Or Will Pay Bargaining Destroy the Single European Market?'. *British Journal of Industrial Relations*, 30: 587–604.

Marsh, I. (1999). 'The State and the Economy: Opinion Formation and Collaboration as Facets of Economic Management'. *Political Studies*, 47: 837–56.

Marshall, J. and Butterworth, S. (2000). 'Pensions Reform in the EU: The Unexploded Time Bomb in the Single Market'. *Common Market Law Review*, 37: 739–62.

Marshall, M. (1999). *The Bank: The Birth of Europe's Central Bank and the Rebirth of Europe's Power*. London: Random House.

Martin, A. 1998. 'EMU and Wage Bargaining: The Americanization of the European Labor Market?'. Paper prepared for the 11th International Conference of Europeanists, Baltimore, 26–8 February.

Maurer, A. (2000). 'Beschäftigungspolitik', in W. Weidenfeld and W. Wessels (eds), *Europa von A—Z. Taschenbuch der europäischen Integration*. Bonn: Europa-Union Verlag.

—— and Wessels, W. (2001). 'Integration Matters: Structuring Self-made Offers and Demands for National Actors and Arenas', in W. Wessels, A. Maurer, and J. Mittag (eds), *Fifteen into One? The European Union and its Member States*. Manchester: Manchester University Press.

Meyer, T. (1999). 'From Godesberg to the Neue Mitte: The New Social Democracy in Germany', in G. Kelly (ed.), *The New European Left*. London: Fabian Society.

Michie, J. (1997). 'Why the Left Should Be Against EMU', in D. Corry and J. Michie (eds), *EMU: The Left Debate*. Sheffield: PERC Policy Papers No. 4.

Midelfart-Knarvit, K., Overman, H., Redding, S., and Venables, A. (2000). *The Location of European Industry* (Economic Papers No. 142). Brussels: Directorate General for Economic and Financial Affairs, European Commission (April).

Mikkelsen, R. (1993). *Dansk pengehistorie 1960–1990*. Copenhagen: Danmarks Nationalbank.

Milesi, G. (1998). *Le Roman de l'Euro*. Paris: Hachette.

Milner, H. (1995). 'Regional Economic Co-operation, Global Markets and Domestic Politics: A Comparison of NAFTA and the Maastricht Treaty'. *Journal of European Public Policy*, 2: 337–60.

Milward, A (1992). *The European Rescue of the Nation-State*. Berkeley: University of California Press.

—— (1996). 'Approaching Reality: Euromoney and the Left'. *New Left Review*, 216: 55–65.

—— (2000). 'The Nature and Future of the European Union: Still Intergovernmental?' (lecture to honours class on European governance), in B. Steunenberg and G. Saeijs (eds), *European Governance*. Leiden: Department of Political Science and Public Administration, Leiden University.

Ministère de l'Économie, des Finances et du Budget (1991). *La contribution française aux progrès de l'union économique et monétaire* (French Draft Treaty). Paris, 16 January. In English, see *Agence Europe*, 28–9 January 1991: 5419.

Ministère de l'Économie des Finances et de l'Industrie (2000). *Politique économique 2000* (rapport économique, social et financier du Gouvernement). Paris: Economica.

Minkkinen, P. and Patomäki, H. (1997). 'Introduction: The Politics of Economic and Monetary Union', in P. Minkkinen and H. Patomäki (eds), *The Politics of Economic and Monetary Union*. Boston, Dordrecht and London: Kluwer.

Mira d'Ercole, M. and Terribile, F. (1998). 'Pension Spending: Developments in 1996 and 1997', in L. Bardi and M. Rhodes (eds), *Italian Politics: Mapping the Future*. Boulder, CO: Westview Press.

Mittag, J. and Wessels, W. (2001). '"One" or "Fifteen"? The Member States between Adaptations and Structural Revolution', in W. Wessels, A. Maurer, and J. Mittag (eds), *Fifteen into One? The European Union and its Member States*. Manchester: Manchester University Press.

Modigliani, F., Baldassarri, M., and Castiglionesi, F. (1996). *Il miracolo possibile. Un programma per l'economia italiana*. Rome: Laterza.

Moran, M. (1989). 'A State of Inaction: The State and the Reform of the Securities Industry in West Germany', in S. Bulmer (ed.), *The Changing Agenda of West German Politics*. Aldershot: Gower.

—— (1991). *The Politics of the Financial Services Revolution*. London: Macmillan.

—— (1992). 'Regulatory Change in German Financial Markets', in K. Dyson (ed.), *The Politics of German Regulation*. Aldershot: Dartmouth.

—— (1994). 'The State and the Financial Services Revolution: A Comparative Analysis'. *West European Politics*, 17: 158–77.

—— (2001). 'Governing European Corporate Life', in G. Thompson *et al.* (eds), *Governing the European Economy*. Buckingham: Open University Press.

Moravcsik, A. (1993). 'Preferences and Power in the European Community: A Liberal Intergovernmentalist Approach'. *Journal of Common Market Studies*, 4: 473–524.

—— (1994). *Why the European Community Strengthens the State: Domestic Politics and International Co-operation* (Working Paper Series No. 52). Cambridge, MA: Centre for International European Studies, Harvard University.

—— (1998). *The Choice for Europe: Social Purpose and State Power from Messina to Maastricht*. Ithaca, NY, and London: Cornell University Press.

—— and Kalypso, N. (1998). 'Federal Ideas and Constitutional Realities in the Treaty of Amsterdam'. *Journal of Common Market Studies, Annual Review*, 36: 13–38.

Morlino, L. (2000). 'The Europeanization of Southern Europe', Third Summer School in Comparative Politics, Sienna, 10–22 July.

Mosely, L. (2000). 'Room to Move: International Financial Markets and National Welfare States'. *International Organization*, 54: 737–73.

—— and Mayer, A. (1999). *Benchmarking National Labour Market Performance: A Radar Chart Approach* (Discussion Paper). Berlin: Wissenschaftszentrum Berlin für Sozialforschung.

Moss, B. and Michie, J. (eds) (1998). *The Single European Currency in National Perspective: A Community in Crisis?* London: Macmillan.

Moutot, P. and Vitale, G. (2001). 'Monetary Policy and Co-ordination in a Globalized World'. *Revue Économique*, 52: 337–51.

Musgrave R. (1969). 'Theories of Fiscal Federalism'. *Public Finance*, 24: 521–32.

Mussa, M. (1997). 'Political and Institutional Commitment to a Common Currency'. *American Economic Review*, 87: 217–20.

Nicholls, A. (1994). *Freedom with Responsibility: The Social Market Economy in Germany 1918–63*. Oxford: Clarendon Press.

Niedermayer, O. and Westle, B. (1995). 'A Typology of Orientations', in O. Niedermayer and R. Sinnott (eds), *Public Opinion and Internationalized Governance* (Beliefs in Government ii). Oxford: Oxford University Press.

Nordjyske Stiftstidende (1999). 'It is about jobs', 21 November .

Notermans, T. (1999). 'Policy Continuity, Policy Change, and the Political Power of Economic Ideas'. *Acta Politica*, 3: 22–48.

—— (2000a). *Money, Markets and the State: Social Democratic Economic Policies since 1918.* Cambridge: Cambridge University Press.

—— (2000b). 'Can Social Democracy Thrive under a Single Currency'. Mimeo, in G. Ross and A. Martin (eds), *EMU and the European Model of Society* (forthcoming).

—— (2000c). 'Social Democratic Policies under the Single Currency'. Paper presented at the mini-workshop 'Social Democracy and Economic Management: Can the Primacy of the Political Be Regained?', Florence, European University Institute, 31 May.

NRC Handelsblad (1996). 'Een kleine EMU is nu het beste begin', 16 November.

—— (1997). 'Het wordt tijd het publiek beter over de euro voor te lichten', 22 February.

Oates, W. (1972). *Fiscal Federalism*. New York: Harcourt Brace Jovanovich.

Oatley, T. (1997). *Monetary Politics: Exchange Rate Cooperation in the European Union.* Ann Arbor: University of Michigan Press.

Odile, Q. (1999). 'From Regulation to a Benchmarking of the Systems', Konferenz der Bundesvereinigung der deutschen Arbeitgeberverbände, Bad Godesberg, 24 September, http://www.europa.eu.int/comm/dgo5/speeches/990992409.pdf.

OECD (1994). *The OECD Jobs Study: Evidence and Explanations. Part II—The Adjustment Potential of the Labour Market.* Paris: OECD.

—— (1997a). *OECD Economic Surveys: Switzerland 1996/1997.* Paris: OECD.

—— (1997b). *Employment Outlook.* Paris: OECD (July).

—— (2000). *Economic Surveys: Italy.* Paris: OECD.

—— (2001). 'Quarterly National Accounts/GDP Statistics'. *Main Economic Indicators*, Online Statistics version, http://www.oecd.org/std/qnagdp/qnagdp.htm.

—— (several years). *Country Survey: France.* Paris: OECD.

Ohmae, K. (1996). *The End of the Nation State: The Rise of Regional Economies.* New York: Free Press.

Økonomi- og Finansministeriet (2000). *Danmark og Euroen.* Copenhagen (April).

Økonomiministeriet (1993). *Økonomisk Oversigt.* Copenhagen (May).

—— (2000a). 'Pressemeddelelse—OECD's vurdering af dansk økonomi'. Copenhagen (22 June).

Økonomiministeriet (2000b). 'Pressemeddelelse—IMF: Danmark godt ristet til den fælles valuta'. Copenhagen (26 June).

Olesen, T. and Laursen, J. (1994). 'Det Europæiske Markedsskisma 1960–72', in J. Laursen et al. (eds), Danmark i Europa, 1945–93. Copenhagen: Munksgaard.

Olsen, J. (1996). 'Europeanization and Nation-State Dynamics', in S. Gustavsson and L. Lewin (eds), The Future of the Nation-State. Stockholm: Nerenius and Santerus.

—— (2000). Organising European Institutions of Governance. A Prelude to an Institutional Account of Political Integration (Arena Working Papers WP 00/2). Oslo: Arena.

Olson, M. (1982). The Rise and Decline of Nations: Economic Growth, Stagflation and Social Rigidities. New Haven, CT: Yale University Press.

Ó Riain, S. and O'Connell, P. (2000). 'The Role of the State in Growth and Welfare', in B. Nolan, P. O'Connell, and C. Whelan (eds), Bust to Boom? The Irish Experience of Growth and Inequality. Dublin: Institute of Public Administration.

Overturf, S. (1997). Money and European Union. New York: St Martin's Press.

Padgett, S. (1999). Organizing Democracy in Eastern Germany: Interest Groups in Post-Communist Society. Cambridge: Cambridge University Press.

Padoan, P. (1994). 'The Changing European Political Economy', in R. Stubbs and G. Underhill (eds), Political Economy and the Changing Global Order. London: Macmillan.

Pagouloulatos, G. (1999). 'European Banking: Five Modes of Governance'. West European Politics, 22: 68–94.

Pakaslahti, J. (1997). 'L'UEM menace-t-elle les systèmes de sécurité sociale?' (Working Paper No. 17). Brussels: European Social Observatory.

—— (1998). 'L'UEM et la protection sociale dans l'union européene', in P. Pochet and P. Vanhercke (eds), Les enjeux sociaux dans l'Union économique monétaire (Travail et Société No. 17). Brussels: Presses Interuniversitaires Européennes.

Palier, B. (2000). 'The Necessity to Negotiate Welfare Reforms in Bismarckian Social Protection Systems: The French Case'. Paper for the IPSA World Congress. Quebec City, 1–5 August.

Pasquino, G. (ed.) (1993). Votare un solo candidato. Bologna: Il Mulino.

Patomäki, H. (1997). 'Legitimation Problems of the European Union', in P. Minkkinen and H. Patomäki (eds), The Politics of Economic and Monetary Union. Boston/Dordrecht/London: Kluwer.

Pedersen, O. and Pedersen, D. (1995). 'The Europeanization of National Corporatism. When the State and Organizations in Denmark went to Europe together' (COS-report, No. 5). Copenhagen: Copenhagen Business School.

Pench, L., Sestito, P., and Frontini, E. (1999). Some Unpleasant Arithmetics of Regional Unemployment in the EU: Are There any Lessons from the EMU? (Economic Papers No. 134). Brussels: Directorate General for Economic and Financial Affairs, European Commission (April).

Perraton, J., Goldblatt, D., Held, D., and McGrew, A. (1997). 'The Globalization of Economic Activity'. New Political Economy. 2: 257–78.

Peters, G. (1999). Institutional Theory in Political Science: The 'New Institutionalism'. London and New York: Pinter.

Petersen, N. (1994). 'Vejen til den Europæiske Union', in J. Laursen et al. (eds), Danmark i Europa, 1945–93. Copenhagen: Munksgaard.

Peterson, J. (1995). 'Decision-making in the European Union: Towards a Framework for Analysis'. *Journal of European Public Policy*, 2/1: 69–93.

Pierson, P. (1998a). 'The Path to European Integration: A Historical Institutionalist Analysis', in W. Sandholtz and A. Stone Sweet (eds), *European Integration and Supranational Governance*. Oxford: Oxford University Press: 27–58.

—— (1998b). 'Irresistible Forces, Immovable Objects: Post-Industrial Welfare States Confront Permanent Austerity'. *Journal of European Public Policy*. 5, 4: 539–560.

—— (1999). 'Coping with Permanent Austerity: Welfare State Restructuring in Affluent Democracies'. Paper presented at the European Forum on 'Recasting the European Welfare States', Florence, European University Institute.

—— (2000). 'Big, Slow Moving, and Invisible: Macro-Social Processes in the Study of Comparative Politics'. Paper delivered to the annual meeting of the American Political Science Association, Washington DC, 30 August 30–1 September.

—— (2001). 'Coping with Permanent Austerity: Welfare State Restructuring in Affluent Democracies', in P. Pierson (ed.), *The New Politics of the Welfare State*. Oxford: Oxford University Press.

Pochet, P. (1998). 'The Social Consequences of EMU: An Overview of National Debates', in P. Pochet and B. Vanhercke (eds), *Social Challenges of Economic and Monetary Union*. Brussels: European Interuniversity Press.

—— (1999). 'Conclusions and Prospects', in P. Pochet (ed.), *Monetary Union and Collective Bargaining in Europe*. Brussels: Peter Lang.

—— and Turloot, L. (1996). 'Economic and Monetary Union–an Incomplete Framework', in O. Jacoby (*sic*) and P. Pochet (eds) (1996). *A Common Currency Area: A Fragmented Area for Wages?* Düsseldorf: Hans Böckler Stiftung.

—— and Vanhercke, B. (eds) (1998). *Social Challenges of Economic and Monetary Union*. Brussels: European Interuniversity Press.

Polanyi, K. (1944). *The Great Transformation*. Boston: Beacon Press.

Pontusson, J. (1992). *The Limits of Social Democracy*. Ithaca, NY: Cornell University Press.

Portillo, M. (1998). *Democratic Values and the Currency*. London: Institute for Economic Affairs.

Prast, H. and Stokman, A. (1999). *De Euro in Nederland: Uitkomsten van de achtste DNB-euro-enquête* (Onderzoeksrapport WO&E nr 580/9913). Amsterdam: De Nederlandsche Bank.

Prodi, R. (1999). *Un'idea dell'Europa*. Bologna: Il Mulino.

Putnam, R. (1988). 'Diplomacy and Domestic Politics: The Logic of Two Level Games'. *International Organisation*, 3: 427–60.

Radaelli, C. (1995). 'The Role of Knowledge in the Policy Process'. *Journal of European Public Policy*, 2: 159–83.

—— (1996). 'Fiscal Federalism as a Catalyst for Policy Development? In Search of a Framework for European Direct Tax Harmonisation'. *Journal of European Public Policy*, 3: 402–20.

—— (1999). *Technocracy in the European Union*. London: Pearson Education.

—— (2000). 'Whither Europeanization? Concept Stretching and Substantive Change'. Paper presented to the annual Conference of the Political Studies Association,

London, 10–13 April; *European Integration online Papers*. 4/8, http://eop.or.at/eiop/texte/2000–008a.htm.

—— and Silva, F. (1998). 'Le parole chiave della regolazione', in A. Boitani, A. Forti, and F. Silva (eds), *Competitività e Regolazione*. Bologna: Il Mulino.

Rasmussen, Anders Fog (2000). 'No More Union'. *Politiken*, 3 May.

Rawnsley, A. (2000). *Servants of the People: The Inside Story of New Labour*. London: Hamish Hamilton.

Regini, M. (1997). 'Still Engaging in Corporatism? Recent Italian Experience in Comparative Perspective'. *European Journal of Industrial Relations*, 3: 259–78.

—— and Regalia, I. (1996). *Italia anni '90: Rinasce la concertazione*. Milan: IRES.

—— (1997). 'Employers, Unions, and the State: The Resurgence of Concertation in Italy?', in M. Bull and M. Rhodes (eds), *Crisis and Transition in Italian Politics*. London: Frank Cass.

Reif, K.-H. (1993). 'Ein Ende des "Permissive Consensus"? Zum Wandel europapolitischer Einstellungen in der öffentlichen Meinung der EG-Mitgliedsstaaten', in R. Hrbek (ed.), *Der Vertrag von Maastricht in der wissenschaftlichen Kontroverse*. Baden-Baden: Nomos Verlagsgesellschaft.

Reland, J. (1998). 'France', in A. Menon and J. Forder (eds), *The European Union and National Macro-economic Policy*. London: Routledge.

Remsperger, H. (1999). 'The Role of Monetary Policy in the Macro Policy Mix'. *Auszüge aus Presseartikeln*. Frankfurt: Deutsche Bundesbank.

Reuten, G., Vendrik, K., and Went, R. (eds) (1998). *De Prijs van de Euro. De Gevaren van de Europese Monetaire Unie*. Amsterdam: Van Gennep.

Rhodes, M. (1998). 'Globalization, Labour Markets and Welfare States: A Future of "Competitive Corporatism"?', in M. Rhodes and Y. Mény (eds), *The Future of European Welfare: A New Social Contract?* London: Macmillan.

—— (2001a). 'Globalization, Welfare States and Employment: Is There a European "Third Way"?', in N. Bermeo (ed.), *Unemployment in the New Europe*. Cambridge: Cambridge University Press.

—— (2001b). 'The Political Economy of Social Pacts: Competitive Corporatism and European Welfare Reform', in P. Pierson (ed.), *The New Politics of Welfare*. Oxford: Oxford University Press.

Rhodes, R. (1997). *Understanding Governance*. Buckingham: Open University Press.

Riker, W. (1964). *Federalism: Origin, Operation, Significance*. Boston: Little Brown.

Risse, T., Green Cowles, M., and Caporaso, J. (2001). 'Europeanization and Domestic Change: Introduction', in M. Green Cowles, J. Caporaso, and T. Risse (eds), *Transforming Europe: Europeanization and Domestic Change*. Ithaca, NY: Cornell University Press.

Risse-Kappen, T. (ed.) (1995). *Bringing Transnational Relations Back In: Non-State Actors, Domestic Structures and International Institutions*. New York: Cambridge University Press.

Robinson, A. (1998). 'Why "Employability" Won't Make EMU Work', in B. Moss and J. Michie (eds), *The Single European Currency in National Perspective: A Community in Crisis?* Basingstoke: Houndmills; New York: St Martin's Press.

Rometsch, D. and Wessels, W. (eds) (1996). *The European Union and Member States: Towards Institutional Fusion?* Manchester: Manchester University Press.

Rood, J. (1990). 'The Position of the Netherlands: A Lesson in Monetary Union', in H. Sherman, R. Brown, P. Jacquet, and D. Julius (eds), *Monetary Implications of the 1992 Process.* London: Pinter/ Royal Institute of International Affairs.

Rosa, J.-J. (1998). *L'erreur européenne.* Paris: Grasset.

Rosamond, B. (1999). 'Discourses of Globalization and the Social Construction of European Identities'. *Journal of European Public Policy,* 6: 652–68.

Ross, G. (1998). 'European Integration and Globalization', in R. Axtmann (ed.), *Globalization and Europe: Theoretical and Empirical Investigations.* Durham, NC: Duke University Press.

Rüdiger, M. (1994). 'Stagnation, 1973–79', in J. Laursen *et al.* (eds), *Danmark i Europa, 1945–93.* Copenhagen: Munksgaard.

—— (1999). 'Denmark Against the EC'. *Berlingske Tidende,* 14 November.

Russell, N. (Nexia International) (2000). *VAT in Europe.* London: Tolley Publishing.

Sabatier, P. (1988). 'An Advocacy Coalition Framework of Policy Change and the Role of Learning Therein'. *Policy Sciences,* 21: 128–68.

Sachs, J. D. and Sala-I-Martin, X. (1992). 'Fiscal Federalism and Optimum Currency Areas: Evidence for Europe from the United States', in M. B. Canzoneri, V. Grilli, and P. R. Masson (eds), *Establishing A Central Bank: Issues in Europe and Lessons from the US.* Cambridge: Cambridge University Press.

Sachverständigenrat zur Begutachtung der gesamtwirtschaftlichen Entwicklung (1996/ 1997). *Jahresgutachten 1996/1997: 'Reformen voranbringen'.* Stuttgart: Metzler-Poeschel.

—— (1997/1998). *Jahresgutachten 1997/1998: 'Wachstum, Beschäftigung, Währungsunion— Orientierungen für die Zukunft'.* Stuttgart: Metzler-Poeschel.

—— (1999). *Wirtschaftspolitik unter Reformdruck. Jahresgutachten 1999/2000.* Berlin.

Salvati, M. (2000). *Occasioni Mancate. Economia e politica in Italia dagli anni 60 a oggi.* Rome and Bari: Laterza.

Sapir, A. and Sekkat, K. (2001). 'Political Cycles, Fiscal Deficits, and Output Spillovers in Europe'. *Public Choice.*

Sartor, N. (ed.) (1998). *Il risanamento mancato. La politica di bilancio italiana, 1986–1990.* Rome: Carocci.

Sbragia, A. (2001). 'Italy Pays for Europe: Political Leadership, Political Choice and Political adaptation', in M. Green-Cowles, J. Caporaso, and T. Risse (eds), *Transforming Europe: Europeanization and Domestic Change.* Ithaca, NY, and London: Cornell University Press.

Scharpf, F. W. (1988). 'The Joint Decision Trap: Lessons from German Federalism and European Integration'. *Public Administration,* 66: 239–78.

—— (1991). *Crisis and Choice in European Social Democracy.* Ithaca, NY: Cornell University Press.

—— (1997). *Games Real Actors Play: Actor-Centred Institutionalism in Policy Research.* Boulder, CO: Westview Press.

—— (1998). 'Demokratische Politik in der internationalisierten Ökonomie', in M. Greven (ed.), *Demokratie—eine Kultur des Westens?.* Opladen: Leske und Budrich.

Scharpf, F. W. and Schmidt, V. (eds) (2000). *Welfare and Work in the Open Economy. Volume I: From Vulnerability to Competitiveness in Comparative Perspective*. Oxford: Oxford University Press.

Schedler, A. and Santiso, J. (1998). 'Democracy and Time: An Invitation'. *International Political Science Review*, 19: 5–18.

Schmidt, V. (1999a). 'Discourse and the Legitimation of Economic and Social Policy Change in Europe'. Paper for Roundtable 4, 'Les effets d'information. Mobilisations, préférences, agendas', Association Française de Science Politique, 6è Congrès. Rennes, 28–31 September.

—— (1999b). 'National Patterns of Governance under Siege: The Impact of European Integration', in B. Kohler-Koch and R. Eising (eds), *The Transformation of Governance in the European Union*. London and New York: Routledge.

—— (2001). 'The Politics of Economic Adjustment in France and Britain: When does Discourse Matter?' *Journal of European Public Policy*, 8: 247–64

—— (forthcoming). *European Economies between Integration and Globalization: Policies, Practices, Discourses*. Oxford: Oxford University Press.

Schmitter, P. (1974). 'Still the Century of Corporatism?'. *Review of Politics*, 36: 85–131.

—— (1999). 'Reflections on the Impact of the European Union upon "Domestic" Democracy in Member States', in M. Egeberg and P. Laegreid (eds), *Organizing Political Institutions: Essays for Johan P. Olsen*. Oslo: Scandinavian University Press.

—— and Grote, J. (1997). *The Corporatist Sisyphus: Past, Present and Future* (EUI Working Papers, SPS 4/97). Florence: European University Institute.

—— and Santiso, J. (1998). 'Three Temporal Dimensions to the Consolidation of Democracy'. *International Political Science Review*, 19: 69–92.

Schofield, N. (2000). 'Constitutional Political Economy: On the Possibility of Combining Rational Choice Theory and Comparative Politics'. *Annual Review of Political Science*, 3: 277–303.

Schor, A.-D. (1999). *Économie politique de l'euro*. Paris: La documentation française.

Schröder, G. (1998). 'German Economic Policy from a European and a Global Perspective', in D. Dettke (ed.), *The Challenge of Globalization for Germany's Social Democracy*. Oxford: Berghahn.

Schulten T. and Stueckler, A. (2000). 'Wage Policy and EMU'. Wirtschafts- und Sozialwissenschaftliches Institut in der Hans-Boeckler-Stiftung and European Foundation for the Improvement of Living and Working Conditions, July.

Schwanhold, E. and Pfender, R. (1998). 'German and European Responses to Globalization', in D. Dettke (ed.), *The Challenge of Globalization for Germany's Social Democracy*. Oxford: Berghahn.

Sciarra, S. (1999). 'The Employment Title in the Amsterdam Treaty: A Multilanguage Legal Discourse', in D. O'Keefe and P. Twomey (eds), *Legal Issues of the Amsterdam Treaty*. Oxford: Hart Publishing.

Semmel, B. (1960). *Imperialism and Social Reform*. London: Allen and Unwin.

SER (Sociaal-Economische Raad) (1986). 'Advies Economische en Monetaire Samenwerking EG' (SER 86/03). Advies inzake voortgang op het gebied van de Europese economische en monetaire samenwerking uitgebracht aan de ministers. The Hague: SER.

—— (1990). 'Economische en Monetaire Union' (SER 90/22). Advies over de Economische en Monetaire Unie uitgebracht aan de ministers. The Hague: SER.

Sidenius, N. (1999). 'Interesseorganisationer og Europa. En status', in K. Ronit (ed.), *Interesseorganisationer i dansk politik*. Copenhagen: Dansk Jurist og Økonomforbund.

Siebert, H. (1998). 'Zehn Regeln für die Wirtschaftspolitik in Euroland'. *Handelsblatt*, 11 May: 47.

Siedentop, L. (2000). *Democracy in Europe*. London: Allen Lane.

Siedentopf, H. and Ziller, J. (eds) (1988). *Making European Policies Work: The Implementation of Community Legislation in the Member States*. London: Sage.

Silvia, S. (1999). 'Every Which Way but Loose: German Industrial Relations since 1980', in A. Martin and G. Ross (eds), *The Brave New World of European Labour: European Trade Unions at the Millenium*. Oxford: Berghahn.

Smith, M. (2000). *The Definitive Regime for VAT*. London: Institute for Fiscal Studies.

Soltwedel, R., Dohse, D., and Krieger-Boden, C. (1999). *EMU Challenges European Labour Markets* (IMF Working Paper WP/99/131). Washington, DC: IMF.

Søndagsavisen (1999). 'The Euro provides security and employment', 31 October.

Soskice, D. (1990). 'Wage Determination: The Changing Role of Institutions in Advanced Industrialized Countries'. *Oxford Review of Economic Policy*, 6: 31–61.

—— (1999). *The Political Economy of EMU: Rethinking the Effects of Monetary Integration on Europe* (Discussion Paper. FS I 99–302). Berlin: Wissenschaftszentrum Berlin.

—— (2000). 'Macroeconomic Analysis and the Political Economy of Unemployment', in T. Iversen, J. Pontusson, and D. Soskice (eds), *Unions, Employers, and Central Banks*. Cambridge: Cambridge University Press.

Spahn, P. (1996). *Budgetkoordinierung und Fiskaldisziplin in der EU*. Project Application in the Priority Area of European Governance of the Deutsche Forschungsgemeinschaft, Frankfurt a.M.

Spaventa, L. and Chiorazzo, V. (2000). *Astuzia o virtu'? Come accadde che l'Italia fu ammessa all'Unione Monetaria*. Rome: Donzelli.

Stadler, R. (1996). *Der rechtliche Handlungsspielraum des Europäischen Systems der Zentralbanken*. Baden-Baden: Nomos Verlagsgesellschaft.

Stark, J. (2001). 'Stark: Ecofin-Rat sollte Irland Tadel erteilen'. *Auszüge aus Presseartikeln*, Frankfurt: Deutsche Bundesbank (14 February): 2–3.

Steinherr, A. (2000). 'Europe's Unemployment: No Policy Issue, a Policy Issue for Europe or for Member States or for Both?'. *CESifo Forum*, 1/1, Spring.

Stephens, P. (1996). *Politics and the Pound*. London: Macmillan.

Stone Sweet, A., Fligstein, N., and Sandholtz, W. (1999). 'The Institutionalization of European Space'. Mimeo.

——, Sandholtz, W. and Fligstein, N. (eds) (2001). *The Institutionalization of Europe*. Oxford: Oxford University Press.

Story, J. and Walter, I. (1997). *Political Economy of European Integration: The Battle of the Systems*. Manchester: Manchester University Press.

—— (1998). *The Political Economy of European Financial Integration: The Battle of the Systems*. Manchester: Manchester University Press.

Strange, S. (1971). *Sterling and British Policy*. Oxford: Oxford University Press.

—— (1988). *States and Markets*. London: Pinter.

Strauss-Kahn, D. (1998). 'Address on the Occasion of the CEPR's 15th Anniversary'. *European Economic Perspectives*. Special 15th Anniversary Issue, November.

Streeck, W. (1994). 'Pay Restraint without Incomes Policy: Institutionalized Monetarism and Industrial Unionism in Germany', in R. Dore, R. Boyer, and Z. Mars (eds), *The Return to Incomes Policy*. London: Pinter.

—— (1995). 'German Capitalism: Does It Exist? Can It Survive?', in C. Crouch and W. Streeck (eds), *Modern Capitalism or Modern Capitalisms?* London: Pinter.

—— (1996). 'On the Beneficial Role of Constraints', in R. Boyer and D. Drache (eds), *States Against Markets: The Limits of Globalization*. London and New York: Routledge.

—— (1998). *The Internationalization of Industrial Relations in Europe: Prospects and Problems* (MPIfG Discussion Paper 98/2). Cologne: Max-Planck-Institut für Gesellschaftsforschung.

—— (1999). *Die Gewerkschaften im Bündnis für Arbeit* (MPIfG Working Paper 99/11). Cologne: Max-Planck-Institut für Gesellschaftsforschung.

—— and Schmitter, P. (1991). 'From National Corporatism to Transnational Pluralism: Organized Interests in the Single Market'. *Politics and Society*, 19/2: 133–64.

Szasz, A. (1988). *Monetaire Diplomatie: Nederlands Internationale Monetaire Politiek 1958–1987*. Leiden/Antwerpen: Stenfert Kroese.

Talani, L. (2000). 'Who Wins and Who Loses in the City of London from the Establishment of European Monetary Union', in C. Crouch (ed.), *After the Euro: Shaping Institutions for Governance in the Wake of European Monetary Union*. Oxford: Oxford University Press.

Teague, P. (1998). 'Monetary Union and Social Europe'. *Journal of European Social Policy*, 8/2: 117–37.

Telegraaf (1996). 'Actiegroep roept op tot boycott van Euro', 28 December.

Teló, M. (2000). 'L'évolution de la gouvernance socio-économique de l'UE et ses implications pour la CIG'. Paper presented at the Symposium of Jean Monnet Chairs, 'The Intergovernmental Conference 2000 and beyond', Brussels, 6–7 July.

Ter-Minassian, M. T. (1997). 'Intergovernmental Fiscal Relations in a Macro Economic Perspective', in M. T. Ter Minassian (ed.), *Fiscal Federalism in Theory and Practice*. Washington, DC: International Monetary Fund.

Thelen, K. (2000). 'Why German Employers Cannot Bring Themselves to Dismantle the German Model', in T. Iversen, J. Pontusson, and D. Soskice (eds), *Unions, Employers and Central Banks*. Cambridge: Cambridge University Press.

—— and Steinmo, S. (1992). 'Historical Institutionalism in Comparative Perspective', in S. Steinmo, K. Thelen, and F. Longstreth (eds), *Structuring Politics: Historical Institutionalism in Comparative Perspective*. Cambridge: Cambridge University Press.

Therborn, G. (1997). *The Western European Welfare State in its Hostile World* (Working Paper No. 109). Madrid: Centro de Estudios Avaznados en Ciencias Sociales, Instituto Juan March.

Thompson, H. (1996). *The British Conservative Government and the European Exchange Rate Mechanism, 1979–1994*. London: Pinter.

Tidow, S. (1999). 'Benchmarking als Leitidee—Zum Verlust des Politischen in der europäischen Perspektive'. *Blätter für deutsche und internationale Politik*, 3: 301–9.

Tiebout, C. M. (1961). *An Economic Theory of Fiscal Decentralization in Public Finance.* Princeton: Princeton University Press.

Tondl, G. (2000). 'Fiscal Federalism and the Reality of the European Union Budget', in C. Crouch (ed.), *After the Euro: Shaping Institutions for Governance in the Wake of European Monetary Union.* Oxford: Oxford University Press.

Traxler, F. (1995). 'Farewell to Labour Market Associations? Organized versus Disorganized Decentralization as a Map for Industrial Relations', in C. Crouch and F. Traxler (eds), *Organized Industrial Relations in Europe: What Future?* Aldershot: Avebury.

—— (1996). 'Collective Bargaining and Industrial Change: A Case of Disorganization? A Comparative Analysis of Eighteen OECD Countries'. *European Sociological Review,* 12: 271–87.

—— (1997). 'Collective Bargaining in the OECD: Developments, Preconditions and Effects'. Paper delivered to European Sociological Association Conference. Colchester, mimeo.

—— (1999). 'Wage-Setting Institutions and EMU', in G. Huemer, M. Mesch, and F. Traxler (eds), *The Role of Employers Associations and Trade Unions in EMU: Institutional Requirements for European Economic Policies.* Aldershot: Ashgate.

—— and Kittel, B. (1998). 'The Bargaining Structure, its Context, and Performance'. Vienna: University of Vienna, mimeo.

Treasury (1978). *The European Monetary System* (Cmnd 7405). London: HMSO.

—— (1997). *UK Membership of the Single Currency: An Assessment of the Five Tests.* London: HM Treasury.

Tsoukalis, L. (1993). *The New European Economy: The Politics and Economic of Integration.* Oxford: Oxford University Press.

—— (2000). 'Economic and Monetary Union', in H. Wallace and W. Wallace (eds), *Policy-Making in the European Union* (4th edn). Oxford: Oxford University Press.

Turner, L. (1998). *Fighting for Partnership: Labour and Politics in Unified Germany.* Ithaca, NY: Cornell University Press.

Underhill, G. (1996). *Financial Market Integration, Global Capital Mobility, and the ERM Crisis 1992–1995* (Working Paper No. 12, Global Economic Institutions Research Programme, Economic and Social Research Council of the United Kingdom). London: Centre for Economic Policy Research for the ESRC.

—— (1997). 'The Making of the European Financial Area: Global Market Integration and the EU Single Market for Financial Services', in G. Underhill (ed.), *The New World Order in International Finance.* Basingstoke: Macmillan.

—— (1999a). 'L'euro et le système financier mondial: prédestination ou temps nouveau d'un libre arbitre?'. *L'Économie Politique,* 1/1: 91–102.

—— (1999b). 'Transnational Financial Markets and National Economic Development Models: Global Structures versus Domestic Imperatives'. *Economies et Sociétés,* série 'Monnaie', ME. 1–2, September–October: 37–68.

—— (2000). 'Global Money and the Decline of State Power', in T. Lawton, J. Rosenau, and A. Verdun (eds), *Strange Power: Shaping the Parameters of International Relations and International Political Economy.* Aldershot: Ashgate.

—— and Zhang, X. (forthcoming 2002). *International Financial Governance under Stress: Global Structures versus National Imperatives* (Cambridge: Cambridge University Press).

UNICE (1991). 'Intergovernmental Conference on Economic and Monetary Union'. Letter to Mr Wim Kok, Dutch Prime Minister, President of the IGC, 13 November.

van der Ploeg, F. (1989). 'Towards Monetary Integration in Europe', in P. De Grauwe *et al.*, *De Europese Monetaire Integratie: Vier Visies*. Wetenschappelijke Raad voor het Regeringsbeleid. The Hague: SDU.

Vanhercke, B. (1999). 'Protection sociale et Union économique et monétaire'. *Revue belge de sécurité sociale*, 1: 5–31.

Vassallo, S. (2000). 'La politica di bilancio: le condizioni e gli effetti istituzionali della convergenza', in G. di Palma, G. Freddi, and S. Fabbrini (eds), *Condannata al successo? L'Italia nell'Europa integrata*. Bologna: Il Mulino.

Vaubel, R., Bernholz, P., and Streit, M. (eds) (1998). *Political Competition, Innovation and Growth: A Historical Analysis*. Berlin: Springer.

Verdun, A. (1990). 'Naar een Economische en Monetaire Unie (1970–1990): een analyse van de politieke beleidsruimte in Nederland' (unpublished manuscript). Amsterdam: University of Amsterdam.

—— (1996). 'An "Asymmetrical" Economic and Monetary Union in the EU: Perceptions of Monetary Authorities and Social Partners'. *Journal of European Integration/ Revue d'Integration européenne*, 20/1: 59–81.

—— (1998a). 'The Institutional Design of EMU: A Democratic Deficit?' *Journal of Public Policy*, 18/2: 107–32.

—— (1998b). 'Understanding Economic and Monetary Union in the EU'. *Journal of European Public Policy*, 5: 527–33.

—— (1999a). 'The Role of the Delors Committee in the Creation of EMU: An Epistemic Community?'. *Journal of European Public Policy*, 6: 308–28.

—— (1999b). 'The Logic of Giving up National Currencies: Lessons from Europe's Monetary Union', in E. Gilbert and E. Helleiner (eds), *Nation-States and Currencies*: London: Routledge.

—— (2000a). *European Responses to Globalization and Financial Market Integration: Perceptions of Economic and Monetary Union in Britain, France and Germany*. Houndmills: Macmillan; New York: St Martin's Press.

—— (2000b). 'Governing by Committee: The Case of the Monetary Committee', in T. Christiansen and E. Kirchner (eds), *Committee Governance in the European Union*. Manchester: Manchester University Press.

—— and Christiansen, T. (2000). 'Policies, Institutions, and the Euro: Dilemmas of Legitimacy', in C. Crouch (ed.), *After The Euro: Shaping Institutions for Governance in the Wake of European Monetary Union*. Oxford: Oxford University Press.

Verzichelli, L. (1999). *La politica di bilancio*. Bologna: Il Mulino.

Victor, B. (1999). *Le Matignon de Jospin*. Paris: Flammarion.

Visser, J. (1998). 'EMU and the Art of Making Social Pacts'. Amsterdam: CESAR mimeograph, University of Amsterdam.

—— and Hemerijck, A. (1997). *A Dutch Miracle: Job Growth, Welfare Reform and Corporatism in the Netherlands*. Amsterdam: Amsterdam University Press.

von Hagen, J. (1993a). 'Monetary Union and Fiscal Union: A Perspective from Fiscal Federalism', in P. Masson and M. Taylor (eds), *Policy Issues in the Operation of Currency Unions*. Oxford: Oxford University Press.

—— (1993b). 'Fiscal Arrangements in a Monetary Union: Evidence from the US', in D. Fair and C. de Boissieu (eds), *Fiscal Policy, Taxation and the Financial System in an Increasingly Integrated Europe*. Dordrecht: Kluwer.

—— (1998). 'Von der Deutschen Mark zum Euro'. *Aus Politik und Zeitgeschichte*. B 24/98: 35–46.

—— and Eichengreen, B. (1996). 'Federalism, Fiscal Constraints and European Monetary Union'. *American Economic Review*, 86: 134–8.

——, Hallett, A., and Strauch, R. (2001). *Budgetary Consolidation in EMU* (Economic Papers No. 148). Brussels: Directorate General for Economic and Financial Affairs, European Commission (March).

—— and Harden, I. (1994). 'National Budget Processes and Fiscal Performance'. *European Economy*, 3: 311–55.

Wallace, H. (2000). 'The Institutional Setting', in H. Wallace and W. Wallace (eds), *Policy-Making in the European Union* (4th edn). Oxford: Oxford University Press.

—— and Wallace, W. (eds) (2000). *Policy-Making in the European Union* (4th edn). Oxford: Oxford University Press.

Wallace, W. (2000). 'Collective Governance', in H. Wallace and W. Wallace (eds), *Policy-Making in the European Union* (4th edn). Oxford: Oxford University Press.

Walsh, J. (1999). 'Political Bases of Macro-Economic Adjustment: Evidence from the Italian Experience'. *Journal of European Public Policy*, 6/1: 66–84.

Weale A. (1996). 'Democratic Legitimacy and the Constitution of Europe', in R. Bellamy, V. Bufacchi, and D. Castoglione (eds), *Democracy and Constitutional Culture in the Union of Europe*. London: Lothian Press.

Webb, M. (1995). *The Political Economy of Policy Co-ordination: International Adjustment since 1945*. Ithaca, NY: Cornell University Press.

Weiler, J. (1995). 'The Transformation of Europe'. *Yale Law Journal*, 100: 2403–83.

Weiss, L. (1998). *The Myth of the Powerless State*. Cambridge: Polity.

Wessels, W. (1997). 'An Ever Closer Fusion? A Dynamic Macropolitical View on Integration Processes'. *Journal of Common Market Studies*, 2: 267–99.

—— (2000). *Die Öffnung des Staates. Modelle und Wirklichkeit grenzüberschreitender Verwaltungspraxis 1960–1995*. Opladen: Leske und Budrich.

—— (2001). 'Nice Results: The Millennium IGC in the EU's Evolution'. *Journal of Common Market Studies*, 39/2: 197–219.

——, Maurer, A., and Mittag, J. (2001). 'The European Union and Member States: Europeanization by the EU system', in W. Wessels, A. Maurer, and J. Mittag (eds), *Fifteen into One? The European Union and its Member States*. Manchester: Manchester University Press.

Whyman, P., Burkitt, B., and Baimbridge, M. (2000). 'Economic Policy Outside EMU: Strategies for a Global Britain'. *Political Quarterly*, 7/4: 1–13.

Willet, T. D. (2000). 'A Political Economy Analysis of the Maastricht and Stability Pact Fiscal Criteria', in A. Hallet, M. Hutchison, and E. Jensen (eds), *Fiscal Aspects of European Monetary Integration*. Cambridge: Cambridge University Press.

Williams, K. (2000). 'From Shareholder Value to Present-day Capitalism'. *Economy and Society*, 29: 1–12.

Wood, S. (2001). 'Labour Market Regimes under Threat? Sources of Continuity in Germany, Britain and Sweden', in P. Pierson (ed.), *The New Politics of the Welfare State*. Oxford: Oxford University Press.

World Bank (1997). *Macroeconomic Management and Fiscal Decentralization*. Washington, DC: World Bank.

Wright, V. (1994). 'Reshaping the State: The Implications for Public Administration'. *West European Politics*, 17/3: 102–37.

Young, B. (2000). 'Diskurse der Globalisierung und die Konstruktion der Europäischen Währungsunion: Die Entstehung einer "Market Citizenship"?'. Paper presented at the Congress of the Deutsche Vereinigung für Politikwissenschaft (DVPW), Halle, 1–5 October.

Young, H. (1998). *This Blessed Plot*. London: Macmillan.

Zaghini, A. (1999). 'The Economic Policy of Fiscal Consolidations: The European Experience'. Banca d'Italia, *Temi di discussione del Servizio Studi*, 35 (June).

Index